An Overview of Health Care
and the
Health Professions

All proceeds from the sale of this book will go to the
Scholarship of Excellence Fund
*which was established by the Association of Schools of Allied
Health Professions (ASAHP) to provide financial assistance to
students at the organization's member institutions.*

An Overview of Health Care and the Health Professions

Thomas W. Elwood

Executive Director
Association of Schools of Allied Health Professions
Washington, DC

SCIENCE &
MEDICINE
2012

An Overview of Health Care and the Health Professions

ISBN 978-0-9758862-3-1

Cover photograph from iStockPhoto.com, © kali 9.

All proceeds from the sale of this book will go to the **Scholarship of Excellence Fund,** which was established by the Association of Schools of Allied Health Professions (ASAHP) to provide financial assistance to students at the organization's member institutions.

Association of Schools of Allied Health Professions
4400 Jenifer Street NW, Ste 333
Washington, DC 20015
Tel 202-237-6481
www.asahp.org

Published by:
Science & Medicine, Inc.
Narberth, PA
www.sciandmed.com

Contents

Acknowledgments

This book has benefited immensely from keen insights furnished by individuals who were kind enough to review it. Collectively, they represent a superb combination of being excellent readers and also being an important part of major developments in health care and higher education over the years. I am most appreciative of the contributions made by the following:

George Cernada (University of Massachusetts at Amherst-retired and Editor, *International Quarterly of Community Health Education*)

Douglas Elwood (New York University Langone Medical Center and Bristol-Myers Squibb)

David Gibson (University of Medicine and Dentistry of New Jersey-retired)

Cecilia Guido-Spano (The World Bank)

Randall Lambrecht (Aurora Health Care)

Beverly Malone (National League of Nursing)

David O'Bryon (Association of Chiropractic Colleges)

Diane Patrick (University of Maryland at College Park-retired)

Ashley Rasmussen (Association of Schools of Allied Health Professions)

Stephen Shannon (American Association of Colleges of Osteopathic Medicine)

John Trufant (Rush University-retired)

A special note of thanks is due book publisher **Michael Bokulich**. His meticulous attention, along with his wise recommendations on how to achieve greater clarity in expressing my thoughts, has been of considerable value.

Lastly, for the past 9 years, I have had the honor and pleasure of teaching a graduate-level course on the topic of health policy to students at the **University of Medicine and Dentistry of New Jersey**. My learning about their wide range of experiences derived from working in many different aspects of health care in various urban and rural areas of the United States has enriched my understanding of the many key dimensions of the health domain.

About the Author

Thomas W. Elwood is Executive Director of the Association of Schools of Allied Health Professions in Washington, DC, where he has been employed since 1988. Earlier positions include serving as a Deputy Director at the Johns Hopkins Comprehensive Cancer Center, Director of Scientific Programs at the American Public Health Association, and chief health lobbyist while on the staff at AARP.

A full scholarship student, he has both a Master's and Doctorate degrees in public health from the University of California at Berkeley and was chosen to represent the School of Public Health in the Berkeley Professional Studies Program in India, where he was assigned to the Ministry of Health in New Delhi.

He has been a World Health Organization Fellow and was selected to study the health systems of England, Denmark, and Sweden. He has served as a consultant to various governmental agencies including the National Cancer Institute, Veterans Health Administration, Health Resources and Services Administration, Administration on Aging, and private sector organizations, including the National Council for International Health.

He also was one of three persons awarded an honorary doctorate from the University of Medicine and Dentistry of New Jersey, the nation's largest academic health science center, in 2000 and the first person in allied health to be so honored by that institution. A Past President of the Federation of Associations of Schools of the Health Professions (FASHP), he also has served on the Executive Committee of the Board of Directors as Treasurer of the National Health Council.

The author of more than 65 professional papers in peer review journals and book chapters, he became Editor of the *Journal of Allied Health* in July 2008 and currently serves on the editorial board of another health publication. In 2009, he had a book published with the title *A View From Washington: Federal Policy in Relation to Allied Health over Two Decades*.

He has been an Adjunct Professor at the University of Medicine and Dentistry of New Jersey since 2004, with responsibility for teaching an online course on health policy issues and trends. An earlier period in academia occurred at the School of Public Health at the University of Massachusetts at Amherst, where he served as a visiting professor from 1982 to 1985. Over the years, he also has been a guest lecturer at: The Ohio State University, University of Maryland at College Park, University of Pennsylvania, The George Washington University, the University of California at Berkeley, the University of Leeds in the U.K., and the University of Applied Sciences in Utrecht in the Netherlands.

He has been a keynote speaker at state and national conferences throughout the United States and in 2009 was the first American to present a keynote address at the annual conference of the Consortium of Institutes of Higher Education in Health and Rehabilitation in Europe, an organization representing 39 academic institutions. As of 2011, he is a member of two advisory committees for health workforce projects funded by the federal government and served as a reviewer for an allied health workshop publication by the Institute of Medicine of the National Academy of Sciences.

Foreword

A lmost nothing is more important to life than its own survival and the quality of its existence. Health is one of the most important measures used to define the quality of life, and although biologically complex, it is influenced by a multitude of variables. The health system in the United States is currently at a crossroads of transformation, whereby the second decade of this 21st century will prove to be a critical time in deciding whether health care in this country is a right or a privilege. Perhaps arguably it is both.

An Overview of Health Care and the Health Professions is one of the most comprehensive and carefully-written, cross-sectional compendium on health care for its time. From demographics, to social determinants, to the environment, workforce, government, financing, technology, and other factors, these influences are like chemical elements that interact together to create a complex system by which the health care system functions. The author masterfully pulls these constructs together in a well-timed invaluable book that couldn't be more appropriate as the nation ventures into an election year with polarizing attitudes towards health care access and delivery in the United States.

The abundance of information, editorials, and literature which dissects and characterizes the health care system involves a sort of dynamic meta-analysis. Polarizing outrage and a growing failure in Washington, DC, to find a unifying compromise to the delivery and access of quality care present a fair-minded assessment of this divisiveness that will likely continue to provoke strong attitudes and emotions.

T he state of health care and health professions has rarely been captured with such sensitivity and objectivity as Dr. Elwood has in this book. Terms are carefully chosen and defined, historical references are appropriately invoked, and statements are accurately referenced. Each chapter is written as an evidence-based approach to seek the truth, yet is not so sanitized to disallow room for debate.

The "Fog of Public Policy," as Dr. Elwood puts it, partly has its origin and roots in "the shape of laws, guidelines, and regulations ... [with] little correlation between the quality of science and the policy derived from it." Whereas researchers systematically test hypotheses which may take years, policymakers have to sell, argue, and react to issues in a time frame dominated by election cycles and constituencies. Communication, languages, and the "View of Health Care Through a Semiotic Veil of Signs" is a chapter focused on the effectiveness of human exchange between patients and health care professionals. On a global level, health care is influenced by the many different languages, cultures, and literacy levels. And while no one would suggest that this multiplicity of languages is the reason there is so little unity, it certainly interferes with the ability to communicate, cooperate, and compromise.

Historically, health has always been an important concern as evidenced in very early writings, yet throughout all the years, "we are still babbling." Throughout the book, Elwood supports his information by supplying numerous findings and conclusions of many analytical papers and research studies. An example is the AHRQ CAHPS report, which states only 12% of U.S. adults have proficient health literacy skills, and the proportion of U.S. population with limited English proficiency is substantial.

Financing a quality health care system is not only a political football, but also a significant challenge. The history-making Affordable Care Act of 2010 was a bold move designed to address Medicare's long-term fiscal crisis by requiring major payment and health care delivery reforms, but many of its elements have yet to be implemented as of the printing of this book. Costs have outpaced the need to adequately provide quality health care for many U.S. residents. The managed-care system, once touted as the solution to health insurance woes, has failed in providing the kind of system that makes health care a right for all people. In addition, personal responsibility and issues surrounding patient compliance are often pitted against the ability of the government and providers to assume and assure accountability.

Dr. Elwood's unique background, expertise, passion, and perspective in public health, health education, and government politics is the foundation for a compelling and informative book. He draws upon the harmonizing events of health care in the U.S., and does so as to not necessarily insert new ideas into the body politic, but to summarize and bring together existing dogma and beliefs into a single, forceful, and unassailable source book. This book offers a basis of truth, a dose of public opinion, and an undisguised sense of wit. It chronicles historical anecdotes and detailed facts, definitions, and explanations that make up the pathology and potential cure of a health care system under assault and perhaps eventually transformation.

RANDALL S. LAMBRECHT, PhD, FASAHP
Dean & Professor Emeritus, University of Wisconsin–Milwaukee
Senior Vice President, Aurora Health Care
January 2012

Introduction

This book is a product of ruminations and observations about health care over more than a six-decade period. Various experiences across that span of time have influenced a personal quest to obtain a more complete understanding of the health enterprise in the United States.

In my youth, it was common for a family doctor to abandon his car and walk the remaining mile in deep snow to our home at 2:00 AM to administer care to a sick child. After performing back surgery and making post-surgical home visits over a 9-month period for an uncle and realizing that our family could not pay the bill, the surgeon agreed to play an all-or-nothing chess game with the patient. He knew full well that my uncle was considered among the best chess players in our hometown, and the outcome was a foregone conclusion. The bill remained unpaid. These two examples are among the many that can be used to indicate how much health care delivery has changed in comparison to what existed in the 1940s and 1950s

Other formative events in my life include being reared in a walk-up tenement in a blue collar neighborhood and witnessing the painfully slow, cigarette smoking-caused deaths of both parents. My working as a shift laborer in a textile mill while being exposed to aerial particulate matter in the form of fine dust, and then 3 years later in a paper mill that involved extensive heavy lifting under high heat conditions and exposure to dangerous machines and odors of several chemicals used in the manufacturing process, has helped to develop an appreciation for important ways in which social and occupational environments can affect health status.

Later on, more than 40 years' experience being employed in various aspects of the health arena provided other insights. Lastly, having suffered a heart attack in 2000, I have benefited greatly from observing health care professionals and facilities from the patient's side of a flimsy gown.

Health care is a highly dynamic component of life in the United States at a time when this country continues to prosper from the steady flow of newcomers from other lands. The gradual aging of the population has an effect on caregivers themselves and on the patients whom they serve. Increasingly, demands are being placed on practitioners to work together in teams more effectively across the different professions and to have the necessary knowledge and skills to apply to a patient base that continues to change as a result of evolving demographic patterns.

The following forces underscore the necessity of making changes in the way health care is provided in the United States. First is the upward cost spiral that is unsustainable and diverts resources that can be used in other sectors of the economy such as education. Second is the need to improve the quality of health care that is provided. Third is the need to increase access for all Americans irrespective of whether they lack health insurance or live in areas that are underserved because of an insufficient supply of health facilities and a proper mix of health professionals.

Unless done properly, trying to improve any single element may conflict with one or both of the other two elements. For example, enhancing access by providing insurance coverage to those who lack it may place more demand on the system of health services, which could end up increasing costs and diminishing quality.

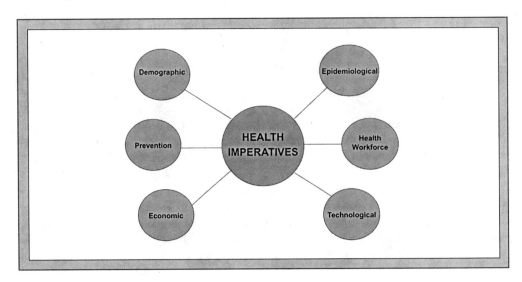

An *imperative* may be defined as something of vital importance. A general framework for the chapters that follow in this book would be to consider them as relating to the following major imperatives:

- Demographic (e.g., Chapters 1, 3, 4)
- Epidemiological (e.g., Chapters 2, 4, 5, 10)
- Economic (e.g., Chapters 6-9, 11, 12)
- Technological (e.g., Chapters 15, 16)
- Health Workforce (e.g., Chapters 10, 11)

Each imperative represents a major driving force that will influence how health care services are delivered in the future and the extent to which they will contribute to improving both individual and population health status. It also should be acknowledged that underlying these imperatives is a *Prevention Imperative*, recognizing that a separate text book or series of books could be devoted to that topic alone. If carried out effectively, prevention efforts would have an impact on the other imperatives such that some portions of the population would experience improved health status, diseases and related problems would be less prevalent, costs would be saved, the necessity of having widespread use of expensive technology would be lessened, and members of the health workforce would be able to focus on preventive as well as curative approaches to health care.

Many prevention initiatives are at the community level and tend to go unnoticed because they are engrained features of daily living. Examples are sanitation, pollution control, and the availability of safe food and water supplies. At the individual level, the impetus is on adopting a lifestyle that emphasizes the necessity of eating a balanced diet, exercising regularly, avoiding the use of harmful substances such as cigarettes, refraining from practices that result in sexually transmitted diseases, maintaining personal weight control, and taking appropriate action upon the appearance of warning symptoms.

While an effort is made in this text to weave the imperatives together and provide some degree of sequential continuity from one chapter to the next, it should be recognized that the book contains several chapters that essentially can stand alone as sources of information. Examples are Chapter 6 on the role of government in the provision and financing of health care services, Chapter 9 on developments in health reform, and Chapter 11 on the health workforce.

More than 400 bibliographical sources are cited and several are drawn from the medical literature. Thus far, physicians have been at the center of providing health care services, but the situation is undergoing significant change. A major contributing factor is that not enough primary care doctors are being produced each year to meet the needs of a growing population. Another key factor is that other health professions such as nursing, physical therapy, and occupational therapy are producing students with clinical doctorates that involve enhanced and expanded scopes of practice.

As more and different kinds of health professionals engage in the provision of essential health care services, the richness of the medical literature can serve as an important guide for them in two ways: (1) it provides examples of favorable interactions with patients that can be repeated in situations involving other kinds of practitioners, and (2) it demonstrates the kinds of interactions that need to be improved.

To the extent that patients and providers differ from one another by age, gender, and race/ethnicity, health care quality can be compromised. As the U.S. population continues to undergo changes resulting from a steady increase in the number and proportion of aged patients and the steady flow of immigrants, meeting the challenge of providing quality care to these groups will continue to be of great importance.

This book should prove of some value to students who want to obtain an overview of certain key components of the health arena. The same may be said for other readers who would like to expand their knowledge of the vast health enterprise that exists in the United States, representing a major component of the largest economy in the world.

Health care has undergone important changes in recent decades and the future should prove to be no different. For example, maternity patients and surgical patients no longer spend many days in bed after babies are born or after surgery has been performed. Moreover, advances in technology can lead to the creation of new types of health professionals. Allied health offers a suitable example of many occupations that have emerged as technological developments occur, just as advances in genomics have led to the need for more professionals who specialize in genetic counseling.

Sometimes, in order to understand the present, it helps to look at what happened during earlier periods. This text represents a blend of some aspects of health care that are current as of December 2011, along with prior efforts in areas such as health reform that provide a foundation for understanding the contemporary scene.

Nobel Prize winning physicist Richard Feynman once made the following observation:

"Perhaps a thing is simple if you can describe it fully in several ways without immediately knowing that you are describing the same thing."

An attempt has been made in the following pages to provide an overview of key dimensions of health in the United States at the beginning of the 21st century. Perhaps in the final analysis, all ongoing action and future developments amount to nothing more than seeking ways to improve the quality of life for everyone who resides here.

Lastly, it is worth noting that all proceeds from the sale of this book will be added to a scholarship account at the Association of Schools of Allied Health Professions. This fund was established to assist students in institutions that are members of the Association. The high costs of education at the college and university level have the potential to dissuade students from enrolling in health professions education programs. This concern is a serious one for individuals from underprivileged backgrounds. Scholarship assistance offers a way of reducing the financial burden of obtaining an education and a hope is that book sales will make it possible for a greater number of students to benefit from the revenue derived.

THOMAS W. ELWOOD, DRPH
Washington, DC
January 2012

Useful Websites

Agency for Healthcare Research and Quality	http://www.ahrq.gov/
Bureau of Labor Statistics	http://stats.bls.gov/
California Healthcare Foundation	http://www.chcf.org/
Congressional Budget Office	http://www.chcf.org/
Centers for Disease Control and Prevention	http://www.cdc.gov/
U.S. Census Bureau	http://www.census.gov/
Center for Studying Health System Change	http://www.hrsa.gov/index.html
Centers for Medicare & Medicaid Services	http://www.cms.gov/
Commonwealth Fund	http://www.commonwealthfund.org/
Department of Health & Human Services	http://www.hhs.gov/
Federal Register	http://www.gpoaccess.gov/fr/
Government Accountability Office	http://www.gao.gov/
Health Policy Picks	http://www.kaiseredu.org/Health-Policy-Picks.aspx
Health Resources & Services Administration	http://www.hrsa.gov/index.html
Institute of Medicine	http://www.iom.edu/
Kaiser Health News	http://www.kaiserhealthnews.org/
Lewin Group	http://www.lewin.com/
Mathematica Policy Research	http://www.mathematica-mpr.com/
McKinsey & Company	http://www.mathematica-mpr.com/
Medicare Payment Advisory Group	http://www.medpac.gov/
Migration Policy Institute	http://www.migrationpolicy.org/
Morbidity and Mortality Weekly Report	http://www.cdc.gov/mmwr/
National Center for Complementary and Alternative Medicine	http://nccam.nih.gov/
National Center for Health Statistics	http://www.cdc.gov/nchs/
National Institutes of Health	http://www.nih.gov/
Population Reference Bureau	http://www.prb.org/
Public Health News	http://www.publichealthnewswire.org/
Public Library of Science Medicine	http://www.plosmedicine.org/home.action
PricewaterhouseCoopers	http://www.pwc.com/us/en/index.jhtml
Rand Corporation	http://www.rand.org/
Urban Institute	http://www.urban.org/
World Health Organization	http://www.who.int/en/

Glossary

AAP	American Academy of Pediatrics	DMEPOS	Durable Medical Equipment, Prosthetics, Orthotics, and Supplies
ACA	Affordable Care Act		
ACF	Administration for Children and Families	DNR	do-not-resuscitate
ACO	accountable care organization	DSHEA	Dietary Supplement and Health Education Act
ACP	advanced care plan		
ACR	American College of Rheumatology	DSM-III	Diagnostic and Statistical Manual, 3rd ed.
ADD	attention deficit disorder		
ADE	adverse drug events	EBP	employee benefit plan
ADHD	attention deficit hyperactivity disorder	EHR	electronic health record
AHEC	Area Health Education Center	EIP	Emerging Infections Program
AHRQ	Agency for Healthcare Research and Quality	EMR	electronic medical record
		EOL	end-of-life care
ALS	amyotrophic lateral sclerosis	EPA	Environmental Protection Agency
AoA	Administration on Aging	ERISA	Employee Retirement Income Security Act
APRN	advanced practice registered nurse		
ART	active antiretroviral therapy	ESI	employer sponsored insurance
		ESRD	end stage renal disease
BCS	breast-conserving surgery		
BHPr	Bureau of Health Professions	FCC	Federal Communications Commission
BRCA1	breast cancer 1 [gene]	FDA	Food and Drug Administration
BRCA2	breast cancer 2 [gene]	FFS	fee-for-service
		FOBT	fecal occult blood test
CAH	critical access hospital	FPL	federal poverty level
CAHPS	Consumer Assessment of Healthcare Providers and Systems	FQHC	federally qualified health center
		FTC	Federal Trade Commission
CBO	Congressional Budget Office		
CDC	Centers for Disease Control and Prevention	GAO	Government Accountability Office
		GTR	Genetic Testing Registry
CER	comparative effectiveness research		
CF	cystic fibrosis	HAI	healthcare-associated infection
CHSI	community health status indicators	HARC	Health Literacy Annual Research Conference
CLASS	Community Living Assistance Services and Supports Act		
		HBOC	hereditary breast and ovarian cancer
CMS	Centers for Medicare and Medicaid Services	HCAHPS	Hospital Consumer Assessment of Healthcare Providers and Systems
CODA	Commission on Dental Accreditation	HCUP	Healthcare Cost and Utilization Project
CON	certificate-of-need	HHS	Department of Health and Human Services
COPD	chronic obstructive pulmonary disease		
CRT	cardiac resynchronization therapy	HICPAC	Healthcare Infection Control Practices Advisory Committee
CT	computed tomography		

HIQR	Hospital Inpatient Quality Reporting Program
HIT	health information technology
HITECH	Health Information Technology for Economic and Clinical Health Act
HPEI	Health Professions Education Institution
HPSA	health professional shortage areas
HQA	Hospital Quality Alliance Program
HRCCT	health resources county comparison tool
HRSA	Health Resources and Services Administration
HSA	Health Systems Agency
HMO	health maintenance organization
HUD	Department of Housing and Urban Development
ICD	implantable cardioverter defibrillator
IDS	integrated delivery systems
IHS	Indian Health Service
IOM	Institute of Medicine
IPAB	Independent Payment Advisory Board
IPPS	Medicare Inpatient Prospective Payment System
IPV	intimate partner violence
IQR	Hospital Inpatient Quality Reporting Program
KS	Kaposi sarcoma
LEP	limited English proficient
LTC	long-term care
MAPD	Medicare Advantage Prescription Drug Plan
MedPAC	Medicare Payment Advisory Commission
MMWR	Morbidity and Mortality Weekly Report
MRI	magnetic resonance imaging
MSP	Medicare savings program
NCAA	National Collegiate Athletic Association
NCQA	National Committee for Quality Assurance
NHIS	National Health Interview Survey
NHSC	National Health Service Corps
NIH	National Institutes of Health
NIMH	National Institute of Mental Health
NLM	National Library of Medicine
NPP	nonphysician practitioner

NSC	National Supplier Clearinghouse
NTD	neural tube defect
OBRA	Omnibus Budget Reconciliation Act
OI	opportunistic infection
OMB	Office of Management and Budget
PAM	patient activation measure
PCMH	patient-centered medical home
PCORI	Patient-Centered Outcomes Research Institute
PDP	prescription drug plan
PGP	physician group practice
PICO	patients, interventions, comparators, outcomes
POC	parole outpatient clinic
PRB	Population Reference Bureau
PRWORA	Personal Responsibility and Work Opportunity Reconciliation Act
PwC	PricewaterhouseCoopers
RCT	randomized clinical trial
RHC	rural health center
RP	radical prostatectomy
RRT	renal replacement therapy
SAMHSA	Substance Abuse and Mental Health Services Administration
SDM	shared decision-making
SES	social economic status
SHOP	small business health options program
SNP	single-nucleotide polymorphisms
SOS	Seattle Obesity Study
SSI	Supplemental Security Income Program
USDA	U.S. Department of Agriculture
USPHS	U.S. Public Health Service
USPSTF	U.S. Preventive Services Task Force
UTI	urinary tract infection
VA	Department of Veterans Affairs
VASCI	violently acquired spinal cord injury
VBP	Medicare value-based purchasing program
VCN	virtual career network
WHO	World Health Organization

CHAPTER 1:
Overview of Health Care
in the United States

The provision of health care services in the United States consumed about 18% of the world's largest economy in 2011. The percentage is expected to increase in coming years. This chapter aims to offer a perspective on health from the standpoint of: (1) how the term health is defined, (2) how social factors such as poverty influence community and individual health status, and (3) how the nation's political, economic, and media sectors affect the realm of health care.

R eaders of this book will come across many items derived from the health literature. Terms that are used interchangeably may not always have the same meaning. For example, *health disparity, health inequality,* and *health inequity* mean different things. Similarly, *comparative effectiveness research, evidence-based medicine,* and *health technology assessment* are not the same. Racial classifications represent another area where sorting out precisely what is meant is not always easy. An example is African Americans and blacks. Not all blacks are African American, but occasionally they are included as if they are. The point is that all references from the literature will stay intact and appear as the authors of various cited articles intended.

Among the many quoted sources appearing in this and coming chapters, most contain acknowledged limitations, a recognition that other studies produced different results and, most importantly, that the findings do not always represent the definitive, final explanation of the phenomenon being investigated.

Some Examples of Limitations

- Cross-sectional designs of surveys limit the ability to derive causal inferences.
- Claimed research findings may simply be accurate measures of the prevailing bias.
- Self-reports by patients are not always reliable.
- Health care encounters are measured during various specified time periods.
- Survey question responses may be influenced by patient recall and patient bias.
- Probability of a research claim being true depends on study power.
- Responses indicate only that interventions occurred, not their depth or quality.
- Direct observation of provider behavior often is not possible.
- A high percentage of data may be missing, which affects conclusions drawn.
- Detailed information about patients' knowledge, beliefs, and attitudes is unknown.
- Clinical and administrative records may be inadequate.
- Process measures used may not reflect clinical outcomes.
- Abstracting race from medical records can lead to misclassification bias.
- Small sample size and lack of statistical power can affect interpretation of study results.
- Race/ethnicity status may be determined by somebody other than patients themselves.

As with much health research in the literature, it is rare to find information that is wholly explanatory and capable of bringing controversy to a complete rest. It is the nature of the research enterprise for studies to build upon previous investigations with the aim of ultimately agreeing upon a given formulation. The same holds true for information that appears in newspapers, magazines, and on the Web. Finally, there always is the risk that more apt references exist, but escaped notice when the current book was prepared. Thus, for any given topic addressed in this chapter and in those that succeed it, readers are advised to conduct their own inquiries and arrive at their own conclusions.

What Is Meant by the Term *Health*?

The word *health* will appear a great many times in this chapter and in those that follow. A time-honored definition from the World Health Organization states that:

Health is a complete state of physical, mental, and social well-being and not merely the absence of disease or infirmity.

The sentiment is quite noble, but is anything of this nature attainable for the vast number of humans who inhabit the earth? Perhaps even more significant is that the definition fails to include the religious, spiritual dimension, which is of central importance in a great many lives.

What constitutes a particular health problem can vary by time and location. For example, in the 1950s and 1960s, anxiety was at the forefront of medical and psychiatric complaints that brought many patients to physicians' offices in the U.S. (Horowitz 2010). Symptoms consisted of headaches, fatigue, back pain, gastrointestinal complaints, and sleep and appetite difficulties. It had many origins such as worrying about exams in school, sitting in traffic jams, and experiencing daily stresses associated with dealing with family members and having to work for a living.

Before the 1970s, "depression was usually considered a relatively rare condition involving feelings of intense meaninglessness and worthlessness often accompanied by vegetative and psychotic symptoms and preoccupations with death and dying. Moreover, depression was more likely to be associated with hospitalized patients than with clients of general physicians or outpatient psychiatrists." A puzzling phenomenon is why beginning in the 1970s, *depression* rather than *anxiety* has become the common term used to indicate complaints associated with stress.

"A revolution in the treatment of mental health problems began in the 1950s when the development of meprobamate (Miltown®) created the first mass market for treating problems of generalized stress." The medication was called a tranquilizer and "became the most popular prescription drug in U.S. history. As early as 1960, about three-quarters of all American physicians were prescribing Miltown. By the late 1960s, however, the spectacular success of the benzodiazepine Librium, which was introduced in 1960, displaced Miltown. In turn, Valium succeeded Librium as a blockbuster antianxiety drug."

"Treatment statistics in the 1970s reflected the growing interest in depression." By the middle of that decade, management of it became as common as that of anxiety. So, what brought about the change in the perceived increase in the incidence and prevalence of depression?

The implementation of the third edition of the *Diagnostic and Statistical Manual* (DSM-III), which the American Psychiatric Association (APA) issued in 1980, was a central turning point leading to the transition from anxiety to depression. The manual radically changed the nature of psychiatric diagnoses. Also, "the psychiatric profession was pressured to embrace the norms of diagnostic specificity accepted in the rest of medicine as the standard for definitions of their subject matter." Biological psychiatrists became concerned about the unscientific nature of psychoanalysis, preferring to study specific diseases rather than amorphous stress conditions.

Pressure from politicians and family advocacy groups led to a transformation in funding research by the National Institute of Mental Health (NIMH) for specific, biologically-based diseases in the 1980s rather than for general psychosocial problems. "Another spur toward specificity of a diagnosis was a mandate from the Food and Drug Administration (FDA) to the pharmaceutical industry to target psychoactive drugs to specific biomedical conditions." Also, growing coverage by private and public insurance resulted in third-party payments, but only for treating specific diseases.

"Psychiatric classifications inevitably reflect social forces prevailing in any particular historical era. Which conditions are diagnosed and how they are treated depend not only on the symptoms displayed by patients, but also on factors that include professional fashions in diagnoses, financial rewards from various treatments, the activities of regulatory and interest groups, cultural values, images of disorder, and the concerns of funding agencies."

"Some signs exist that anxiety could replace depression, recapture its hold on the stress tradition, and return again to the forefront of the stress tradition. The boundaries between depression and anxiety are permeable enough that the same drugs easily can be marketed as responses to anxiety rather than to depressive disorders. The diagnosis of depression is no longer as useful to psychiatry as it was over the past quarter century. The profession's scientific credibility is now far greater than it was in the 1970s; its diagnostic system is generally regarded as reliable; and its biological models are widely accepted. Most important, the drugs used to treat depression have lost their patents." [1]

Classification provides a foundation for the recognition and study of illness (Jutel 2011). The assignment of particular disease labels is linked to both therapeutic and social responses. Diagnosis is both framed by and, in turn, frames the social reality of patients and those who provide them with health care. "Overweight is a new disease, not because individuals are fatter than they once were, but because in the 19th century 'overweight' could not exist as a category of analysis because scales were too expensive for doctors' offices or for personal use. As a result, weight (in contradistinction to fatness) was not a feature of obesity. Yet, even as scales became a standard feature of the medical rooms, and a range of weight classification systems became both available and implemented, the social shaping of diagnostics options continued to vary."

"From 1942 to 2000, no fewer than 18 different 'ideal,' 'desirable,' 'normal,' 'suggested,' 'acceptable,' or other categorical formulations for weight were implemented by a range of official classificatory documents. A weight considered 'ideal' in 1942 would have been 'desirable' in 1959, 'acceptable' in 1985, and 'overweight' in 2000. Today, the gold standard for weight assessment in the Western world is the body mass index (BMI). However, even using this assessment tool, from 1990 to 2000 the upper limit of healthy weights has changed from 27.8 kg/m^2 to 24.9 kg/m^2 and has variably modified its cut-off range for healthy weight on the basis of age and gender."

"The changes to the classification system are due to increasing scientific input relative to risks and benefits of particular classificatory groupings, yet, such science cannot be assumed to

---

1.   Horwitz, A.V. How an Age of Anxiety Became an Age of Depression, *The Milbank Quarterly*, Vol. 88, No. 1, 2010, pp. 112-138.

be either universally accepted or unproblematic." Some obesity scholars "argue that the concern about an alleged obesity epidemic actually is a moral panic, fueled by economic interests, neoliberal philosophy, shoddy science, but also by beliefs in an aesthetic of health and the desirability of slender and compact bodies. Each and every classification engages some social perspectives and shuts down others, but once a classification is established it reproduces itself in an intuitive way that silences debate." [2]

Pathologies That Seemingly Disappear

1960 Nobel Prize winner Sir Macfarlane Burnet was quoted as follows:

> *One can think of the middle of the 20th century as the end of one of the most important social revolutions in history, the virtual elimination of the infectious diseases as a significant factor in social life.* [3]

Exuberance may have been premature, but several factors contributed to a sense of complacency back then. New vaccines were developed for serious diseases such as poliomyelitis and more effective antibiotics became available. Nutritional conditions improved in many parts of the world. The quality of housing was enhanced at a time when there were widespread improvements in sanitation. A sign of optimism was evidenced by decisions made at many schools of medicine to close microbiology departments and end infectious disease training programs.

Recent decades, however, have led to countervailing developments. Human and animal populations continue to grow. Foods are imported into the U.S. from all over the world. Urbanization and the production of huge crowded slums have continued apace. Humans keep spreading themselves geographically, moving to what previously were wild, uninhabited areas. Air and cargo ship traffic increase at regular intervals. The threat of terrorism represents just one more possibility that must be taken into account when conceiving measures to protect the public's health.

"On June 5, 1981, the *Morbidity and Mortality Weekly Report* (MMWR), published by the Centers for Disease Control and Prevention (CDC), described *Pneumocystis carinii* (now *P. jiroveci*) pneumonia in five homosexual men in Los Angeles, California, USA, documenting for the first time what became known as acquired immunodeficiency syndrome (AIDS) (De Cock 2011). An accompanying editorial suggested that the illness might be related to the men's sexual behavior. A month later, the MMWR reported additional diagnoses of *P. carinii* pneumonia, other opportunistic infections, and Kaposi sarcoma in homosexual men from New York City and California. These articles were sentinels for what became one of history's worst pandemics, with >60 million infections, 30 million deaths, and no end in sight."

"The 30th anniversary year of the first description of AIDS [in 1981] is also the 15th anniversary of the introduction of highly active antiretroviral therapy (ART). Henceforth, AIDS will have been a treatable condition longer than it was the inevitably fatal disease first recognized."[4]

---

2.   Jutel, A. Classification, Disease, and Diagnosis, *Perspectives in Biology and Medicine*, Vol. 54, No. 2, Spring 2011, pp. 189-205.

3.   Burnet M. 1962. *Natural History of Infectious Disease*. Cambridge: Cambridge University Press.

4.   De Cock, A.M. et al. Reflections on 30 years of AIDS, *Emerging Infectious Diseases*, Vol. 17, No. 6, June 2011, pp. 1044-1048.

Health Care in Relation to Segmentation of the Population

An important report from the Institute of Medicine (IOM) that was published in 2001 is entitled *Crossing The Quality Chasm*.[5] It specifies six aims for health care: it must be safe, effective, efficient, patient-centered, timely, and equitable. As a way of meeting patients' needs effectively, an approach would be to stratify the population into groups that are sufficiently homogeneous to enable arranging a set of commonly needed supports and services (Lynn 2007). The proposed segments are:

"Healthy (e.g., 37-year-old male who goes for annual check-ups)
Maternal and infant health (e.g., 26-year-old female needing pregnancy and newborn care)
Acutely ill (e.g., 18-year-old athlete who breaks a leg)
Chronic conditions, normal function (e.g., 49-year-old female with diabetes and hypertension)
Stable, but serious disability (e.g., 56-year-old male quadriplegic with suicidal tendencies)
Short period of decline before dying (e.g., 68-year-old female hospice patient)
Limited reserve and exacerbations (e.g., 75-year-old male with severe emphysema)
Frailty, with or without dementia (e.g., 88-year-old female with dementia who cannot walk)"

Over the course of a lifetime, except for pregnancy, males can appear in any of these classifications and females in all of them. Each segment entails different priority concerns, components of health care, and personal health goals. Accordingly, matching them with the six IOM aims will call for different arrays of treatment modalities and practitioners. An important consideration is the cost of health care and the payment mechanisms used for that purpose.

The above classification is not perfect. For example, Medicare law and financing make end-stage renal disease patients (ESRD) a distinct group needing a different mix of services that may cut across the segments. Nevertheless, the framework is one that can be used to think about health in a more specific way that reflects a population with enormous variability among individuals.[6]

Even when certain members of a population subgroup appear similar in fundamental ways, challenges are involved in characterizing them from a health standpoint as shown in the following example. Gesualdo and Luchino are first-generation Italian-Americans whose parents come from Acci Trezza in Sicily. Both men are 51 years old and are the same height and weight. They both underwent an angioplasty in the same month at the same academic health science center hospital.

Gesualdo	Luchino
Has a low stress job	Has a highly stressful job
Has good health insurance	Has substantial out-of-pocket costs
Happily married	Divorced
Non-smoker	Smoker
Optimistic	Fatalistic
Has many friends	Is a loner
Plavix worked satisfactorily	Plavix did not work to offset platelet formation
Faithful medication adherent	Takes occasional drug holidays
Exercises regularly	Doesn't exercise
Father still active at age 81	Father died of a heart attack at age 61

5.   Institute of Medicine. 2001. *Crossing The Quality Chasm*, Washington, DC: National Academy Press.
6.   Lynn, J. et al. Using Population Segmentation to Provide Better Health Care for All: The "Bridges to Health" Model. *Milbank Quarterly*, 2007, Vol. 85, No. 2, pp. 185-208.

Both men may be candidates for additional heart problems such as atrial fibrillation, but if an actuarial estimate had to be surmised, it is probable that Gesualdo will live longer and have fewer episodes that require hospitalization. Although physicians play an important role in each of their lives, it should be evident that Luchino in particular would benefit from the interventions of a more well-rounded health care team drawn from public health, allied health, nursing, and other professions.

Geographical Variation in Health Problems and Health-Related Problems

Washington, DC is bounded on its borders by Montgomery County and Prince George's County, both of which are in the state of Maryland and both of which are contiguous to each other. The Robert Wood Johnson Foundation is collaborating with the University of Wisconsin Population Health Institute to develop rankings for each state's counties. The following rates and percentages as of June 2011 furnish a description of conditions in each jurisdiction:

Condition	Montgomery County	Prince George's County
Population in poor/fair health	9%	12%
High school graduates	85%	70%
Teen birth rate*	20	38
Low-birthweight babies	8.0%	10.5%
Single-parent homes	22%	40%
Violent crime rate*	240	940
Adult smoking	10%	16%
Motor vehicle crash death rate*	7	17
Sexually transmitted infections*	207	638
Access to recreational facilities*	15	8

* Rate per 100,000 population; teen birth rate per 1,000 female population. Data from County Health Rankings, 2011 data. Available at www.countyhealthrankings.org. Accessed Jan 18, 2012.

Similar comparisons of interest can be made throughout the United States. Based on these criteria and related indices such as rates of substance abuse, premature death, access to healthy foods, excessive drinking, and adult obesity, counties are ranked within each state. Differences among counties can be quite stark.

Another valuable resource used in discerning county differences is the *Health Resources County Comparison Tool* (HRCCT), which was developed to enable local health planners, administrators, and researchers to compare health status indicators and available health resources for their county (or county equivalents) to peer counties nationwide. Peer counties are those that are similar in population size, density, age distribution, and poverty.

The tool links health resource data from the *Area Resource File* with *Community Health Status Indicators* (CHSI) data. The ability to compare similar counties directly may assist analysts and health planners in identifying areas in which they lack vital community resources to address health problems. By selecting a state, a county of interest within that state, and a peer county-grouping criterion of interest, a list of peer counties is displayed. After selecting counties for comparison, the user can choose between summary or detailed views of county data.

Health professionals have a vital role to play in dealing with some aforementioned conditions that are listed, but not all of them. The provision of health care services alone will not suffice to prevent morbidity and mortality. Poverty is an overriding concern that creates many situations not conducive to health care interventions. Improvements are dependent upon circumstances in other domains such as education, social services, and law enforcement. Each domain has its own resource capabilities in the form of state and local support and each has its own highly detailed bureaucracy. Pulling them all together to improve personal and community health status poses a major challenge.

Health and the Economy

Health considerations touch upon vital aspects of life in the United States. Consequently, the public policy arena is permeated with issues that require constant attention. A vibrant economy affects the willingness and ability of a national government to meet the health needs of its inhabitants. A stagnant economy in the U.S. creates demands to solve problems such as lowering a distressingly high unemployment rate that has persisted for more than 2 years and shows few signs of becoming lower as 2011 comes to a close. The preservation of existing jobs and the creation of new ones are viewed as desirable objectives. A healthy economy generates tax revenue from individuals and corporations that help to underwrite the costs of providing health care services. A less than vibrant economy adds to publically financed health and social welfare costs as more workers become unemployed.

The creation and preservation of jobs relate to income earned by individuals and families. Being employed offers workers an opportunity to obtain health insurance as part of an organization's benefit structure. Having enough disposable income makes it possible to purchase healthy foods, live in a neighborhood that has advantages leading to the improvement of health status, and be able to pay the costs of achieving higher levels of education. All these factors have a bearing on the ability to sustain healthy lives. An important task confronting policymakers is to contend with the uncertainty of knowing where in a cycle to intervene, when to do so, and how to deal with any unanticipated negative consequences that might result.

For many Americans, economic conditions in the United States are worse than they have been since the Great Depression of the 1930s. Job loss has been substantial. Even when new employment opportunities become available, they are for positions involving lower pay combined with negligible benefits. In June 2011, a report by McKinsey & Company based on a survey of more than 1,300 businesses found that 30% of employers are likely to stop offering workers health insurance after the bulk of the health reform act takes effect in 2014.[7] Hundreds of thousands of workers already have lost the health insurance coverage that they enjoyed while employed. Meanwhile, the oldest segments of the population continue to grow both numerically and proportionately.

The Cycle of Health in Relation to Incarceration

During the past 40 years, the number of prison inmates has increased dramatically. "An estimated 10 million Americans are incarcerated each year (Rich 2011). For black Americans, especially men with no college education, incarceration has become an alarmingly common life experience. By middle age, black men in the United States are more likely to have spent time

---

7.   Kaiser Health News Daily Report, June 8, 2011. On the Web at http://www.kaiserhealthnews.org/Daily-Report. aspx?reportdate=6-8-2011#Health Reform-1. Accessed on June 8, 2011.

in prison than to have graduated from college or joined the military and they are far more likely than whites to be sent to prison for drug offenses despite being no more likely than whites to use drugs."

"Deinstitutionalization of the mentally ill over the past 50 years and severe punishment for drug users starting in the 1970s have shifted the burden of care for addiction and mental illness to jails and prisons. The largest facilities housing psychiatric patients in the U.S. are not hospitals, but jails. The problem is that correctional facilities are designed to confine and punish rather than treat disease. The harsh and socially isolated conditions in jail or prison exacerbate mental illness, especially when inmates are placed under solitary confinement. Moreover, substance use and dependence are highly prevalent among prisoners. With growing numbers of drug users in correctional facilities, the prevalence of infectious diseases has increased correspondingly. As many as a quarter of all Americans infected with HIV and one in three with hepatitis C pass through one of these facilities each year."

In low-income minority communities where a large portion of the male population is in correctional facilities at any given time, incarceration delivers a devastating blow to stable relationships, resulting in risky sexual partnerships that lead to increased rates of sexually transmitted diseases and HIV transmission. The likelihood of unwanted pregnancies is another possible outcome. When prisoners return home, many lack the education and skills required to obtain decent paying jobs. They may be ineligible for Medicaid, supplies of medications given upon their release may run out prematurely, and the only recourse for seeking health care is in hospital emergency rooms, which produces uneven services lacking any semblance of continuity.[8]

States are burdened with the ever-rising costs of their Medicaid programs, a jointly financed partnership between them and the federal government. An intended by-product of the Affordable Care Act (ACA) of 2010 is to reduce the number of uninsured individuals by adding 16 million of them to the Medicaid rolls. Over time, the cost burden for states will increase, which makes it increasingly unlikely that they can devote more resources for supporting higher education, providing an adequate range of social services, and maintaining a criminal justice system effectively.

On May 23, 2011, the U.S. Supreme Court ruled on a 5-4 vote that California must reduce the size of its prison population by one-fourth during a 2-year period. A technical report stands as a model of prescience regarding the potential outcomes of this judicial ruling (RAND 2009). The document states that California's prison population is "disproportionately sicker on average than the U.S. population in general, with substantially higher rates of infectious diseases such as HIV/AIDS, tuberculosis, and hepatitis B and C), serious mental illness, and substance abuse disorders." Inmates also bear a high burden of chronic diseases such as asthma and hypertension, which in common with the aforementioned health problems, require regular use of health care for effective management.

"About two-thirds of California inmates reported having a drug abuse or dependence problem. Yet among California inmates reporting drug use or dependence, only 22% reported receiving treatment since admission to prison. More than half of California inmates reported a recent mental health problem, and about half of them received treatment in prison." Upon release from incarceration, their access to health care services varied by facility type, geographic area (across and within counties), and race/ethnicity. For example, in Los Angeles and Alameda

---

8.   Rich, J.D. et al. Medicine and the Epidemic of Incarceration in the United States, *New England Journal of Medicine*, Vol. 364, Number 22, June 2, 2011, pp. 2081-2083.

counties, more African American parolees resided in areas with lower levels of accessibility than did Latino or white parolees.

In the realm of mental health services, California has established a network of Parole Outpatient Clinics (POCs). Given that many facilities are understaffed with long waiting lists, their role as gatekeepers to county mental health services may be undermined, which in turn will have an impact on parolee efforts to reenter society. Also, based on anecdotal reports, it appears that there is a strong disincentive for parolees to report mental health problems to their parole officers for fear of being labeled as troublemakers or at high risk of recidivism. In California, African Americans and Latino parolees in particular tend to return to disadvantaged neighborhoods and communities, defined by high poverty rates, high unemployment rates, low educational attainment, and a higher share of households in which English is not the primary language.[9]

Children of Dysfunctional Families

"The most disadvantaged U.S. parents are also most likely to have children with more than one partner, creating complex family relationships and potentially exacerbating poverty (Scommegna 2011)." As part of the *2010-2011 Policy Seminar Series* of the Population Reference Bureau (PRB), analysis revealed that among the married parents surveyed, 21% had a child by another partner. Among unmarried parents, 63% already had a child with another partner, which means that more than half of children with unmarried parents are "born into families with at least one half-sibling." By the time those children celebrated their fifth birthdays, 71% had a half-sibling, reflecting the instability of unwed relationships.

"In 2010, 41% of U.S. births were to unmarried parents. As a result, the share of U.S. children whose family lives are shaped by multi-partner fertility is substantial." Overall, the findings suggest that "having children with more than one partner is most common among parents who are young, African American, lived with one parent at age 15, and have lower education levels. The fathers were more likely to have spent time in jail and the birth was more likely to be the result of an unintended pregnancy."

"One concern is the impact on parents' investment in children." Fathers who later have a child with a new partner "tend to reduce the time and money they spend on previous biological children. There is early evidence that the complex family dynamics may take an emotional toll on both children and parents. Children whose parents have offspring by other partners tend to show more 'externalizing behaviors' such as acting out and aggression, which psychologists find are related to dropping out of high school and delinquency later on. Also, parents who have children by more than one partner seem more likely to experience depression." [10]

It should be apparent that each factor relates to other important facets of life that impinge on health status. Low educational attainment and lack of English as a primary language do not correlate positively with health literacy. The lower the level of health literacy, the greater the likelihood that health care will not be delivered and received optimally, leading to non-adherence to prescribed regimens, which can produce deleterious outcomes.

---

9.   Davis, L.M. et al. 2009. *Understanding the Public Health Implications of Prisoner Reentry in California, Phase 1 Report*, Santa Monica, CA: Rand Corporation.

10. Scommegna, P. Population Reference Bureau, Washington, DC: Viewed on the Web at http://www.prb.org/Journalists/Webcasts/2011/multipartner-childbearing-policy-seminar.aspx. Accessed on June 14, 2011.

Economic and Political Aspects of Health Care

Hospitals remain a source of health care, jobs, and economic growth for communities across the country, but they are not immune to the negative impact of a declining economy. Medicaid enrollment and unemployment are increasing, but federal funding continues to fail to cover the costs of care. Hospitals' financial health through the current downturn hinges upon adequate funding from governmental programs.

Amid great controversy, the Affordable Care Act became law in March 2010 without the support of congressional Republicans. As of 2011, many Republicans in both chambers are in favor of repealing the law. The House of Representatives, which has a Republican majority, approved a bill in 2011 to repeal the law. Even if the Senate votes to scuttle health reform, it is unlikely that President Obama will sign this kind of a bill and there probably will not be enough votes to override his veto. Also, even if a Republican is elected President in 2012 and both the House and Senate are controlled by Republicans, it still may be enormously difficult to reverse what has been set in motion.

Factors that will create numerous supporters of retaining the health reform law include enhanced drug benefits under Medicare, elimination of the practice by insurance companies of denying coverage to children because of preexisting health conditions, and providing an opportunity for young adults as old as 26 to remain on their parents' health plan. Human beings tend to be loss-averse and they rarely are happy when something beneficial is taken away from them.

Health Care and Health Status

Elected officials may be prone to viewing health status as part of a simple equation:

Availability of health care = good health

Much more than health care is needed to achieve positive health status of individuals and communities. Providing every inhabitant of the U.S. with a health insurance card offers no guarantee that everybody will enjoy good health. Other factors such as the amount of disposable income, type of employment, adequate housing, marital status, safe neighborhoods, physical fitness, health beliefs, immigration status, and genomics/family health history also have a role in determining health outcomes.

The contents of this chapter and subsequent chapters may be open to different kinds of interpretation, depending upon the reader's level of education, family background, and political orientation. For example, arguments exist about the extent of the role that government should play in financing and assuring that health care is available for all who need it. Heated debates arise when costs are shared by all for the provision of health care to individuals who may be perceived as not deserving it (e.g., substance abusers, obese persons, vehicular drivers whose speeding causes accidents, and smokers). Mandatory vaccination of children is just another example of controversy that easily is generated.

One postulate holds that "pessimistic expectations over the future of an epidemic reduce incentive to avoid current risk. Concentrating attention on dire forecasts may have the unintended consequence of increasing risky behavior." Making cars safer may lead to more accidents because it results in riskier driving behavior; or a vaccine, which makes risky sexual practices less likely to transmit a disease, may lead to more risky sex.[11]

---

11.   Auld, M. Choices, Beliefs, and Infectious Disease Dynamics, *Journal of Health Economics*, Vol. 22, Issue 3, May 2003, pp. 361-377.

It is useful to reflect on other ways in contemporary American society in which products or practices that are intended to remedy a problem instead may exacerbate the situation. For example, supermarkets are flooded with low-fat or no-fat items on food shelves. Does their presence lead to greater consumption than would otherwise occur were they not labeled as such?

Personal Versus Governmental Responsibility

Since the early days of the U.S. republic, political thinkers have debated the role of government in the lives of Americans. Clearly, there must be a balance struck between the concomitant responsibilities of individuals and the obligations of society as expressed by government policies to make life safer and of a higher quality.

Cigarette package warning labels may not have stopped anybody from lighting up, but there is a correlation between a decrease in smoking and higher taxes and restrictions imposed by cities on smoking in bars, restaurants, and indoor arenas. Higher taxation in New York City led to bootleg cigarettes being brought in from North Carolina. Prohibition of alcohol in the 1920s helped fuel an increase in organized crime. Some illegally produced alcoholic beverages were poisonous and resulted in death, blindness, and other debilitating conditions. Despite the danger and illegality of imbibing, Americans continued to drink during those years.

Surely, there cannot be many college-age youth who have not heard about the harmful effects of smoking. Yet, smoke they do. Part of youthful behavior may be attributed to a sense of invulnerability and being unable to compute the association between actions performed during one's late teens and health sequelae four and five decades later.

In the 1970s, seat belt use was mandated. Many car owners paid extra money to deactivate their seat belts and resented the government forcing them to do something to which they were opposed. If a serious effort were made to reduce deaths and injuries caused by auto accidents, an argument might be made for mandating that occupants of a car wear crash helmets. Since many deaths are attributable to head trauma, lives would be saved.

Fast food eateries play a role in the ever-increasing corporeal rotundity of the U.S. populace. A culprit in the larger portions being served is the fact that commodity prices have dropped. It presently is possible to serve larger helpings of French fries at either the same or lower cost than smaller portions. Nobody is required to consume everything on the plate, but it happens. Meanwhile, as the unemployment rate stays high, low-cost fast food chains will attract more customers.

Depending on the kind of health problem to be tackled, it is not always an easy task to decide where to allocate primary responsibility for slowing or reversing trends. Should the emphasis be exclusively on one set of actors such as individuals or on the health care system? Parenthetically, it is worth noting that there really is no health system *per se* in the U.S. If anything, there are several different systems, such as Medicare, Medicaid, the Indian Health Service, the Veterans Health Administration, the Department of Defense, and various forms of managed care. Also, the Affordable Care Act (ACA) of 2010 will result in the creation of a new entity known as *accountable care organizations*, which will be described in more detail in Chapter 13 on delivery of health care services.

Individual responsibility can be taken only so far. A point often is reached when some kind of governmental intervention must occur through a stricter regulatory environment when industry is guilty of undermining the health and well-being of individuals through pollution and shoddy manufacturing practices.

A huge issue confronting the United States and other industrialized nations around the world is how to meet and pay for the emerging health care needs of an aging population. In October 2007, the first of 77 million baby boomers collected a Social Security benefit check. On January 1, 2011, the oldest of the baby boomers (born 1946-1964) reached age 65. Every day for the next two decades, another 10,000 individuals will do so and become eligible for Medicare benefits, which poses a major challenge to the ability to sustain entitlement programs of this nature. The number of workers who will pay the bill for these programs in the form of taxes is shrinking relative to the size of the number of beneficiaries. Solutions will entail some combination of higher taxes, fewer benefits, or raising the entitlement age. None of these prescriptions will be popular and can be expected to cause more battles to be waged by various interest groups.

Worth noting is that Barack Obama began his presidency in 2009 with a pledge to take action to correct the financial strains resulting from Social Security and Medicare. It remains to be seen, however, if he will be successful in doing so given the entrenched interests that will oppose any effort to introduce changes in these programs. President George W. Bush wanted to make alterations in Social Security during his stay in office in 2000-2008, but his plan never advanced in Congress due to fierce resistance.

Schools often are identified as having an important role to play in contributing to the improved health status of children. Many school districts are the objects of criticism because youngsters are performing below grade level in areas such as reading, math, and science. Superimposed on these failings is a belief that these same institutions also should be proficient in raising self-esteem of students, bettering their health, improving race relations, and providing classroom safety.

It is important to keep in mind that health and education represent two entirely separate domains in the governmental sphere. Much of what health experts would like to occur in schools is subject to the approval of local educational authorities. Separate budgets and governing structures are involved and it is not always easy for the two domains to be in harmony with one another. Education spending at the local level is one of the few areas where voters have direct control. Although many citizens support the concept of increasing the number of government services and programs, they are unwilling to pay higher taxes.

Health and the Media

The health behavior of clinicians and patients can be influenced by what appears in the media. Fast food chains devote substantial resources to television advertisements. Pharmaceutical ads ranging from medications for erectile dysfunction to dry eye problems appear on television and in print publications. Typically, a laundry list of possible harmful side effects is presented. Names of diseases are mentioned to alert potential users to the dangers that might ensue if patients with any particular conditions take the medication. The advice in both cases is that if side effects are experienced or certain diseases are present, then users should ask their doctor for advice before proceeding any further. For older patients with comorbidities who are under the care of several physicians, a good question to ask is which doctor? A related aspect is that if patients begin demanding particular medications that they see advertised, then their caregivers need to know enough about these substances to provide accurate advice.

Major news media in the form of newspapers, magazines, and ads on radio and television are among the many avenues that provide health information to consumers and patients. The world of the Internet opens up a vast array of support groups and other kinds of information about the best way of treating health problems.

The Washington Post furnishes an example of a big-city newspaper that has devoted a section in one edition each week to discuss health matters. All too often, however, what is reported in the newspaper and on radio and television is wrong or misleading (Dentzer 2009). "Some distortion is attributable to ignorance or an inability to interpret and convey the nuanced results of clinical studies. More broadly, a problem that is worsening in the era of the 24/7 news cycle is the frequent failure to put new developments into any kind of reasonable context for readers or viewers. Journalists sometimes feel the need to play carnival barkers, hyping a story to draw attention to it. Doing so leads them to frame a story as new or different—depicting study results as counterintuitive or a break from the past—if they want it to be featured prominently or even accepted by an editor at all." [12]

"One of every two men and one of every three women will be diagnosed as having cancer in their lifetime, and approximately half of all patients with cancer will die of their illness or of related complications. Annually, 555,500 Americans are expected to die of cancer, and as the population ages, these rates are expected to rise significantly" (Fishman 2010). Thus, cancer has a prominent place in news reporting.

"Cancer news coverage may offer an unrealistic view if reports emphasize survival rather than mortality, cures rather than treatment failure and adverse events, and aggressive treatment rather than palliative alternatives. A study of large-readership newspapers and national magazines found that there are few reports about death and dying. Even those that do generally do not mention palliative and hospice care," which is significant given numerous well-documented benefits for patients and family members. [13]

Cultural values can influence how stories in the media are portrayed. A comparative case study was done of American news reporting on eating disorders and overweight/obesity between 1995 and 2005 (Saguy 2010). In the contemporary United States, thinness is prized and is associated with high social status and taken as evidence of moral virtue. In contrast, fatness is linked to low status and seen as a sign of sloth and gluttony. Drawing on an original data set of news reports, an examination was conducted of how social and moral meanings of body size inform news reporting on eating disorders and overweight. "The results show that the news media typically discuss how a host of complex factors beyond individual control contribute to anorexia and bulimia, thus mitigating individual blame. Insofar as anorexics and bulimics are typically portrayed as young white women or girls, cultural images of young white female victims are reinforced. Accordingly, the news articles were much less likely to hold these individuals responsible for curing eating disorders."

In contrast, the media predominantly attribute overweight to bad individual choices and tend to treat binge eating disorder as blameworthy. Given that the poor and minorities are more likely to be overweight, such reporting reinforces social stereotypes of fat individuals, ethnic minorities, and the poor as being out of control and lazy. Yet, diet and exercise are viewed as within their power to choose to do something about being overweight. While appreciation for bigger female bodies among African Americans is hailed as protecting against thinness-oriented eating disorders, this same cultural preference is partially blamed for overweight and obesity among African American women and girls. [14]

---

12. Dentzer, S. Communicating Medical News—Pitfalls of Health Care Journalism, *New England Journal of Medicine*, Vol. 360, No. 1, January 1, 2009, pp. 1-3.
13. Fishman, J. et al. Cancer and the Media: How Does the News Report on Treatment and Outcomes? *Archives of Internal Medicine*, Vol. 170, No. 6, March 22, 2010, pp. 515-518.
14. Saguy, A.C. and Gruys, K. Morality and Health: News Media Constructions of Overweight and Eating Disorders, *Social Problems*, Vol. 57, Issue 2, May 2010, pp. 231-250.

A gigantic industry exists for the purpose of dealing with the problem of being overweight. Diet guides fill the shelves of bookstores. Other interventions entail surgery and the use of drugs. Some individuals who least can afford the luxury of paying for these kinds of services still go ahead and do so from a sense of desperation. Sadly, the remedies may have just a temporary effect. Not only does the problem recur, but some interventions pose their own health risks.

Concluding Thoughts

The term *health* embraces an extensive range of considerations. This chapter may serve as a useful aid in identifying certain key features that entail how health is defined, how different kinds of individuals are affected by health problems, the role the economy plays in furnishing resources to address health care needs, individual and governmental influences on health care, and how the media can offer a perspective on the onset of particular health problems.

CHAPTER 2:
Viewing Health Care Through
a Semiotic Veil of Signs

An old joke goes as follows. A patient is admitted to an emergency room and, while lying there, over-hears a conversation about his case by a group of health professionals. One asks, "Should we treat him or should we let him live." Fear of the unknown upon entering the health care arena is an important ele-ment in life for many patients. Apart from a sense of anxiety that may result from the appearance of a suspicious lump or stomach pain, patients bring a host of important attributes to the health care setting. Depending on the degree of similarity, or lack thereof, between patients and providers on factors such as age, gender, and race/ethnicity, their interaction might be more of a social collision than a satisfactory encounter. This chapter touches upon certain elements that have the potential to influence the quality of their interaction.

Taxonomy of Factors Influencing Patient–Health Professional Interaction Effectiveness

Verbal
- Tone of voice
- Speech rate
- Loudness
- Jargon and incomprehensible terminology used by health professionals

Nonverbal
- Eye contact
- Silence on part of patients
- Facial expressivity such as smiling or frowning
- Nodding in agreement
- Looking at a computer instead of at patients
- Open or closed body posture
- Leaning forward or backward during patient-provider interaction
- Nervous reactions by patients such as rubbing of hands or tugging at hair
- Conveying boredom or coldness toward patients
- Use of hand gestures

Unstated and Often Unacknowledged Intangibles
- Race/ethnic/gender/religious concordance between patients and health professionals
- Quality of patients' relationship with significant others such as one's spouse
- Loneliness
- Trust placed in health professionals and vice versa
- Mutual frustration on part of patients and health professionals
- Respect shown to patients
- Empathy displayed by health professionals
- Bias toward certain kinds of patients
- Age differences between patients and health professionals
- Clothing and accessories such as large tattoos and tongue studs
- Patients' health literacy

The provision of health care services is a necessary, but insufficient, way of ensuring improvement of personal and community health. Nevertheless, health status can be influenced positively by the quality of interactions between patients and health care professionals. The effectiveness of such human exchanges is mediated by cultural differences involving patterns of verbal and non-verbal communication. The accompanying list indicates various attributes that can affect the quality of interaction between patients and health professionals.

Fundamentals of Semiotics

From the perspective of semiotics, a sign is something that stands symbolically to somebody for something (Burnham 1993). An example is a flag, which is not a nation but serves to designate one. "By interpreting and giving meaning to signs, we make sense of the world around us. Signs are ubiquitous in human affairs."

"Language is the cardinal sign, but whatever else stands for something and says something to us is also a sign." Touching a patient can be considered a sign of caring. Failure to touch may be perceived by a patient as a radically different kind of sign, especially when caregiver and patient differ by race, ethnicity, or skin color. Failure to interpret signs correctly may produce hazardous consequences. In Homer's *Iliad*, "Hector, vacillating between whether to give battle, misread and failed to heed the flight of an eagle as an omen of disaster and led his Trojan warriors into bloody defeat."

"In diagnosis and in relating to patients, we physicians are on the receiving end of communication and must assign meaning to signs," including the patient history and physical examination, test results, and all other bits of pertinent information. "Semiotics warns us that if we are to minimize errors in interpretation, we must remember that medical signs are but symbolic, often ambiguous proxies of truth whose meaning furthermore is shaped by its contexts and whose interpretation lies at the mercy of inference and the experience, and bias of the individual physician." [15] Nietzsche may have been close to the truth when he asserted that there are no facts, only interpretation.[16]

Charles Sanders Peirce (1839-1914) played a pivotal role in the development of semiotic theory. He "differentiated signs into three categories: *symbolic signs*, *indexical signs*, and *iconic signs*" (Nessa 1996). Human language provides an example of a *symbolic sign*, and in health care, "history-taking is primarily a collection of symbolic signs. The *indexical sign* is causally related to its object." Bodily gestures, body language, and signs explored through physical examinations are indexical signs. An *iconic sign* is one that has "some character in itself showing what it is. x-rays or other technological visualizations are medical examples of iconic signs."

The distinction among these three categories is arbitrary and not exact. It would be difficult to find an absolutely pure index or to find any sign absolutely devoid of the indexical quality. In the realm of semiotics, "these difficulties are seen especially regarding the symbolic and indexical sign *pain*." [17]

---

15. Burnham, J.F. Medical Diagnosis through Semiotics. *Annals of Internal Medicine*, Vol. 119, Number 9, November 1, 1993, pp. 939-943.
16. Nietzsche, F. 1967. *The Will to Power*, Kaufman, W, Hollingsdale, R.J., eds. New York: Random House.
17. Nessa, J. About Signs and Symptoms: Can Semiotics Expand the View of Clinical Medicine? *Theoretical Medicine and Bioethics*, Vol. 17, No. 4, December 1996, pp. 363-377.

Non-Verbal Signs

Most semiotic studies focus on linguistics. "Other semiotic resources that contribute to or even alter the meaning made via linguistic semiotics, albeit significant in importance, are often neglected." Clothing provides an example of an item that might be taken for granted when health professionals interact with patients (Owyong 2009). Different articles of clothing such as a white coat worn in a clinical setting convey messages to observers. For example, the individual who wears such apparel can be viewed as establishing "an asymmetrical power relationship" from the standpoint of health knowledge and expertise.[18] When that expertise is expressed by using medical language, problems can arise when interacting with patients with limited health literacy skills (Koch-Weser 2009). "Patients who may not understand all the medical terminology being used in their role as patient may be deferential to the doctor's expertise and hesitate to interrupt to ask that terminology be explained." [19]

It's also possible that from the perspective of the patient, anyone who is wearing a white coat can be seen as being a physician. The same holds true for anyone possessing a stethoscope. "A new Pennsylvania law aims to make it clear for patients who is taking their blood pressure, giving them an injection or preparing to operate on a loved one" (Krupa 2010). Under the law signed November 23, 2010, by Governor Edward Rendell, physicians, nurses, and other health care professionals are required to wear photo identification badges that state their credentials in large block letters, with descriptions such as "physician" or "registered nurse." [20]

Since physicians may not always wear their white coats and nurses don't necessarily wear caps, patients cannot always tell who is taking care of them. Depending on a patient's cultural background, the presence of a physician or other health professional attired in jeans and a polo shirt may convey a lack of seriousness that can jeopardize the quality of interactions taking place. Conversely, caregivers may form negative impressions of how patients present themselves. For example, the presence of accessories in the form of tongue studs, navel rings, large tattoos, or toe rings might lead to biases that on a subconscious level could affect the desirability of wanting to treat such individuals.

The term *disgust* may be an exceptionally strong one to employ in certain situations, but it also is an emotion that could be aroused. Emergency rooms are the portal of entry for some individuals who may not be considered by health professionals as ideal patients. Vagrants and homeless persons who are heavily inebriated or victims of a drug overdose, who appear not to have bathed in a considerably long period of time, and who may have serious lacerations and skin lesions typically are not high on the list of patients whom health professionals may want to treat.

Disgust is an adaptive system for disease-avoidance behavior (Curtis 2011). "Available data suggest that there is a universal set of disgust cues" that can be elicited by stimuli in the form of bodily wastes and by deformed or unhygienic individuals. Contact with these elicitors can result in withdrawal, distancing, and even nausea.[21] "Darwin was the first to propose that disgust is expressed universally." [22]

---

18. Owyong, Y.S.M. Clothing Semiotics and the Social Construction of Power Relations, *Social Semiotics*, Vol. 19, No. 2, June 2009, pp. 191-211.

19. Koch-Weser, S. et al. Medical Word Use in Clinical Encounters, *Health Expectations*, Vol. 12, Issue 4, December 2009, pp. 371-382.

20. Krupa, C. New Pennsylvania Law Requires Physicians to Wear Photo IDs. amanews.com, December 20, 2010.

21. Curtis, V. et al. Disgust as an Adaptive System for Disease Avoidance Behaviour, *Philosophical Transactions of The Royal Society B: Biological Sciences*, Vol. 366, No. 1563, February 12, 2011, pp. 389-401.

22. Darwin, C. 1872. *The Expression of the Emotions in Man and Animals*, London, UK: Murray.

Even when meeting what would be considered standards for an appropriate physical appearance, in approaching a medical encounter, patients are entering an unusual social situation (Lepper 1995). Often, they must present themselves while dressed only in paper gowns. "They may be required to disclose intimate details of their lives to someone they do not know well. They are expected to answer all questions asked of them." Little, if any, of the encounter consists of the direct expression of expectations and feelings such as fear, embarrassment, and uneasiness about the encounter.

"Since it is known that other types of feelings and emotions are conveyed by means of nonverbal cues such as voice tone and quality, touch, gaze, posture, and facial expressions, it may be that expectations regarding the optimal level of patient involvement also are transmitted and understood nonverbally. Examples of nonverbal expressions by patients are leaning forward to the physician, maintaining eye contact, smiling and head nodding, or doing just the opposite, plus displaying anxiety by self-touching gestures such as rubbing hands together or pulling at hair strands. Practitioners convey messages by gazing toward a patient, head nodding, and sitting or standing close to the patient with a forward lean. Opposite gestures would include writing in the medical record while the patient is speaking and refraining from nodding in response to answering questions being asked." [23]

Nonverbal expressions become a central part of the context and should be viewed as making meaningful statements in their own right (Gallagher 2005). Examples of ways in which health professionals convey meaning are by communicating coldness rather than warmth, creating a sense of distance with patients, acting bored or inattentive, showing enthusiasm, appearing to be sincere, demonstrating an interest in listening to a patient's narrative, and not applying an upper-hand in conversing.[24]

"Talk is incomplete (Knight 2007). What is meant during interaction goes far beyond the meaning of individual utterances themselves. Indeed, the rationality of conversations comes from the intentions of speakers, while understanding depends partly on the recognition of implicit and unstated intentions by the hearer." Inferences augment understanding because natural language often omits aspects that the responder is assumed to be able to infer. As such, arguments are sometimes incomplete. Aristotle called these *enthymemes*. An enthymeme is an argument in which one or more premises (or a conclusion) are missing and need to be filled in because it has not been explicitly expressed." The term *argument* is used here to mean "a form of logical inference based on a deductive syllogistic reasoning process." Typically, this process takes the form of a major premise, a minor premise, and a conclusion. When all three are not present, the incomplete syllogism is an enthymeme.[25]

Concerns do not always have to be expressed verbally (Lang 2000). For example, "when a patient pauses for a long moment or appears to be struggling to respond, a clue that significant problem-solving, self-censoring, or reflection may be occurring." A grimace is a nonverbal feeling clue. A routine visit without cause or expression of dissatisfaction with previous medical care may be a signal that the real reason for the visit has not surfaced yet.[26]

---

23. Lepper, H.S. et al. A Model of NonVerbal Exchange in Physician-Patient Expectations for Patient Involvement, *Journal of Nonverbal Behavior*, Vol. 19, No. 4, Winter 1995, pp. 207-222.

24. Gallagher, T.J. et al. Further Analysis of a Doctor-Patient Nonverbal Communication Instrument, *Patient Education and Counseling*, Vol. 57, Issue 3, June 2005, pp. 262-271.

25. Knight, L.V. and Sweeney, K. Revealing Implicit Understanding through Enthymemes: A Rhetorical Method for the Analysis of Talk, *Medical Education*, Vol. 41, Issue 3, March 2007, pp. 226-233.

26. Lang, F. et al. Clues to Patients' Explanations and Concerns About Their Illnesses: A Call for Active Listening, *Archives of Family Medicine*, Vol. 9, No. 3, March 2000, pp. 222-227.

Among the words that a patient hears when learning of a diagnosis, perhaps cancer is the one that is most feared. Just as cancer is often referred to as the "Big C," sound symbolism is associated with cancer medication names (Abel 2008). The concept of sound symbolism proposes that even the tiniest sounds comprising a word may suggest qualities of the object which the word represents. For example, "common voiced consonants such as *b, d, g, v,* and *z* are thought to be associated with slowness and heaviness" while voiceless consonants "such as *p, t, k, f,* and *s* are believed to be associated with fastness and lightness." Medication trade names are marketing devices, unlike chemical and generic names. "Trade naming considers many factors, including the ease which consumers can recall the name, the name's potential impact on patients, and how reminiscent it is of its generic counterpart."

Medications have been portrayed as: a physician's power to heal, capabilities of technology, patient status of being ill, or an effort to exert self-control. "Not only the type of medication but also the physical form it takes has been shown to have strong symbolism (e.g., blue pills are more tranquilizing than red pills)." Analyzing sounds in the names of 60 cancer-related medications prescribed at the Dana-Farber Cancer Institute in Boston, investigators found that the names of these medications differed systematically from standard American English.

"Trade names possessed an increased frequency of voiceless consonants, which psycholinguistic literature has shown to be associated with the concepts of lighter, smaller, and faster, and in the cancer context might be translated into 'more tolerable.' Moreover, as recent research has shown that physicians often fail to communicate vital information about new medications to patients, we suggest that, imbued with symbolic power, the names themselves—partly created by marketers (in designing trade names) and partly by providers (in adopting common usage names)—may be filling this gap." [27]

Racial and Ethnic Dimensions of Patient-Provider Interaction

Public transit systems provide a venue for overhearing conversations even when doing so is not the intention of listeners. Loudly voiced complaints can be made by the occasional patient who is returning home or going back to work after having spent time in a clinic or health practitioner's office. An example is "I don't know if they pay any attention to me. I tell them what's wrong, but nobody is helping me get any better."

While it is uncertain if such comments are about patients' interactions with health personnel who are not of the same racial or ethnic group, "there is evidence that (1) health care providers hold stereotypes—based on patient race, class, sex, and other characteristics—that influence their interpretation of behaviors and symptoms and their clinical decisions; (2) application of such stereotypes frequently occurs outside conscious awareness; and (3) providers interact less effectively with minority than with white patients. Whites often feel anxious when interacting with blacks. In the context of the clinical encounter, this may translate into white providers' engaging in avoidance behaviors. Non-white patients who may be particularly vigilant for signs of prejudice or rejection, may interpret signs of anxiety displayed by white providers as reflecting negative attitudes. Nonverbal behaviors associated with anxiousness overlap considerably with cues of dislike" (Burgess 2007). [28]

27. Abel, G.A. and Glinert, L.H. Chemotherapy as Language: Sound Symbolism in Cancer Medication Names, *Social Science & Medicine*, Vol. 66, No. 8, April 2008, pp. 1863-1869.
28. Burgess, D. et al. Reducing Racial Bias among Health Care Providers: Lessons from Social-Cognitive Psychology, *Journal of General Internal Medicine*, Vol. 22, No. 6, June 2007, pp. 882-887.

Variability in physicians' communication and perceptions may be related to patients' demographic characteristics (Street 2007). "Even the most well-meaning and egalitarian physicians may have stereotypes or biases based on a patient's demographic status. Racial bias, in particular, has been implicated in research showing that some physicians associate more negative attributes (e.g., non-compliant, less intelligent, more likely to abuse drugs and alcohol) to minority and less educated patients, perceptions that in turn may affect medical decision-making."

In the opposite direction, patients' "communication style can have a powerful effect on physician behavior and beliefs. The medical encounter like other forms of social interaction, requires that participants cooperate and coordinate their talk. Thus, any one interactant can exert influence over the other. For example, physicians typically are more informative, accommodating, and supportive when patients ask questions, make requests, offer opinions, and express their fears and concerns." [29]

Most physicians do not admit to any racial biases explicitly (Green 2007). In a study "on the implicit measures of bias, most non black physicians demonstrated some degree of bias favoring whites over blacks." The study was designed to determine whether physicians' implicit biases predicted different patterns of thrombolysis recommendations for black and white patients with acute coronary syndromes.[30]

"Research has shown that doctors have poorer communication with minority patients than with others" (Ashton 2003). The race and ethnicity of doctor and patient can affect their ability to communicate and negotiate." The most obvious is language or dialect discordance. Even when they speak the same language, "they may use and interpret terms, idioms, and metaphors differently. Patients from different ethnic groups may be more or less inclined to provide a health narrative to the doctor, may use different terms to describe the same phenomenon, and may screen out items in their explanatory model they think the doctor will find unacceptable." [31]

Distrust may "contribute to problems with health and health care in the U.S., including rising health care costs, ineffective or low quality care, and poor patient outcomes (Armstrong 2008). Health care distrust is commonly cited as an important contributor to racial disparities in health and health care, following the argument that higher distrust among racial minorities interferes with seeking medical care and adherence with medical recommendations." [32]

The quality of patient-physician communication is associated with better processes and outcomes, including patient self-management behaviors, adherence, satisfaction, health status and blood pressure control (Cené 2009). Racial disparities in patient-physician communication have been documented. "Physicians provide less information, engage in more narrowly biomedical conversations, spend less time building rapport, and are more verbally dominant and less patient-centered with black patients." [33]

In a study of the provision of information by physicians, "black patients received less information from their doctors, were less active participants, and were less likely to bring a companion to consultations for lung cancer or a pulmonary nodule" (Gordon 2006). While not direct-

29.   Street, R.L. Jr. et al. Physicians' Communication and Perception of Patients: Is it How They Look, How They Talk, or Is it Just the Doctor? *Social Science & Medicine*, Vol. 65, No. 3, August 2007, pp. 586-598

30.   Green, A.R. et al. Implicit Bias among Physicians and its Prediction of Thrombolysis Decisions for Black and White Patients, *Journal of General Internal Medicine*, Vol. 22, No. 9, September 2007, pp. 1231-1238.

31.   Ashton, C.M. et al. Racial and Ethnic Disparities in the Use of Health Services: Bias, Preferences, or Poor Communication, *Journal of General Internal Medicine*, Vol. 18, No. 2, February 2003, pp. 146-152.

32.   Armstrong, K. et al. Differences in the Patterns of Health Care System Distrust between Blacks and Whites, *Journal of General Internal Medicine*, Vol. 23, No. 6, June 2008, pp. 827-833.

33.   Cené, C.W. The Effect of Patient Race and Blood Pressure Control on Patient-Physician Communication, *Journal of General Internal Medicine*, Vol. 24, No. 9, September 2009, pp. 1057-1064.

ly negating the possibility that racial disparities in care are due to doctor bias or patient preferences, they suggest that disparities in medical care are related in part to the communicative dynamics of the encounter, particularly the degree to which patients are actively involved. Communication may be more difficult for black patients because some of them "may have difficulty connecting with doctors if their explanatory models about health and illness are dramatically different."

For example, black patients were more likely to believe that exposure of lung cancer to air during surgery would cause a tumor to spread. As a result, they would be more likely to decline a recommendation for potentially curative surgery. Another possible explanation is that doctors who have less favorable attitudes toward black patients "may subtly communicate distance or less interest in ways that make patients more cautious." [34]

Patients' ethnicity may be related to how well physicians understand them. Compared to the beliefs of white patients in one study, "physicians had a poorer understanding of African-American patients' preferences for a partnership (Street 2011). Doctors also had a poorer understanding of patients' sense of control over health when the patient was of a different race. Other studies have shown that, even when taking into account racial differences in patient participation, minority patients feel less trust and are sometimes perceived by clinicians more negatively. Taken as a whole, these results suggest that understanding the patient's perspective is more complex when physicians and patients come from different cultural and ethnic backgrounds, and they underscore the need for skills training in narrative medicine, history building, and other forms of cultural competence." [35]

"Approximately 10-30% of persons with type 2 diabetes have been reported to withdraw from prescribed regimens within one year of diagnosis and long-term persistence in use of lipid-lowering and anti-hypertensive therapies is low (Traylor 2010). Barriers to the patient-physician relationship such as physician stereotypes and biases and disparities in the quality of interpersonal care may create even greater obstacles to medication adherence for patients of color." They are "more likely to face language barriers and miscommunication with providers and have shorter and less patient-centered office visits than white patients. Patients of color are also more likely to be perceived negatively. Patient race is associated with physicians' assessment of patient intelligence, feelings of affiliation toward the patient, and beliefs about the patients' likelihood of risk behavior and adherence with medical advice." [36]

"Racial and ethnic disparities in health care remain prevalent in the United States. To help track and address these disparities, policymakers and pundits have urged physicians to collect data on the race and ethnic group of patients (Wynia 2010). A landmark 2003 Institute of Medicine (IOM) report recommended the collection of data on the 'race, ethnicity, socioeconomic status, and where possible, primary language' of patients, and in September 2009, the IOM recommended standards for collecting and reporting data on patients' race, ethnic group, and language. Recent health reform proposals also encourage data collection. Yet, most physicians do not collect data on their patients' race and ethnic group. Reliable collection is uncommon even in large group practices and community health centers." [37]

34. Gordon, H.S. et al. Racial Differences in Doctors' Information-Giving and Patients' Participation, *Cancer*, Vol. 107, No. 6, September 15, 2006, pp. 1313-1320.
35. Street, R.L. and Haidet, P. How Well Do Doctors Know Their Patients? Factors Affecting Physician Understanding of Patients' Health Beliefs, *Journal of General Internal Medicine*, Vol. 26, No. 1, January 2011, pp. 21-27.
36. Traylor, A.H. et al. Adherence to Cardiovascular Disease Medications: Does Patient-Provider Race/Ethnicity and Language Concordance Matter, *Journal of General Internal Medicine*, Vol. 25, No. 11, Nov 2010, pp. 1172-1177.
37. Wynia, M.K. et al. Collection of Data on Patients' Race and Ethnic Group by Physician Practices, *New England Journal of Medicine*, Vol. 362, No. 9, March 4, 2010, pp. 846-850.

In one study (Nápoles-Springer 2005), it was noted that "for many African-Americans the potential for racial discrimination and biased care existed in any first encounter with a racially discordant physician. Based on certain nonverbal cues such as maintaining physical distance from the patient or hesitancy to touch the patient or an object touched by the patient, respondents appraised physicians as acting on prejudice. Some African-American participants felt that physicians sometimes made assumptions that they were intellectually inferior or drug users based on their race. African-Americans perceived that physicians treated them as equals, however, when they were included in decision-making." [38]

Religion and Spirituality

"One way or another, religion plays an important role in our lives—be it is as active believers, as targets or victims of religiously motivated actions, or as interested observers of conflicts nurtured by differing religious convictions (Colzato 2010). The impact may be more fundamental than commonly assumed, namely, that religious practice may affect basic perceptual processes in such a way that followers of different religions literally see the same things differently. Members of different religions and atheists differ specifically and systematically in the way they attend to the global and local features of visual stimuli. This divergence can stand in the way of effective communication between people with different religious background." [39]

"Patient views regarding the importance of various aspects of depression care were similar for African Americans and whites, except for the importance of spirituality" (Cooper 2001). In one study, "African American patients were more likely than whites to rate spirituality as an extremely important aspect of care for depression." Prayer is viewed as an important means of coping with serious personal problems. [40]

Faith is a major resource for African American/black men, helping them move from a perception of cancer as a death sentence to the integration of their cancer into their lives (Maliski 2010). In the health care context, faith can be placed in health care providers, family, self, and others such that there is a congruence of belief, trust, and obedience in relation to these entities. For men treated for prostate cancer, as they deal with the shock of their diagnosis, faith gives them "a framework to reframe perceptions such that they integrate the illness experience into their lives through purposeful acceptance or resignation. As these men dealt with treatment and symptom management, faith was used as an empowering force that freed them to be active participants in their treatment." [41]

Do religion and spirituality affect patients' health? Physicians might be a good source to answer that question, but it is unlikely that they view the religious and spiritual domain "through uncolored lenses. They also have their own religious beliefs and practices, which may shape the way they interpret their own clinical experiences and the empirical data regarding the relationship between religion/spirituality and health" (Curlin 2007). In the clinical domain, patients are likely to encounter different ideas about the relationship between their religion/spirituality and their health, depending on the religious frameworks of their physicians. "What the secular physician may not notice or may ignore, the religious physician may emphasize or

38. Nápoles-Springer, A.M. et al. Patients' Perceptions of Cultural Factors Affecting the Quality of Their Medical Encounter, *Health Expectations*, Vol. 8, Issue 1, March 2005, pp. 4-17.
39. Colzato, L.S. et al. God: Do I Have Your Attention, *Cognition*, Vol. 117, Issue 1, October 2010, pp. 87-94.
40. Cooper, L.A. How Important Is Intrinsic Spirituality in Depression Care? *Journal of General Internal Medicine*, Vol. 16, No. 9, September 2001, pp. 634-638.
41. Maliski, S.L. Faith among Low-Income, African American/Black Men Treated for Prostate Cancer, *Cancer Nursing*, Vo. 33, No. 6, November-December 2010, pp. 470-478.

exaggerate. The influence that one may interpret as weak and negative, the other may view as strong and positive." [42]

Shift in the Culture of Health Care

"As the molecular and chemistry-oriented sciences became the predominant 20th century medical paradigm, historians of modern medicine have tracked an undeniable decline in the centrality of face-to-face communication in the care process. Not only were unstructured medical histories replaced by narrow system reviews, but it can be argued that physicians lost confidence in the significance of any but the most explicit hypothesis-driven exchanges and quantified findings" (Roter 2006).

Medicine can be seen as having undergone a shift in the nature of its culture from a high to low communication-context endeavor. High-context communication depends on sensitivity to nonverbal behaviors and environmental cues to decipher meaning, while low-context changes are more verbally explicit, with little reliance on the unstated or nuanced. A manifestation of this shift in medicine is diminished attention to emotion and its role in the care process. "Greater patient satisfaction was associated with nonverbal indicators of physician interest, including less time reading the patient's chart (probably associated with more eye contact), more physical immediacy (e.g., forward lean), and more head nods and gestures. And closer interpersonal distance." [43]

Apart from these circumstances, an important contributing factor that serves to lessen the opportunity for more effective interaction between patients and their caregivers is the reduced amount of time available in the clinical setting. For reasons of economy, it is common for many kinds of health professionals to have strict limits on the amount of time that can be spent with each patient.

A shift in patient care is occurring. Shortages of primary care physicians at a time when the overall U.S. population is growing in size, with dramatic increases among the oldest cohorts, means that health professionals such as physician assistants and advanced nurse practitioners will be called upon to fill the breach. They will have to demonstrate a host of skills necessary to deal effectively with patients, such as recognizing and overcoming potential biases against those who have a different racial or ethnic background. They also will have to be attentive to clues furnished by patients that are not strictly biomedical in nature.

The *concordance model* was conceived originally "to define a process of prescribing and medicine-taking based on a partnership" between patients and health professionals aimed at "reaching an agreement on when, how, and why to use medicines, drawing on the expertise of the health care professional as well as the experiences, beliefs, and wishes of the patient" (Stevenson 2004). A systematic review of the research on communication between patients and health care professionals indicated that "patients may withhold information about nonadherence for fear of incurring the wrath of doctors." Practitioner behavior may act as a barrier to concordance if it entails spending more time talking to, rather than listening to, patients. "If concordance is to be achieved, it is necessary for both practitioners and patients to disclose and discuss their concerns and views." Practitioners need to listen carefully and empathetical-

42.   Curlin, F.A. et al. Physicians' Observations and Interpretations of the Influence of Religion and Spirituality on Health, *Archives of Internal Medicine*, Vol. 167, No. 7, April 9, 2007, pp. 649-654.
43.   Roter, D.L. et al. The Expression of Emotion through Nonverbal Behavior in Medical Visits: Mechanisms and Outcomes, *Journal of General Internal Medicine*, Vol. 21, Supplement 1, January 2006, pp. S28-S34.

ly. Yet, much of the research identified describes an asymmetrical relationship typical of paternalistic interactions.[44]

Doctors are faced with the dilemma of appearing to pay full attention to patients while simultaneously shifting their gaze and even their body posture away from them to record information in the medical record or to examine diagnostic test results (Ruusuvuori 2001). Unlike patients, doctors have to divide their attention among a multiplicity of sources of diagnostic information. The temporal dimension is important during the patient narrative because the doctor's disengagement from interaction could be interpreted as lack of attention when it specifically is viewed by the patient as most needed. "Considering the importance of the phase of problem presentation for the outcome of the visit, doctor's withdrawal of gaze at moments proposed by the patient as relevant for recipiency, could result in the patient leaving out a particularly important part of his/her symptom description." [45]

The Importance of Empathy

"Empathy is not only an important ingredient in patient-centered care, but also has been recognized as absolutely essential when treating chronic pain (Matthias 2010). Empathic, patient-centered care is associated with better health outcomes, in part because seeking to understand a patient's pain and actively involving a patient in his or her care fosters trust, thereby encouraging the patient to reveal important diagnostic information and to participate more fully in treatment." Empathy also can "defuse moments of conflict and reduce the need for each party to feel as if he/she needs to dominate."

"Patients view medical experiences as intertwined with the issues of their everyday lives" (Levinson 2000). They "view their physicians as individuals whom they can trust with their most intimate information, including the stresses of their daily lives and their personal worries. Patients often do not verbalize their anxieties directly; rather, they raise these issues indirectly by offering clues or hints about these psychological and social concerns" such as growing older, loss of a family member, and youngest child leaving home to go to college.[46]

Presentation of clues provides "opportunities for physicians to express empathy and understand patients' lives. In both primary care and surgery, physicians tend to bypass these clues, missing potential opportunities to strengthen the patient-physician relationship. Outcomes of care become optimal when physicians can address concerns that go beyond the biomedical problem."[47]

Rapport building via the use of empathy and effective communication skills is critical to forming effective and trusting relationships with patients (Ferguson 2002). Positive nonverbal and verbal expressions to patients that demonstrate active listening and respect also improve the practitioner-patient relationship. Unfortunately, evidence shows that race, ethnicity, and language all affect the quality of that relationship. "Minority patients, especially those not proficient in English, are less likely to engender empathic responses from physicians, establish rap-

44. Stevenson, F.A. et al. A Systematic Review of the Research on Communication between Patients and Health Care Professionals about Medicines: The Consequences of Concordance, *Health Expectations*, Vol. 7, Issue 3, September 2004, pp. 235-245.

45. Ruusuvuori, J. Looking Means Listening: Coordinating Displays of Engagement in Doctor-Patient Interaction, *Social Science & Medicine*, Vol. 52, No. 7, April 2001, pp. 1093-1108.

46. Matthias, M.S. et al. The Patient-Provider Relationship in Chronic Pain Care: Providers' Perspectives, *Pain Medicine*, Vol. 11, 2010, pp. 1688-1697.

47. Levinson, W. et al. A Study of Patient Clues and Physician Responses in Primary Care and Surgical Settings, *Journal of the American Medical Association*, Vol. 284, No. 8, August 23/30, 2000, pp. 1021-1027.

port with physicians, receive sufficient information, and be encouraged to participate in medical decision-making." [48]

One study at a single medical school revealed that a significant decline in empathy occurs during the third year of education (Hojat 2009). Among the reasons for this erosion was that "modern medical education promotes physicians' emotional detachment, affective distance, and clinical neutrality as emphasized through a focus on the science of medicine and a benign neglect of the art of patient care. Students can easily misinterpret these lessons as an endorsement of avoiding interpersonal engagement in patient care." [49]

Several months later in the same journal, a paper was published to the effect that reports of the decline of empathy are greatly exaggerated (Colliver 2010). A critique of the research methods used to arrive at conclusions about the extent of empathy loss was provided. Fundamentally, the problem is that "self-report empathy instruments are basically self-assessments" and their accuracy may be poor. Rather than focus on the elusive empathy concept, "medical educators might be better served shifting their focus from the elusive empathy concept and concentrating more on good interpersonal behaviors." [50]

Electronic Medical Records

Electronic medical records increasingly are being used in health care organizations, in general and ambulatory settings in particular (Shachak 2009). Benefits include "comprehensive documentation of a patient's medical history, easy access to medical data from remote sites, improved communication among the various providers involved in health care, and easy access to medical information and state of the art resources on the Internet" such as journals and treatment guidelines. Computer use during a session with patients can involve the transmission of nonverbal clues, such as turning one's gaze to or from the screen, typing, or placing a hand on the mouse, to indicate changes in conversation topic or as a signal that the visit is concluded.

Spatial organization of equipment also might have a negative impact, such as restricting eye contact with patients or requiring a practitioner "to move the chair to face patients." [51] As the use of electronic medical records becomes more prevalent, it will be worth studying the extent to which they have an effect on the quality of patient-practitioner interactions.

Depending on one's point of view, the use of electronic medical records can help or hinder communications between patients and practitioners (O'Malley 2010). For example, it is unlikely that nuanced information can be obtained easily from medical records, such as "social context, values, preferences, and issues specific to complex patients such as how health problems affect their lives. On the benefit side, their use allows clinicians to focus on the patient rather than gathering information from a variety of various paper sources."

A challenge is to maintain focus on the patient rather than be tempted to seek information or respond to instant messages or alerts in the electronic medical record. Another potential downside is that the plentiful amount of information from the medical record could "lull clini-

---

48. Ferguson, W.J. and Candib, L.M. Culture, Language, and the Doctor-Patient Relationship, *Family Medicine*, Vol. 34, No. 5, May 2002, pp. 353-361.

49. Hojat, M. et al. The Devil Is in the Third Year: A Longitudinal Study of Erosion of Empathy in Medical School, *Academic Medicine*, Vol. 84, No. 9, September 2009, pp. 1182-1191.

50. Colliver, J.A. Reports of the Decline of Empathy During Medical Examination Are Greatly Exaggerated: A Reexamination of the Research, *Academic Medicine*, Vol. 85, No. 4, April 2010, pp. 588-593.

51. Shachak, A. and Reis, S. The Impact of Electronic Medical Records on Patient-Doctor Communication During Consultation: A Narrative Literature Review, *Journal of Evaluation in Clinical Practice*, Vol. 15, Issue 4, August 2009, pp. 641-649.

cians into believing that they have all the information needed." Although patients may feel more comfortable knowing that a practitioner has information available from other practitioners, a risk is that the wealth of data could lead to a belief that all necessary information is available, which could result in less direct communication with the patient. Also, using a computer may be as much of a distraction as any other gesture that results in a loss of gazing at patients and interacting with them.[52]

Pain in Its Many Manifestations

In Chapter 1 the question was asked, "What is health?" A similar question can be posed about pain. What is it? More specifically, when does acute or chronic pain result in a patient seeking care from a health professional or by taking matters in hand personally such as through self-medication by using over-the-counter products or taking pills left over from a previous episode of experiencing pain?

To what extent will the ability to participate in a given activity influence a decision to do what is prescribed by health providers? Will a football player who hurt his hip when tackled be willing to rest and stay out of the lineup for 3 weeks, knowing that he may never win back his position if his replacement plays well during the interim? In a tight economy where jobs are few, will a day laborer who hurt herself refrain from going to work, knowing full well that there will be no salary obtained for each day missed and that the chances of being rehired will diminish with every passing day?

Will two patients who have the same degree of pain react in the same way, or will factors such as age, gender, race, and ethnicity produce different responses? Does it matter in which part of the body that pain occurs such as the head, stomach, genitalia, lower back, or shoulder? If the latter, what kind of health professional's aid will be sought: primary care physician, chiropractor, physical therapist, athletic trainer, acupuncturist, nurse, physical medicine and rehabilitation physician, or kinesiotherapist?

Upper extremities may be held in deference. We walk arm in arm, shoulder burdens, elbow our way through situations, and dismiss with a flick of the wrist (Hadler 2003). When annoyed with others, it is common to say that they are a pain in the neck, or that a task can be back-breaking. "Coping with upper limb pain is never a passive activity." On a personal level, "how and how much is function restricted and how and how much is comfort compromised?" Is the pain bearable?[53]

Self-reported chronic pain, defined as pain that is not fleeting or minor and lasting for at least 6 months, is common in the U.S. population (Johannes 2010). "A quarter of the population experienced chronic pain of at least 6 months duration and moderate-to-severe intensity. The majority (89%) of individuals had experienced the pain for a year or more, most (86%) experienced pain frequently (two to three times per week or more), and about a third reported severe average pain intensity in the 3 months" prior to a study that was conducted.[54]

"An abundant literature attests to the clinical difficulties faced by patients with pain, secondary to the issue of symptom uncertainty" stemming from medically unexplained symptoms such as cardiac complaints and gastrointestinal symptoms (Tait 2009). "Health care providers tend to

---

52. O'Malley, A.S. et al. Electronic Medical Records and Communication with Patients and Other Clinicians: Are We Talking Less, *Issue Brief from the Center for Studying Health System Change*, No. 13, April 2010, 4 pp.

53. Hadler, N.M. The Semiotics of "Upper Limb Musculoskeletal Disorders in Workers," *Journal of Clinical Epidemiology*, Vol. 56, Issue 10, October 2003, pp. 937-939.

54. Johannes, C.B. et al. The Prevalence of Chronic Pain in United States Adults: Results of an Internet-Based Survey, *The Journal of Pain*, Vol. 11, No. 11, November 2010, pp. 1230-1239.

under-assess, underestimate and under-treat symptoms. These patterns have been found across a range of providers, including nurses, physicians, and other professionals. Likewise, they have been found across a range of settings, including inpatient, outpatient, emergency department, and long-term care. Under-treatment of pain appears to be affected significantly by social characteristics of patients, including race/ethnicity, gender, and age. Characteristics of health care providers such as their training and experience and of the environments in which they practice may affect the extent to which pain is under-assessed, underestimated, and under-treated." [55]

A challenge is to be able to distinguish between someone who actually is experiencing pain and someone who is in pursuit of a disability claim. If the latter is the primary goal, exchanges between patients and providers may be characterized by skepticism and distrust that lead to strained, even hostile interactions and ultimately to provider frustration, stress, and burnout. Such reactions can compromise effective patient care that drain energy and reduce capacity to show empathy for patients.

"Social constructionism provides the means of addressing the multiplicity of meanings available in culture in understanding chronic pain (Eccleston 1997). From this viewpoint it is assumed that within any culture and at any time, there always will be a diversity of ways that pain can be constructed, i.e., that pain always can and always does mean different things." [56]

In *Birth of the Clinic*, Foucault points to the separation in the late 18th century of the anatomical sign and the symptom (Foucault 1994). It was at this time that a discourse of "sign without symptom" began to construct illness, i.e., the belief that illness must show itself through pathology. With this "medical gaze" one can explore the body for signs without the corroboration of the interrogated subject. At the same time, the converse also became possible. The symptom could be supported or cast in medical doubt by the existence or nonexistence of the sign.[57]

Research has shown that "the odds of prescribed activity restrictions are 3.6 times higher for female patients than for males with equivalent characteristics (Safran 1997). The observed differential is not explained by differences in male and female patients' health or role responsibilities. Gender differences in illness behavior and physician gender biases both appear to contribute to the observed differential. Female patients exhibit more illness behavior than males and these behaviors increase physicians' tendency to prescribe activity restrictions. After accounting for illness behavior differences and all other factors, the odds of prescribed activity restrictions among female patients of male physicians is four times that of equivalent male patients of those physicians." The findings are consistent with previous studies indicating that where patient and physician differ in age, gender, race, or culture, communications barriers occur more readily and may result in failed perception of patient preferences.[58]

Other studies indicate that pain complaints of women and minorities receive less attention from health professionals leading to variability in pain assessment and treatment (Green 2010). Despite chronic pain's increasing prevalence and many therapeutic modalities used to manage pain adequately, inadequate chronic pain assessment and treatment occur. This consideration is important in light of the U.S. population's becoming increasingly older and more diverse because pain management will present significant health care challenges.[59]

55.   Tait, R.C. et al. Provider Judgments of Patients in Pain, *Pain Medicine*, Vol. 10, No. 1, Jan/Feb 2009. pp. 11-34.
56.   Eccleston, C. et al. Patients' and Professionals' Understandings of the Causes of Chronic Pain: Blame, Responsibility and Identity Protection, *Social Science & Medicine*, Vol. 45, No. 5, September 1997, pp. 699-709.
57.   Foucault, M. 1994. *The Birth of the Clinic: An Archaeology of Medical Perception*. New York: Vintage Books Edition.
58.   Safran, D.G. et al. Gender Differences in Medical Treatment: The Case of Physician-Prescribed Activity Restriction, *Social Science & Medicine*, Vol. 45, Issue 5, September 1997, pp. 711-722.
59.   Green, C.R. and Hart-Johnson, T. The Adequacy of Chronic Pain Management Prior to Presenting at a Tertiary Care Pain Center: The Role of Patient Socio-Demographic Characteristics, *The Journal of Pain*, Vol. 11, No. 8, August 2010, pp. 746-754.

Fibromyalgia is a common and complex syndrome characterized by chronic and widespread musculoskeletal pain, fatigue, sleep disturbance, and physical and psychological impairment. An assertion is that "physicians are unable to demonstrate fibromyalgia as a visible disease (Hazemeijer 2003). It occurs in the context of unrevealing physical examination and laboratory and radiological examination. The typical sufferer is a middle-aged person, most often a woman, who seeks help from the family doctor because of complaints experienced over a period of several months. The pain is vague and affects the whole body and it usually is accompanied by constipation or abdominal pains. When the diagnosis is made, the patient may respond with hostility to any suggestion that psychological factors may be contributing." [60]

"Studies indicate that treatment of acute pain remains suboptimal due to attitudes and educational barriers on the part of both physicians and patients, as well as the intrinsic limitations of available therapies (Sinatra 2010). Inadequate management of acute pain has a negative impact on numerous aspects of patient health, and may increase the risk of developing chronic pain." [61]

"Men diagnosed with prostate cancer are faced with uncertainties about the best treatment option (Schumm 2010). Patients vary in the amount of information they want and the extent to which they appear to want to be involved in treatment decisions. There has been a tendency to view decision-making as a dyadic process involving patients and their health care professional." Meta-ethnography has been used to synthesize findings from qualitative studies about the influence of having couples involved in making such decisions. The rationale is "that treatment decision-making occurs within the context of wider social networks and is not necessarily a dyadic process between the patient and the health care provider." Adding a patient's significant other to the process adds a further level of complexity.[62]

"Marriage is the central personal relationship for many adults, with important consequences for health and well-being (Smith 2011). Married people live longer than the unmarried and are less prone to serious illnesses, although this benefit often is greater for men than for women. Marital quality is also important, as marital strain and conflict, separation, and divorce confer risk of emotional difficulties and serious physical illness." Physiological stress responses are a key mechanism including "cardiovascular, neuroendocrine, and immune changes reflecting the sympathetic nervous system and the hypothalamic-pituitary-adrenocortical system." [63]

Relationships may influence adjustment to chronic pain conditions such as rheumatoid arthritis" (Reese 2010). Findings underscore the importance of considering not only marital status, but also degree of marital adjustment. The association between marital status and health status depends on the quality of the marriage. Being in a well-adjusted marriage is linked with better health status, whereas being in a distressed or low adjustment marriage is similar to being unmarried.[64]

60. Hazemeijer, L. and Rasker, J.J. Fibromyalgia and the Therapeutic Domain. A Philosophical Study on the Origins of Fibromyalgia in a Specific Social Setting, *Rheumatology*, Vol. 42, Issue 4, April 2003, pp. 507-515.

61. Sinatra, R. Causes and Consequences of Inadequate Management of Acute Pain, *Pain Medicine*, Vol. 11, Issue 12, December 2010, pp. 1859-1871.

62. Schumm, K. et al. "They're Doing Surgery on Two People": A Meta-Ethnography of the Influences on Couples' Treatment Decision Making for Prostate Cancer, *Health Expectations*, Vol. 13, Issue 4, December 2010, pp. 335-349.

63. Smith, T.W. et al. Matters of the Variable Heart: Respiratory Sinus Arrhythmia Response to Marital Interaction and Associations with Marital Quality, *Journal of Personality and Social Psychology*, Vol. 100, No. 1, January 2011, pp. 103-119.

64. Reese, J.B. et al. Pain and Functioning of Rheumatoid Arthritis Patients Based on Marital Status: Is a Distressed Marriage Preferable to No Marriage, *The Journal of Pain*, Vol. 11, No. 10, October 2010, pp. 958-964.

Loneliness

A broken ankle or an earache is a physical condition that is apparent and treatable. Other kinds of health problems may be less clearly defined, making it more difficult to produce a satisfactory remedy. These conditions represent the soft underbelly of health care. An example of a factor that appears to have a strong relationship with more visible health problems is loneliness, which is a prevalent and serious social and public health concern.

According to some measures, society is changing in ways that may make individuals even lonelier. The U.S. Census Bureau estimates that approximately 29 million persons live alone in the U.S., a 30% increase from 1980 to 2009.[65]

A widely cited study in the *American Sociological Review* asked a representative sample of the U.S. population how many would feel comfortable discussing an important personal issue with someone else (McPherson 2006). Between 1985 and 2004, the average number dropped from three to two confidants and the percentage who reported having no confidants rose from 10% to 25%. The American population has lost discussion partners from both kin and outside the family. The largest losses have come from ties that bind to the community and to the neighborhood. The finding is significant because the closer and stronger the tie with others, the greater the likelihood that they will provide help in a crisis.[66]

"Loneliness in adolescence and young adulthood predicted how many cardiovascular risk factors (e.g., body mass index, waist circumference, blood pressure, cholesterol) were elevated in young adulthood and that the number of developmental occasions (i.e., childhood, adolescence, young adulthood) at which participants were lonely predicted the number of elevated risk factors in young adulthood (Cacioppo 2009). Loneliness has also been associated with the progression of Alzheimer's disease, obesity, increased vascular resistance, elevated blood pressure, increased hypothalamic-pituitary-adrenocortical activity, less salubrious sleep, diminished immunity, reduction in independent living, alcoholism, depressive symptomatology, suicidal ideation and behavior, and mortality in older adults."

"What might appear to be a quintessential individualistic experience—loneliness—is not only a function of the individual, but is also a property of groups. People who are lonely tend to be linked to others who are lonely, an effect that is stronger for geographically proximal than distant friends yet extends up to three degrees of separation (friends' friends' friends) within the social network. Longitudinal analyses also indicated that nonlonely individuals who are around lonely individuals tend to grow lonelier over time. Longitudinal results suggest that loneliness appears in social networks through the operation of induction (e.g., contagion), rather than simply arising from lonely individuals finding themselves isolated from others and choosing to become connected to other lonely individuals (i.e., the homophily hypothesis)." [67]

"At any given time up to 32% of adults over the age of 55 report feeling lonely and 5%-7% report feeling intense or persistent loneliness (Hawkley 2010). Socially isolated individuals tend to feel lonely, but loneliness is not synonymous with being socially isolated." Although no effective therapy for loneliness has been documented yet, a cognitive-behavioral therapist should be able to identify and address specific sources of problems in patients' social experiences. Regard -

65. U.S. Census Bureau, "America's Families and Living Arrangements: 2009, Table A2. Family Status and Household Relationship of People 15 Years and Over, by Marital Status, Age, and Sex: 2009," On the Web at http://www.census.gov/population/www/socdemo/hh-fam/cps2009.html. Accessed June 16, 2011.

66. McPherson, M. et al. Social Isolation in America: Changes in Core Discussion Networks over Two Decades, *American Sociological Review*, Vol. 71, Issue 3, June 2006, pp. 353-375.

67. Cacioppo, J.T. et al. Alone in the Crowd: The Structure and Spread of Loneliness in a Large Social Network, *Journal of Personality and Social Psychology*, Vol. 97, No. 6, December 2009, pp. 977-991.

ing blood pressure, there is no evidence that reducing loneliness will lower blood pressure. The more important goal may be to detect and treat loneliness early in life before it has an opportunity to take a toll on physical and mental health and well-being. [68]

"Social behavior has a profound influence on health and well-being (Norman 2011). This is particularly apparent in the study of cardiovascular disease, for which social isolation and stress are risk factors comparable to smoking and obesity. Indeed, social isolation is associated with increased incidence and poorer prognosis among individuals with coronary heart disease." One study examined the role of perceived social isolation in moderating the effects of oxytocin on cardiac autonomic control in humans. "Intranasal administration of 20 IU oxytocin resulted in a significant increase in autonomic (parasympathetic and sympathetic) cardiac control. The effects of oxytocin on cardiac autonomic control were significantly associated with loneliness ratings. Higher levels of loneliness were associated with diminished parasympathetic cardiac reactivity to intranasal oxytocin. The effects of [oxytocin] on autonomic cardiac control were independent of any effects on circulating pro-inflammatory cytokine or stress hormone levels. Thus, lonely individuals may be less responsive to the salubrious effects of oxytocin on cardiovascular responsivity." [69]

"Social and demographic trends are placing an increasing number of adults at risk for loneliness, an established risk factor for physical and mental illness (Masi 2011). The growing costs of loneliness have led to a number of loneliness reduction interventions. Qualitative reviews have identified four primary intervention strategies: (a) improving social skills, (b) enhancing social support, (c) increasing opportunities for social contact, and (d) addressing maladaptive social cognition. An integrative meta-analysis of loneliness reduction interventions was conducted to quantify the effects of each strategy and examined the potential role of moderator variables. Results revealed that single-group pre-post and non-randomized comparison studies yielded larger mean effect sizes relative to randomized comparison studies. Among studies that used the latter design, the most successful interventions addressed maladaptive social cognition." [70]

Closing Thoughts

Semiotics provides a mechanism for examining important nonverbal factors that can influence the effectiveness of the interaction between patients and health professionals. While necessary to focus on the physical symptoms presented by patients, other aspects of their lives such as feelings of loneliness, job dissatisfaction, or marital discontent may be associated with an important underlying problem. Taking into account social factors that might not be apparent or easily discoverable could be a necessary adjunct to efforts to achieve improved health status. Differences between patients and providers may create a level of distrust that can interfere with the effective delivery of health care services.

68.   Hawkley, L.C. et al. Loneliness Predicts Increased Blood Pressure: 5-Year Cross-Lagged Analyses in Middle-Aged and Older Adults. *Psychology and Aging*, Vol. 25, No. 1, March 2010, pp. 132-141.

69.   Norman, G.J. et al. Oxytocin Increases Autonomic Cardiac Control: Moderation by Loneliness, *Biological Psychology*, Vol. 86, No. 3, March 2011, pp. 174-180.

70.   Masi, C.M. et al. A Meta-Analysis of Interventions to Reduce Loneliness, *Personality and Social Psychology Review*, Vol. 15, Issue 3, August 2011, pp. 219-266.

CHAPTER 3:
Determinants of
Health Status

3

This chapter describes socioeconomic factors pertaining to age, gender, race/ethnicity, level of educa-tion, marital status, occupation, and income that have an impact on health status and the ways in which patients interact with health professionals. Women represent a group deserving of special attention. Pregnancy and the consequences of the entire lifespan of a woman leading up to childbearing will have a strong influence on her health and on the health of her children.

The health status of individuals and society as a whole is a complex affair (Elwood 2009). "One way of envisioning the various determinants of health status is to consider a five-layer chessboard arrangement. Each individual chessboard is independent of the other four, and within each board, dynamic interactions occur among the constituent parts. In addition, although they differ markedly from one another, all five layers are related in essential ways. They are:

- Health care services
- Individual behavior
- Social environment
- Physical environment
- Genetics" [71]

Socioeconomic factors permeate each layer and a great amount of research has been con-ducted for the purpose of understanding the impact of socioeconomic inequalities on health sta-tus. Many studies produce conflicting or unclear results about the various factors that work either singly or in combination to produce unfavorable health outcomes. The result is a tangled web that not always is easy to unravel.

Nevertheless, even on an intuitive level it appears highly likely that the social conditions under which one is born, raised, and lives during the period of adulthood will influence health in fundamental ways. Given the voluminous nature of the professional literature, this chapter by necessity will focus on only a limited portion of studies that purport to explain the relation-ship between health status and a host of pertinent social and cultural factors.

As a prelude, certain terms used in this chapter should be clarified. "*Health disparities* are dif-ferences in health outcomes and their determinants between segments of the population, as defined by social, demographic, environmental, and geographic attributes. *Health inequalities,* which is sometimes used interchangeably with the term *health disparities,* is used more often in the scientific and economic literature to refer to summary measures of population health asso-ciated with individual- or group-specific attributes (e.g., education, income, or race/ethnicity). *Health inequities* are a subset of health inequalities that are modifiable, associated with social dis-

---

71. Elwood, T.W. Health Status Determinants in Relation to Federal Health Policy, *Journal of Allied Health,* Vol. 38, Number 1, Spring 2009, pp. 3-7.

advantage, and considered ethically unfair" (Truman 2011). The three terms serve as important indicators of community health and provide information for decision-making and for implementing interventions to reduce preventable morbidity and mortality.[72]

Socioeconomic Correlates and Causality

"Income, education, occupation, age, sex, marital status, and ethnicity are all correlated with health in one context or another," but difficulties are encountered in "deriving robust scientific conclusions from these correlations or drawing reliable policy applications" (Fuchs 2004). Some reasons for this uncertainty are that many socioeconomic variables are correlated with each other and sometimes it is difficult to estimate the independent relationship of each one with health. A big problem is establishing causality. "Even when a causal connection appears to be particularly robust, the mechanism of action usually is unknown. All of these problems are exacerbated by the fact that health is multi-dimensional. Frequently used measures such as morbidity, mortality, disability, and self-reported health status are usually positively correlated, but sometimes the correlations are weak and occasionally even are negative. For example, holding age constant, women report worse health and disability than men but they have higher life expectancy."

Inconsistencies abound. To cite another example, high income correlates with better health, but if that income is the result of working longer hours in high-stress or dangerous occupations, then it may offset the possibility of being in good health. One level of income could be achieved in an occupation that offers several weeks of vacation and a work week involving fewer hours than another occupation that provides the same level of income but with little vacation time and much longer work weeks. It would not be surprising if life expectancy were shorter in the latter situation.

"Another illustration is that married men and women tend to be healthier than their unmarried peers." Instead of causality running from marriage to health, it could go in the other direction such that healthier men and women do better in the marriage market.[73] Although it appears that marital status often correlates with income and education, it will be shown later in this chapter that such a connection may not always be true as evidenced by teen marriages of high-school dropouts.

Since Fuchs published his views on how various factors do not clearly explain causal relationships, more studies have been conducted to shed light on these issues. A position maintained by the Centers for Disease Control and Prevention (CDC) is that "socioeconomic circumstances of persons and the places where they live and work strongly influence their health (Beckles 2011). The risk for mortality, morbidity, unhealthy behaviors, reduced access to health care, and poor quality of care increases with decreasing socioeconomic circumstances. This association is continuous and graded across a population and cumulative over the life course."

Education and income commonly are used to assess the influence of these circumstances. "Education is a strong determinant of future employment and income." The availability of a suitable amount of "income can influence health by its direct effect on living standards (e.g., access to better quality food and housing, leisure-time activities, and health-care services)." [74]

72. Truman, B.I. et al. Rationale for Regular Reporting on Health Disparities and Inequalities—United States, *Morbidity and Mortality Weekly Report*, Vol. 60, No. 1, January 14, 2011, pp. 3-10.

73. Fuchs, V. Reflections on the Socioeconomic Correlates of Health, *Journal of Health Economics*, Vol. 23, Issue 4, July 2004, pp. 653-661.

74. Beckles, G.L. and Truman, B.I. CDC Health Disparities and Inequalities Report—United States, 2011, *Morbidity and Mortality Weekly Report*, Supplement/Vol. 60, January 14, 2011, pp. 12-17.

"Ripple effects of income on health extend beyond its direct influence on access to care and personal efforts to modify behavioral risk factors (Woolf 2007). For example, individuals with limited incomes often lack the resources to remove themselves from unhealthy communities, jobs, and schools. They cannot afford to live in neighborhoods where they can exercise safely; shop at markets with healthy food choices; escape advertising for fast foods, tobacco, and liquor; and avoid violent crime."

"Perhaps the most enduring characteristics of income are mediated by education. Parents with limited income are more likely to live in poorly funded school districts and their children are less able to obtain a college education, a good job, and sufficient earnings to avoid repeating the cycle with their own children. Individuals with inadequate education are less likely to have the necessary knowledge and health literacy to successfully modify behaviors, recognize warning symptoms, and manage complex chronic illnesses amid a highly fragmented health care system." [75]

The Affordable Care Act (ACA) that became law in March 2010 aims to expand the number of individuals covered by health insurance. Until all its provisions become effective, a sizable portion of the population with reduced economic means will continue to have "less access to adequate health insurance or to receive optimal preventive or therapeutic medical care, have lower literacy, and are less likely to seek timely medical attention, or successfully navigate the health system" (Jemal 2008). In one investigation, blacks and Hispanics were disproportionately represented in the lowest education group, more likely to be uninsured, and less likely to receive optimal care. "Socioeconomic status, race, and ethnicity are closely interrelated and difficult to disentangle." [76]

Research efforts to sort out the influence of socioeconomic facts are not confined to the United States. An extensive body of investigations has been conducted in the United Kingdom and in several nations belonging to the European Union. Closer to home, Canada has been the scene of a comprehensive report that was built around a model involving 14 social determinants of health as shown below (Mikkonen 2010).

Social Determinants Having Strong Effects upon the Health of Canadians	
Aboriginal status	Gender
Disability	Housing
Early Life	Income and income distribution
Education	Race
Employment and working conditions	Social exclusion
Food insecurity	Social safety net
Health services	Unemployment and job security

The report provides information on the importance and policy implications of each factor.[77] Similar analyses are conducted in the United States, with one difference being aboriginal status is not considered in this country. Instead, parallel designations such as Native Americans and recent immigrants are more likely to be the focus of different investigations.

75. Woolf, S.H. Future Health Consequences of the Current Decline in US Household Income, *Journal of the American Medical Association*, Vol. 298, No. 16, October 24/31, 2007, pp. 1931-1933.

76. Jemal, A., et al. Mortality from Leading Causes by Education and Race in the United States, 2001, *American Journal of Preventive Medicine*, Vol. 34, No. 1, January 2008, pp. 1-8.

77. Mikkonen, J. and Raphael, D. *Social Determinants of Health: The Canadian Facts*, Toronto: York University School of Health Policy and Management, May 2010, 62 pp. On the Web at http://www.thecanadianfacts.org/ Accessed on May 31, 2011.

The Robert Wood Johnson Foundation has played an important role in providing mechanisms for improving health status. A major step in that direction was the Foundation's creation of a *Commission to Build a Healthier America*. The work of the Commission was enhanced by findings from various analyses, which indicate that "in the U.S., where education and income are the most frequently used socioeconomic measures, Americans who are poor and who have not graduated from high school experience considerably worse health on average than more affluent or educated Americans. Health disparities across income and education groups are seen in a range of health conditions from the beginning of life to old age" (Braveman 2011). The following six figures show evidence of these disparities by education level and income for selected conditions.

"Infant mortality and life expectancy are important indicators of a population's health, and both vary markedly across U.S. groups defined by education and/or income. For example, babies born to mothers who have completed fewer than 12 years of schooling are nearly twice as likely to die before their first birthdays as babies born to mothers who have completed 16 or more years of schooling (Figure 1). More education is also linked with longer life. Men and women who have graduated from college can expect to live at least 5 years longer on average than their counterparts who have not completed high school (Figure 2)." A similar pattern in life expectancy can be seen with income, as higher-income men and women live longer than those with lower incomes (Figure 3).

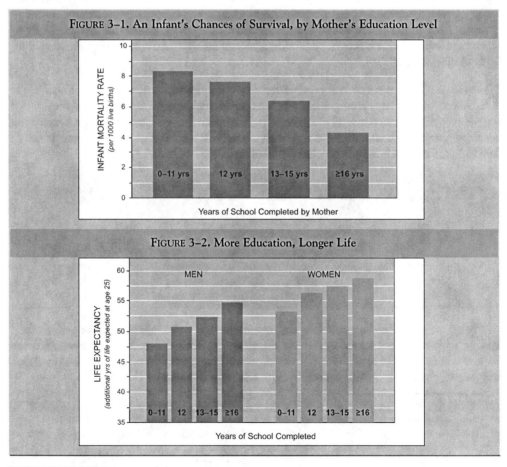

FIGURE 3–1. An Infant's Chances of Survival, by Mother's Education Level

FIGURE 3–2. More Education, Longer Life

Source: Figures 1-4 adapted from Braveman et al., *American Journal of Preventive Medicine* (Braveman 2011).

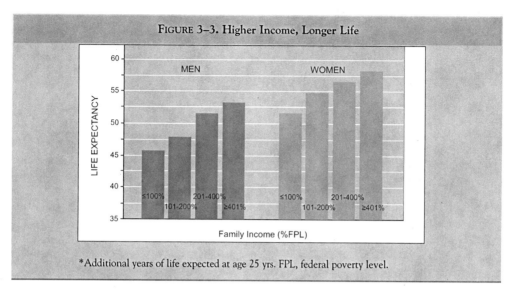

FIGURE 3–3. Higher Income, Longer Life

*Additional years of life expected at age 25 yrs. FPL, federal poverty level.

"Individuals' reports of whether their health is poor, fair, good, very good, or excellent are generally considered to be reliable indicators of their health status. The percentage of U.S. adults who report being in poor or only fair (rather than good or better) health increases as levels of income (Figure 4) and education decrease. For example, poor adults are nearly five times as likely to report being in poor or only fair health as adults with family incomes above 400% of the federal poverty level" (FPL).

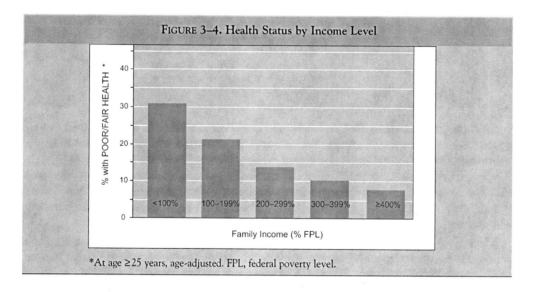

FIGURE 3–4. Health Status by Income Level

*At age ≥25 years, age-adjusted. FPL, federal poverty level.

Children's health status (as reported by parents or guardians) also reflects family income and education levels. As shown in Figure 5, "the prevalence of poor or fair health among U.S. children increases dramatically with decreasing parental education; children whose parents have not completed high school are approximately six times more likely to be in poor or fair health as children with at least one college-graduate parent."

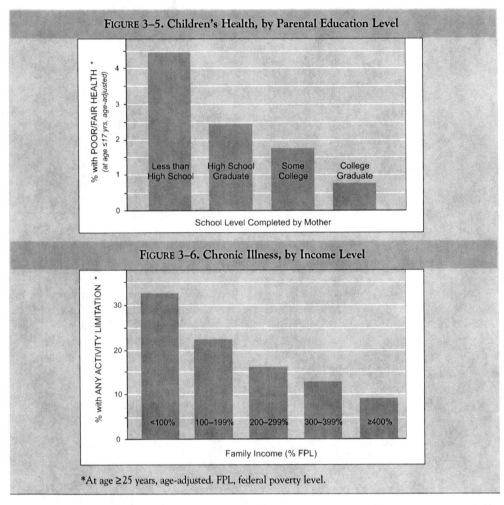

FIGURE 3–5. Children's Health, by Parental Education Level

FIGURE 3–6. Chronic Illness, by Income Level

*At age ≥25 years, age-adjusted. FPL, federal poverty level.

Similarly, chronic disease that limits an individual's activity is much more common in persons in more disadvantaged groups. For example, as compared with higher-income adults, "adults with family incomes below the federal poverty level are more than three times as likely to report activity limitation (inability or limited ability to work, requiring help with personal care, inability to perform activities usual for individuals their age) due to chronic illness (Figure 6), more than twice as likely to have diabetes, and nearly 1.5 times as likely to have coronary heart disease."

While these six figures show that the largest disparities in health are seen when comparing the worst-off to the best-off groups, they also show health differences between each level of income or education, including health differences between the next-to-highest income or education group and those with the highest incomes/education. "These examples—and evidence from other studies in the U.S. and elsewhere—illustrate an important point: the effects of socio - economic disparities in health are not limited to those in the most disadvantaged groups."

"Although individuals in the poorest or least educated groups typically experience the poorest health, even Americans who by most standards are considered to be 'middle-class' are on

Source: Figures 5-6 adapted from Braveman et al., *American Journal of Preventive Medicine* (Braveman 2011).

average less healthy than Americans with greater advantages. Socioeconomic disparities in a wide range of health conditions typically follow a gradient pattern, with greater social and economic advantage corresponding to better health. The gradient does not necessarily follow a straight line. Increases in income for individuals at the lower end of the income scale tend to translate into larger increases in health, while increases in income among already very high-income individuals may not be associated with better health."

"Results of these observational and unadjusted analyses certainly do not establish a causal role for income or educational attainment per se." What they do, however, is "add to and support a large and growing body of evidence, including research identifying pathways and physiologic mechanisms, that suggests likely causal roles in many health conditions for factors tightly linked with income and education. Though reverse causation—with poor health leading to lower income—may in part explain income gradients in health, it is a less likely explanation for the education gradients."

Racial or ethnic differences in health, rather than reflecting biological differences that would explain the large, widespread health disparities, are more likely to reflect differences in personal experiences from birth on, based on the relatively advantaged or disadvantaged position in society of the race or ethnic group of the families.

The importance of considering both socioeconomic and racial/ethnic groups in assessing health disparities is underscored when income or education and racial/ethnic group are considered together. "Poor or fair health is less prevalent both among higher-income adults and among whites, which could lead to the erroneous inference that poorer health among blacks and Hispanics is the primary explanation for both observed gradients. When income and racial or ethnic group are considered jointly, however, income gradients in fair or poor health are seen within each racial or ethnic group, and racial or ethnic differences are seen at each level of income. The racial/ethnic differences within each income group could reflect unmeasured socioeconomic differences; at the same level of income, black and Hispanic adults have far less wealth, are more likely to have grown up in households with fewer socioeconomic advantages, and are more likely to live in socioeconomically disadvantaged neighborhoods where conditions such as inadequate housing, crime, noise, pollution, and lack of services may have health impacts above and beyond those associated with the income or educational attainment of individual residents." [78]

Socioeconomic Status and Environmental Risk Exposure

Income is viewed as being inversely correlated with exposure to suboptimal environmental conditions such as "physical properties of the ambient and immediate surroundings" of individuals, "including pollutants, toxins, noise, and crowding, as well as exposure to settings such as housing, schools, work environments, and neighborhood settings (Evans 2002). The poor are most likely to be exposed not only to the worst air quality, the most noise, the lowest-quality housing and schools, but to lower-quality environments on a wide array of multiple dimensions."

Substandard housing is common in poor neighborhoods, increasing the likelihood of infestation by rodents and cockroaches, along with inadequate heating systems and the presence of dampness, mold, and other allergens. Children in low-income families also are more likely to be

---

78.   Braveman, P.A. et al. Broadening the Focus: The Need to Address the Social Determinants of Health, *American Journal of Preventive Medicine*, Vol. 40, Issue 1, Supplement 1, January 2011, pp. S4-S18.

exposed to lead in the home. Exposure to dust mites and pollens has negative health consequences. Those who rent are more likely to be exposed to these hazards than those who own their homes. Meanwhile, the national housing bubble has burst and the number of foreclosures is rising steeply. Home ownership for many Americans is quickly on its way to becoming an issue of being able to find a suitable alternative in the form of rental lodging.

Members of disadvantaged racial and ethnic groups are more likely to live in poor neighborhoods. The characteristics of such locales—factors like limited access to nutritious food, living near toxic wastes and abandoned or deteriorating factories, freeway noise and fumes, and exposure to crime, violence, and other hazards—increase the chances of serious health problems. All these factors that increase illness or risk of injury are more common in the daily lives of poor and minority families. Living in health-damaging situations often means that individuals and families don't have healthy choices they can afford to make.

Schools in low-income neighborhoods may be overcrowded. Lack of a sufficient level of education can lead to taking the only available jobs, which may entail heavy lifting, repetitive strains, and exposure to "toxins, fumes, dust, explosives, and vibration." Many public school systems in large urban areas are not models of high performance. If parents are not involved, dropout rates are high, and police have to patrol the corridors to provide safety, then it is hard to imagine how such institutions are going to be able to meet expectations.[79]

"Socioeconomic status (SES) exposures during childhood are powerful predictors of adult cardiovascular morbidity, cardiovascular mortality, all-cause mortality, and mortality due to a range of specific causes" (Cohen 2010). Little is known, however, about "when childhood SES exposures matter most, how long they need to last, what behavioral, psychological, or physiological pathways link the childhood SES experience to adult health, and which specific adult health outcomes are vulnerable to childhood SES exposures. While early childhood exposures seem to be potent predictors of a range of health outcomes, later childhood and adolescent exposures are risks for other health outcomes." [80]

An analysis conducted in 2010 using data from participants in the 2008–2009 survey of the Seattle Obesity Study "compared the relative strength of the association between the individual-level neighborhood wealth metric (assessed property values) and area-level SES measures (including education, income, and percentage above poverty as single variables, and as the composite Singh index) on the binary outcome fair/poor general health status (Moudon 2011). The neighborhood wealth measure was more predictive of fair/poor health status than area-level SES measures." The investigators believe that "the proposed individual-level metric of neighborhood wealth, if replicated in other areas, could replace area-based SES measures, thus simplifying analyses of contextual effects on health." [81]

Apart from any hazards posed by environmental defects, individuals sometimes contribute to their own health risks. Parental smoking, which is related inversely to income levels, increases exposures to a wide variety of indoor toxins. In parts of the United States where cold weather prevails in the winter months, storm windows are used on homes. They might be installed in early October and remain there until April. If any inhabitants are smokers, whatever benefits are derived by reducing the baleful effects of cold weather are offset to an appreciable extent by the accumulation of smoke in an airtight cage suffused with indoor toxins.

---

79.   Evans, G.W. and Kantrowitz, E. Socioeconomic Status and Health: The Potential Role of Environmental Risk Exposure, *Annual Review of Public Health*, Vol. 23, 2002, pp. 303-331.

80.   Cohen, S. et al. Childhood Socioeconomic Status and Adult Health, *Annals of the New York Academy of Sciences*, Vol. 1186, February 2010, pp. 37-55.

81.   Moudon, A.V. et al. A Neighborhood Wealth Metric for Use in Health Studies, *American Journal of Preventive Medicine*, Vol. 41, Issue 1, July 2011, pp. 88-97.

Social Relationships

Evidence from observational studies has documented the association between social relationships and beneficial effects on health outcomes such as mortality (Barbour 2010). "The precise size of the effect, and of which aspects that form part of social relationships are most strongly linked with positive outcomes, remains unclear. A systematic review and meta-analysis of the literature shed further light on these questions. Researchers examined studies carried out in both community populations and patient samples, and examined only the hardest endpoint—mortality (excluding studies in which only suicide or injury-related mortality was reported). Stronger social relationships were associated with a 50% increased chance of survival over the course of the studies, on average."

"The effect was similar for both 'functional' (e.g., the receipt or perception of receipt of support within a social relationship) and 'structural' measures of relationships (e.g., being married, living alone, size of social networks). The degree of mortality risk associated with lack of social relationships is similar to that which exists for more publicized risk factors, such as smoking." [82] This finding would seem to be in harmony with the points made in the previous chapter about the impact that loneliness has on health status.

Maternal Factors that Have an Influence on Health Outcomes

What has emerged from research efforts "is a rather complex picture of how individuals in the lower socioeconomic strata are exposed over their lifetime to a wide variety of unfavorable and interacting material, cultural, and psychological conditions, and how these exposures lead to ill-health—either directly or indirectly through unhealthy behaviors or psychosocial stress (Mackenbach 2003). The basis of health inequalities is evident in the womb because low socioeconomic status of the mother is associated with lower birthweight of the child. Low birthweight not only is associated with infant health, but surprisingly also with adult health. Early life influences on inequalities in adult health are not limited to fetal programming of growth patterns. Childhood experiences leave their mark on adult health as measured by both all-cause mortality and specific mortality rates for conditions such as coronary heart disease." [83]

An example of a social problem that can have a dramatic effect on a woman's health is being a victim of intimate partner violence, a calamitous occurrence with 44% of women reporting exposure in their adult lifetime, depending on the population sampled, definitions of partner violence, and data-collection methods (Thompson 2006). Intimate partners could be current or former spouses, non-marital partners, or dating partners in a relationship lasting longer than 1 week. Intimate partner violence types are "physical, sexual, and psychological." [84]

Compared with never-abused women (Bonomi 2009), "abused women had significantly increased relative risks of the following disorders: psychosocial/mental (substance abuse, family and social problems, depression, anxiety/neuroses, tobacco use), musculoskeletal (degenerative joint disease, low back pain, trauma-related joint disorders, cervical pain, acute sprains and pains), and female reproductive (menstrual disorders, vaginitis/vulvitis/cervicitis)."

82. Barbour, V. et al. Editorial: Social Relationships Are Key to Health, and to Health Policy, *PLoS Medicine*, Vol. 7, No. 8, August 31, 2010

83. Mackenbach, J. and Howden-Chapman, P. New Perspectives on Socioeconomic Inequalities in Health, *Perspectives in Biology and Medicine*, Vol. 46, No. 3, Summer 2003, pp. 428-444.

84. Thompson, R.S. et al. Intimate Partner Violence: Prevalence, Types, and Chronicity in Adult Women, *American Journal of Preventive Medicine*, Vol. 30, Issue 6, June 2006, pp. 447-457.

"Abused women had a more than 3-fold risk of being diagnosed with a sexually transmitted disease and a 2-fold increased risk of lacerations, as well as an increased risk of acute respiratory tract infection, gastroesophageal reflux disease, chest pain, abdominal pain, urinary tract infections, headaches, and contusions/abrasions." [85] Assuming that women who have encountered abuse bear children, the offspring would appear to be at increased risk of developing health problems that would not otherwise have occurred.

"While ancient Roman, Catholic, English, and early American law may have allowed marriage at age 12 for girls and 14 for boys, many questioned the advisability of such early unions" (Dahl 2010). Around the turn of the 20th century, "it became recognized that teens may be especially ill-prepared to assume the familial responsibilities and financial pressures associated with marriage. As a result of the changing economic and social landscape in the United States, in the latter part of the 19th century and throughout the 20th century, individual states began to slowly raise the minimum legal age at which individuals were allowed to marry."

"Previous research points to a variety of social, family, health, and financial outcomes that are correlated strongly with early teen marriage and low education. Women who marry in their teens are two-thirds more likely to divorce within 15 years of their wedding compared with women who postpone marriage. In addition, women who marry in their teens tend to have more children and to have those children earlier. Teenage marriage is also associated with much lower educational levels; women who marry before the age of 19 are 50% more likely to drop out of high school and four times less likely to graduate from college. Low education, in turn, correlates with lower wages, higher unemployment rates, worse health, and higher crime rates. The negative outcomes associated with early marriage and dropping out of high school have the potential to affect not only the individual making the decision, but also her children and the rest of society. A high divorce rate combined with low wages and a larger family size increases the number of children living in poverty and receiving state assistance."

Estimates imply that women who marry young are 31 percentage points more likely to live in poverty when they are older. Similarly, women who drop out of school are 11 percentage points more likely to be in families below the poverty line. These results suggest that "decisions women make early in life can have long-lasting consequences. Legal restrictions that prevent early marriage and mandate high school completion have the potential to greatly reduce the chances of future poverty for a woman and her family. The implication is that legal restrictions on teenagers' choices can reduce external costs imposed on society and it also is possible they prevent some teens from making decisions they will regret later." [86]

"Some of the most powerful influences on pregnancy outcome are related to influences on women's health that occur long before pregnancy begins (Misra 2003). For example, nutritional status may be strongly influenced by childhood practices. To achieve sufficient folate in early pregnancy, nutrition may need to be ensured not just in the few weeks or months prior to pregnancy, but possibly years before childbearing begins. Similarly, although infection during pregnancy is a strong risk factor for preterm delivery, the problem of infections may need to be addressed beginning in adolescence and between pregnancies to be effective in preventing adverse outcomes."

A "lifespan" approach to pregnancy outcome identifies the antecedents of poor perinatal outcome and links behaviors and risks across time, not solely during those periods in which a

---

85. Bonomi, A.E. et al. Medical and Psychosocial Diagnoses in Women With a History of Intimate Partner Violence, *Archives of Internal Medicine*, Vol. 169, No. 18, October 12, 2009, pp. 1692-1697.
86. Dahl, G.B. Early Teen Marriage and Future Poverty, *Demography*, Vol. 47, No. 3, August 2010, pp. 689-718.

woman is pregnant. "As in the case of chronic disease programs, efforts to improve the outcome of pregnancy may need to adopt a "multiple determinants" model that integrates the social, psychological, behavioral, environmental, and biological factors that shape pregnancy." The postponement and continuation of childbearing by women into their 30s and 40s underscores the importance of addressing chronic diseases in the context of pregnancy-related care and services. [87]

Another point of view maintains that "many epidemiologists interested in life course issues hypothesize that most adult disease is not likely the result of early childhood or prenatal exposure, but rather the result of a lifetime of accumulated exposure (Berkman 2009). Such a model can relate to early exposures and simultaneously to adult exposures because it is the impact of cumulative exposures across the life course that takes a toll at later ages. Early experiences may produce some independent impact on outcomes but that is not the central issue in this model. In this model the etiologic period is long and covers decades of an individual's life, starting in early childhood or in adulthood. Even if early experiences set individuals up for adult experiences, it is the cumulative impact that is critical." [88]

The Role of Government in Promoting Better Health Conditions

M any efforts are made by researchers and policy analysts to define problems and propose solutions that involve action by different levels of government or by other parties, including individual consumers and patients. When polled, respondents may demonstrate a high amount of agreement when it comes to assessing such factors as health care quality, costs, and the necessity of providing coverage for the uninsured. Then, when given various alternatives regarding what to do about any of these conditions such as raising taxes, there is a tremendous amount of disagreement.

The creation of government support programs often results in unintended consequences. County-operated mental hospitals were a standard feature of the American landscape until the 1960s. A facility with thousands of patients might have had only a handful of psychiatrists to provide mental health care. In many instances, these hospitals were nothing more than huge holding pens. One incentive that helped to empty them was when the federal government created the Supplementary Security Income (SSI) program in 1974. Benefits were aimed at the blind, aged, and disabled in an effort to standardize a base of financial support as a means of eliminating the difference between what poor states and wealthier states were capable of providing in the form of public assistance.

Almost simultaneously as mental patients were released from county hospitals, unlicensed personal care facilities came into existence. Much of what was offered turned out to be worthless for those who were now on the street trying to survive. Whereas previously they were fed and had a roof over their heads, now many had neither and were prey to those who wished to harm or take advantage of them. Some of these patients then joined the ranks of the homeless and were forced to contend with daily challenges of obtaining food and shelter. The reform of today may sometimes prove to be the disaster of tomorrow.

Economic downturns are among the many factors leading to increased stress in life. Individuals react to stress in different ways, starting with the various conditions that are determined

---

87. Misra, DP. et al. Integrated Perinatal Health Framework: A Multiple Determinants Model with a Life Span Approach, *American Journal of Preventive Medicine*, Vol. 25, Issue 1, July 2003, pp. 65-75.
88. Berkman, L.F. Social Epidemiology: Social Determinants of Health in the United States: Are We Losing Ground? *Annual Review of Public Health*, 2009, Vol. 30, pp. 27-41.

as stressful in the first place. Nobel Prize winning author Luigi Pirandello referred to *l'arco della bestia* (Italian for the beast in the cave) or *la bestia originaria acquatatta dentro a ognuno di noi* (the primordial beast that lurks within us). As an example, simply observe how different individuals react at airports when a departing flight is delayed because of inclement weather. Scratch away the thin veneer of civilization and the result is quite interesting to behold when the beast inevitably surfaces and anger is inflicted on a ground agent who has no control over the fate of the scheduled flight.

Many determinants are within the purview of individuals to change while other factors are dependent upon societal action, but the line dividing the two areas of intervention occasionally proves to be quite "gray." Ignorance breeds poor choices. Even if individuals want to make positive changes in their lives, they may be unaware of the best alternatives and how to pursue them. Growing up in a family where all the adults are obese may not be a predisposing factor for children to structure their lives any differently. During their early years, they have no control over the kind of food and the amount placed on the dining table by adults.

It is difficult to assess what is in the individual's power to change, because so much is influenced by how that individual was raised and what was available to him or her. Several determinants can be changed by individuals that affect well-being and health outcomes. Education would be one of the most important factors. Still, growing up in a slum neighborhood where the schools are not of the highest quality and being raised in a poverty-stricken, single-parent family means that it takes an enormous amount of personal motivation to overcome such impediments to achieving an education that leads to social advancement.

The debate over whether to blame the individual or society for various health problems has a long and rich history. Factors that play a role in shaping personal outlook regarding such matters are where individuals are raised, where they reside now and did so in the past, their level of education, and their sources of information.

The following represent the kinds of governmental action that often are recommended to improve the health of the population: establish parks and recreational facilities, curtail food advertising directed at children, develop alternate transportation systems, restrict gun ownership, prevent unemployment and job insecurity, restore individuals to lost jobs, provide insurance discounts for the healthy, impose mandatory immunization schedules for children, have the government subsidize healthy foods, eliminate "for profit" insurers/hospitals/clinics, and furnish living wages.

Any single proposal immediately can become enmeshed in a political thicket involving such basic questions as who will pay and who will benefit from such a change? Given that resources are limited, in what other areas should spending cuts occur in order to pay for a new service or facility? How much authority should the government have when it comes to infringing on personal rights such as whether a child should be vaccinated? What is it about not-for-profit entities that supposedly render them superior to their for-profit counterparts? The last question cuts across many dimensions. Should an important package be delivered by the U.S. Post Office or by FedEx? Is it better to have a child in a public school, a private school, or to be educated at home? When seriously ill, which is viewed as the more desirable place for the ambulance to rush to: an inner-city hospital operated by the municipality or a private academic health science center?

To cite another common example of a controversial issue, women who have to walk dark streets at night may feel more secure owning and knowing how to use a handgun. Should they be denied the right to take action that they see as crucial in relation to personal safety? States, cities, and towns across the U.S. are the scene of heated discussions over such matters.

Policy Interventions Viewed from the Bottom Upwards

Once a problem is diagnosed, it is not uncommon for interventions to be designed by policy-makers with expertise in the area of what might be done successfully. Recognizing that social services also may need to be provided in conjunction with health care services, budget constraints may limit how much can be furnished. A group of Washington, DC, residents living under 200% of the federal poverty threshold "was recruited to engage in a hypothetical exercise to prioritize interventions designed to ameliorate the social determinants of health within the constraints of a limited budget" (Pesce 2011).

Following the deliberation, participants became "more likely to agree that a broad number of determinants contribute to their health." They prioritized interventions that would provide for basic necessities and improve community conditions "while at the same time addressing more macro-structural factors such as homelessness and unemployment." The investigators concluded that "engaging small groups in deliberation about ways to address the social determinants of health can both change participant attitudes and yield informed priorities that might guide public policy aimed at most affordably reducing health disparities." [89]

The Important Role Played by How Health Issues Are Framed

Widespread agreement exists about the wisdom of reducing the nation's ever-growing budget deficit, but there is great reluctance to cut spending on defense, health programs, and education. Easy solutions are not readily available. The success of proposed remedies often will depend on how health issues are framed. Whether the cause of a given health problem is perceived as stemming from individual or societal reasons will affect how political opponents decide what must be done or what must be avoided in the form of government interventions.

"Substantial theoretical and empirical evidence supports the conventional wisdom that when the public believes that a health problem results from external factors (i.e., from social or environmental determinants) instead of from individuals' own behaviors or shortcomings, they will be more likely to support social or governmental attempts to address the problem (Gollust 2009). Research indicates that attitudes about social groups are powerful influences on public opinion toward health and social policy. When particular groups are highlighted in the media, people draw attitudes and prejudices toward these populations when making judgments about policies relevant to the problem at hand." Research has shown that "Republicans are less likely to acknowledge the role of social structural factors in influencing socioeconomic status than Democrats and believing more strongly in personal responsibility for social status."

Consequently, "political partisans may respond differently to messages about the social determinants of health because of their differing underlying attitudes about those in poverty and the role of personal responsibility." Type 2 diabetes provides a suitable example of how perceptions might differ. The disease is associated with poor diet, lack of physical activity, and obesity. One side of the argument is that these factors are in the realm of personal responsibility, with the onus of doing something about them resting with individuals themselves. In the context of poverty, opponents would argue that neighborhood environments characterized by

---

89. Pesce, J.E. et al. Deliberation to Enhance Awareness of and Prioritize Socioeconomic Interventions for Health, *Social Science & Medicine*, Vol. 72, No. 5, March 2011, pp. 789-797.

low availability of wholesome foods and social stressors that can affect insulin resistance also play a role.[90]

Since the beginning of the 21st century, obesity has achieved prominence as a serious condition with dire health implications both in this nation and abroad. It has been argued that "how issues are framed, or presented in public discussion, is important to which policy approaches are adopted as well as whether a topic reaches the legislative agenda (Kersh 2009). Over time, a host of competing perspectives tend to cohere around a few, or even just one or two, basic frames." One well-established frame involving obesity is personal responsibility. Overeating and consuming high-fat, low-nutrition foods are the concerns of individual consumers. This frame points "away from robust legislative solutions. Instead, voluntary action by industry and measures like government-sanctioned nutrition education and exhortations to exercise are considered the most effective kinds of intervention."

A second frame views "an unhealthy or obesogenic food environment as being at least partly responsible for rising obesity rates." This environment involves expanding food portion sizes, the widespread availability of food in places such as gas stations and drugstores, and incessant advertising of high-fat, low-nutrition foods. Advocates of this frame view the following kinds of policy interventions as necessary: protecting children from industry advertising campaigns, subsidizing healthy foods, limiting sales of unhealthy foods, and taxing junk foods. A national labeling law would be another type of remedy. A version of labeling was adopted at Harvard University; its cafeterias provided calorie information but later "removed it in response to concern about potential deleterious effects on students with eating disorders and body-image concerns." [91]

It is highly unlikely that consensus ever will be reached about whether the individual or society should be held accountable for devising solutions to particular health and health-related social problems. Motor vehicle operators who drink heavily and speed on the nation's highways create mayhem and carnage. Gays who frequent bathhouses and have unprotected sex with other males are highly prone to experience sexually transmitted diseases such as AIDS. Adults use the Internet to prey on children with the intention of engaging in sexual acts with them. Genetics, failure to live by a religious code of conduct, poverty, and suffering abuse of one kind or another in childhood are among the many variables offered as explanations for aberrant behavior.

The movie *Rashomon* by the Japanese filmmaker Akira Kurosawa involves the commission of a crime, which is explained by four different versions of what occurred. At its essence, the movie focuses on the inability of any one person to know the truth, no matter how clearly everything appears.

A tendency in the U.S. is to view different kinds of deviance in medical terms. If something can be classified as a disease, then the perpetrator becomes a sick person deserving of therapeutic intervention. How one views such phenomena relates to political beliefs, spiritual inclinations, and notions of personal responsibility. In a nation as large as the United States, it is inevitable that a cultural divide will continue to exist about the responsibility of the individual versus the responsibility of society. Whichever group holds sway at the ballot box will help to determine the degree to which societal remedies in the form of health care and related social services will be applied to solve nettlesome problems.

---

90. Gollust, S.E. et al. The Polarizing Effect of News Media Messages about the Social Determinants of Health, *American Journal of Public Health*, Vol. 99, No. 12, December 2009, pp. 2160-2167.
91. Kersh, R. The Politics of Obesity: A Current Assessment and Look Ahead, *The Milbank Quarterly*, Vol. 87, Issue 1, March 2009, pp. 295-316.

The Individual, Society, and Health Behavior

Cancer is a major cause of mortality and remains the second leading cause of death in the U.S. It is not a single disease, but a group of different diseases with different etiologies. "Cancer registries report approximately 80 types of malignant neoplasm, and define them by their location and cell types" (Hiatt 2008). Lung cancer is associated with tobacco use. "Individual behavior related to tobacco is intimately tied to the social context." Social-level interventions to control tobacco use have been effective. Changes in social policies such as "federal excise taxes, workplace bans on smoking, media campaigns, clean-indoor-air policies, and the enforcement of restrictions on tobacco use by minors" are interventions that have produced a positive impact.[92]

The proliferation of tobacco-control policies led to reduction in tobacco use (Meara 2008). "In the four decades following the 1964 Surgeon General's report, per capita consumption of cigarettes among adults fell by half. However, declines were greatest among the most educated groups. The growing education-related gap in mortality for smoking-related causes supports the long-standing paradox that prevention can widen disparities in health across education and income groups."[93]

It has been "hypothesized that educated individuals produce health more efficiently, thus providing one explanation for the observed gaps in health by education level" (Lange 2011). One purported reason for this efficiency is that more educated individuals may be better at processing information related to health, a conjecture known as the *allocative efficiency hypothesis*.

Results of one investigation show that "both screening and individual risk assessments are more closely related to objective risk factors among educated individuals." The simplest explanation is "that the educated make better health decisions because they are better at processing health information." The data do not allow, however, "to determine whether education causes individuals to become better at processing information or whether education simply correlates with the ability to process information." It also is possible that the observed information advantage is the outcome of a prior investment decision. "In that case, it might be that the educated know more about their cancer risk, but only because they expended more resources to learn about health. Information advantages might simply reflect differences in the demand for health that lead to more efforts to collect information at an earlier stage."[94]

"Health and disease are widely understood as being influenced by many factors and contending perspectives are not necessarily incompatible (Mechanic 2007). The focus and the relative focus on one or another of these perspectives affects research funding and the research agenda, the types of interventions developed, and the social policies seeking to promote health and prevent disease." The challenge for science and society is to decide the extent to which upstream (e.g., socioeconomic status, environmental factors) and nonmedical determinants should become more central in conceptualizing health challenges and how they translate into the nation's research and health agenda.[95]

92. Hiatt, R.A. and Breen, N. The Social Determinants of Cancer: A Challenge for Transdisciplinary Science, *American Journal of Preventive Medicine*, Vol. 35, Issue 2, Supplement 1, August 2008, pp. S141-S150.
93. Meara, E.R. et al. The Gap Gets Bigger: Changes In Mortality And Life Expectancy, By Education, 1981–2000. *Health Affairs*, Vol. 27, Issue 2, March/April 2008, pp. 350-360.
94. Lange, F. The Role of Education in Complex Health Decisions: Evidence from Cancer Screening, *Journal of Health Economics*, Vol. 30, Issue 1, January 2011, pp. 43-54.
95. Mechanic, D. Population Health: Challenges for Science and Society, *The Milbank Quarterly*, Vol. 85, Issue 3, September 2007, pp. 533-559.

I t is improbable that children have not been exposed to messages about the dangers of smoking, which is even more unlikely among youngsters from higher socioeconomic backgrounds.
A visit to any college campus should dispel myths about the degree to which these warnings
have been incorporated into student health behavior. In June 2011, the federal government
announced that it is going to step up its effort to curb smoking by requiring tobacco manufacturers to place more dramatic warnings on cigarette packages. The effect is unknown, but it is
safe to assert that renewed efforts to advertize the catastrophic effects of smoking will not prevent all tobacco users from lighting up their cigarettes.

The consequences of inappropriate consumption of alcoholic beverages can be observed in
any emergency room or morgue throughout the nation. The popularity of televised athletic
events continues to attract large audiences, which consists in part of youth who are below legal
drinking age. Yet, it is the rare contest that is not subsidized by the alcohol beverage industry.
Cigarette ads were banned in the early 1970s. Would it make sense to treat alcohol in the same
manner? A host of political and economic factors would prevent that outcome from happening
any time soon. Commercial interests are important and will figure into any discussion about
advertising, marketing, tax revenues, and the availability of many substances.

H ealth is an individual and community affair. An old adage about the poor always being
present would seem to apply equally to the notion of the ubiquitous nature of health problems. Individuals and the society in which they live will continue to grapple with the most effective ways of mitigating the effects of these health problems

The best clinical care in the world will not ensure the best health outcomes (Parekh 2011).
"It is estimated that 40% of deaths in the United States are caused by behavior patterns that
could be modified by prevention-oriented interventions. Tobacco use continues to be the number one cause of preventable disease and 20.6% of adults currently smoke cigarettes, plus 34.0%
of Americans 20 years of age or older are considered obese and 28.1% of U.S. adults surveyed
report having drunk excessive amounts of alcohol in the previous 30 days." Lack of adherence
to medication and noncompliance with therapeutic regimens also have substantial effects on
outcomes such as preventable hospitalizations, disease progression, premature disability, and
death. Additional deficiencies pertain to following referral advice, keeping follow-up appointments with health professionals, and maintaining care regimens in the face of chronic impairments.[96]

The extent of health problems does not seem to recognize any bounds. Modifying personal
health behavior is a key to achieving more favorable outcomes. Clearly, health care has a role
to play in improving the current state of affairs. By definition, health care requires the presence
of health professionals. The problems are significant enough in scope that there is plenty of
room for many kinds of health researchers, educators, and practitioners to be involved in bringing about improvements in individual and community health status. Chapter 11 will focus on
the contributions that fall within the realm of the health professions.

Closing Thoughts

A long-standing debate is whether society or individuals themselves are responsible for many
kinds of poor health outcomes. Some health problems arise from the intemperate use of
harmful substances such as tobacco or from overeating. Still, poverty helps to create many situ-

---

96.   Parekh, A.K. Winning Their Trust, *New England Journal of Medicine*, Vol. 364, No. 24, June 16, 2011, p. e51.

ations that are not conducive to good health status. A faltering economy that produces high unemployment coupled with low paying jobs affects the ability to live in better neighborhoods with good schools, recreational facilities, stores that sell wholesome foods, and an environment that has low exposure to pollutants.

CHAPTER 4:

Race/Ethnicity, Culture, and Geography

4

This chapter broadens the focus on factors such as health disparities that relate directly to an individual's race and ethnicity and the environments in which they live. Neighborhoods characterized by poverty serve as breeding grounds for the generation of many kinds of health problems. An inability to obtain a quality education has an impact on health literacy, which may have decisive effects on the ability of patients to understand and adhere to treatment protocols.

Race and ethnicity, however so defined, exert themselves in a variety of ways. Health status differences can be found among various groups. The reason why this assertion is true is a function of many interrelated variables. In addition to poverty, housing, nutrition, level of education, the environment, and a host of other pertinent concerns, members of various groups also may be distinguished by: their respective beliefs about medical care, health care-seeking behaviors, differences in patient preferences for treatment, and willingness to accept procedures recommended by health professionals.

This chapter should help to illustrate the inherent complexities entailed in any discussion of major factors that have an impact on the health of individuals and communities. Many ideas expressed in what follows pertain to the previous two chapters that focused on patient-provider interaction and socioeconomic determinants of health status. There also is a connection with the next chapter, which will provide details about an important population subgroup—immigrants.

The terrain of the U.S. population is quite broad and any effort to arrange it into coherent segments will at best be quite arbitrary. In this instance, an emphasis will be placed on some overall aspects of race and ethnicity, culture, language, geographic locations where residents live and where health care services are provided, and some specific disease aspects. Within these broad classifications, as an alternative it would have been just as convenient to treat each racial and ethnic group separately, segregate the population by age group, and cover a wide range of diseases. Instead, this chapter will involve more of a blend of these kinds of considerations. As was done in the previous chapter, it may be useful to furnish some comments about terminology that is not always employed consistently in the professional literature.

Race and Ethnicity

"Since the 1970s, there have been substantial increases in the numbers of U.S. immigrants from Africa, Asia, and Latin America (Ford 2010). Researchers have responded to demographic trends in several ways. Increasingly, they use the term *ethnicity* instead of *race*. They often do so inconsistently or inappropriately. Some use ethnicity as a euphemism for race, but the two constructs are not synonymous." Typical classifications such as those used by the U.S. Office of Management and Budget (OMB) are a blend of ethnicity (e.g., Hispanic/Latino and *not* Hispanic/Latino) and race (e.g., white and black). Confusion is common. Mexicans, Puerto Ricans, and Spaniards are different from one another, and even though different nations are classified under the Hispanic rubric, Latin America has non-Spanish-speaking countries such as Brazil.

Although on the basis of skin color society may define individuals as being black, rather large differences exist between foreign-born and native-born blacks. Among the latter, distinctions can be made on the basis of "racial subordination or privilege, internalization of American racial ideology, and the health implications of exposure to discrimination." Sociocultural differences can be used to differentiate Islamic Senegalese from black-identified Brazilians and rural Nigerians.

Asian populations are segmented according to where they were born or by ancestral national origin. Chinese-Americans whose families have been in this country for several generations are not the same as recent Chinese immigrants.[97] "The number of Asian-born women living in the United States is growing rapidly (Zhao 2010). They represent more than 43 different ethnic groups and speak more than 100 different languages." Health beliefs, attitudes, and perspectives about health, illness, and health care services stemming from the unique culture of one ethnic group cannot be generalized to other groups.[98] Chapter 12 on the topic of Complementary and Alternative Medicine will provide specific examples of the ways in which Asian Indians differ from other groups.

Satisfaction is never complete in trying to sort out differences among groups when classifications prove to be somewhat murky. Consequently, on June 29, 2011, the Department of Health and Human Services (HHS) issued proposed standards for collecting and reporting data on race, ethnicity, sex, primary language, and disability status as required by the Affordable Care Act. The proposed standards are intended to help federal agencies refine their population health surveys to understand better health disparities and how to eliminate them. Comments on the draft standards were to be accepted through August 1. The agency also announced plans to integrate questions on sexual orientation into national data collection efforts by 2013 and begin a process to collect information on gender identity to identify health disparities in lesbian, gay, bisexual, and transgender populations.

Race and Genetics in Relation to Health Disparities

A matter of debate is "whether an understanding of the unique patterns of genes across patient populations defined by race will help identify groups at risk of developing particular diseases" (Fine 2005). One premise is that "race is an inherent biological characteristic that accurately reflects human ancestry and the flow of common threads of genetic material in biologically distinct populations over time and geography." Others have come to view "race as a social and cultural construct rather than a biological construct. They posit that race is not useful for distinguishing polygenic phenotypes such as height, let alone complex diseases where there is little evidence that specific susceptibility-gene variants occur more frequently in differ-

---

97. Ford, C.L. and Harawa, N.T. A New Conceptualization of Ethnicity for Social Epidemiologic and Health Equity Research, *Social Science & Medicine*, Vol. 71, No.2, July 2010, pp. 251-258.
98. Zhao, M. et al. Cultural Beliefs and Attitudes toward Health and Health Care among Asian-Born Women in the United States, *Journal of Obstetrics, Gynecologic, and Neonatal Nursing*, Vol. 39, Issue 4, July/August 2010, pp. 370-385.

ent populations." Apart from its potential to stigmatize whole communities, "they argue that an unintended consequence of genetic reductionism or categorizing biological risk by race might be the exclusion of other, more relevant social or environmental factors as potential explanations for the expression of health or disease." [99]

When the U.S. Food and Drug Administration (FDA) in 2005 granted formal approval to BiDil® as a race-specific drug to treat heart failure among African Americans, it led to a controversy over whether the initiative should be viewed as an advance or a setback in the struggle to address disparities in health status associated with race (Sankar 2005). Critics asserted that the "push to bring this drug to market (it is a combination of two generics long recognized as benefiting patients with heart failure) as a race-specific treatment was motivated by the peculiarities of U.S. patent law and a willingness to exploit race to gain commercial and regulatory advantage." [100]

A policy perspective on this issue suggests that "analyses rarely addressed the practical factors the FDA had to consider in reaching a decision" (Carlson 2005). A proposition was advanced that "much of the literature simply assigned the question to the domain of racial politics, failing to consider the ethics of professional care, the Hippocratic Oath, and marketplace efficiency in moving drugs quickly to those who might benefit most." [101]

Apropos of the relationship between race and genetics, colleges and universities with Division I programs are requiring top student athletes (Stein 2010) as of August 1, 2010, to submit to testing for the sickle cell anemia gene. This mandate by the National Collegiate Athletic Association (NCAA) in April 2010 was in response to a lawsuit filed by the family of a football player who had the trait and died after an intense football workout. The purpose of testing is to prevent sudden death associated with intense physical exertion. Objections have been raised because identifying someone as a carrier could be discriminatory. "For decades, blacks were stigmatized by sickle cell because they carried it more commonly than whites, marking them as supposedly genetically inferior, barring them from jobs, the military, insurance coverage, and even discouraging them from marrying and having children." [102]

Ernest Hendon once stood in front of the Alabama House of Representatives to hear legislators express regret for what had been done to him. The son of a poor black sharecropper in Macon County, he was enrolled in the infamous Tuskegee Syphilis Study, which began in 1932. The purpose of the investigation was to study the effects of this disease in blacks. Penicillin became an effective treatment for syphilis in 1943, but was not administered to the Tuskegee subjects unless they requested it. No serious questions about the study were asked until 1972, which led to its termination. By then, more than 100 subjects had died of the disease, along with at least 40 unwitting wives and 19 children who contracted syphilis at birth. A legacy of the study is a level of African American distrust that may continue to the present day.[103] One of the lucky survivors of the Tuskegee enterprise, Mr. Hendon died on January 16, 2004, at age 96.

---

99. Fine, M.J. et al. Editorial: The Role of Race and Genetics in Health Disparities Research, *American Journal of Public Health*, Vol. 95, No. 12, December 2005, pp. 2125-2127.

100. Sankar, P. and Kahn, J. BiDil: Race Medicine or Race Marketing? *Health Affairs Web Exclusive*, October 11, 2005, pp. W5-455 to W5-463.

101. Carlson, R.J. Perspective: The Case of BiDil: A Policy Commentary on Race and Genetics, *Health Affairs Web Exclusive*, October 11, 2005, pp. W5-464 to W5-468.

102. Stein, R. Sickle Cell Testing for Athletes Stirs Old Fears, *Washington Post*, September 20, 2010.

103. Elwood, T.W. The Influence of Words as Determinants of U.S. International and Domestic Health Policy: Part I, *Journal of Allied Health*, Vol. 34, No. 3, Fall 2005, pp. 125-129.

Culture and Health

Culture is another term that tends to be bandied about indiscriminately. The word often is used to characterize subgroups. A common expression is a "culture of poverty." Within that broad classification, there may be individuals who are poor because they are disabled. Those particular terms have been criticized in some quarters because of their negative connotations. Advocates of something more positive would prefer that "differently abled" be used instead.

The term *cultural* often is used as an adjective when making the case for the importance of health professionals becoming *culturally sensitive* and *culturally competent*. Given the vast range of different kinds of individuals who seek health care in large cities such as New York and Los Angeles and who may differ by gender, age, race, and ethnicity, that order can prove to be a tall one, especially when many non-English languages are involved.

A problem is that while various groups include elements of culture (e.g., ethnicity and values), "they share the general limitation of conceiving culture as a categorization variable that is relatively simple and fixed rather than a complex, dynamic, and adaptive system of meaning (Kreuter 2004). The cultural characteristics of any given group may be directly or indirectly associated with health-related priorities, decisions, behaviors, and/or with acceptance and adoption of health education and health communication programs and messages." [104]

"During the past two decades, a debate about disability definitions, concepts, models, and policies has been led primarily by Western white middle class disability activists and scholars" (Devlieger 2007). Attention has shifted to defining disability culture, examining whether it is experienced by and applies to all disabled individuals and whether it develops in a monolithic or multicultural forms. "When viewing young African-American men with violently acquired spinal cord injuries, disability culture is not monolithic. Under conditions of non-violence, disability in the African-American community may not be a unifying experience."

Chronic illnesses such as diabetes and asthma may take years to develop, allowing time for individuals, families, caregivers, and the larger community to adjust and respond. That luxury does not exist for gang members wounded by bullets. A hospital becomes the only source of protection. Parents and family members may be unable to care for a son who recently became wheelchair-bound. A change in identity occurs among these men, and a shared disability culture emerges that is represented through signs, symbols, language, rules, and ceremonies. [105]

"Automobile collisions are a major source of injury, death, and disability worldwide. Roadway injuries are affected by societal and cultural influences as much as any other health-related event, but have historically received relatively little attention from the medical anthropology community (Forman 2011). The development of safety intervention strategies is affected by notions of responsibility for preventive care, including a balance between regulation, technology, and personal choice. This balance may be affected by perceptions of the risks associated with roadway use, potentially related to notions of individual control and the portrayal of collisions in the popular media and lexicon."

"Prevention efforts are also affected by the definition of injury as a disease—a biological phenomenon requiring research and intervention efforts from the medical and public health communities. Injury prevention priorities and strategies also differ across cultures and locales, dependent in part on economic constraints, native mobility practices, and the quality and expe-

---

104.   Kreuter, M.W. and McClure, S.M. The Role of Culture in Communication, *Annual Review of Public Health*, Vol. 25, 2004, pp. 439-455.
105.   Devlieger, P.J. et al. The Production of Disability Culture among Young African-American Men, *Social Science & Medicine*, Vol. 64, No. 9, May 2007, pp. 1948-1959.

diency of post-trauma care. Progressing injury prevention worldwide requires multidisciplinary action, including an examination of these various cultural and societal influences." [106]

Health Disparities and Symbolic Interactionism

Similar to many ideas expressed in Chapter 2 on the topic of semiotics, a related perspective that may prove useful in considering health disparities was developed by Herbert Blumer (Disclosure: this book's author was enrolled in a course in 1969 taught by Professor Blumer at the University of California at Berkeley), who focused on *symbolic interactionism*. Influenced by George Herbert Mead, under whom he studied at the University of Chicago, Blumer used the term to refer to the peculiar and distinctive character of interaction as it takes place between human beings.

> "The peculiarity consists in the fact that human beings interpret or 'define' each other's actions instead of merely reacting to each other's actions. Their 'response' is not made directly to the actions of one another but instead is based on the meaning which they attach to such actions. Thus, human interaction is mediated by the use of symbols, by interpretation, or by ascertaining the meaning of one another's actions. This mediation is equivalent to inserting a process of interpretation between stimulus and response in the case of human behavior." [107]

In a survey of 4,157 randomly selected U.S. adults, perceptions of health care disparities were compared "among fourteen racial and ethnic groups to those of whites (Blendon 2007). Findings suggest that many ethnic minority groups view their health care situations differently, and often more negatively than whites. A substantial proportion perceived discrimination in receiving health care and many felt that they would not receive the best care if they were sick. The variety of responses across racial groups demonstrates the importance of examining subgroups separately rather than combined into a single category." For example, "compared to whites, African-Americans born in either the Caribbean region or Africa provided more positive ratings of the health care system and had fewer problems than did U.S.-born African Americans." [108]

Findings of this nature lead to intriguing questions. Even if they do so unconsciously, do non-Hispanic white health professionals act in a way that is perceived by non-Hispanic black patients as being biased? If so, is the bias conveyed selectively so that African Americans not born in the U.S. fail to experience what their American-born counterparts are able to detect, or is the bias the same but one group is more skilled than the other in detecting it? Whatever the answers are to such questions, the important point is that symbols are being transmitted and interpreted at the receiving end that can affect the quality of the interaction between patients and those who provide health care services to them.

Annual *National Healthcare Disparities Reports* developed by the Department of Health and Human Services (HHS), seek to address three questions critical to guiding Americans toward the optimal health care they need and deserve:

- "What is the status of health care quality and disparities in the United States?
- How have health care quality and disparities changed over time?
- Where is the need to improve health care quality and reduce disparities greatest?" (AHRQ 2011)

---

106. Forman, J.L. et al. Death and Injury from Automobile Collisions: An Overlooked Epidemic, *Medical Anthropology*, Vol. 30, No. 3, May 2011, pp. 241-246.
107. Blumer, H. 1969. *Symbolic Interactionism: Perspective and Method*, Berkeley: University of California Press.
108. Blendon, R.J. et al. Disparities in Health: Perspectives of a Multi-Ethnic, Multi-Racial America, *Health Affairs*, Vol. 26, No. 5, September/October 2007, pp. 1437-1447.

"A key function of the reports is to summarize the state of health care quality, access, and disparities for the nation. This undertaking is difficult, as no single national health care data-base collects a comprehensive set of data elements that can produce national and state estimates for all population subgroups each year. Rather, data come from more than three dozen databases that provide estimates for different population subgroups and data years. While most data are gathered annually, some data are not collected regularly or are old." Despite the data limita-tions, "analyses indicate that health care quality in America is suboptimal. The gap between the best possible care and that which is routinely delivered remains substantial across the United States."

On average, "patients received appropriate acute care services three-quarters of the time. Rates of receipt of acute care services ranged from a low of 8% among patients who needed and received treatment for an alcohol problem at a specialty facility to a high of 94% of hospitalized patients who indicated that communication with their doctors was good. On average, patients received recommended chronic disease management services three-quarters of the time. Receipt of chronic disease management services varied widely, from 17% of dialysis patients being regis-tered on a kidney transplant waiting list to 95% of hospice patients receiving the right amount of pain medication."

"Access to care is also far from optimal. On average, Americans report barriers to care one-fifth of the time, ranging from 3% of people saying they were unable to get or had to delay get-ting prescription medications to 60% of people saying their usual provider did not have office hours on weekends or nights. All Americans should have equal access to high-quality care." Instead, "racial and ethnic minorities and poor people often receive poorer quality of care and face more barriers when trying to access care." [109]

Important barriers to mental health care for African American and Hispanic patients "include patients' perceptions of stigma, beliefs that life experiences are the cause of depression, that problems should not be discussed outside one's family, mistrust of health care professionals, and concerns about the effects of psychotropic medication (Cooper 2003). Both antidepressant medication and counseling have been found to be effective treatment for depression." The odds of finding the medication acceptable were lower "for those two groups compared with white individuals because these medications are viewed as being addictive. The odds of finding coun-seling acceptable were somewhat lower for African-Americans and higher for Hispanics than for white persons." Counseling is viewed as bringing up "bad feelings." African Americans were more likely to state a preference for seeing a mental health professional who belonged to their same race or ethnicity. [110]

As demonstrated in the chapters of this book thus far, many journal articles are based on an examination of disadvantaged patients' beliefs and attitudes toward health care. General ly, these investigations aim to explain "how these beliefs and attitudes influence adherence and utilization (Malat 2006). This approach fails to consider whether patients use specific strategies to overcome providers' potentially negative perceptions of them."

In contrast, positive self-presentation has been examined as a "strategy that may be used by disadvantaged groups to improve their medical treatment." Examples of positive self-presenta-tion would be exhibiting a friendly manner and wearing nice clothing, which relates back to Chapter 2 on the influence of semiotics on the quality of patient-provider interactions. Findings

---

109. Agency for Healthcare Research and Quality. *2010 National Healthcare Disparities Report*, AHRQ Publication No. 11-0005, March 2011. On the Web at www.ahrq.gov/qual/qrdr10.htm. Accessed on June 15, 2011.
110. Cooper, L.A. et al. The Acceptability of Treatment for Depression among African-American, Hispanic, and White Primary Care Patients, *Medical Care*, Vol. 41, No. 4, April 2003, pp. 479-489.

support the hypothesis that African Americans and lower socioeconomic individuals are more likely to think that self-presentation strategies are important. [111]

A construct known as *John Henryism* has been used to differentiate a particular kind of health-related behavior by blacks (Fernander 2005). In an effort to understand the ethnic/racial disparity in the risk factor of high blood pressure, the John Henryism Active Coping Scale was developed as a culturally sensitive tool to help delineate the influence of stress and coping.

"While, John Henry active coping is defined as a strong behavioral predisposition to cope in an active, determined, and hard-working manner with the stressors of daily life, John Henryism is an interactive construct which suggests that blacks of low [socioeconomic status] who frequently address psychosocial stress by actively coping will be vulnerable to negative health outcomes, including high blood pressure." Smoking and nicotine dependence are viewed as a way to cope with stress.[112] Whether or not the construct has value in understanding health behavior by a population subgroup, studies of this nature exemplify the kinds of efforts undertaken by researchers to understand more fully the characteristics that may distinguish one group from another.

Various studies "have generally found higher rates of hospitalization resulting from ambulatory care-sensitive conditions for blacks compared to whites (Biello 2010). After adjustment for sociodemographic characteristics, blacks were hospitalized earlier than whites across all conditions combined and for chronic and acute conditions separately. The largest differences were seen for uncontrolled diabetes (adjusted difference = –12.0 years) and bacterial pneumonia (adjusted difference = –7.5 years). Difference in age at hospitalization places an undue burden on individuals, families, and society with long-term health and financial sequelae." [113]

Black patients tend to "receive more life-prolonging measures at the end of life (EOL) than white patients (Mack 2010). End-of-life discussions and communication goals seem to assist white patients in receiving less life-prolonging EOL care, but black patients do not experience the same benefits of EOL discussions. Instead, black patients tend to receive life-prolonging measures at the EOL even when they have do-not-resuscitate orders or state a preference for symptom-directed care." Among the alternatives to explain this difference, one is that racial bias on the part of health care providers about patient preferences could play a role.[114]

"In the decade following an organizational transformation, the Veterans Affairs (VA) health care system achieved substantial improvements in quality of care with minimal racial disparities for most process-of-care measures, such as rates of cholesterol screening. These improvements in clinical performance were not accompanied by meaningful reductions in racial disparity for clinical outcomes such as blood pressure, glucose, and cholesterol control" (Trivedi 2011). Because cardiovascular disease and diabetes are major contributors to racial disparities in life expectancy, what is occurring in the VA system underscores "the urgency of focused efforts to improve intermediary outcomes among black Americans in the VA and other settings." [115]

111. Malat, J.R. et al. Race, Socioeconomic Status, and the Perceived Importance of Positive Self-Presentation in Health Care, *Social Science & Medicine*, Vol. 62, No. 10, May 2006, pp. 2479-2488.
112. Fernander, A.F. et al. Exploring the Association of John Henry Active Coping and Education on Smoking Behavior and Nicotine Dependence among Blacks in the USA, *Social Science & Medicine*, Vol. 60, No. 3, February 2005, pp. 491-500.
113. Biello, K.B. et al. Racial Disparities in Age at Preventable Hospitalization among U.S. Adults, *American Journal of Preventive Medicine*, Vol. 38, Issue. 1, January 2010, pp. 54-60.
114. Mack, J.W. et al. Racial Disparities in the Outcomes of Communication on Medical Care Received Near Death, *Archives of Internal Medicine*, Vol. 170, No. 17, September 27, 2010, pp. 1533-1540.
115. Trivedi, A.N. et al. Despite Improved Quality of Care in the Veterans Affairs Health System, Racial Disparity Persists for Important Clinical Outcomes, *Health Affairs*, Vol. 30, No. 4, April 2011, pp. 707-714.

Geographical Influences on Health

A case can be made that segregation occurs along cultural and political dimensions. Fox television network aficionados probably would not feel too comfortable living in an area where all their neighbors love to quote what they hear on MSNBC or on National Public Radio. The same holds true in reverse. Voters who love President Obama more than likely would not want to spend a lot of time listening to devotees of his White House predecessor, President George W. Bush. Sentiments of this nature may spill over to wanting to reside in locales that are compatible with an individual's beliefs and values about whether a school should promote abstinence or distribute condoms to students, whether marijuana use for nonmedical purposes should be legalized, and whether creationism should be taught alongside evolution.

Related factors may influence patient preferences for specific health care facilities and practitioners. Examples are location, accessibility, convenience, reputation of the health care facility or practitioner, insurance company requirements, and whether insurance coverage exists. Other influences may include income/poverty levels, cultural values, and beliefs.

Department of Health and Human Services (HHS) Secretary Kathleen Sebelius released a new report in May 2009, *Hard Times in the Heartland: Health Care in Rural America*, outlining health care challenges facing rural communities (Seshamani 2009). The report was developed by HHS staff from across the department. "Throughout rural America, there are nearly 50 million people who face challenges in accessing health care. The past several decades have consistently shown higher rates of poverty, mortality, uninsurance, and limited access to a primary health care provider in rural areas. With the recent economic downturn, there is potential for an increase in many health disparities and access concerns that already are elevated in rural communities." The report provides insight into the current state of health care in rural areas.[116]

Where a patient lives can itself have a large impact on the level and quality of health care obtained, which matters in the measurement and interpretation of health and health care disparities since black or Hispanic populations tend to live in different areas than the non-Hispanic white population (Baicker 2005). "Blacks tend to live in parts of the country that have a disproportionate share of low-quality providers. Within those hospitals, both whites and blacks tend to receive low-quality care, but since blacks are over-represented in such areas, the quality of the hospital will cause an overstatement of the role that race plays in disparities at the level of the health care provider."

"Racial disparities in health care are a local phenomenon. Hospitals and regions of the country vary enormously in the extent to which such health care disparities are present." Some health care markets that serve large numbers of minorities "do not have disparities, although a plurality do. This finding limits the extent to which anecdotal evidence or even detailed quantitative studies from a given hospital, city, or state may be used to shed light on the larger problem of racial disparities at the national level." Also, it is not "entirely clear to what extent some regions are systematically worse, or systematically better, at eliminating health care disparities."

"Overall health and health care disparities should be considered to be the sum of two components: (1) unequal treatment within a hospital or by a given provider, and (2) unequal treatment because of where patients live. The reason that this distinction is important is because the sources of inequity are quite different: in the first case it is either at the level of the health care

---

116. Seshamani, M. et al. *Hard Times in the Heartland: Health Care in Rural America*, U.S. Department of Health and Human Services, May 4, 2009, 5 pp. On the Web at http://healthreform.gov/reports/hardtimes/ruralreport.pdf. Accessed on June 15, 2011.

interaction (whether because of bias by the provider or poor information or preferences of the patient), while in the second case it is related to differences in where individuals live, which is dependent on factors such as wage and income as well as barriers to housing that are less likely to be associated with the health care system per se." [117]

One study revealed that the "5% of hospitals with the highest volume of black patients cared for nearly half of all elderly black patients, and the hospitals in the top quartile by volume of patients cared for nearly 90% of black patients (Jha 2007)." Facilities with a high volume of black patients were larger and were more often teaching hospitals located in the southern United States. These hospitals differ in their characteristics from those of other hospitals and they often provide lower quality of care, especially for patients admitted with pneumonia. The variation in performance among hospitals that care for high volumes of black patients represents a critical opportunity. Targeting quality improvements efforts to these hospitals can improve the care of all Americans who receive care in these hospitals." [118]

An observational study using patient-level data acquired from hospitals for acute myocardial infarction (five care measures), congestive heart failure (two measures), community-acquired pneumonia (two measures), and patient counseling (four measures) revealed that "there were consistent unadjusted differences between minority and nonminority patients in the quality of care across eight of 13 quality measures (Hasnain-Wynia 2007). Disparities were most pronounced for counseling measures. Reasons for disparities may vary with the services being provided. Some services may be of low quality because of where they are provided and others because of bias, racism, or difficulties with intercultural communication." [119]

M any poor areas lack suitable recreational opportunities. Physical exercise often is promoted as a way of enhancing personal health status. One alternative means of trying to stay fit consists of walking. A factor that acts as a disincentive in some neighborhoods in the suburbs is the absence of sidewalks. Urban areas have such walkways, but it is unlikely they will be used if residents have a fear of crime and disorder (Roman 2008). One analysis examined "the degree to which individual-level demographic characteristics and neighborhood-level physical and social characteristics are associated with increased fear of crime. Age and female gender were associated with an increase in fear" in a section of Washington, DC. "The percentage of a resident's life spent in the same neighborhood was associated with a decrease in fear. Results of cross-level interactions showed that at the neighborhood level, women were more fearful than men in neighborhoods without violence, but the difference in fear between men and women shrinks as neighborhood violence increases." [120]

In a related study, residents of the most hazardous neighborhoods in Baltimore were nearly twice as likely to be obese compared to residents in the least hazardous neighborhoods (Glass 2006). Neighborhood deprivation may operate through different pathways. One of them may be that walking and outdoor physical activity may be reduced due, in part, to perceptions of safety and fear of crime.[121]

---

117. Baicker, K. et al. Geographic Variation in Health Care and the Problem of Measuring Racial Disparities, *Perspectives in Biology and Medicine*, Vol. 48, Number 1 Supplement, Winter 2005, pp. S42-S53.

118. Jha, A.K. et al. Concentration and Quality of Hospitals That Care for Elderly Black Patients, *Archives of Internal Medicine*, Vol. 167, June 11, 2007, pp. 1177-1182.

119. Hasnain-Wynia, R. et al. Disparities in Health Care Are Driven by Where Minority Patients Seek Care, *Archives of Internal Medicine*, Vol. 167, June 25, 2007, pp. 1233-1239.

120. Roman, C.G. and Chalfin, A. Fear of Walking Outdoors: A Multilevel Ecologic Analysis of Crime and Disorder, *American Journal of Preventive Medicine*, Vol. 34, Issue 4, April 2008, pp. 306-312.

121. Glass, T.A. et al. Neighborhoods and Obesity in Older Adults: The Baltimore Memory Study, *American Journal of Preventive Medicine*, Vol. 31, Issue 6, December 2006, pp. 455-463.

As is the case in many aspects of the professional literature, the complete picture rarely proves to be 100% clear. In a study of four Maryland counties and the City of Baltimore, private recreation facilities were found to be equitably distributed by race/ethnicity and income (Abercrombie 2008). The distribution of public parks, while not truly equitable, did not appear to contribute substantially to racial and income disparities in access to facilities that could be used for physical activity.[122]

From the standpoint of a specific health problem such as coronary heart disease, approximately 40 published studies have investigated associations between social characteristics of the residential environment and this disease (Chaix 2009). A significant number of them reported "an increased risk among residents of socially deprived areas after controlling for individual socioeconomic characteristics." [123]

Finally, interactive maps display regional variation at the state and county levels for several indicators of hospital performance, including measures tracking delivery of recommended care, patient experience, mortality rates, and readmission rates for common conditions (Commonwealth Fund 2010). The unique maps are a first step toward viewing performance at the local level-where much of the important work of building collaboration and accountability across health care organizations is beginning to happen, with incentives from the health reform legislation that was enacted in March 2010.[124]

Environmental Influences on Health

Living in some communities increases exposure to multiple environmental hazards and stressors, including poverty, poor housing quality, and social inequality:

- "Health disparities between groups of different racial or ethnic makeup or socioeconomic status are significant and persistent, and exist for diseases linked to social and environmental factors.
- Inequalities in exposure to environmental hazards also are significant and persistent, and are linked to adverse health outcomes.
- Intrinsic biological and physiological factors—for example, age or genetic makeup—can modify the effects of environmental factors and contribute to differences in the frequency and severity of environmentally-related disease.
- Extrinsic social vulnerability factors at the individual and community levels—such as race, gender, and socioeconomic status—may amplify the adverse effects of environmental hazards and can contribute to health disparities." (Morello-Frosch 2011)

A disproportionate number of hazardous waste sites, industrial facilities, sewage treatment plants, and other locally undesirable and potentially polluting land uses are located in communities of racial or ethnic minorities and in socially disadvantaged neighborhoods. Residents also are more likely to live near busy roads where traffic-related air pollutants concentrate.[125]

"The study of neighborhood health effects has grown exponentially" in recent years (Diez Roux 2010). Although there is substantial evidence that health is spatially patterned, questions

122. Abercrombie, L.C. et al. Income and Racial Disparities in Access to Public Parks and Private Recreation Facilities, *American Journal of Preventive Medicine*, Vol. 34, Issue 1, January 2008, pp. 9-15.

123. Chaix, B. Geographic Life Environments and Coronary Heart Disease: A Literature Review, Theoretical Contributions, Methodological Updates and a Research Agenda, *Annual Review of Public Health*, Vol. 30, 2009, pp. 81-105.

124. Commonwealth Fund. Interactive Maps. On the Web at http://whynotthebest.org/. Accessed on July 6, 2011.

125. Morello-Frosch, R. et al. Understanding the Cumulative Impacts of Inequalities in Environmental Health: Implications for Policy, *Health Affairs*, Vol. 30, No. 5, May 2011, pp. 879-886.

remain regarding causal importance and the health effects of changing neighborhood factors through intervention or more distal policy changes. "Fundamentally, work on neighborhoods and health highlights the potential impact of policies often thought to be unrelated to health, such as community development policies, urban planning, zoning, and transportation policies. It also highlights the broader role of a continuum of interacting environmental determinants in shaping behaviors and biology through dynamic interactions with the characteristics of individuals."[126]

The United States has "more than 53 million schoolchildren and more than 135,000 public and private schools (Mohai 2011). Unfortunately, not all of these schools are safe and healthy places for children to grow, play, and learn. Children are known to be more vulnerable than adults to the effects of pollutants. Moreover, they have little or no choice about where they live or go to school. A large and growing body of evidence shows that pollution burdens fall disproportionately on low-income and racial or ethnic minority communities."

In a study conducted in Michigan, "schools located in areas with the highest pollution levels also had the lowest attendance rates (a potential indicator of poor health) and the highest proportion of students failing to meet the state's educational testing standards." These associations remained statistically significant even when there were confounding variables, such as urban, suburban, or rural locations, spending per student, and school socioeconomic characteristics.

One concern was that variables such as parental education and school crowding were not controlled. A picture emerges, however, of key elements in life interacting to produce unfavorable health outcomes. Poor classroom attendance and an inability to meet state educational testing standards are not going to provide a smooth path to higher education and good paying jobs. Low income can impede the opportunity to live in safer and healthier neighborhoods, and there may not be enough discretionary cash to afford higher quality and more accessible health care. An endless cycle of poverty with all its dire consequences may be an outcome that stems partly from exposure to environmental pollutants during the important period of child development.[127]

Racial and Ethnic Disparities Involving Specific Kinds of Disease

Leading causes of mortality in the United States are heart disease and cancer. Large numbers of studies have been conducted on both kinds of disease as well as other serious conditions such as diabetes. Cancer furnishes an illustration of an appropriate starting point to begin any discussion of the ravages of disease.

"Cigarette smoking is associated with substantial morbidity and mortality. Almost one-third of tobacco users will die prematurely because of their use of tobacco. Members of racial and ethnic minority populations bear a disproportionate share of the adverse health consequences of tobacco use (Cokkinides 2008). The identification and counseling of smokers is among the most consequential and cost-effective intervention in clinical practice" through the use of health care encounter-based interventions such as screening, smoking-cessation advice, and use of smoking-cessation aids.[128]

---

126. Diez Roux, A.V. and Mair, C. Neighborhoods and Health, *Annals of the New York Academy of Science*, Vol. 1186, February 2010, pp. 125-145.

127. Mohai, P. et al. Air Pollution around Schools Is Linked to Poorer Health and Academic Performance, *Health Affairs*, Vol. 30, No. 5, May 2011, pp. 852-861.

128. Cokkinides, V. E. et al. Racial and Ethnic Disparities in Smoking-Cessation Interventions: Analysis of the 2005 National Health Interview Survey, *American Journal of Preventive Medicine*, Vol. 34, Issue 5, May 2008, pp. 404-412.

Compared to other kinds of providers, those at the primary care level have ongoing, unique opportunities to deliver preventive services (Sonnenfeld 2009). In an analysis of data from the National Ambulatory Medical Care Survey (2001-2005), it was shown that tobacco screening and counseling were less common at visits made by Hispanics compared to non-Hispanic whites. "Traditional barriers to care among Hispanic patients, such as lack of insurance and more new-patient visits, did not explain the observed differences." Similar results occurred for screening and counseling among non-Hispanic black and non-Hispanic Asian patients.[129]

Males can have a strong influence and play dominant roles in situations involving the health behavior of their spouses in Latino communities (Erwin 2010). As cancer control initiatives are pursued by health authorities, there is "a need to understand how the nuances of different Latino cultures translate to opportunities and barriers for access to cancer screening and care. The diversity by country of origin" for this group often is overlooked. Findings demonstrate that both country of origin and current geographic residency in the United States are significant determinants of women's perspectives on community-based religious organizations, knowledge of anatomy, experiences with the medical system, and access to services that are essential factors to consider in developing effective cancer control interventions.

Whatever terms are used to discuss this group, Latino or Hispanic, it is evident that there is much intergroup diversity, stemming partly from variation in migration patterns. Puerto Ricans have "consisted of laborers or middleman merchants or domestic workers" who settled in urban areas like New York City. Most Cubans moved to Miami. Many Central Americans "immigrated as political refugees." Mexicans have headed to southern and Midwestern destinations where low-paying jobs are available in meat-processing plants, hotels, and other settings where residential services are provided.

Among women, lack of support from male partners can lead to situations where they will not have a Pap smear because their husbands will not allow them to do so. For example, a husband may be opposed to having other males look at his wife's body. Unless these women perceive themselves to be in a position to control their environment or be empowered to seek health care on their own, they will fail to take recommended action. Although breast and cervical cancer are considered women's health issues, they cannot be addressed outside the sociopolitical structures of local communities.[130]

"A prominent public health disparity is the lack of mammogram screening among low-income Hispanic women (Deavenport 2010). They have "the lowest rates of mammogram usage compared to women of other race/ethnicities." Apart from such factors as lack of health insurance and high copayments to have this procedure performed, additional reasons for the disparity in screening may be due to "lack of knowledge, fear of screening, and cost." Associated with an insufficient level of knowledge, influential beliefs include perceptions that breastfeeding may result in cancer and that either injury or infection from the common cold or the flu can result in breast cancer. Other disincentives are that screening will be too painful, it may discover something wrong, or is too embarrassing. Low perceived susceptibility may be the result of a belief that God will prevent them from being afflicted with breast cancer. If they are to experience a different outcome, then screening will not make a difference in their ultimate fate.[131]

---

129. Sonnenfeld, N. et al. Racial and Ethnic Differences in Delivery of Tobacco-Cessation Services, *American Journal of Preventive Medicine*, Vol. 36, Issue 1, January 2009, pp. 21-28.
130. Erwin, D.O. et al. Contextualizing Diversity and Culture within Cancer Control Interventions for Latinas: Changing Interventions, Not Cultures, *Social Science & Medicine*, Vol. 71, No. 4, August 2010, pp. 693-701.
131. Deavenport, A. et al. Health Beliefs of Low-Income Hispanic Women: A Disparity in Mammogram Use, *American Journal of Health Studies*, Vol. 25, Issue 2, 2010, pp. 92-101.

Given the rapid growth in the number and proportion of Hispanics in the United States, there is merit in devoting more attention to the health needs of this group. Members differ in many fundamental ways such as country of origin, whether they recently arrived here or are the offspring of immigrants, whether they are here legally or illegally, and the degree to which they speak English, possess sufficient knowledge to be able to navigate a complex array of health care services, and have a satisfactory level of health literacy.

Another prominent subgroup in the population that is increasing in size at a rapid pace is Asian Americans. Cancer is a major cause of death among Asian American females, but their screening rates are low (Ma 2009). Never-screened rates are high for all subgroups of Chinese, Korean, Vietnamese, and Cambodian Americans, "ranging from 20.1% to 78.5% for mammo - graphy, 28% to 75.6% for Pap test, 56.7% to 97% for prostate cancer, and 65.3% to 94.9% for colorectal cancer. Koreans had the highest never-screened rate for health checkups (34.7%)." Differences were found by age, years lived in the United States, education level, employment status, annual household income, having health insurance, having a regular physician, having a language-concordant physician," ability to speak English, having an opportunity to view health information sources on the Internet in one's native language, and frequency of visits to primary providers in the last year.[132]

"Cancer genetics is one of the most developed areas of clinical genetics. Testing for BRCA1 and BRCA2 mutations to assess the risk of hereditary breast and ovarian cancer is among the most established genetics tests in clinical use. Guidelines and commercial testing for BRCA1/2 mutations have been available for more than a decade and most health insurers reimburse at least partially for these tests in individuals at high risk for mutations (Levy 2011). National guidelines recommend that women diagnosed with early-onset breast cancer receive BRCA1/2 testing to guide treatment decisions."

"Among patients newly diagnosed with cancer, a positive test result will often prompt more aggressive surgical treatment (e.g., bilateral salpingo-oophorectomy or prophylactic contralateral mastectomy) with the goal of minimizing the potential for secondary primary cancers. A positive test result also may prompt consideration of BRCA1/2 testing among at-risk relatives of the cancer patient so that those testing positive can benefit from more aggressive prevention and screening."

In a study that assessed the degree to which BRCA1/2 testing occurred among a group of commercially-insured newly-diagnosed early-onset-risk breast cancer patients, low rates were found. "The testing rates were significantly lower for black, Hispanic, and low-income women compared with others being served in the same large commercial health plans. It is these underserved populations that experience poorer treatment and higher mortality rates for breast cancer." [133]

"More than 200,000 women are diagnosed with breast cancer each year in the United States and it is projected that approximately 40,000 will die with the disease annually" (Amirikia 2011). Mortality rates have declined over the past two decades. The improvement in outcome is explained largely by the combination of earlier detection and screening mammography coupled with the use of more effective systemic therapy.

Yet, "population-based data demonstrated that African-American women had a more advanced stage distribution for breast cancer compared with white American women and high-

132. Ma, G.X. et al. Cancer Screening Behaviors and Barriers in Asian Americans, *American Journal of Health Behavior*, Vol. 33, Issue 6, 2009, pp. 650-660.

133. Levy, D.E. et al. Underutilization of BRCA1/2 Testing to Guide Breast Cancer Treatment: Black and Hispanic Women Particularly at Risk, *Genetics in Medicine*, Vol. 13, No. 4, April 2011, pp. 349-355.

er incidence rates for triple-negative breast cancer. These patterns were observed for women ages 40 to 49 years and for older women, and they suggest that mammographic screening for the early detection of breast cancer will be particularly relevant for younger African-American women."[134]

"Definitive local therapy of early stage breast cancer includes adjuvant radiotherapy after breast-conserving surgery (BCS). As mastectomy rates have decreased over time, the challenge has been to ensure adequate therapy with consistent delivery of radiotherapy after BCS, especially among vulnerable populations who may lack access to oncology services (Dragun 2011). Despite widespread knowledge of the benefit of radiotherapy after BCS, the rate of undertreatment remains high, with significant disparities for elderly, rural, minority, and uninsured women."

"Multidisciplinary management strategies, including accelerated and hypofractionated radiation regimens, are needed to eliminate disparities and improve outcomes. Several factors exist in rural communities that contribute to disparities, including higher percentages of uninsured patients, disproportionate elderly populations, higher levels of medical comorbidities, physician shortages, and lack of transportation options and assistance." [135]

While prevention of cancer represents the most ideal goal, early detection and treatment are most important in the quest to achieve favorable outcomes. Unfortunately, those interventions do not always produce the desired results and mortality occurs. "Culturally sensitive end-of-life (EOL) care is a national priority (Smith 2008). The National Quality Forum and National Consensus Project for Quality Palliative Care both identify provision of culturally sensitive care as one of eight core domains of high-quality palliative care." Yet, compared with white patients, black and Hispanic patients were less likely to have an advanced care plan, which involves having "patients, in conjunction with their physicians and loved ones, establish goals and preferences for future care and codify these preferences in written documents such as a living will, durable power of attorney for health care decision-making (health care proxy), or Do-Not-Resuscitate order." Although black and Hispanic patients are less likely to consider themselves terminally ill and more likely to want intensive treatment, these factors did not explain observed disparities in advanced care planning.[136]

English Language Proficiency and Health Literacy

The quality of health care in the United States is not optimal and the pace of improvement is slow. In addition, disparities persist for specific population groups. A fundamental step in identifying which populations are most at risk is to collect data on race, ethnicity, and English-language proficiency. A large body of research has documented disparities in access to and quality of health care that are revealed when quality of care measures are examined by these variables.

Level of education pertaining to literacy and poor literacy skills, along with innumeracy, affect many persons and the result is that medication errors can and do occur. Many patients fail to acknowledge that they are at a poor reading level, and for many reasons, providers either do not ascertain that a satisfactory ability to read exists on the part of patients or they feel

134. Amerikia, K.C. et al. Higher Population-Based Incidence Rates of Triple-Negative Breast Cancer among Young African-American Women, *Cancer*, Vol. 117, Issue 12, June 15, 2011, pp. 2747-2753.

135. Dragun, A.E. et al. Disparities in the Application of Adjuvant Radiotherapy after Breast-Conserving Surgery for Early Stage Breast Cancer, *Cancer*, Vol. 117, Issue 12, June 15, 2011, pp. 2590-2598

136. Smith, A.K. et al. Racial and Ethnic Differences in Advance Care Planning among Patients with Cancer: Impact of Terminal Illness Acknowledgment, Religiousness, and Treatment Preferences, *Journal of Clinical Oncology*, Vol. 26, No. 25, September 1, 2008, pp. 4131-4137.

uncomfortable becoming involved in such discussions (Zahnd 2009). Include as a second complicating factor that English is a second language for many patients and it is not hard to envision why medical errors and noncompliance occur. Health literacy skills among inhabitants of rural areas represent another area of analysis.[137]

"The Institute of Medicine (IOM) formed the Subcommittee on Standardized Collection of Race/Ethnicity Data for Healthcare Quality Improvement to examine approaches to standardization. In its 2009 report, *Race, Ethnicity, and Language Data: Standardization for Health Care Quality Improvement,* the subcommittee recommends collection of more granular ethnicity and language need according to national standards in addition to the U.S. Office of Management and Budget (OMB) race and Hispanic ethnicity categories (Ulmer 2009). The presence of data on race, ethnicity, and language does not, in and of itself, guarantee subsequent actions regarding quality-of-care data to identify health care needs or actions to reduce or eliminate disparities that are found. The absence of data, however, essentially guarantees that none of those actions will occur." [138]

Patients who cannot speak English may not take necessary steps to seek health care assistance without a reassurance that language barriers have been removed. If an alternative is not available or the obstacle is not reconciled, then patients will not receive the medical care and medication needed, which will cause the disease to possibly progress towards a more serious condition and lead to a more severe burden for the patient, society, and the health care system. Being able to understand health professionals brings a level of trust and security to a patient. It also brings to the patient a sort of ethnicity-type feeling where a social bond is built between the patient and the practitioner. This bond may be even stronger if the practitioner has the same racial or ethnic background as the patient. Beyond health care, they may be able to relate to other things because of that similarity, all of which helps build a strong relationship so that the primary goal of health care may be realized.

The proportion of the U.S. population with limited English proficiency is substantial. Health professionals may find themselves in situations where language services are limited. Apart from any other disadvantages that may arise when communication barriers exist, there is a danger that misinterpretation of what a patient has to say may lead to unfavorable consequences (Flores 2006). For example, a "Spanish-speaking woman told a medical resident that her two-year-old daughter had 'hit herself' when she fell off a tricycle. The two words were misinterpreted as meaning the fracture resulted from physical abuse. Subsequently, a worker from the Department of Social Services, "without an interpreter present, had the mother sign over custody of her two children."

In another case, after a man stumbled into his Spanish-speaking girlfriend's home, before collapsing, he said that he was "intoxicado." While the intended meaning was nauseated, "non-Spanish-speaking paramedics believed the patient was intoxicated. After 36 hours in the hospital being worked up for a drug overdose, the "comatose patient was reevaluated and given a diagnosis of intracerebellar hematoma with brain-stem compression and a subdural hematoma secondary to a ruptured artery." The hospital later had to pay a $71 million malpractice settlement.[139]

---

137. Zahnd, W.E. et al. Health Literacy Skills in Rural and Urban Populations, *American Journal of Health Behavior,* September/October 2009, Vol. 33 Issue 5, pp. 550-557.

138. Ulmer, C. et al, Editors. 2009. *Race, Ethnicity, and Language Data: Standardization for Health Care Quality Improvement,* Washington, DC: National Academy Press.

139. Flores, G. Perspective: Language Barriers to Health Care in the United States, *New England Journal of Medicine,* Vol. 355, No. 3, July 20, 2006, pp. 229-231.

The past two decades of research in health literacy have done much to raise awareness about problems associated with low health literacy, which may be defined as the degree to which individuals have the capacity to obtain, process, and understand basic health information and services needed to make appropriate health decisions. Nearly 9 out of 10 adults have difficulty using everyday health information that is available in health care facilities, retail outlets, media, and communities (Kutner 2006). Moreover, the impact of low health literacy disproportionately affects lower socioeconomic and minority groups.[140]

The *Institute of Medicine Roundtable on Health Literacy* focuses on building partnerships to move the field of health literacy forward by translating research findings into practical strategies for implementation. The roundtable serves to educate the public, press, and policymakers regarding issues of health literacy. The roundtable sponsors workshops for members and the public to discuss approaches to resolve key challenges in the field.

A workshop in October 2009 was designed to explore areas for research in health literacy, including the relationship of health literacy to health disparities and information technology applications (Vancheri 2011). The event began with a presentation about the first annual Health Literacy Annual Research Conference (HARC). Discussion focused on two recurring themes of the HARC meeting: the integration of research on health literacy and health disparities, and the role of information technology and health literacy research. For the workshop, a panel was convened to address each of the two themes. A third workshop panel focused on professional development in health literacy research. The fourth panel entailed having leaders of three government agencies offer the first public presentation of the new *National Action Plan to Improve Health Literacy*. The final workshop panel addressed the role of health literacy research in the National Action Plan. The workshop ended with a discussion of lessons learned from the workshop.[141]

The *National Action Plan to Improve Health Literacy* from the Centers for Disease Control and Prevention (CDC) envisions a restructuring of ways to create and disseminate all types of health information in the U.S. (HHS 2010). It seeks to engage organizations, professionals, policymakers, communities, individuals, and families in a linked, multisector effort to improve health literacy. The plan includes seven broad goals with multiple high level strategies and provides a focal point for the field. It is based on the principles that:

- "Everyone has the right to health information that helps to make informed decisions.
- Health services should be delivered in ways that are understandable and beneficial to health, longevity, and quality of life." [142]

Low health literacy in older Americans is linked to poorer health status and a higher risk of death, according to an evidence report from the HHS Agency for Healthcare Research and Quality (Berkman 2011). "In 2003, approximately 80 million adults in the United States (36%) had limited health literacy," making it difficult for them to understand and use basic health information. A 941-page report released in March 2011 is an update of a 2004 literature review featuring findings from more than 100 new studies. It found an association between low health

140. Kutner, M. et al. *The Health Literacy of America's Adults: Results From the 2003 National Assessment of Adult Literacy* (NCES 2006-483). Washington, DC: U.S. Department of Education, National Center for Education Statistics, 2006.

141. Vancheri, C. Rapporteur. *Innovations in Health Literacy*, Institute of Medicine, Washington, DC: 2011. On the Web at http://www.nap.edu/catalog.php?record_id=13016#toc. Accessed on June 28, 2011.

142. U.S. Department of Health and Human Services, Office of Disease Prevention and Health Promotion. *National Action Plan to Improve Health Literacy*, Washington, DC: 2010. On the Web at http://www.health.gov/communication/hlactionplan/pdf/Health_Literacy_Action_Plan.pdf. Accessed on June 10, 2011.

literacy in all adults, regardless of age, and more frequent use of hospital emergency rooms and inpatient care, compared with other adults.[143]

The Agency for Healthcare Research and Quality (AHRQ) released the Consumer Assessment of Healthcare Providers and Systems (CAHPS) Item Set for Addressing Health Literacy in English and Spanish (AHRQ 2008). The primary purpose of the CAHPS Item Set for Addressing Health Literacy is to measure, from the patients' perspective, how well health care professionals communicate with their patients. Only 12% of U.S. adults have proficient health literacy. Over one-third of U.S. adults—77 million individuals—could have difficulty with common health tasks such as following directions on a prescription drug label or adhering to a childhood immunization schedule using a standard chart. The Item Set for Addressing Health Literacy offers:

- "Ability to identify specific topic areas for quality improvement (e.g., communication about test results, medications, and forms)
- Measure of health care professionals' health literacy practices
- Ability to recognize behavior that inhibits effective communication (e.g., talking too fast)
- Assistance in designing a safer, shame-free environment where patients feel comfortable discussing their health concerns (e.g., showing interest in questions)." [144]

"As the focus on health care delivery continues to shift from inpatient to outpatient settings, the practice of quality control over medication use is becoming more the responsibility of the patient and less the responsibility of the provider (Davis 2006). Yet, patients do not always take medications as prescribed, and as a result, outpatient adverse drug events are common." As an example, one study indicated that "correct understanding of instructions on 5 labels ranged from 67.1% to 91.1%. Patients reading at or below the sixth-grade level (low literacy) were less able to understand all 5 label instructions. Although 70.7% of patients with low literacy correctly stated the instructions, 'Take two tablets by mouth twice daily,' only 34.7% could demonstrate the number of pills to be taken daily. After potential confounding variables were controlled for, low and marginal literacy were significantly associated with misunderstanding. Taking a greater number of prescription medications also was associated statistically significantly with misunderstanding." [145]

Detecting patients who have a low level of health literacy may prove difficult. "For many patients, the stigma of low literacy may lead to compensatory behaviors by patients that make their level of literacy hard to characterize (Kelly 2007). Physical characteristics such as appearance and speaking ability are often always inaccurate indicators of a patient's literacy level." The risk is that "physicians often might make instantaneous, subconscious, and inaccurate judgments about what their patients can understand." [146]

Health literacy skills can be measured accurately in a relatively short amount of time (Powers 2010). "Despite the important health implications of literacy, physicians are often unaware of their patients' literacy levels and the effects on outcomes. Patients may not volunteer they have

143. Berkman, N. et al. *Health Literacy Interventions and Outcomes: An Updated Systematic Review*, *Evidence Report Technology Assessment Number 199*, Agency for Healthcare Research and Quality, March 2011, 941 pp. On the Web at http://www.ahrq.gov/downloads/pub/evidence/pdf/literacy/literacyup.pdf. Accessed on May 4, 2011.
144. Agency for Healthcare Research and Quality, Clincian & Group Survey and Reporting Kit 2008, On the Web at https://www.cahps.ahrq.gov/cahpskit/CG/CGChooseQX.asp. Accessed on May 3, 2011.
145. Davis, T.C. et al. Literacy and Misunderstanding Prescription Drug Labels. *Annals of Internal Medicine*, Vol. 145, No. 12, December 2006, pp. 887-894.
146. Kelly, P.A. and Haidet, P. Physician Overestimation of Patient Literacy: A Potential Source of Health Care Disparities, *Patient Education and Counseling*, Vol. 66, Issue 1, April 2007, pp. 119-122.

a problem because nearly one-half of patients with limited literacy express shame over their inability to read. Although education attainment can be a proxy for literacy, it often is misleading, with many patients reading below their highest level of education and up to 20% of high school-educated patients having limited literacy. The implication for clinicians is that many patients will be unable to interpret prescription instructions, understand patient education materials, or use written information to prepare for clinical tests, however, clinicians often do not detect these limitations." [147]

"Great enthusiasm exists over the use of emerging interactive health information technologies—often referred to as eHealth—and the potential these technologies have to improve the quality, capacity, and efficiency of the health care system. Many doctors, advocacy groups, policy makers, and consumers are concerned, however, that electronic health systems might help individuals and communities with greater resources while leaving behind those with limited access to technology" (Hernandez 2009).

Even if it were possible to ensure equal access to technology, some user groups find it extremely difficult to take advantage of such technology. The average U.S. adult reads on just an eighth-grade level, for example, while most health websites are designed for individuals whose reading level is much higher. In particular, it is the elderly and those with limited literacy and numerical skills who are most likely to have low health literacy and thus be least able to take advantage of new health technologies. [148]

Closing Thoughts

Many individuals because of their race and ethnicity are marginalized in the United States. If they are of low socioeconomic status, they often lack the resources necessary to obtain an education and have access to quality health care. The care that they do receive may lack coordination and continuity, especially if reliance is placed on the use of emergency rooms and urgent care centers. The level of educational attainment will be a determining factor in being able to achieve a high degree of health literacy.

---

147. Powers, B.J. et al. Can This Patient Read and Understand Written Health Information? *Journal of the American Medical Association*, Vol. 304, No. 1, July 7, 2010, pp. 76-84.
148. Hernandez, L.M. Rapporteur. *Health Literacy, eHealth, and Communication: Putting the Consumer First*, Workshop Summary, Roundtable on Health Literacy; Institute of Medicine, Washington, DC: 2009. On the Web at http://www.nap.edu/openbook.php?record_id=12474&page=1. Accessed January 17, 2011.

CHAPTER 5:
Demographic Patterns in the Context of Immigration

5

Immigration has been a steady feature of life in the United States for more than two centuries. A controversial issue revolves around the number of immigrants who have no legal authorization to be in this country. Their ability to obtain health care can prove to be a significant challenge. Migrant agricultural workers represent a special population subset that lives under poor conditions. Assimilation into the American way of life may not be an easy thing to do. A consequence may be the onset of mental health problems.

Population Definitions

Native Born—Born in the United States or one of its territories or, if born abroad, to at least one parent who is a U.S. citizen.

Foreign Born—Born outside the United States or one of its territories to parents who are not U.S. citizens.

Immigrant—A synonym for foreign born. The term refers to individuals who choose to leave their own country to seek employment and education opportunities that either are not present or are inadequate in their native land.

Naturalized Citizen—A foreign-born individual who has become a U.S. citizen by fulfilling requirements set forth in the Immigration and Nationality Act, including, in most cases, having resided in the United States for at least 5 years.

Legal Permanent Resident—A noncitizen resident of the U.S. authorized to live, work, and study in this country permanently. Such status is granted to immediate relatives of U.S. citizens, including spouses, minor children, and parents. Another category that is eligible for this status consists of refugees and asylum seekers. After becoming a legal permanent resident, a noncitizen immigrant receives a permanent resident card called a "green card," which serves as proof of permission to live and work in the U.S.

Legal Temporary Resident or Visitor—A noncitizen of the U.S. who is admitted to the country with a temporary visa or who is allowed to enter without a visa. Individuals in this category include visitors who are in the U.S. for short periods and temporary residents who are in the U.S. for longer, although time-limited stays.

Unauthorized Resident—A noncitizen of the U.S. who is in the country without legal authorization. The group includes individuals who enter the country illegally and those who enter the country with valid visas but overstay their authorized time.

Refugee—An individual who owing to a well-founded fear of being persecuted for reasons of race, religion, nationality, membership in a particular social group or political opinion, is outside the country of his or her nationality and is unable to, or owing to such fear, is unwilling to avail himself or herself of the protection of that country.

Asylee—An alien living in the United States as a result of fear of persecution in one's native country. The difference between asylees and refugees is that the former seek asylum after they enter the United States whereas refugees are granted their status abroad.

Depending on country of origin and amount of time residing in the United States, from a health standpoint different groups of immigrants represent a wide range of beliefs about the causes of and remedies for health problems, access to health care services, ability to converse in English, degree of health literacy, and ability to pay for health care. These variations place different kinds of demands on the health care system in each geographical area of this nation, especially from the perspective of having a health workforce capable of providing effective levels of care.

Certain topics such as abortion and capital punishment are highly controversial. The topic of immigration also can produce heated discussions. Opponents tend to focus on illegal immigrants. They are viewed as low-paid workers who crowd out other Americans in the quest for employment, especially at a time of recession when unemployment rates are high in the United States. They also are accused of producing a cost burden for taxpayers who have to finance health, health-related social services, and education. The state of Arizona was in the news regularly in 2011 because its methods of dealing with illegal immigrants are not always in harmony with federal policy on the most effective means of ensuring border control.

The general public is somewhat ambivalent about such matters. According to one poll, many Americans favor a fairly restrictive Arizona immigration law that expands the role of local law enforcement authorities in enforcing immigration laws. The same poll also reveals that large majorities would support a bill that offered a pathway to legal residency for individuals who have been living and working in the United States.[149] Other polls produce conflicting results.

Although immigration is not as salient an issue as health reform, Congress has tried at different times to pass immigration reform legislation, but these efforts failed to reach fruition. Consequently, states have been attempting to fill the vacuum with their own immigration enforcement bills. "One of the first efforts by states to regulate immigration was the passage of Proposition 187 in California in 1994" (Human Rights Watch 2011).

Proposition 187 attempted to require local law enforcement to verify the immigration status of anyone "suspected of" being in the U.S. unlawfully and also required schools to verify the immigration status of students. Proposition 187 was later found unconstitutional, but it set the stage for statewide immigration enforcement bills in Oklahoma in 2007 and Arizona in 2010. It is an explosive trend. The National Conference of State Legislatures reports that in 2010, 208 immigration bills were enacted at the state level and over 1,400 were introduced.[150]

Estimating the Numbers

A disputable point is how many illegal immigrants there are, what countries they are from, when they came to the United States, where they are living, and what their demographic, family, and other characteristics are (Bruno 2010). What is known is that they enter this country in three main ways:

- "Some are admitted to the United States on valid nonimmigrant (temporary) visas (e.g., as visitors or students) or on border-crossing cards and either remain in the country beyond their authorized period of stay or otherwise violate the terms of their admission.
- Some are admitted based on fraudulent documents (e.g., fake passports) that go undetected by U.S. officials.
- Some enter the country illegally without inspection (e.g., by crossing over the Southwest or northern U.S. border)."

---

149. CNN/Opinion Research Corporation Poll. Taken July 16-21, 2010. On the Web at www.pollingreport.com/immigration.htm. Accessed July 5, 2011.
150. Human Rights Watch. Q & A: State Immigration Legislation and Human Rights, April 13, 2011.

Over the years, a range of options has been offered for addressing problems associated with this group. "In most cases, the ultimate aim is to reduce the number of aliens in the United States who lack legal status." For example, one option would be to require or encourage these individuals to depart from the United States. An opposing strategy would grant them various benefits, including an opportunity to obtain legal status. The issue is so controversial that it poses major obstacles to having comprehensive immigration reform legislation passed by Congress.[151]

Estimates vary of the number of illegal immigrants. Main sources of information about them are the U.S. Department of Homeland Security; the Center for Immigration Studies, a think tank based in Washington, DC; and the Pew Hispanic Center, which is part of the Pew Research Center, another Washington, DC-based organization. In 2009, an estimated 10.8 million individuals (4% of the 307 million U.S. inhabitants) were unauthorized, according to the Congressional Budget Office (CBO 2011) based on data from the Department of Homeland Security and the *Current Population Survey* conducted by the Census Bureau.

As of mid-October 2011, the overall U.S. population was 312 million. If the 4% figure were applied to that number, it would produce an even greater number of unauthorized individuals. As of March 2010, the Pew Hispanic Center estimated that there were 11.2 million unauthorized immigrants in the U.S. Since all these figures are the equivalent of educated guesses, it is assumed for purposes of this chapter that the number is in the range of 11 million.

Although a small fraction of the overall population, these individuals may live under circumstances that have an adverse impact on their health and well-being. "Most unauthorized immigrant adults reside with immediate family members—spouses or children (Passel 2009). About half of undocumented adults live with their own children under 18. Nearly half of unauthorized immigrant households (47%) consist of a couple with children. That is a greater share than for households of U.S.-born residents (21%) or legal immigrants (35%). The difference stems in large part from the relatively youthful composition of the unauthorized population. Most children of unauthorized immigrants, 73% in 2008, are U.S. citizens by birth."

These youngsters are a growing share of students in kindergarten through grade 12. In five states (Arizona, California, Colorado, Nevada, and Texas), perhaps 10% or more of students are children of undocumented immigrant parents. Some other findings are:

- "Adult unauthorized immigrants are disproportionately likely to be poorly educated. Among unauthorized immigrants ages 25-64, 47% have less than a high school education. By contrast, only 8% of U.S.-born residents ages 25-64 have not graduated from high school.
- An analysis of college attendance finds that among unauthorized immigrants ages 18 to 24 who have graduated from high school, half (49%) are in college or have attended college. The comparable figure for U.S.-born residents is 71%."
- Less educated than other groups, they are "more likely to hold low-skilled jobs and less likely to be in white collar occupations."
- "The 2007 median household income of unauthorized immigrants was $36,000, well below the $50,000 median household income for U.S.-born residents. In contrast to other immigrants, undocumented immigrants do not attain markedly higher incomes the longer they live in the United States."
- "Poverty rates are much higher than for other U.S.-born or legal immigrant residents."
- "A third of the children of unauthorized immigrants and a fifth of adult unauthorized immigrants live in poverty, which is nearly double the poverty rate for children of U.S.-born parents (18%) or for U.S.-born adults (10%)."

---

151. Bruno, A. 2010. Unauthorized Aliens in the United States. Washington, DC: Congressional Research Service.

> • More than half of adult unauthorized immigrants (59%) "had no health insurance during all of 2007. Among their children, nearly half of those who are unauthorized immigrants (45%) were uninsured and 25% of those who were born in the U.S. were uninsured." [152]

Largely as a result of their higher uninsured rate, "noncitizen immigrants (lawfully residing and undocumented) face greater barriers to accessing care and obtain less health care than citizens" (Artiga 2009). Undocumented immigrants are particularly less likely to receive care. Even though they face greater barriers to care and receive less primary care, "noncitizens, particularly undocumented immigrants, are less likely than citizens to use the emergency room for care." When noncitizen immigrants do receive health care, they tend to "rely on safety-net providers, such as clinics and health centers. These providers tend to be limited in the smaller urban and rural areas that are experiencing some of the most rapid growth of immigrant populations." [153]

Female Immigrants

Another factor that may lead to a disinclination to seek health care is a fear of drawing the attention of immigration authorities. Women in particular may find it difficult to obtain care, especially once they are detained. Most immigration detainees in the United States are held for administrative rather than criminal infractions (Rhoad 2009). Research in detention facilities in Florida, Arizona, and Texas found that these women, held for periods ranging from a few days to several months or even years, often have limited access to adequate basic health care.

Instances were documented "where women's health concerns went unaddressed by facility medical staff or were addressed only after considerable delays." Women reported struggling to obtain important services such as Pap smears to detect cervical cancer, mammograms to check for breast cancer, prenatal care, counseling for survivors of violence, and even basic supplies such as sanitary pads or breast pumps for nursing mothers. A host of problems obstructed access to health services, including inadequate communication about available services, unexplained delays in treatment, unwarranted denial of services, breaches of confidentiality, failure to transfer medical records, and ineffective complaint mechanisms.[154]

Overall Demographic Profile

"In 2009, about 39 million foreign-born people lived in the U.S., making up more than 12% of the overall population—the largest share since 1920 (CBO 2011). The breakdown is as follows: 17 million naturalized citizens and 22 million noncitizens among whom about half have no authorization to live or work in the U.S. either temporarily or permanently. Increased enforcement by immigration officials and the economic recession are factors that result in holding the number of unauthorized individuals steady or even below what it was 2-3 years ago. The size of the group remains near an historical peak."

---

152. Passel, J.S. and Cohn, D. 2009. A Portrait of Unauthorized Immigrants in the United States. Washington, DC: Pew Hispanic Center.
153. Artiga, S. and Tolbert, J. Immigrants Health Coverage and Health Reform, The Henry J. Kaiser Family Foundation, December 2009, 7 pp.
154. Rhoad, M. *Detained and Dismissed: Women's Struggle to Obtain Health Care in United States Immigration Detention,* Human Rights Watch, March 17, 2009, 78 pp.

"The foreign-born represent a substantial fraction of the population in certain states. In 2009, more than one in four in California and more than one in five in New York and New Jersey were born in another country."

"Some additional characteristics as of 2009 are:

- Only 15% of the foreign-born population was under age 25 compared with 37% of the native-born population.
- Nearly three-quarters of the foreign-born population was of working age (between 25 and 64 years old) compared with half of the native-born population.
- 29% of the foreign-born population between the ages of 25 and 64 had not completed high school compared with 8% of the native-born population."
- Marked differences in education occur, depending on country of origin, e.g., "55% of individuals from Asia had at least a bachelor's degree compared with 32% of the native-born population while 56% of individuals from Mexico and Central America had not finished high school.
- Median annual earnings for male workers from: Mexico and Central America ($22,000), Asia ($48,000), Europe and Canada ($53,000), and $45,000 among the native-born."

"The United States is in the midst of its fourth wave of mass immigration, with newcomers arriving from Asia, Latin America, and the Caribbean.

- The 1st wave consisted of early colonial settlers until the outbreak of the Revolutionary War in 1775.
- The 2nd wave lasted from the 1820s to the 1870s.
- The 3rd wave went from 1880 to the early 1920s.
- The 4th wave began in 1965."

"Until the last wave began, most immigrants were from the United Kingdom and Europe. Wars and economic events such as depressions were the main factors that ended the first three waves. Among the fourth wave group of immigrants, an item of interest is that the 2010 U.S. Census enumerated 3.7 million persons living in Puerto Rico, which was down from 3.8 million in 2000. By contrast, in the 50 U.S. states and the District of Columbia, the population of Hispanics of Puerto Rican origin increased from 3.4 million in 2000 to 4.6 million in 2010, surpassing Puerto Rico's Hispanic population." These figures help to demonstrate the dynamic nature of the ever-growing and ever-changing nature of this nation's population.[155]

"Hispanics of Mexican, Puerto Rican, and Cuban origin or descent remain the nation's three largest Hispanic country-of-origin groups, according to the 2010 U.S. Census (Lopez 2011). However, the relative position of these three groups has remained unchanged since 2000; the next four Hispanic subgroups grew faster during the decade. Hispanics of Salvadoran origin, the fourth largest country-of-origin group, grew by 152% since 2000. The Dominican population grew by 85%, the Guatemalan population by 180%, and the Colombian population grew by 93%. Meanwhile, the Cuban and Puerto Rican populations grow more slowly—44% and 36% respectively."

Geographical diversity characterizes these different groups. For example, even though about two-thirds of all Hispanics nationwide are of Mexican origin, in many of the nation's metropolitan areas Mexicans are not the largest Hispanic-origin group. "Puerto Ricans are the largest Hispanic-origin group in the New York area and Cubans are the largest in the Miami area." In the Washington, DC metropolitan area, "Salvadorans are the single largest Hispanic group, comprising 33.7% of the area's more than 700,000 Hispanics." Absolute numbers fail to tell the

---

155. Congressional Budget Office. 2011. A Description of the Immigrant Population: An Update, Washington, DC.

whole story, however, because "even though Salvadorans are the largest Hispanic-origin group in the Washington, DC area, there are almost twice as many Salvadorans in the Los Angeles–Long Beach metropolitan area. In 2009, 414,000 Salvadorans resided in Los Angeles–Long Beach, compared with 240,000 in the Washington, DC area. However, in Los Angeles–Long Beach, Salvadorans make up just 7% of the Hispanic population, putting them a distant second to Hispanics of Mexican origin, who comprise 79.3%." [156]

"A substantial amount of research has documented that, overall, immigrants are more likely to be uninsured than U.S.-born citizens and, as such, face increased barriers to accessing needed care (Cunningham 2009). Immigrants are a diverse group, ranging in country of origin, race/ethnicity, citizenship status, length of time in the country, and socioeconomic characteristics. Reflecting these differences, health coverage and access vary across immigrant cohorts. Further, the socioeconomic circumstances of immigrants change over the course of time they reside in the U.S. and often improve for adult children of immigrants (second generation Americans), which also has implications for their health coverage and ability to access care."

"Uninsured rates among non-elderly adult immigrants are more than twice that of U.S.-born residents. However, the uninsured rate for recent immigrants is almost three times that of immigrants who have been in the U.S. for more than 20 years (63% vs 22%). Controlling for differences in socioeconomic characteristics, health status, and levels of assimilation (e.g., citizenship, language use) essentially eliminates the difference in the uninsured rate between U.S.-born residents and immigrants who have been residing in the U.S. for at least 5 years. The higher uninsured rate for recent immigrants persists after controlling for these differences, likely reflecting lower availability and take-up of employer-sponsored coverage among recent immigrants." [157]

Children of Immigrants

At the beginning of 2011, the Census Bureau released its new statistics on the nation's children and school enrollment, which showed something momentous (Frey 2011). "For the first time since this annual data series has been released, fewer than half of all the children (49.9%) in the youngest age group shown, three-year-olds, were white. These data finally confirm the beginning of an oft-predicted trend—a truly multiethnic minority school age population that will continue to pour into U.S. primary grade schools, high schools, and beyond in the coming decade. The trend is most pronounced in eight states and the District of Columbia, where the pre-k and kindergarten populations already are minority majority. In an additional nine states, minorities—Hispanics, blacks, Asians, and other races—comprise over four in ten students."

"These dramatic shifts in the child population result from the aging and low fertility rates of whites, coupled with immigration and often higher fertility rates of younger Hispanics and other minority groups. Today, most Hispanic growth is due to births to U.S. families rather than immigration."

Additionally, much of the demographic momentum for this change is already set in place. Even if immigration stopped tomorrow, "we will achieve a national minority majority child population by 2050 (by around 2023 if current immigration trends continue)." This dramatic transformation in child and school-age populations should lead to an increase in efforts to provide a

156. Lopez, M.H. and Dockterman, D. 2011. U.S. Hispanic Country-of-Origin Counts for Nation, Top 30 Metropolitan Areas. Washington, DC: Pew Hispanic Center.
157. Cunningham, P. and Artiga, S. How Does Health Coverage and Access to Care for Immigrants Vary by Length of Time in the U.S.? The Henry J. Kaiser Family Foundation, June 2009, 18 pp.

quality education for racial and ethnic groups with traditionally lower achievement rates in American schools.[158]

"Children in immigrant families are the fastest growing segment of the nation's population of children (Fortuny 2009). While the number of children in native families grew by 2.1 million between 1990 and 2007, children of immigrants increased by 8.1 million during this period. The share of children that have at least one foreign parent rose rapidly and now as a result, children of immigrants represent more than one in five U.S. children. In 2007, 56% of children of immigrants were of Hispanic origin. Equal shares of children were Asian and white (18% each), and fewer children of immigrants (8%) were black."[159]

"Despite better overall health indices at birth, young children who are U.S. citizens and whose mothers are recent immigrants are at greater risk for food insecurity and for reported fair or poor health than are young children of U.S.-born mothers (Chilton 2009). Although women who had lived in the United States for more than 10 years were at a lower risk of household food insecurity than were newly arrived immigrants, the risk for all immigrants, regardless of their duration of residence, was significantly higher than that among households with U.S.-born mothers."

"Increased odds of food insecurity and poor health among children of immigrants raise concerns about future difficulties associated with development, socioemotional status, and school performance that could be passed on to the next generation of U.S.-born children. Elevated rates of food insecurity are an indication that immigrant families and their young children face preventable health risks that may jeopardize children's ability to achieve in school, develop to their full potential, and contribute to the future economy as productive workers."[160]

Integration of Immigrants into U.S. Society and Their Health Care

Fears about immigrants' ability to integrate have accompanied each new influx and this fourth wave is no exception (Jiménez 2011). "When they first arrive, immigrants face some natural barriers to full social, economic, and political participation." The gap narrows over time as they and "their children learn English, interact with members of host communities, and become involved in the political process. For the most part, full integration usually takes more than one generation." The children of immigrants tend to outperform their parents in "educational attainment, occupational status, wealth, and home ownership. Residential segregation tends to decrease over time and intermarriage with members of other groups becomes more common." Progress is uneven, however, among different groups. Based on the aforementioned education data, "Latinos are not faring as well as those with Asian, black, and non-Hispanic white immigrant backgrounds."[161]

"The suspected burden that undocumented immigrants may place on the U.S. health care system has been a flashpoint in health care and immigration reform debates (Stimpson 2010).

158. Frey, W.H. A Demographic Tipping Point among America's Three-Year-Olds, State of Metropolitan America, No. 26, Brookings Institution, Washington, DC: On the Web at http://www.brookings.edu/opinions/2011/0207_population_frey.aspx?p=1. Accessed on February 15, 2011.

159. Fortuny, K. and Chaudry, A. Children of Immigrants: Immigration Trends, The Urban Institute, Fact Sheet No. 1, October 2009, 4 pp.

160. Chilton, M. et al. Food Insecurity and Risk of Poor Health among US-Born Children of Immigrants, *American Journal of Public Health*, Vol. 99, No. 3, March 2009, pp. 556-562.

161. Jiménez, T. Immigrants in the United States: How Well Are They Integrating into Society? Migration Policy Institute, May 2011, Washington, DC: 25 pp.

An examination of health care spending during 1999-2006 for adult naturalized citizens and immigrant noncitizens (which includes some undocumented immigrants) finds that the cost of providing health care to immigrants is lower than that of providing care to U.S. natives and that immigrants are not contributing disproportionately to high health care costs in public programs such as Medicaid."

Immigrants were affected profoundly by a major policy shift in 1966, the Personal Responsi - bility and Work Opportunity Reconciliation Act (PRWORA). It "denied Medicaid eligibility to immigrants until they had lived in the United States for at least five years." Despite this hin-drance, "both legal and undocumented immigrants may be eligible for emergency care services under Medicaid, which are available only to certain classes of Medicaid-eligible groups such as children, pregnant women, families with dependent children, and elderly or disabled people who meet specific income and residency requirements." [162]

"Immigrants often are identified as a vulnerable population, i.e., a group at increased risk for poor physical, psychological, and social health outcomes and inadequate health care (Derose 2007). Addressing the health care needs of this group is challenging both because of the hetero-geneity of this group and because recent federal and state policies have restricted some immi-grants' access to health care."

"Educational attainment, type of occupation, and earnings directly and indirectly influence immigrants' access to health care resources." Within immigrant subgroups, there also are large variations based on country of origin, perhaps greatest among Asian immigrants. "For example, educational attainment is much higher among immigrants from India (89% high school gradu-ates) than among those from Laos (46%)."

"Limited English proficiency is also likely to affect the quality of care immigrants receive. Those with limited proficiency report lower satisfaction with care and lower understanding of their medical situation. Those who need an interpreter, but do not receive one, fare the worst, followed by those who have an interpreter and those who have a language-concordant provider or speak English well enough to communicate with the provider. Limited English proficiency also affects patient safety, increasing the probability of an adverse medication reaction resulting from problems in understanding instructions. Providing written instructions in patients' native language not always is an effective solution, given that some immigrants—particularly those who are older and have less formal education—have limited literacy in their native languages as well."

Immigrants' vulnerability also can be influenced by factors related to stigma and marginal-ization. Contributing factors are: "differences in appearance (for example, wearing traditional dress), cultural and religious practices, language barriers, speaking with an accent (even among immigrants who speak English), and skin tone. Stigmatization of immigrant populations can be exacerbated by community concerns regarding the effects of immigration on community resources. Being part of a stigmatized group can make immigrants reluctant to seek care because of concerns about poor treatment. If providers do not have adequate resources to serve immi-grant groups, longer waits and frustration adversely affect both patients and providers. Further, immigrants are more likely than U.S.-born populations to report discrimination in health care. Perceptions of being discriminated against can reinforce feelings of stigmatization and lead to decreased use of health services in the future." [163]

162. Stimpson, J.P. et al. Trends in Health Care Spending for Immigrants in the United States, *Health Affairs*, Vol. 29, No. 3, March 2010, pp. 544-550.
163. Derose, K.P. et al. Immigrants and Health Care: Sources of Vulnerability, *Health Affairs*, Vol. 26, No. 5, September 2007, pp. 1258-1268.

An example of vulnerability is provided by the situation of furnishing care for undocumented immigrants with end-stage renal disease (ESRD). "The absence of uniform policy for their health care has created a unique challenge for nephrologists, a medical group consulted to provide life-sustaining renal replacement therapies (RRTs) because there may be no mechanism available to reimburse these services" (Campbell 2010). Renal replacement therapy has been guaranteed for U.S. citizens since passage of the Social Security Amendments of 1972 (Public Law 92-603).

Hispanics represent the majority of unauthorized immigrants and are reported to have an "approximately 33% higher rate of progression from intermediate stages of chronic kidney disease to ESRD and an adjusted incidence rate approaching 500 cases/1,000,000 population. This suggests that there may be 5,500 of these individuals with ESRD. The landscape for provision of ESRD care to undocumented immigrants is difficult to define, however, because coverage for this vulnerable population differs among states and even among hospitals in the same state." [164]

Immigration and Mental Health

An old Italian story posted in the Ellis Island Museum is as follows:

> *"I came to America because I heard the streets were paved with gold. When I got here, I found out three things:*
>> *First, the streets were not paved with gold.*
>> *Second, they weren't paved at all.*
>> *Third, I was expected to pave them." (Sher 2010)*

Living the American dream may not always be what it is portrayed to be. Learning to adjust to life in a new country can prove to be a highly stressful undertaking. Many health professionals who arrive here are confronted with the fact that the education and training obtained in their country are no guarantee that a comparable occupational position will be secured in the United States. A dentist may have to settle for being a dental assistant, for example, unless steps are taken to meet licensing and practice requirements for being a practitioner in this country.

Loneliness and homesickness are common. Language barriers pose many challenges to successful integration into American society. Cultural differences may be substantial enough to produce uneasiness. Some newcomers may become targets for ridicule, abuse, and the prospect of being swindled. Apparently, vulnerability to suicidal behavior among immigrants is influenced by genetic factors, childhood experiences, psychiatric and medical problems, availability of social support, cultural acceptability of suicide, extent of pre-immigration, immigration, and post-immigration stress, and other factors. "Precipitants for suicidal behavior include financial problems, relationship problems, mood instability, alcohol intoxication, abuse/assault, and acute medical illness."

Suicidal behavior among immigrants usually does not receive much attention. They "often face significant obstacles to receiving quality mental health care, including financial difficulties, lack of insurance, lack of culturally- and linguistically-appropriate services, and mistrust of mental health providers." [165]

---

164. Campbell, G.A. et al. Care of the Undocumented Immigrant in the United States with ESRD, *American Journal of Kidney Disease*, Vol. 55, No. 1, January 2010, pp. 181-191.
165. Sher, L. Editorial: Immigration, Mental Health and Suicidal Behavior, *Medical Hypotheses*, Vol. 74, Issue 6, June 2010, pp. 966-977.

"Cultural factors intrinsic to different immigration groups play a role in help-seeking behaviors (Saechao 2011). Mental health is understood differently by diverse immigrant populations on account of cultural differences and the availability of mental health services in their country of origin. In many cultures, mental illness is highly stigmatized. For example, among Chinese-American female immigrants, the cultural value placed on the avoidance of shame acts as a barrier to using mental health services." One source of stress may be enculturation, particularly the preservation of one's native culture and the transmission of traditions and values to the next generation. A list of stressors and barriers is shown in the accompanying figure. [166]

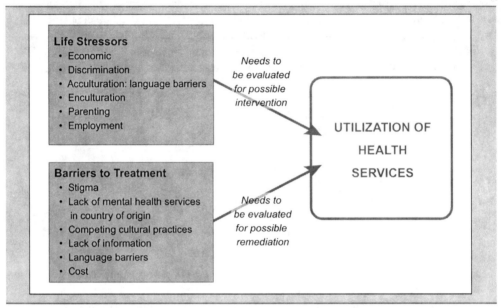

Source: Adapted from Saechao et al., *Community Mental Health Journal* (Saechao 2011).

"Poor young women are at risk of depression and those who are from an ethnic minority group are particularly unlikely to obtain care (Nadeem 2007). Fewer than 9% of U.S.-born Latinos seek care from mental health settings, and fewer than 20% seek such care in general health care settings. Immigrant Latinos are even less likely to get mental health treatment. African-Americans are more likely than Latinos to obtain depression care, but they are underserved compared with their white counterparts. Stigma about mental illness may keep poor women from ethnic minority groups from seeking treatment for common mental disorders and might therefore be an important factor in explaining disparities in care."

In one study, "differences in stigma were most pronounced among women with depression, with black women, particularly immigrant black women, reporting the most stigma concerns. Among women with depression, compared with U.S.-born white women, immigrant African women had over three times higher odds and immigrant Caribbean women had over six times higher odds of reporting stigma concerns. Ethnic differences were also evident among women without depression, suggesting broader community-based differences in stigma-related concerns between immigrant black and Latina women and U.S.-born white, Latina, and black women." Immigrant women were most likely to report stigma-related concerns about care. "Depressed

---

166. Saechao, F. et al. Stressors and Barriers to Using Mental Health Services among Diverse Groups of First-Generation Immigrants to the United States, *Community Mental Health Journal*, Published online June 7, 2011. Accessed on June 12, 2011.

immigrant women with stigma concerns were least likely to state that they wanted care. Stigma appears to dampen women's desire to obtain needed mental health care." [167]

As is often the case, it is advisable to use caution in drawing firm, definitive conclusions (Alegria 2008). Other evidence shows that "in the aggregate, risk of most psychiatric disorders was lower for Latino subjects than for non-Latino white subjects. Consistent with the immigrant paradox, U.S.-born Latino subjects reported higher rates for most psychiatric disorders than Latino immigrants. However, rates varied when data were stratified by nativity and disorder and adjusted for demographic and socioeconomic differences across groups. The immigrant paradox consistently held for Mexican subjects across mood, anxiety, and substance disorders, while it was only evident among Cuban and other Latino subjects for substance disorders. No differences were found in lifetime prevalence rates between migrant and U.S.-born Puerto Rican subjects. Aggregating Latino subjects into a single group masks significant variability in lifetime risk of psychiatric disorders, with some subgroups, such as Puerto Rican subjects, suffering from psychiatric disorders at rates comparable to non-Latino white subjects. Some findings suggest that immigrants benefit from a protective context in their country of origin, possibly inoculating them against risk for substance disorders, particularly if they emigrated to the United States as adults." [168]

Cultural differences influence mental health help-seeking strategies, affecting variables such as problem identification, problem definition, and treatment or provider choices. "Culture influences what is defined as a problem, how the problem is understood, and which solutions to the problem are acceptable (Hernandez 2009). Culture also affects mental health services when there are cultural differences between providers and individuals receiving services. When unacknowledged and unaddressed, these differences have been found to perpetuate disparities through misdiagnosis and mistreatment."

"Individuals with lower socioeconomic status tend to face significantly more service access barriers, including a lack of insurance, time constraints, and transportation limitations. These patterns underscore the importance of attending to both the joint and the independent effects of socioeconomic status and culture." [169]

Migrant Workers

A portion of the immigrant population is involved in agricultural production. One estimate is that "approximately 95% of agricultural workers in the United States were born in Mexico and 52% are undocumented" (Holmes 2006). Apart from being exposed to pesticides and harsh working conditions, they often are victims of prejudice and even violence. Immigrants who enter the country illegally from Mexico may find it increasingly more hazardous to do so. As more efforts to prevent illegal border crossing are implemented in the form of increasing the number of enforcement agents, the erection of more barriers, and added technology, the routes that immigrants are inclined to take can be highly dangerous and have been known to lead to fatalities.[170]

---

167. Nadeem, E. et al. Does Stigma Keep Poor Young Immigrant and U.S-born Black and Latina Women from Seeking Mental Health Care? *Psychiatric Services*, Vol. 58, No. 12, December 2007, pp. 1547-1554.
168. Alegria, M. et al. Prevalence of Mental Illness in Immigrant and Non-Immigrant U.S. Latino Groups, *American Journal of Psychiatry*, Vol. 165, No. 3, March 2008, pp. 359-369.
169. Hernandez, M. et al. Cultural Competence: A Literature Review and Conceptual Model for Mental Health Services, *Psychiatric Services*, Vol. 60, No. 8, August 2009, pp. 1046-1050.
170. Holmes, S.M. An Ethnographic Study of the Social Context of Migrant Health in the United States, *PLoS Medicine*, Vol. 3, No. 10, October 2006, p. 1776-1793.

Working on farms and type of residence often go hand-in-hand. Migrant farmworkers are among the few occupational groups whose housing quality is linked directly to their employment, often as part of their compensation (Vallejos 2011). Poor housing quality has a negative impact on health. Substandard conditions such as "inadequate bathing, laundry, or storage facilities are common in migrant farmworker camps." Crowded living conditions are associated with increased rates of depression, anxiety, and social withdrawal. An inadequate supply of shower-heads is of particular importance to workers exposed to pesticides. The fewer showers available, the longer workers must wait to take a shower, potentially resulting in higher doses of pesticide entering the body.[171]

Human Trafficking

Often hidden from view, but important nevertheless, are migrants who arrive in the United States as victims of human trafficking. "Trafficked persons are defined as 'individuals who are coerced, tricked or forced into situations in which their bodies or labor are exploited, which may occur across international borders or within their own country'" (Barbour 2011). While their vulnerability is considerable, "the true magnitude of the problem is still unknown. Attempts to understand the scale of the problem are further hampered by differences between countries in defining what constitutes trafficking, in their efforts to protect those exploited by it and prosecute the traffickers, and in reporting data."

"Coercion into the sex trade, overwhelmingly of women and children, comprises the largest proportion of all those trafficked internationally, with a smaller minority trafficked for labor or other forms of exploitation. Such estimates tend to be based around analysis of the very small numbers of cases reported to, or investigated by, national authorities, and it has been suggested that only 0.4% of likely victims of trafficking are ever identified as such. Health implications for those affected by trafficking, and particularly for sexual exploitation, are severe during any phase of migration. Individuals face enormous barriers in many countries in accessing health services and other forms of support, and many health problems or risks arise directly from marginalization, insecurity, and difficulties obtaining care."[172]

The U.S. Bureau of Justice Statistics has a reporting system that began in 2007 to collect data on alleged human trafficking incidents from state and local law enforcement agencies. Highlights of a report are that 1,229 alleged incidents of human trafficking were recorded from January 1, 2007 to September 30, 2008 (Kyckelhahn 2009). Most (83%) involved allegations of sex trafficking. Labor trafficking accounted for 12% of incidents. The rest were unknown.[173]

Health Experiences of Different Racial/Ethnic Groups

The U.S. continues to be a nation of immigrants who tend to bring their beliefs with them. Problems can arise from language differences in the health care setting and from generational differences in cultural background. India is a fascinating place to behold these days. Out - sourcing of jobs from the U.S. and Europe to that country in the form of the establishment of

171. Vallejos, Q.M. et al. Migrant Farmworkers' Housing Conditions across an Agricultural Season in North Carolina, *American Journal of Industrial Medicine*, Vol. 54, Issue 7, July 2011, pp. 533-544.
172. Barbour, V. et al: Editors. Human Trafficking: The Shameful Face of Migration, *PLoS Medicine*, Vol. 8, No. 6, June 2011.
173. Kyckelhahn, T. et al. *Characteristics of Suspected Human Trafficking Incidents, 2007-2008*, Bureau of Justice Statistics Special Report, January 2009, 16 pp.

call centers has made it possible for large numbers of young persons to migrate to urban locales to work all night in these venues.

They are well-educated, articulate, and eager to achieve financial independence from their parents. Young women are able to live in their own apartments and do not feel bound to accept time-honored arrangements that result in having parents choose their spouse and subsequently compel them to move in with in-laws after the marriage takes place. Similar clashes occur in the U.S. between first-generation Americans and their immigrant parents. Social changes of this nature also can have a major impact on health beliefs and practices and can help to determine the kinds of practitioners sought when health problems occur. For immigrants, the sources of health information relied upon and discrepancies that exist between traditional health beliefs and Western medicine will influence personal health practices.

Hispanic Immigrants

In the United States, "the prevalence of obesity is increasing and higher rates of obesity are found in Hispanics than non-Hispanic whites (Wolin 2009). Adjusting for age, education, smoking status, hours per day spent sitting, and occupational status, women who had lived in the U.S. for greater than 20 years had twice the odds of being obese as women who had lived in the U.S. for 10 years or less." There was no difference between women who had lived in the U.S. for 11–20 years and women in the U.S. for 10 years or less.[174]

"Data are emerging that show large numbers and high rates of occupational fatality among Hispanic and foreign-born workers over the last two decades, despite downward trends for the U.S. workforce. The work-related death rate for foreign-born Hispanics was 5.9 per 100,000 compared to a rate of 3.5 for U.S.-born Hispanics (Forst 2010). In 2006, the fatality rate was 5.0 per 100,000 Hispanic workers, 4.0 for all U.S. workers, 4.0 for non-Hispanic white workers, and 3.7 for non-Hispanic black workers. The percent of Hispanic decedents that were foreign-born went from 52% in 1992 to 67% between 2003 and 2006." The increase has "been attributed to work in hazardous economic sectors and in low-skill occupations, temporary employment situations, poor communication due to inability to speak English, lack of training, low educational attainment, cultural norms and beliefs about vulnerability and prevention, poor access to health care, economic insecurity, fear of deportation, and other socioeconomic factors. While overrepresentation of Hispanics in hazardous work settings has been demonstrated, the relative importance of other factors is not well-characterized in the published literature." [175]

"Researchers have been intrigued by studies indicating that Latinos experience health outcomes that are equal to or better than those of whites, despite having lower socioeconomic status (Viruell-Fuentes 2011). One important exception to this paradox is self-rated health. Latino's assessments of their overall health status are lower than those of whites and below what would be expected from more objective measures." The explanation may be that "the usual Spanish translation of response categories to the self-rated health question induces Spanish-speaking respondents to report poorer health than if they were responding to the question in English."

Response categories are "conventionally translated into Spanish as *excelente* (excellent), *muy buena* (very good), *buena* (good), *regular* (fair) and *mala* (poor). Findings suggest that the trans-

---

174. Wolin, K.Y. et al. Obesity and Immigration among Latina Women, *Journal of Immigrant Minority Health*, Vol. 11, No. 5, October 2009, pp. 428-431.
175. Forst, L. et al. Traumatic Occupational Injuries in Hispanic and Foreign Born Workers, *American Journal of Industrial Medicine*, Vol. 53, Issue 4, April 2010, pp. 344-351.

lation of the English word 'fair' to *regular* induces Spanish-language respondents to report poorer health than they would in English. Self-related health should be interpreted with caution, especially in racial/ethnic comparisons." [176]

The dangers of a wide variety of prescription diet pills have been documented clearly over the past four decades. "In the late 1960s, an epidemic of pulmonary hypertension with a 50% mortality rate was traced to the diet pill Aminorex (Cohen 2009). In the 1990s, pulmonary hypertension and valvular heart disease were found to be caused by the combined use of fenfluramine and phentermine.

Currently dangerous compounded diet pills are commonly prescribed in Brazil. Since the 1990s, many Brazilian physicians, usually advertising themselves as weight loss specialists in private practices, have prescribed these compounded diet pills. These compounded appetite suppressants contain an average of three to six prescription medications that often include amphetamines, benzodiazepines, selective serotonin reuptake inhibitors, diuretics, levothyroxine, laxatives, or other substances.

A study demonstrated that compounded diet pills banned by the U.S. Food and Drug Administration (FDA) have been used "in the U.S. by nearly one-fifth of female Brazilian immigrants presenting to a primary care practice. Most pill users reported significant physical symptoms attributed to the component medications of the pill."

"Health risks may be magnified when these pills are exported to the U.S. where health care providers may not be knowledgeable about their use. This lack of knowledge potentially could lead to misdiagnosis of side effects and inappropriate medical care." Attainment of a college education was associated with compounded diet pill use among Brazilian women.[177]

Asian Immigrants

Among the *Hmong*, a group of immigrants from Laos, concepts of health, disease, and treatment modalities are a blend of traditional and Western ideas. "Disease causation has natural and supernatural etiologies (Culhane-Pera 2003). Natural sicknesses are caused by wind, heredity, germs, bad food or water, chemicals in food, and an imbalance in metaphysical forces. Treatments include releasing built-up wind or bad blood with massage, cupping, coining, or medicines; enticing illnesses to mature; and directing healing energy through magical healing." [178]

These ideas are similar to concepts found in China and Southeast Asia that revolve around the necessity of achieving balance in *yin/yang* elements. "Each individual has unique amounts of *yin* (female, hot, wet, dark) and *yang* (male, cold, dry, light). Illness is caused by disrupting the balance. Treatment restores it. The influence of *yin/yang* imbalance can be seen in post-partum women. They are cold as they have lost hot blood and they need to follow prohibitions to restore balance" (Cha 2003).

For Hmong refugees, moving to the U.S. created imbalance in their lives. In Laos they ate rice and worked in the fields, which allowed them to sweat out the salts from their diet in a

---

176. Viruell-Fuentes, E.A. et al. Language of Interview, Self-Rated Health, and the Other Latino Puzzle, *American Journal of Public Health*, Vol. 101, No. 7, July 2011, pp. 1306-1313.

177. Cohen, P.A. et al. Imported Compounded Diet Pill Use among Brazilian Women Immigrants in the United States, *Journal of Immigrant and Minority Health*, Vol. 11, No. 3, June 2009, pp. 229-236.

178. Culhane-Pera KA and Xiong P. Hmong culture: tradition and change. In: Culhane-Pera KA, Vawter DE, Xiong P, Babbitt B, Solberg M, editors. *Healing by Heart: Clinical and Ethical Case Stories of Hmong Families and Western Providers*. Nashville, TN: Vanderbilt University Press; 2003.

country where the weather was suitable for them. In the U.S., they eat what they consider to be contaminated foods, don't do as much physical work, and experience weather that is different. Their animistic beliefs create additional dissonance. "Physical and spiritual worlds co-exist. Land spirits interact with souls and humans travel between the two worlds. Upon their arrival in the U.S., they wondered where the land spirits resided and which were friendly and which were evil. A failure to make offerings to land spirits can result in illness. A major concern was whether Americans had driven spirits from the land." [179]

In addition to beliefs about balance and being out of balance, other notions carried over to how well they could interact successfully with American health practitioners. Head touching, eye contact, and complimenting children were viewed by them as practices that were insulting, offensive, or dangerous. In order for effective treatment to be provided, accommodations must take place between Hmong and U.S. culture.

"Rates of liver and cervical cancer are 3 to 4 times as high among the Hmong in California as they are as among other Asians/Pacific Islanders in California (Baker 2010). The Hmong are also much less likely than are other ethnic groups in California to have their cancers diagnosed at an early, treatable stage; prevention is key to reducing the cancer burden in this population. Up to 60% of liver cancer and 70% of cervical cancer can be prevented by adequate immunization, but the Hmong are the least likely among Asian/Pacific Islander groups to obtain these immunizations for their children."

Research has demonstrated that Hmong in the United States blend and adapt traditional animism with Western medicine to interpret the role and possible failure of immunization in an outbreak. They "often use a multifaceted, hybrid pathway in seeking health care that incorporates Western medicine (for acute physical illness) and consultation with a shaman (for illnesses presumed to be spiritual or for which Western medicine has failed to provide an adequate cure or explanation). Despite shamans' acceptance of immunization, Hmong parents who consult a shaman for health care may be blending ways of understanding health and may be distrustful of aspects of Western medicine, including immunizations."

"Another explanation is that parents who seek services from shamans and herbalists may not seek (or may seek less often) routine medical care from Western health care providers. As a result, they may experience barriers arising from inconsistent health care or from the absence of a trusting relationship with a primary care provider. Studies have found that individuals who do not have regular care providers are more likely to be underimmunized or behind schedule in receiving immunization." [180]

Korean Americans are one of the recently arrived and rapidly growing ethnic groups in the U.S. (Jo 2009). "Colorectal cancer is the most common cancer in Korean American males, followed by stomach and lung cancers; the second most common cancer in Korean American females, after breast cancer; and the incidence is rising in this population. Although screening, using the fecal occult blood test (FOBT), sigmoidoscopy or colonoscopy is well established as an effective means of reducing the burden of colorectal cancer, screening rates are low across populations and even lower among Korean Americans. According to the 2005 California Health Interview Survey, about 77% of Korean adults 40 and older have never received any colorectal cancer screening as compared to 55% of Asian Americans, 46% of the general population, and 39% of whites living in California."

179. Cha, D. 2003. *Hmong American Concepts of Health, Healing, and Conventional Medicine*, New York: Routledge.
180. Baker, D.L. et al. Perception of Barriers to Immunization among Parents of Hmong Origin in California, *American Journal of Public Health*, Vol. 100, No. 5, May 2010, pp. 839-845.

The majority of Korean Americans are foreign-born and approximately 54% of Koreans aged 18 and over living in California do not speak English well. Thus, many seek care from Korean American physicians if they have the opportunity. "Contrary to the belief that among under-represented populations ethnic concordance between physician and patient should result in higher quality care, one study suggested that Korean physicians very rarely recommended colo - rectal cancer screening for their Korean patients. This finding is consistent with two previous studies that showed ethnic minority patients are less likely to receive certain preventive servic-es such as pap smears, mammograms, and clinical breast exams from ethnic minority physicians compared to care received from Caucasian physicians."

"Physicians identified the following barriers for recommending colorectal cancer screening: barriers directly attributable to the physicians themselves (i.e., lack of knowledge, fear of medico-legal liability), barriers associated with their patient characteristics (i.e., patient's unfa-miliarity with the concept of screening and prevention), and barriers that result from the limi-tations of the health care system or local clinics (i.e., lack of referral network, poor reimburse-ment)." Study findings elucidated themes "that may be unique to this group and perhaps to other immigrant or underserved groups. In particular, the lack of concept of 'screening' may be common in immigrant populations from countries where preventive medicine is not widely practiced. Additionally, heavier involvement of the extended family in the patient's health practices and treatment decisions resulting in additional physician burden may be found more commonly in the Latin American and many of the Asian cultures." [181]

Muslim-Arab Immigrants

The terms *Muslim* and *Arab* often are used interchangeably, but they should not be. Al-though many Arabs are Muslims, not all Muslims are Arabs. Muslims who are not Arabs and do not speak Arabic have a substantial presence in Bangladesh, Pakistan, India, and Indonesia.

Arab Americans are residents of the United States who trace their ancestral, cultural, or lin-guistic heritage or identity back to one of 22 Arab countries (El-Sayed 2009). Many reasons exist why health indicators among Arab Americans may be different than those in the general population at large. First, they "are disproportionately recent immigrants to the U.S. Second, they share a set of cultural norms, heavily influenced by Islamic behavioral restrictions, that may substantially influence health behaviors. Third, this group has in the past few decades been mar-ginalized from the general population, and increasingly so in the past several years."

Arab immigrants living in the United States total between 1.5 million and 3.5 million. They also have been growing in number each decade. New York's Arab population of 405,000 ranks third in this country after those of California and Michigan. [182]

In a study conducted in New York City, "the language barrier was often named as one of the most profound and pervasive obstacles to health care access by both male and female partici-pants" (Shah 2008). Arabic-speaking health care providers and Arab primary care doctors were preferred by many respondents. "The women indicated that they could not fully explain their symptoms and health concerns in English, and along with males, commented on the lack of

181. Jo. A.M. et al. Why Are Korean American Physicians Reluctant to Recommend Colorectal Cancer Screening to Korean American Patients? Exploratory Interview Findings, *Journal of Immigrant and Minority Health*, Vol. 11, No. 4, August 2009, pp. 302-309.
182. El-Sayed, A.M. and Galea, S. The Health of Arab-Americans Living in the United States: A Systematic Review of the Literature, *BMC Public Health*, Vol. 9, 2009, pp. 272-280.

translated materials in Arabic and Arabic-speaking interpreters at medical visits. Women who had to bring male family members as interpreters did not feel comfortable discussing certain female-specific health issues, including gynecologic care and they reported that they did not mention such topics during their health care visit."

"Among the women, all of whom were Muslim, there was a strong sense of thankfulness to God ('Al hamdulallah') for one's good health. God was thanked whenever a woman reported a positive health diagnosis or result. God also was identified as the omnipotent protector. The phrase, 'All is in the hands of God,' was mentioned many times." Several males in the study believed that cancer was a punishment by God or that the prospect of a cure was only known by God.[183]

Fasting during the month of Ramadan is "one of the five pillars of Islam" (Kridli 2011). The other pillars are "announcement of faith, praying five times a day, Zakat (giving to the poor), and Hajj (pilgrimage once in a lifetime). Ramadan is the ninth month of the Islamic Lunar calendar and is an important period because it was the month in which the Qur'an, the holy book of Islam, was revealed. During this month, Muslims abstain from eating and drinking from sunrise to sunset. Since Ramadan is based on a Lunar calendar, it begins 11 or 12 days earlier each year and it lasts 29 to 30 days. Ramadan can occur in any of the four seasons; it is considered more difficult to fast in the summer than the winter due to the heat and longer day hours. The purpose of fasting for Muslims is to: learn self-restraint from indulgence in everyday pleasures, develop God-consciousness, develop self-control, purify the body, and empathize with the poor and hungry."

"Islamic law is very clear about the exemption from fasting for the sick, menstruating, traveling, elderly, the breastfeeding and pregnant, and those unable to understand the purpose of fasting during Ramadan. Yet, some Muslim women still may choose to fast while sick, pregnant, and breastfeeding because of a confluence of social, religious, and cultural factors. American-born Muslim women are less likely to fast than immigrant Muslim women." Also, "multiparous women were found to be more likely to fast compared to primigravidas, which could be related to first-time mothers tend to be more worried about the effect of fasting." Little is known about the physiological effects of fasting on the mother or her unborn baby, Thus, nurses and other health care providers are faced with the difficult task of providing appropriate advice.

The role of gender must be incorporated into treatment protocols and educational plans when counseling women about fasting. Men such as fathers, brothers, husbands, and religious leaders may have a powerful influence in the life of women. Some pressure on women to fast can be linked to pervasive gender roles and to lack of understanding by men about what exactly are the tenets of Islamic law about fasting while pregnant or breastfeeding.[184]

Closing Thoughts

Immigration is a fact of life in the United States. Since the early days of the republic, newcomers have arrived in this country. They bring with them a wide assortment of health beliefs about the causes of disease. Their approaches to treating various conditions may not conform to western standards of health care. Inability to converse in the English language poses another

183. Shah SM, et al. Arab American Immigrants in New York: Health Care and Cancer Knowledge, Attitudes, and Beliefs, *Journal of Immigrant Minority Health*, Vol. 10, No. 5, October 2008, 429-436.
184. Kridli, S.A. Health Beliefs and Practices of Muslim Women During Ramadan, MCN, *The American Journal of Maternal Child Nursing*, Vol. 36, No. 4, July/August 2011, pp. 216-221.

obstacle that can interfere with the provision of high-quality care. One remedy is to produce a health workforce that mirrors the racial and ethnic background of different groups. Because that option is not always available, the next best approach is to have a health workforce that possesses a keen understanding of cultural differences and has acquired the knowledge necessary to bridge the kinds of gaps that can interfere with the provision of effective patient care.

CHAPTER 6:

Government's Role in Health Policy and Provision of Services

6

A preponderant role is played by the federal government in health care for the nation's population, directed by several key agencies in the executive branch. Congress appropriates funds to conduct an extensive range of activities and provides legislative oversight of how these activities are implemented and maintained. Political controversy often centers around the extent of governmental reach into the private sector that is considered necessary and desirable.

Health in the United States represents approximately 18% of the largest economy in the world. It should come as no surprise that the provision of health care services and various aspects of financing would be a major part of the responsibility of government at all levels—federal, state, county, city, and town. Much of what occurs goes unnoticed by the general public and consists of basic services to protect health such as inspection of food and water supplies to ensure safety. Data gathering through epidemiology studies provides a basis for developing programs to enhance the health of the entire population or particular segments that are at greatest risk.

For example, the Foodborne Diseases Active Surveillance Network (FoodNet) is the principal foodborne disease component of the Emerging Infections Program of the Centers for Disease Control and Prevention (CDC). FoodNet is a collaborative project of the CDC, 10 state health departments (California, Colorado, Connecticut, Georgia, Maryland, Minnesota, New Mexico, New York, Oregon, and Tennessee), the U.S. Department of Agriculture (USDA), and the Food and Drug Administration (FDA).

Foodborne diseases monitored through FoodNet include infections caused by the bacteria *Campylobacter*, Shiga toxin-producing *Escherichia coli*, *Listeria*, *Salmonella*, *Shigella*, *Vibrio*, and *Yersinia*; and the parasites *Cryptosporidium* and *Cyclospora*. In 2010, the FoodNet surveillance area covered a population of approximately 46 million individuals or 15% of the U.S. population. Epidemiology studies help public health officials better understand the nature of foodborne diseases. FoodNet also provides a network for responding to new and emerging foodborne diseases, monitoring this burden, and identifying their sources. Most importantly, FoodNet surveillance provides the data necessary for measuring progress in disease prevention.

Officials of many health departments and organizations want the federal government to become more involved in food matters (Silver 2011). They would like the government "to track nutrients in the U.S. food supply by building a public and product-specific national nutrition database. The database would provide consumers with easy access to nutrition information already required by the FDA on packaged food labels. Such a system would make it possible to track changes in key determinants of health such as sodium, trans-fat, and saturated fat over time. It also would foster competition for healthier products, driving the entire food supply to be healthier."

In some instances, the leading causes of death across the nation are preventable, including cardiovascular disease, cancer, and diabetes. The food consumed is an important factor that can protect against—or increase the risk of—chronic disease. "Much of the U.S. food supply is undergoing a significant shift in product formulation, but no existing nutrition database is publicly available, product-specific, up-to-date, and comprehensive." [185]

History of U.S. Involvement in the Health Arena

The federal government became involved in health affairs when legislation was enacted in 1798, authorizing the provision of medical care for merchant seamen and for establishing the U.S. Marine Hospital. By 1799, federal-state cooperation was evident in efforts to enforce various quarantine laws to stem the spread of infectious diseases such as cholera and yellow fever. Other milestone events were:

1887	Establishment of a Hygienic Laboratory at the Staten Island Marine Hospital
1902	Biologic Controls Act for Licensing and Regulating Production and Product Sales
1935	Social Security Act authorizes Health Grants to States for Tuberculosis and Other Diseases
1937	National Cancer Institute created by the National Cancer Act
1946	National Institute of Mental Health created
1946	National Hospital Survey and Construction Act (Hill-Burton Programs)
1946	Transfer of Office of Vital Statistics from Census Bureau to Public Health Service
1948	Water Pollution Control Act
1948	National Heart Institute created
1950	National Institutes of Arthritis, Metabolic Diseases, and Neurological Diseases and Blindness created
1955	National Institute of Allergy and Infectious Diseases created
1955	Air Pollution Control Act
1956	Public Health Service authorized to provide student traineeships
1956	National Health Survey authorized by Congress
1960	National Center for Health Statistics established
1961	Community Health Services and Facilities Act
1963	Mental Retardation Facilities and Community Health Centers Construction Act
1963	Health Professions Education Assistance Act for Construction of Health Professions Schools
1964	Nurse Training Act for Nursing School Construction or Rehabilitation
1965	Medicare and Medicaid Programs created
1965	Regional Medical Programs created
1965	Older Americans Act
1966	Comprehensive Health Planning and Public Health Services Act
1972	End Stage Renal Disease Program created under Medicare
1974	National Health Planning and Resources Development Act
1973	Health Maintenance Organization Act
1990	Ryan White Act AIDS Relief Program
1996	Health Insurance Portability and Accountability Act
2003	Medicare Prescription Drug, Improvement, and Modernization Act
2007	State Children's Health Insurance Program created

---

185. Silver, L.D. and Farley, T.A. Sodium and Potassium Intake: Mortality Effects and Policy Implications, *Archives of Internal Medicine*, Vol. 171, No. 13, July 11, 2011, pp. 1191-1192.

Interplay of Different Levels of Government

National and state initiatives help to guide efforts launched at the county and municipal levels of government. Many essential activities usually are the responsibility of local health departments. Separate agencies may be involved in programs such as meals-on-wheels, an important component of efforts to enhance the health status of home-bound, aged individuals. Contracts with agencies such as the Visiting Nurses Association make it possible to furnish services that enable the aged and the disabled to remain in their homes instead of being institutionalized. States, counties, and cities that house inmates in correctional facilities have to be able to provide basic health services such as dental care or make arrangements for them to be provided.

Municipalities sometimes can take steps that have the potential to become more widespread. More than a century ago, the landmark Supreme Court case of *Jacobsen v. Massachusetts* validated a program of compulsory vaccination against smallpox in the City of Cambridge. Some public resistance to vaccination programs continues to the present day and the issue will be discussed in Chapter 16 of this book, which focuses on perspectives on the future.

Another example of a local initiative occurred in Los Angeles (Sturm 2009). A regulation banning new fast-food establishments for one year was passed unanimously by the city council in July 2008. The ordinance was applied to South Los Angeles, which officials believed had an over-concentration of fast-food eateries. The premises for the ban were questioned on many accounts. For example, the density of fast-food chain restaurants was higher in other parts of that city. A stated goal was the hope that sit-down restaurants would become more common replacements for their fast-food counterparts, but they too are known to provide meals with an excess of calories.[186]

Government involvement in initiatives that can have an effect on health status occurs in many other ways. Cigarette smoking is the cause of major diseases such as lung cancer and emphysema. Many cities and states have enacted laws and ordinances that prohibit smoking in public establishments such as restaurants, taverns, and both indoor and outdoor sports arenas. Another way of discouraging smoking is to levy taxes on tobacco products, an initiative that may make it difficult to purchase these items because of their high prices.

For reasons pertaining to safety, state and local law enforcement personnel act in ways to discourage being alcohol-impaired while driving a motor vehicle. Motorists suspected of having consumed above the legal limit can be stopped and administered a breathalyzer test. Failure to pass can result in stiff fines and loss of driving privileges.

Some government initiatives spark fiery opposition. Fluoridation of water supplies in the eyes of many was viewed as part of a Communist plot. The perspective was satirized in the 1964 film *Doctor Strangelove or: How I Learned to Stop Worrying and Love the Bomb*. The plot involves a crazed U.S. Air Force base commander who sets in motion a plan to annihilate the Soviet Union by unleashing a fleet of planes armed with nuclear explosives. He looks upon fluoridation as a post-World War II international communist conspiracy to sap and impurify precious bodily fluids, which explains why he will mix only rain water with his alcoholic beverages.

Typically, every state either has it own health department or it is part of a larger agency that encompasses both health and related social services. Over the decades, important services in the form of mental hospitals and tuberculosis hospitals were operated under the direction of these health departments. Deinstitutionalization led to the closing of large state mental hospitals across the United States. Better health care and improved living conditions helped to convert tuberculosis from a major scourge to a disease that is less prominent today.

---

186. Sturm, R. and Cohen, D.A. Zoning for Health? The Year-Old Ban on New Fast-Food Restaurants in South LA, *Health Affairs*, Web Exclusive, October 6, 2009, pp. w1088-w1097.

The latter change had an impact in other ways. Voluntary health agencies have played an important function in supplementing the work of governmental agencies. One such group was the National Tuberculosis Association. As that disease receded in importance, the focus shifted to other respiratory ailments and the organization became the National Tuberculosis and Respiratory Disease Association in 1968. Five years later, it was transformed into the American Lung Association with a particular emphasis on air quality, tobacco control, and asthma.

Similarly, the National Foundation for Infantile Paralysis, more commonly known as the March of Dimes Foundation, was established to combat polio. The development of an effective vaccine against polio meant that the organization either had to disappear altogether or shift its attention to other health areas. It began to do so initially by devoting its resources to fighting birth defects. That mandate eventually was broadened to focus on the health of mothers and babies.

The Federal Governmental Arena

B ecause of the huge and growing national debt, a great deal of attention is directed toward devising ways to sustain the Medicare and Medicaid programs. Those two entities will be addressed more fully in Chapter 8, while noting that an entire book of considerable size could be written about them alone. Moreover, simply to describe the vast panoply of activities hosted and financed by the federal government would take several volumes.

Instead, this chapter will focus on some essential aspects of the federal role in health activities. Given the huge scope of action undertaken at the national level, a basic taxonomy may be useful in delineating what transpires within different jurisdictions. A keystone cabinet-level department is Health and Human Services (HHS). It comprises:

- Office of the Secretary
- Administration on Aging (AoA)
- Administration for Children and Families (ACF)
- Agency for Healthcare Research and Quality (AHRQ)
- Centers for Disease Control and Prevention (CDC)
- Food and Drug Administration (FDA)
- Health Resources and Services Administration (HRSA)
- Indian Health Service (IHS)
- National Institutes of Health (NIH)
- Substance Abuse and Mental Health Services Administration (SAMHSA)

Within any of these categories, there is a broad range of activities. For example, in the Office of the Secretary at HHS, the following responsibilities are housed:

- Office of the Civil Rights
- Office of Intergovernmental Affairs
- Office of Consumer Information and Insurance Oversight
- Office of Global Health Affairs
- National Coordinator for Health Information Technology
- Office of Public Health and Science
- Office of Disease Prevention and Health Promotion
- Office of HIV/AIDS Policy
- Office of Minority Health
- Office of Population Affairs
- Office of Inspector General

A similar breakdown could be provided for any of the other entities within HHS. For example, the NIH represents a significant amount of federal investment in health. Its major components include the following:

- Office of Intramural Research
- Office of Extramural Research
- Office of Legislative Policy and Analysis
- Office of Science Policy
- Office of AIDS Research
- Office of Behavioral and Social Sciences Research
- Office of Disease Prevention

Important Centers include:

- Center for Information Technology
- Center for Scientific Review
- National Center for Complementary and Alternative Medicine
- National Center for Research Resources
- Fogarty International Center

Also, there are 22 institutes, with some of the more well-known components being the National Cancer Institute and the National Heart, Lung and Blood Institute. In order of progression, depending upon the amount of money appropriated, groups may begin as Offices, evolve into Centers, and eventually become Institutes. Many Institutes have a focus on a particular part of the body such as the National Eye Institute. Others concentrate on a profession such as the National Institute of Nursing Research. Still others embrace a broad research agenda such as the National Institute of Child Health and Human Development. Some institutes came into existence because of the particular interest of a powerful senator or group of senators on Capitol Hill, while other institutes had their provenance stemming from the demands of one or more interest groups that were successful in garnering national media attention.

Although it is neither an office nor a center nor an institute, the National Library of Medicine (NLM) plays an important role, serving as the largest medical library in the world. A popular service produced by the Library is *PubMed*, which comprises more than 20 million citations in the biomedical literature. Apart from information aimed at the community of scholars in the health sciences, the general public has an opportunity to use the NLM to learn about diseases, drugs, and medical terminology by browsing the Library website.

Health Involvement Throughout the Federal Establishment

Beginning with the Executive Office of the President of the United States, important health functions are the responsibility of staff in the Office of Legislative Affairs, the Domestic Policy Council, Office of National Drug Control Policy, Office of National AIDS Policy, Council on Environmental Quality, and the Office of Management and Budget (OMB).

Within departments, there are entities that directly or indirectly through statistics-gathering functions have an impact on the health of the inhabitants of this nation:

Department of Agriculture
- Center for Nutrition Policy and Promotion
- Food and Nutrition Service
    Special Nutrition Programs
    Supplemental Nutrition Assistance Program
- Food Safety and Inspection Service

Department of Defense
- Force Health and Readiness
- Defense Centers of Excellence for Psychological Health and Traumatic Brain Injury
- Uniformed Services University of the Health Sciences
- TRICARE Management Activity

Department of Education
- National Center for Education Statistics
- Office of Postsecondary Education
- Rehabilitation Services Administration
- National Institute on Disability and Rehabilitation Research

Department of Energy
- Office of Health, Safety, and Security

Department of Health and Human Services—Health Resources and Services Administration
- Office of Rural Health Policy
- Bureau of Clinician Recruitment and Service
- Bureau of Health Professions
- Bureau of Healthcare Systems
- Bureau of HIV/AIDS
- Bureau of Maternal and Child Health
- Bureau of Primary Health Care

Department of Homeland Security
- Office of Health Affairs
- Office of Immigration Statistics
- Federal Emergency Management Agency
- U.S. Immigration and Customs Enforcement

Department of Housing and Urban Development
- Office of Healthy Homes and Lead Hazard Control

Department of Justice
- National Drug Intelligence Center
- INTERPOL Drug Division
- Bureau of Alcohol, Tobacco, Firearms and Explosives
- Drug Enforcement Administration

Department of Labor
- Office of Disability Employment
- Bureau of Labor Statistics
- Mine Safety and Health Administration
- Occupational Safety and Health Administration
- Employment and Training Administration

Department of State
- Bureau of Population, Refugees, and Migration

Department of Transportation
- Run Way Safety
- Office of Aerospace Medicine
- National Highway Traffic Safety Administration
- Pipeline and Hazardous Materials Safety Administration

Department of Veterans Affairs
- Veterans Health Administration

Apart from departments, several independent entities also are involved in different aspects of health such as:

- U.S. Agency for International Development
- U.S. Chemical Safety and Hazard Investigation Board
- Consumer Product Safety Commission
- Environmental Protection Agency
- Federal Mine Safety and Health Review Commission
- Federal Trade Commission
- National Council on Disability
- U.S. Occupational Safety and Health Review Commission

Clearly, the health domain is a large one in the United States, but how each of the aforementioned groups participates may not be immediately evident. An example is the Federal Trade Commission (FTC). Officials there have a keen interest in scope of practice disputes among the health professions. When requested to do so, Commission personnel will comment on proposed state legislation aimed at broadening the inclusion of professions that seek to provide a given set of health services, such as advanced practice nurses who want to be engaged in a level of service delivery that is compatible with their skills and educational preparation.

The Affordable Care Act of 2010 will result in the creation of accountable care organizations (ACOs). Chapter 12 on health delivery will provide more information about them, but for now it suffices to acknowledge that both the FTC and the Department of Justice will be involved in compliance monitoring of ACOs.

Apart from all the coordination that is necessary for different groups to work in harmony when multiple kinds of intervention are required in the face of a major disaster, there always is the possibility that competition and turf battles may arise. A good example of the confusion that can ensue when decisions must be made quickly and not all facts about a situation are known occurred in 1976. In mid-January of that year, a large number of cases of respiratory disease was reported among Army recruits at Fort Dix, New Jersey.

A few weeks later, after leaving his sick bed and making a forced, 5-mile night march, a recruit collapsed and died. From that point forward until the middle of December, a train of events unfolded to create, implement, and ultimately suspend a national influenza vaccination program. An excellent analysis of these events and a description of the main characters involved in launching this program, from the President of the United States down, is available (Neustadt 2005). The text offers valuable lessons to take into account when similar problems arise.[187]

Less dramatic are examples of the proverbial right hand not knowing what the left hand is doing. Large governmental bureaucracies may contain an enormous number of separate units. In the case of the Health Resources and Services Administration (HRSA), different appropriations funding streams finance the activities of various groups. What happens within each portion of a large bureaucracy may not always be known to personnel in other units. One group may undertake a particular endeavor such as developing a survey instrument when much can be learned from how to do so by staff in another unit who previously engaged in a similar exercise.

Everything becomes even murkier when totally different agencies are carrying out their respective functions such as the Bureau of Health Professions (BHPr) within HRSA and the Centers for Medicare and Medicaid Services (CMS). As an example, staff at the latter may

---

187. Neustadt, R.E. and Fineberg, H.V. 2005. *The Swine Flu Affair: Decision-Making on a Slippery Disease*. Honolulu, HI: University Press of the Pacific.

decide to conduct a survey about a specific profession such as clinical laboratory scientists, but not be aware of the skills and knowledge that are available at the Bureau to develop such tools.

The Legislative Branch of Government and Health Programs

Thus far, the focus of this chapter has been on the executive branch of government. Some problems and challenges that result at that level are a direct reflection of decisions made in Congress about levels of funding and assignment of jurisdictional responsibilities. That branch has its own major challenges to confront in producing legislation that effectively responds to health problems.

The passage of bills often depends on which political party is in the majority in both the House and the Senate when there is an inability to have a sufficient amount of bipartisan agreement. Matters become complicated when one chamber is controlled by one political party and the other chamber is dominated by its opponents. The result often is a stalemate. A good example in 2011 is what to do about the spiraling costs of the Medicare, Medicaid, and Social Security programs and the cost of national defense in the context of a federal deficit that continues to increase at an unacceptable pace.

Generally, Republicans view spending as the main problem and are reluctant to raise taxes as a means of having revenues more in line with expenditures. Democrats tend to assess the problem from an opposite point of view. They cannot conceive of any solution that does not entail raising taxes, especially on the most wealthy individuals and corporations. Even if legislation makes its way through Congress, the President may fail to sign the measure into law. That occurrence sometimes results when the chief executive belongs to one political party and the Congress is controlled by the other party.

Congress is a complicated institution with a large number of committees and subcommittees that work assiduously to protect their own turf. President Clinton was forced to appreciate the extent of that obstacle in 1993-94 when his Administration favored the enactment of major health reform legislation. Although he was a Democrat and both chambers were controlled by Democrats, his proposal never made it to the stage of voting. Powerful committee chairpersons in both houses of Congress insisted on having their respective committees become the primary source of jurisdiction. In the House, there was competition among the Ways and Means Committee, Energy and Commerce Committee, and the Education and Labor Committee. Competition in the Senate resulted from disagreements between the chairmen of the Finance Committee and the Labor and Human Resources Committee.

Successful in 2008 in winning enough votes to control the House and Senate, Democrats also won the grand prize of seeing one of their own become the occupant of the White House after an 8-year hiatus. The result was a heady brew of optimism about the prospect of enacting major health reform legislation. They were successful in achieving that goal in March 2010, albeit without the support of a single Republican.

Opposition to the legislation had manifested itself, but early signs of disfavor became even more pronounced once legislative details became more apparent. In several parts of the country, this dissatisfaction was considered a main reason why many Democrats became losing candidates in the 2010 election. Republicans seized on the issue as a way of defeating their Democrat opponents. Many ran on a platform of promising to repeal the health reform law.

Dissent also emerged at the state level when state attorneys general around the United States filed suit, declaring that the individual mandate to compel individuals to purchase health insurance was unconstitutional. Since then, different courts have produced conflicting rulings. More often than not, judges who were appointed by Democrats voted in favor of retaining the mandate while Republican appointees viewed it as unconstitutional. Ultimately, the matter is going to the U.S. Supreme Court for a final adjudication in 2012.

A related mantra that characterizes the opposing positions of the two political parties is whether health reform will lower or increase health care costs that will be borne by taxpayers. Democrats believe that costs will be lowered while access and quality will be improved. Republicans are disinclined to accept this assessment.

Congressional Dynamics

Concerns about the impact of health reform are couched inside larger issues such as producing mechanisms for controlling the burgeoning costs of Medicare and Medicaid. Both cannot be sustained in their present configuration, which spills over to the debate about raising the national debt level. If it is not raised, as it was in August 2011, then the federal government is at risk of reneging on some of its obligations such as paying interest to bond holders around the globe and issuing monthly checks to Social Security beneficiaries.

Furthermore, every debate on how to proceed is within the context of the upcoming 2012 election. Many Republicans have been opposed to increasing the debt limit absent major reductions in federal spending. Democrats prefer to raise the debt limit while also insisting that the huge and growing deficit can only be dealt with effectively by increasing some taxes.

Legislators who aspire to remain in office often are confronted with situations characterized by uncertainty and indeterminancy (Elwood 2001). Apart from what polling data suggest, they never can be entirely sure how voters will react to their policy decisions. They don't know if supporters will outnumber naysayers who go to the voting booth on election day. It also can be difficult to gauge what their colleagues eventually will do. Some will hold true to their convictions and vote the party line, but others may find it necessary to compromise because of their own need to survive an election.[188]

Congress is characterized by a level of complexity that makes it difficult to move bills forward. The production of legislation involves a dilemma that confronts each member in both legislative chambers (Elwood 1999). Every legislator is beholden to voters who made election to office possible. When campaigning for reelection, they will be judged by how well their actions proved beneficial to the residents of a congressional district or a state. Essentially, what transpires is that individual elected officials find it in their rational self-interest to behave in ways that are detrimental to the collective interest of Congress as an institution and to the collective good of society. Individual rationality often produces collectively irrational institutional and policy results.[189]

An example of indeterminancy is the Part D Medicare drug bill that was enacted and went into effect in January 2006. Once implemented, anecdotes were common regarding the tremendous confusion that resulted as beneficiaries tried to have prescriptions filled under the new plan. Even when such bureaucratic problems are resolved, what continues to be worrisome is that Congress still has to figure out how to pay for this add-on provision and for the Medicare program as a whole in the years ahead. Obviously, in January 2011 when the first group of beneficiaries in the form of the baby boomer generation became eligible, they could add 77 million to the benefit rolls over a 19-year period, creating additional finance challenges for the program.

---

188. Elwood. T.W. Congress from the Perspective of Quantum Physics, *Journal of Allied Health*, Vol. 28, No. 3, Fall 1999, pp. 184-190.
189. Elwood, T.W. Fractals and the Making of Laws, *Journal of Allied Health*, Vol. 28, No. 4, Winter 1999, pp. 257-260.

Any good story has the potential to have listeners poised on the edge of their seats while bursting with the question, "And then what happened?" This book will be published before the fate of the individual mandate is sealed by the U.S. Supreme Court in 2012. If Republicans can control both chambers as a result of the 2012 election and elect one of their own to the White House, then maybe the entire health reform law will be repealed. Already, there are beneficiaries of that law who will be most averse to losing what they currently enjoy.

An example is the families of children with preexisting conditions who previously were denied health insurance coverage. If that benefit were to disappear after repeal of the law, will dissatisfaction be enough to create a backlash that results in the eventual ouster of Republicans from public office? If so, will it be a return to, "and then what happens?"

Elected officials should be wary about playing fast and loose with the electorate. Bills should not be passed by legislators who are unfamiliar with their contents. Unfortunately, the press of business and the necessity of moving on a timely basis for certain kinds of legislation such as appropriations means that huge bills will be voted on favorably before all their contents are digested properly. Unless a legislative session is ready to expire, it would be in the best interests of all concerned parties to provide the additional time needed to read and comprehend major bills. Yet, as long as there is a tendency to tuck into a bill at the last minute some additional elements that benefit particular constituencies, it is unrealistic to expect that this aspect of behavior will be subject to radical change.

Recognizing that there are serious limitations in making prognostications, legislators are obliged to pay more attention to both ends of the range of cost projections for any given proposed endeavor. While drawing attention to the low side of cost makes sense politically in the short run, over the long-term, discontent among the electorate may be a serious barrier to developing badly needed programs and services.

Congress may pass legislation and the President may sign it, but those steps do not represent the end of the whole process. Legislation usually is written in broad terms and it is the job of staff in federal agencies to fill in the blanks by specifying exactly how the law is to be implemented.

Implementation language appears in the *Federal Register*, a publication that appears each business day to publicize proposed regulations, final rules, grants and contracts, and related kinds of announcements. This document amounted to 82,424 pages of small print in triple columns per page in 2011. An important set of proposed rules that will affect the development of accountable care organizations (ACOs) under the Affordable Care Act was published on April 7, 2011. It amounted to 127 pages. On July 15, a proposed set of rules for establishing health information exchanges under that same legislation amounted to 62 pages. As is customary, the government invited comments for both sets of rules prior to issuing them in final form. A final set of rules was issued in late October 2011.

Another publication that sometimes proves helpful in determining the intention of lawmakers is the *Congressional Record*, which reports happenings on Capitol Hill. It amounted to 22,579 pages in 2011 in the form of comments made in the House and Senate, along with an extension of remarks and a daily digest. Oftentimes, the rationale for proposed legislation appears in the *Record*, along with hearty testimonials from congressional sponsors and cosponsors.

The Politics of Obesity

Two of the most important words in the national discourse about obesity are "personal responsibility." Much rests on how these words are interpreted and how the concept of personal responsibility affects national policy (Brownell 2010). As a bulwark against governmental involvement in policing the food industry in any way, representatives from that sector of the economy point to the irresponsibility of individuals or counterproductive government policies rather than to corporate behavior. A related sentiment is that "government intervention unfairly demonizes industry, promotes a nanny state, and intrudes on personal freedom." These arguments have had some effect. Policy reforms such as restricting junk food in schools and menu labeling were successfully blocked for years in many jurisdictions.[190]

The food and beverage industries have a significant presence in the United States, which manifests itself through extensive advertising campaigns. Meanwhile, the rise of obesity in this country has reached alarming levels. A report produced in 2011 by the Trust for America's Health with financial support from the Robert Wood Johnson Foundation indicates that adult obesity rates increased in 16 states in the previous 12 months and did not decline in any state (Levi 2011). Twelve states have obesity rates above 30%. Four years earlier, only 1 state was above 30%.

Obesity is one of the most challenging health crises the country has ever faced. Two-thirds of adults and nearly one-third of children and teens are currently obese or overweight, placing them at increased risk for more than 20 major diseases, including type 2 diabetes and heart disease. It's not just personal health that is suffering. Obesity-related medical costs and a less productive workforce are hampering America's ability to compete in the global economy.[191]

Much of the food and beverage advertising effort is directed toward children. Critics fear that some ads contribute to what youngsters eat and how their dietary habits exacerbate the pediatric obesity problem. Issues of this nature usually lead to prominent divides along the political spectrum, depending on whether one is liberal or conservative, Democrat or Republican. The industry side of the ledger prefers self-regulation. Advocates of governmental involvement perceive that approach as sometimes being less than satisfactory. Their preference is to have increased oversight and more regulatory authority on the part of the government.

Apart from industry opposition to governmental intrusion into the private sector, there is a lengthy tradition of having the government intervene in ways that affect individual behavior. Prohibition was enforced by the federal government in the early part of the 20th century to prevent the consumption of alcoholic beverages. Bans on cigarette advertising represent another example. Whether to allow the use of marijuana for medical purposes remains a controversial issue in many states.

The Federal Trade Commission (FTC) is in a position to play a constructive role in thwarting the dissemination of ads that are viewed as compounding the obesity problem. The deception doctrine and the unfairness doctrine provide a legitimate basis for the FTC to intervene when advertisements are deemed as misleading (deception doctrine) or likely to cause substantial injury to consumers (Mello 2010). Even though it has the authority to propose and enforce rules, it still has to demonstrate the likelihood of consumer injury resulting from advertising and show an inability of consumers to take reasonable steps to avoid harm (unfairness doctrine). Opponents of regulation point out that nutritional information and advice are available in venues other than advertising and that parents have a role in deciding what food their children will eat.

---

190. Brownell, K.D. et al. Personal Responsibility and Obesity: A Constructive Approach to a Controversial Issue, *Health Affairs*, Vol. 23, No. 3, March 2010, pp. 379-387.
191. Levi, J. et al. 2011. *F as in Fat: How Obesity Threatens America's Future.* Washington, DC: Trust for America's Health.

The extent to which the agency is likely to wade into the thicket of preventing inappropriate advertising sometimes relates to whoever at a given time occupies the White House and serves on key committees in Congress. Similar to all other federal agencies, the FTC "depends on Congress for its funding and scope of authority, and its budget and agenda are heavily driven by the priorities and ideology of the reigning presidential administration." [192]

Federal and state agencies have been deeply involved in the production, distribution, and consumption of food over the course of a great many years. The U.S. Department of Agriculture (USDA) was established during Abraham Lincoln's presidency. Nutritional issues currently are overseen by that department along with the Federal Trade Commission (FTC), the U.S. Department of Commerce, and several components of the U.S. Department of Health and Human Services (HHS) such as the Food and Drug Administration (FDA) and the National Institutes of Health (NIH).

On matters that involve advertising, there is some overlap between what the FTC does and what is within the authority of the FDA and the Federal Communications Commission (FCC). The latter has broad powers to regulate in domains such as broadcast advertising. The FDA has overlapping jurisdiction with the FTC in food marketing, with the former involved in matters involving food labeling. In the best of all worlds, these agencies work in harmony with one another, but the potential for conflict and competition can arise when jurisdictional lines are blurred.

Distribution of Governmental Responsibility and Power

Few policy areas unequivocally belong to one level of government; almost any policy initiative requires legal powers, money, or resources such as staff that belong to another level of government (Greer 2010). "Areas with a confused division of power are as diverse as environmental regulation, reproductive rights, and transportation spending. Health care itself is suffused with this tension. Aside from Medicaid, an explicitly state-federal program, states have had responsibility for regulating insurance, but the Employee Retirement Income Security Act of 1974 (ERISA) has preempted state regulation of employee benefit plans," which meant that state laws purporting to regulate employee benefit plans may not be enforced in any court. "In this context, state laws include legislation and regulations such as those mandating particular benefit coverage, and most medical liability actions targeting health plans." ERISA has provided only "minimal federal regulation in place of state laws, but it does not prevent a state from regulating the underlying insurance coverage that an individual purchases in either the commercial market or as provided to an employer group plan." [193]

Health reform legislation enacted in March 2010 raises a host of issues about federal and state roles. Approximately 16 million uninsured individuals are destined to become enrolled in the Medicaid program, a topic that will be discussed in Chapter 8. Many states already are becoming financially unstable because of the burden of financing care for eligible patients. If anything, they want to reduce the number of clients they serve rather than expand the base. Despite financial support from the federal government to implement the expansion, their concern is that the aid will not be permanent and that they will be left to shoulder the weight of a program that already is considered to be unsustainable.

---

192. Mello, M.M. Federal Trade Commission Regulation of Food Advertising to Children: Possibilities for a Reinvigorated Role, *Journal of Health Politics, Policy and Law*, Vol. 35, No. 2, April 2010, pp. 227-276.
193. Greer, S.L. and Jacobson, P.D. Health Care Reform and Federalism, *Journal of Health Politics, Policy and Law*, Vol. 35, No. 2, April 2010, pp. 203-226.

As mentioned in a previous section of this chapter, state attorneys general have filed suit to oppose the imposition of individual mandates to purchase health insurance. Many Republicans in Congress have stated a desire to overturn the law by repealing it completely. Until that opportunity presents itself, they will oppose the provision of funds to implement various provisions of the law. Thus, the whole notion of the future of health insurance and the role of government will continue to be unclear for the foreseeable future.

Interaction Among the Three Branches of Government

The U.S. Supreme Court occasionally becomes involved as the final arbiter of many disputes that involve health issue, such as abortion and safety matters involving the right to own firearms. Whenever the final vote is 5-4 on any major decision, the court stands accused of allowing politics and personal ideologies to dictate its outcomes. At the heart of any debate is each justice's interpretation of the constitution. Critics then contend that all that is necessary is to add one more conservative or one more liberal to tilt the decision in the other direction. Such perceptions do not enhance the image of the court as an objective referee, acting in the best interests of the nation. A way to counteract this impression is to produce more opinions that achieve or approach unanimity. The key is to have less grandstanding by individual justices and more collegiality in reaching decisions that improve the common good and also have a greater likelihood of standing the test of time.

This chapter provides only a flavor of the various kinds of activities in the governmental sector that have an impact on individual and community health status. The ship of state has many compartments. Understanding what occurs at any level can prove to be an exhaustive task. Sometimes events move slowly or not all. Efforts to achieve overall health reform in the United States required an entire century. The American Medical Association (AMA) initially displayed an interest in the issue of financing national health insurance as early as 1910 (Elwood 1992).[194] Instead, a series of incremental adjustments occurred with the major examples being the creation of the Medicare and Medicaid programs in 1965.

Members of each branch of the federal government represent and are accountable to different constituencies, and the staggering of terms (2 years in the House of Representatives, 6 years in the Senate, 4 years as president, and lifetime appointments as federal judges) "cools all but the most potent of temporary passions (Oliver 2006). No one branch of government can act alone in the design and execution of public policy. The separate institutions share powers by virtue of the legislative power of the purse, executive vetoes and legislative veto overrides, and judicial review of legislative and executive actions. The power of minorities is enhanced further by extra-constitutional rules and norms allowing filibusters and individual holds on bills and nominations in the Senate. The built-in constraints on policy initiatives are compounded by frequent periods of divided government, during which neither of the major political parties controls both houses of the legislature and the presidency."

"Through his command of media attention, leadership of his party, political appointments, and other institutional resources, the president is effective in setting the national agenda, including health policy. In contrast to many other political systems, however, the power of the chief executive in policy formulation is particularly weak and the chief source of influence is not the formal authority but the power to persuade others inside and outside of government. It is

---

194. Elwood, T.W. The Federal Role in Allied Health Workforce Data, *Journal of Allied Health*, Vol. 21, No. 4, Winter 1992, pp. 31-37.

common for presidential initiatives to die or undergo substantial alterations in the hands of the legislature or the courts." [195]

During the Administration of President George Bush Sr., he advocated the implementation of ergonomic regulations to improve safety in the workplace. Approximately 10 years later, at the close of his service in the White House, President William Clinton pushed through a set of regulations that were much more ambitious in scope. Two months after they went into effect, they were nullified by the Congressional Review Act passed by a Republican Congress and signed into law by President George W. Bush.

A major responsibility of Congress is to provide oversight of programs that it has produced through legislation. Sometimes agencies can become the center of political controversy if they are viewed as overstepping their responsibilities or not performing as originally envisioned. The investigative arm of Congress known as the Government Accountability Office (GAO) has the responsibility of determining if programs operate effectively as set forth in the law.

For example, in a report to congressional requesters entitled *Health Professional Education Programs: Action Still Needed to Measure Impact*, officials at the GAO indicated that the Health Resources and Services Administration (HRSA) spent about $2.7 billion to fund health professions education programs authorized under Titles VII and VIII from 1995 to 2005 (Elwood 2008). Funding for Title VII programs rose by about one fourth, while the amount for Title VIII programs (nursing) more than doubled. The number of programs increased from 46 to 50, with the addition occurring in Title VIII nursing.

HRSA has published performance goals for Titles VII and VIII programs, but cannot fully assess their effectiveness, because the goals do not apply to all the programs and the data for tracking progress are problematic. According to the GAO, reviews of these programs have raised questions about the ability of HRSA to assess their effectiveness. For example, although one performance goal is to increase the proportion of health professionals who enter practice in underserved areas, data are insufficient to track the practice location of these individuals. In reporting on progress toward meeting its published goals, HRSA relies in part on grantees' self-reported data, which the agency acknowledges are problematic. Grantees depend on the voluntary provision of practice location information by their graduates, and some do not furnish it. One reason for noncompliance is a concern related to state privacy laws. [196]

Information of this nature could have toxic effects in Congress. Advocates of reducing the size of the federal budget might seize on this report to conclude that since it cannot be proven that a given set of programs is working in the intended manner, then perhaps it would be wise to reduce or terminate funding. Program supporters will resist such action, which adds to the uncertainty of what the final outcome will be. During the interim, government relations staff from professions that would be affected by terminating or reducing the scope of funding will attempt to prevent any decisions that would have an adverse impact.

Health Planning

During the decades of the 1960s through the 1980s, planning was viewed as an effective means of improving the distribution of health care facilities and the health workforce. The need to control health care spending became paramount. "Difficulties in carrying out the intent of Congress stemmed from the inaccessibility to regulatory agencies of the causes behind cost

---

195. Oliver, T.R. The Politics of Public Health Policy, *Annual Review of Public Health*, Vol. 27, 2006, pp. 195-233.
196. Elwood, T.W. Politics of the Federal Budget Process, *Journal of Allied Health*, Vol. 37, No. 1, Spring 2008, pp. 3-7.

escalation, the fragmented structure of agencies and their vague lines of authority, the tendency of agencies to take up bargaining and unaccountable politics, and the subversion of agency goals by staff" (Melhado 2006).

"Different forms of resistance such as evasion of cost controls by providers drew strength from the pro-growth orientation of hospital interests and local economic boosters. The conviction among community members of agency boards that more—as well as more advanced—care was better, their deference to representatives of providers seeking expansion and growth, and the broad desire of community interests to increase the supply of health services and obtain the benefits of additional economic activity they generated routinely carried the day in agency deliberations over proposals to constrain the growth of providers and thus limit the availability of health facilities and services."

Another important factor was that "health policy in the late 1970s and early 1980s had become inhospitable to planning. Additional factors included:

- Original congressional backers were gone.
- Declining community ties eliminated the traditional context for planning.
- Planning and regulation, once touted as the last best hope for cost control, increasingly appeared ineffective; their giving way to politics and their preservation of the status quo seemed illegitimate and irremediable.
- Cost containment and market improvements eclipsed the rationalization of health care and expanded entitlement as the main goals of health policy." [197]

The following anecdote may help to shed light on human dimensions that often come into play involving health issues and help to explain why what may look good on paper in the form of health planning is not always viable in real life:

In the early 1980s, a network of health systems agencies (HSAs) had been established in states throughout the United States as a result of the National Health Planning and Resources Development Act of 1974. This book's author served as a board member of an HSA in a New England state. On one occasion, at issue was whether to reverse a decision to shut down a long-term care facility and transfer the patients to a new location several miles away from the present site.

Petitioners consisted of elderly spouses of these patients. They described all the steps they had taken to improve the physical condition of the facility to make it conform to all regulations. Time, money, and personal effort went into repainting the interior and performing similar tasks. They stated that the most important aspect of the quality of care was their ability to visit their loved ones. Relocating patients would mean that some older family members would not be able to do so. Public transportation was unavailable to the new site, which meant that they had no other way of traveling there.

Similar claims were made about other defects in the plan to close the current site. Their petition was buttressed by statements made by local public elected officials who pleaded that the decision be reversed so that patients could remain where they are at present rather than experience the trauma of moving to a new place and losing important social ties. Shortly thereafter, a unanimous vote reversed the original decision.

---

197. Melhado, E.M. Health Planning in the United States and the Decline of Public-Interest Policymaking, *The Milbank Quarterly*, Vol. 84, No. 2, June 2006, pp. 359-440.

The Fog of Public Policy

Some public policy as expressed in the shape of laws, guidelines, and regulations is the product of punctilious research and the meticulous application of findings. Yet, even when results of studies are clear and consistent, there often are multiple options (Brownson 2006). As a consequence, there may be little correlation between the quality of science and the policy derived from it.

Multiple reasons exist for this incongruity. An important one is the decision-making processes for researchers and policymakers, i.e., individuals elected or appointed at some level of government. "Researchers test hypotheses, relying on experimental and observational studies conducted systematically. Policymakers have to sell, argue, advocate, and be re-elected in light of available capital. Even when data are solid, political action may not occur because ideas may not be ready for action due to competing policy issues. Research can take years whereas policymakers have to react to issues in a timeframe dominated by the election cycle."

Policymakers want precise evidence, but only estimates may be the best that researchers can provide. Information overload can prove challenging to policymakers because they can be bombarded with information from many sources. Consumer-oriented groups and industry groups can produce studies with conflicting results. Policymakers have to decide which side of any issue best serves the public good and also enhances the prospect of being able to remain in public office.[198]

Sometimes, the states take action before anything significant happens at the federal level. Massachusetts enacted comprehensive health reform legislation well in advance of the Obama Administration's Affordable Care Act. Several features of the state law such as the imposition of an individual mandate served as models for the federal version. In Oregon, an attempt was made to prioritize services that would be covered by payment. Critics viewed it as rationing health care.

In the state of Washington, an initiative was launched to use formal methods to conduct critical appraisals of surgical devices and procedures, medical equipment, and diagnostic tests. Results of these evaluations can be used to produce coverage recommendations (Franklin 2009). Some opposition can be expected to arise from device manufacturers whose products cannot be afforded without insurance coverage. Patients who are satisfied with their treatment and physicians who prize their autonomy also may offer resistance.[199]

Libertarians and other citizens have voiced disapproval over the steady encroachment of government on a broad range of individual activities. A less well-known observation is that the private sector can have a profound influence on how the public sector operates. Because of a combination of economic, social, and legal factors, considerable power over health care has effectively been delegated to medical societies, research organizations, and other institutions, enabling them to function in some respects like government rather than agents in a free market (Sessions 2010). "In particular, the issuance of official statements setting the criteria for the diagnosis and treatment of disease can have much the same effect as the enactment of legislation or promulgation of regulations."

The influence of clinical guidelines goes beyond the interaction between individual patients and clinicians. A variety of federal and state laws, rules that govern private insurance arrange-

---

198. Brownson, R.C. et al. Researchers and Policymakers: Travelers in Parallel Universes, *American Journal of Preventive Medicine*, Vol. 30, No. 2, February 2006, pp. 164-172.
199. Franklin, G.M. and Budenholzer, B.R. Implementing Evidence-Policy in Washington State, *New England Journal of Medicine*, Vol. 361, No. 18, October 29, 2009, pp. 1722-1725.

ments, and judicial standards for medical malpractice rely on the determinations of medical authorities to define disease and specify appropriate treatment. The issuance of new formal guidelines might increase the risk of iatrogenic harm. "For example, lowering numerical thresholds for the diagnoses of diabetes, hypertension, overweight, and hypercholesterolemia increased the prevalence of these diseases by 14%, 35%, 42%, and 86%, respectively. The change in the definition of hypercholesterolemia alone added nearly 43 million cases to this disease category. Although such changes can and often do result in improvements in both prevention and treatment, they also expose the enlarged class of patients to risks of long-term medication exposure."

"Sellers of medical goods and services are motivated by economic interests and not only patient needs. Both academic research and the development of guidelines are prone to significant conflicts of interest." As an illustration, "pharmaceutical manufacturers can fund the development of some guidelines either directly or indirectly by funding the clinical societies that promulgate the guidelines." [200]

M any politicians campaigning for public office run on a platform of promising to tame the regulatory beast once elected. Sometimes within government, a self-diagnosis is conducted. As a result, it is discovered that the patient would benefit from the application of some therapy. When he served as Secretary of Health and Human Services, Tommy Thompson created an Advisory Committee on Regulatory Reform to carry out the following mission:

> To improve the quality of and access to health care and human services for patients and consumers by (1) removing regulatory obstacles to smoothly functioning relationships in the health care system and by (2) promoting appropriate regulatory approaches so time and resources can be redirected toward patient care. [201]

The product was a report that uncovered how the complexity of laws and regulations creates problems for beneficiaries and other consumers, health plans, medical directors, providers, and regulated industries. Other findings demonstrated that certain issues are complicated and require more than a regulatory solution. Instead, unraveling the complexity might entail a legislative solution, significant structural changes, or additional fiscal resources.

Programs touted as being of great importance come and go. Some are highly valuable while others have to be abandoned when they fail to produce desired results. Perhaps a sounder approach would be to view new ways of doing business not as programs but as experiments. Trying them out across different kinds of states and regions of the country could provide a basis for sound judgments leading to expansion, modification, or even termination if the results do not produce anything worthwhile apart from the knowledge gained of why the intervention failed.

T he extent of government involvement in personal life is likely to remain a contentious issue. As problems arise, proponents of governmental activity will cite reasons why it is necessary to have official intervention. An example is the growing problem of obesity, especially among children. Parents are seen as playing an important mediating role in preventing child obesity. Inadequate or unskilled parental supervision, however, can leave children vulnerable to

---

200. Sessions, S.Y. and Detsky, A.S. The Shadow Government, *Journal of the American Medical Association*, Vol. 304, No. 24, December 22/29, 2010, pp. 2742-2743.

201. Report of the Secretary's Advisory Committee on Regulatory Reform. Bringing Common Sense to Health Care Regulation, Washington, DC: 2002, on the Web at http://www.regreform.hhs.gov/finalreport.pdf. Accessed on April 14, 2011.

harmful influences such as lack of opportunity to engage in physically active recreation (Murtagh 2011). "Even relatively mild parenting deficiencies, such as having excessive junk food in the home or failing to model a physically active lifestyle, may contribute to a child's weight problem."

As an alternative approach, involvement of state protective services might be considered, including placement into foster care in carefully selected situations. According to this point of view, "state intervention may serve the best interests of many children with life-threatening obesity, comprising the only realistic way to control harmful behaviors." [202] It is highly unlikely that this approach will receive universal approbation by the American public. Once again, it raises the thorny issue of what is the best way of protecting the vulnerable in society. National history is replete with examples of measures that governmental agencies have had to take to achieve this aim.

Moreover, is foster care so beneficial in every case that it merits funneling more children into that particular venue? It is over such issues that individuals sort themselves into categories such as liberal, conservative, or libertarian. At another time during the early decades of the last century, anarchists were content with trying to tear down the whole societal edifice. Today, apart from the occasional bombing of an abortion clinic or the slaying of a physician who works there, the U.S. is a relatively calm place in comparison. An ongoing challenge for a well-functioning democracy is to produce ways of accommodating many different points of view while continuing to move forward in a constructive manner.

Closing Thoughts

This chapter describes the many ways in which the government influences the provision of services that benefit individuals and the population as a whole. Given the essential role that health professionals play, there is a justification for placing more emphasis on health workforce policy and planning to deal with matters pertaining to recruitment and retention, geographic distribution of providers, financing of health professions education, scope of practice, and cultural competence.

202. Murtagh, L. and Ludwig, D.S. State Intervention in Life-Threatening Childhood Obesity, *Journal of the American Medical Association*, Vol. 306, No. 2, July 13, 2011, pp. 206-207.

Financing Health Care

7

A steady rise in the cost of health care appears to defy the law of gravity. Programs such as Medicare and Medicaid continue to dwarf other kinds of governmental expenditures. Polling of the general public shows considerable support for reducing federal spending except for these two programs and Social Security benefits, which comprise a major share of overall spending. Also, a substantial amount of uncompensated health care and related social services is supplied by family caregivers. The changing nature of American families offers no guarantee that relatives will be able to care for one another as they do so presently.

The second quarter of 2011 "marked a return to heavy downgrade pressure for credit ratings in the not-for-profit hospital sector, with credit downgrades outpacing upgrades four to one, according to a report" released by Moody's Investors Service (AHA 2011). "In addition to bad economic and unemployment news, large federal and state budget deficits and cuts to Medicaid and Medicare funding have contributed to flat or softening patient volumes, a weaker payer mix, and higher levels of uncompensated care that limit top-line revenue growth." [203]

Looming over every discussion in Congress about how to deal with the national debt limit problem is the issue of reducing spending, raising taxes, or some combination of both approaches. Major targets for spending reductions would have to include Medicare, Medicaid, Social Security, and national defense. As a share of total outlays, these items are as follows: Medicaid, (8%), Medicare (15%), Social Security (20%), and national defense (20%). For Medicaid, the percentage does not include what the states spend on this program (CBO 2011).[204]

Thus, to focus exclusively on other areas of the federal budget such as expenditures for the arts would not amount to much more than taking cosmetic steps to control spending.

Health Care Expenditure and the Economy

The impact of health on the overall economy is shown in the following tables. Table 1 presents the total annual spending for health care by the federal government for selected years from 1960 to 2011. By themselves, these figures do not convey much information. They become more salient when viewed in the context of the overall economy as shown in Table 2.

---

203. AHA News.com. Moody's: Hospital Credit Downgrades on the Rise, July 15, 2011. On the Web at http://www.ahanews.com/ahanews_app/jsp/display.jsp?dcrpath=AHANEWS/AHANewsNowArticle/data/ann_071511_Moodys&domain=AHANEWS. Accessed on July 18, 2011.
204. Congressional Budget Office, The Budget and Economic Outlook, Fiscal Years 2011 to 2021, Washington, DC: January 2011. On the Web at http://www.cbo.gov/ftpdocs/120xx/doc12039/01-26_FY2011Outlook.pdf. Accessed on July 18, 2011.

TABLE 1. National Health Spending, 1960–2011 (in Billions)	
Year	Amount Spent
1960	$27
1970	$75
1980	$256
1990	$724
2000	$1,378
2005	$2,021
2008	$2,391
2009	$2,486
2010	$2,600*
2011	$2,710*

*Years 2010 and 2011 are CMS projections based on a September 2010 data release.

TABLE 2. National Health Spending as a Share of Gross Domestic Product (GDP), 1960–2019	
Year	Percentage
1960	5.2%
1970	7.2%
1980	9.2%
1990	12.5%
2000	13.8%
2005	16.0%
2008	16.6%
2009	17.6%*
2019	19.6%**

*The percentage for 2009 reflects a 1.7% contraction in GDP, a 4.0% increase in health spending, and revisions to the national health expenditure accounts, which resulted in recognition of higher spending levels.
**The percentage for 2019 is a projection.

In 2009, national health care spending grew at the slowest pace seen in half a century. The 4.0% increase over prior-year spending extended a slowing trend that has been underway since 2003. Yet, the modest growth in health spending still outpaced the economy and health care's share of GDP rose to 17.6%, a full percentage point above 2008. Total health care spending in 2009 reached nearly $2.5 trillion, or $8,086 per individual as shown in Table 3.

TABLE 3. National Health Spending per Individual, 1999–2011	
Year	Amount per Individual
1999	$4,599
2001	$5,240
2003	$6,098
2005	$6,827
2007	$7,561
2009	$8,086
2011	$8,666*

*The amount for 2011 is a projection.

Source: Data for Tables 1–3 and 5 are from the Centers for Medicare and Medicaid Service (CMS), Office of the Actuary; Table 4, as shown. Compiled by the California HealthCare Foundation. *California Health Care Almanac, Health Care Costs 101,* May 2011. On the Web at http://www.chcf.org/chart-cart/presentations/health-care-costs-101. Accessed on July 19, 2011.

Standing by themselves, these figures do not convey a complete picture. As a means of comprehending them more fully, it helps to examine how much is spent per capita for health in other countries. Table 4 provides this comparison.

TABLE 4. Health Care Spending in Selected Developed Countries, 2008		
Country	Per Capita Spending	Percentage of GDP
Korea	$1,801	6.5%
Spain	$2,902	9.0%
U.K.	$3,129	8.7%
Germany	$3,737	10.5%
France	$3,696	11.2%
Canada	$4,079	10.4%
Switzerland	$4,627	10.7%
Norway	$5,003	8.5%
U.S.	$7,538	16.0%

Source: Organization for Economic Co-Operation and Development, OECD Health Data 2010, October 2010.

The first thing to note is that there is some discrepancy between OECD and CMS figures for the United States in Tables 3 and 4. One reason is that they reflect different time periods. Nevertheless, it is clear that the U.S. exceeds other developed nations both in per capita spending and as a percentage of GDP. Although not shown in Table 4, the public sector accounts for the majority of health spending in other countries, which is not the case in the U.S. A useful breakdown is to examine the purposes for which health dollars are spent in the United States.

Table 5 provides this information based on $2.486 trillion in expenditures.

TABLE 5. Health Spending (in Billions) by Category of Expenditure, 2009, and Growth Over 2008			
Category	2009 Amount	(% Growth)	2009/2008
Hospital care	$759	(31%)	5.1%
Physician and clinical services	$506	(20%)	4.0%
Dental and other care	$292	(12%)	4.5%
Nursing care facilities	$137	(6%)	3.1%
Home health care	$ 68	(3%)	10.0%
Prescription drugs	$250	(10%)	5.3%
Other medical products	$ 78	(3%)	0.8%
Administration	$163	(7%)	–0.6%
Public health activities	$ 77	(3%)	5.9%
Investment	$156	(6%)	–0.6%

"The 4.0% increase in health spending in 2009, to approximately $2.5 trillion—or $8,086 per person—represented the slowest rate of growth in the 50-year history of the National Health Expenditure Accounts. This historically low rate followed growth of 4.7% in 2008—the second-slowest rate during the past 50 years (Martin 2011). Nonetheless, the share of U.S. gross domestic product (GDP) devoted to health care rose one percentage point—to 17.6% in 2009, which is the largest 1-year increase in the history of the national health accounts. The increase was mainly due to a 1.7% decline in the current-dollar GDP, its largest drop since 1938. For purposes of comparison, the health spending share of GDP increased 0.7 percentage point in 1991 and 2001, during the two most recent recessions, and 0.8 percentage point in the recession of 1982."

"The recession that ended officially in June 2009 profoundly influenced total health spending in 2009. Many consumers decreased their use of health care goods and services partly because they had lost employer-based private health insurance coverage, and partly because their household income had declined. The slowdown in the growth of overall health spending in 2009 was primarily due to a deceleration in private health insurance spending, a decline in spending on structures and equipment in the health care system, and slower growth in out-of-pocket spending."

"Several factors partially offset the slowdown—most notably, a rapid increase in Medicaid enrollment, which increased the program's rate of spending. Additionally, other private revenues—which include non-operating revenue of health care providers—increased in 2009, after declining in 2008, when hospitals' investment income fell. Prescription drug spending growth was another factor: Spending growth increased more rapidly in 2009 than in 2008, as a result of more rapid growth in the prices of drugs and in the number of prescriptions dispensed."

Other findings are:

- "The federal government's share of health care spending increased just over three percentage points in 2009, to 27%.
- Federal health spending increased 17.9% between 2008 and 2009 and 9.6% between 2007 and 2008.
- In contrast, the shares of spending of households (28% in 2009), private businesses (21%), and state and local governments (16%) fell by roughly one percentage point each between 2008 and 2009.
- The substantial number of jobs lost since the beginning of the recession contributed to a higher rate of unemployment than in recent recessions. In December 2009, the unemployment rate reached 10.0%—an increase of 2.6 percentage points over the December 2008 rate of 7.4%. Additionally, between December 2007 and December 2009, nonfarm employment fell 3.1%. These job losses caused many people to lose employer-sponsored health insurance and, in some cases, to forgo health care services they could not afford.
- In response to the recession, Congress passed the American Recovery and Reinvestment Act, informally known as the stimulus package or the Recovery Act. Although enacted in February 2009, it contained some provisions that were retroactive for Medicaid to October 1, 2008. This legislation provided funding for various programs related to health care, including an estimated $34 billion in additional federal matching funds for Medicaid in 2009.
- Faster growth in Medicaid spending—from 4.9% in 2008 to 9.0% in 2009—was driven by the addition of 3.5 million new enrollees; it partially offset the slower growth experienced by most other payers. These changes in enrollment occurred at the same time that the number of uninsured increased by 3.8 million (from 42.7 million in 2008 to 46.5 million in 2009).
- Like households, the federal government faced declining revenues in 2009. Revenues went down 18.2% in 2009, while spending for health care grew 17.9%. Thus, health spending as a share of total federal revenue increased from 38% in 2008 to 54% in 2009. Although slight, state and local government health care spending as a share of total state and local revenue also increased, from 26% in 2008 to 27% in 2009. The change was mainly due to decreased revenue."[205]

Given the unsettled nature of the economy over a 3-year period, as of May 2011 employers have feared the worst about their health benefit costs and worried about a rebound of health costs in 2012. According to PricewaterhouseCoopers Health Research Institute, medical costs for workers are expected to increase 8.5% in 2012, up from an 8% increase in 2011. The esti-

---

205. Martin, A. et al. Recession Contributes to Slowest Annual Rate of Increase in Health Spending in Five Decades, *Health Affairs*, Vol. 30, No. 1, January 2011, pp. 11-21.

mate stems from a survey of 1,700 employers from 30 industries and interviews with hospital executives, health plan actuaries, and other executives whose companies have more than 80 million in covered lives.

Factors that will inflate costs in 2012 are:

- "Provider consolidation continues. More and more physicians and hospitals are merging. Although consolidation is promoted as a way to increase efficiency and reduce costs in the long-term, payers are concerned about the impact of increased consolidation of payment rates.
- Cost shifting from Medicare and Medicaid increases. In 2012, the increase in Medicare inpatient hospital rates is expected to be 3.3 percentage points below the expected growth in their costs.
- Post-recession stress builds up on workers. Health plans and employers are reporting that they are beginning to notice post recession stress taking its toll on workers' health as well as medical utilization deferred during the depth of the recession." [206]

Early detection and treatment continue to be mechanisms for trying to prevent health problems from occurring. Once such problems manifest themselves, providing necessary treatment prevents them from becoming worse. Patients who lack insurance coverage either go without these procedures or they obtain health care that is episodic and lacks continuity.

Health Exchanges and CLASS

The Affordable Care Act became law in March 2010 with the major objective being to add 32 million individuals to the ranks of the insured. The Department of Health and Human Services will work with states to enable them to create and operate their own health insurance exchanges where consumers and small businesses can compare and shop for health plans starting in 2014.

As expressed by a proposed rule appearing in the *Federal Register* on July 15, 2011, the framework would offer states a roadmap and flexibility for establishing the competitive exchanges. Another feature is that consumers and small businesses would be given more choice in deciding their health insurance coverage.

The rule offers guidance and options for states in their efforts to structure and deploy the exchanges, including setting standards for putting them in place and aligning their information systems, setting up a small business health options program (SHOP), performing the basic functions of an exchange, and certifying health plans for participation in the exchange. The framework also details how to assure premium stability for insurance plans and enrollees in the exchange, especially in the early years as the effort takes shape and absorbs new enrollees.

Many states and the District of Columbia have accepted grants to help plan and operate exchanges. Certain states also are taking additional action beyond receiving a planning grant such as passing legislation or taking administrative action to begin building exchanges. States will continue to implement exchanges on different schedules through 2014. Consumers who qualify for assistance will use the exchanges to receive federal subsidies or tax credits to purchase insurance or to gain access to Medicaid, the state-federal program for the poor. Industry groups, consumer advocates and others have 75 days to weigh in with comments on the proposed rules

---

206. PricewaterhouseCoopers Health Research Institute. Behind the Numbers: Medical Cost Trends for 2012, May 2011, 30 pp. On the Web at http://pwchealth.com/cgi-local/hregister.cgi?link=reg/behind-the-numbers-medical-cost-trends-2012.pdf. Accessed on May 31, 2011.

once they are issued. Whenever a rule is proposed, it generates many unanswered questions. In this instance, some examples are:

- Who should govern the exchanges?
- Should a state become part of a multi-state exchange?
- How will states facilitate enrollment in exchanges?
- Who will seek to be enrolled in an exchange?

Although the deadline for implementation is 2014, states have to submit their plans for developing exchanges and the federal government has to approve them in 2013. States will be required to offer a minimum set of benefits, but final rules for benefits may not be issued until 2013. Proposed rules, including the one issued in 2011, cite the necessity of producing more proposed rules. The situation conjures up images of a *babushka doll* or a *matryoshka doll*. Popular among Russian children, it is a set of wooden dolls of increasing size placed one inside the other. Oftentimes, the smallest doll is a baby. The July 15, 2011 proposed rule may be the equivalent of such a baby.

As stated earlier, the health reform law of 2010 will add 16 million uninsured persons to the ranks of coverage through the Medicaid program, a joint federal-state endeavor. States already are capsizing financially under the weight of the Medicaid program. In 2011, Arizona was trying to obtain a federal waiver to remove thousands from being eligible to participate. Typically, the bulk of expenditures is for long-term care. Meanwhile, the portion of the population entering the ranks of the aged is proceeding at a rapid pace.

The new law also has a feature in it known as CLASS (Community Living Assistance Services and Supports Act) to finance long-term care. The idea is to select a group of younger citizens, charge them a monthly premium, and then 10-years later begin to provide benefits. By September 2011, no agreement had been reached on such issues as what the premium should be to sustain the program and whether somebody can drop out and return when it appears services are needed.

CLASS provides a good example of why not a single Republican in the House of Representatives voted in favor of the health reform law. They sneered at the proposed cost-saving projections that would result as a consequence of collecting money for 10 years before paying any benefits and by a failed plan to reduce Medicare payments to physicians by 29% in December 2010/January 2011. Concerning the latter, they know such cuts are highly unlikely to occur because they would lead to a massive exodus of physicians from the program.

Then in October 2011, Kathleen Sebelius (Secretary of the Department of Health and Human Services) announced that CLASS was terminated. Significantly, the revenue it would have produced as projected over the 10-year period has to be eliminated from overall revenue projections that were made originally. Critics of the health reform law jumped on the news, pointing out that the demise of this part of the legislation simply helped to reinforce their claim that health reform ultimately would cost money rather than save money as Democrat supporters predicted when the bill became law.

Reducing Health Spending

"The case that the United States spends more than is optimal on health care is overwhelming" (Aaron 2011). To lower spending without lowering net welfare, "it is necessary to identify what procedures are effective at reasonable cost, to develop protocols that enable providers to identify in advance patients in whom expected benefits of treatment are lower than costs, to design incentives that encourage providers to act on those protocols, and to provide research support to maintain the flow of beneficial innovations." [207] A related set of views was advanced in an Institute of Medicine (IOM) Roundtable on Evidence-Based Medicine in a three-part workshop series (Yong 2010).[208]

Should a limit be placed on the proportion of the nation's economy devoted to health care expenditures? Typically, there is considerable disagreement over this matter, which comes as no surprise. Is there any such thing as an ideal limit? Is the 19.6% of GDP projected for 2019 too high or should that figure be even higher? Clearly, there is no correct answer unless elements such as the following are taken into account:

- How much the U.S. population values and desires high-quality health care as opposed to spending money for other purposes such as larger homes and more upscale personal consumer goods.
- The extent to which the entire population becomes eligible to obtain care.
- The quality of that care as demonstrated by the availability of evidence-based practices and technologies.
- Demographic factors that include the ratio between wage earners who pay taxes and aged/disabled beneficiaries who consume services.
- Geographical mobility patterns that separate individuals from family members who could serve as informal caregivers.
- The extent to which healthcare expenditures crowd out other vital areas of the economy.

As described in Chapter 5, a segment of the population that is somewhat obscured from view in discussions of use of health care services consists of the millions of illegal immigrants. What kind of health care do they receive, if any, and how will meeting their needs affect health care spending?

Rather than attempting to define an ideal percentage of GDP that would be devoted to health care expenditures, perhaps it would be more productive to place greater focus on how to curtail those aspects of health care that fail to provide valuable increments in health benefits. A delicate balance exists between a desire for medical advancement and the application of new technology. An ever-growing variety of tests, procedures, and medications continues to become available, but are they all needed and are they effective?

Health services research on effectiveness and outcomes could play a huge role in this respect, especially on the value obtained by implementing new technologies. Initiating a move in that direction begs the question of whether the nation has the requisite number of researchers who possess the kinds of skills needed to conduct such investigations. If not, resources would have to be devoted to produce an adequate cadre of researchers and provide them with the resources needed to conduct studies.

Any effort to reduce the federal deficit undoubtedly will require policymakers to consider what can be cut in health spending. Teaching hospitals are allocated an estimated $6.4 billion in the form of indirect medical-education payments. The funds are the main financial support for graduate medical education. They are used to subsidize the training of physicians and other health care personnel and they help to underwrite the costs of sophisticated equipment and

207. Aaron, H. J. and Ginsburg, P.B. Is Health Spending Excessive? If So What Can We Do about It? *Health Affairs*, Vol. 28, No. 5, September/October 2009, pp. 1260-1275.
208. Yong, P.L. et al, Editors. *The Healthcare Imperative: Lowering Costs and Improving Outcomes*, The National Academies Press, Washington, DC: 2010. On the Web at http://books.nap.edu/openbook.php?record_id=12750. Accessed on August 3, 2011.

treatment in specialized units such as those established for the care of burn patients. A proposal by President Obama's bipartisan National Commission on Fiscal Responsibility and Reform would reduce support by $3.9 billion, or about 61%.

Chapter 11 will focus on the health force, but for now, it is worth mentioning that any serious effort to reduce the nation's debt has the potential to affect support for health professions students and the institutions in which they obtain their education. The federal Pell Grant Program has proved of vital importance to many students. Unlike a loan, it does not have to be repaid. The maximum grant for the 2010-2011 award year (July 1, 2010 to June 30, 2011) is $5,550. The amount depends on financial need, costs to attend school, status as a full-time or part-time student, and plans to attend school for a full academic year or less. The program in 2011 was at a spending level of $44 billion.

An austere budget climate places the Pell Program at risk of a spending reduction, one of many federal programs liable to undergo cuts in spending. Since it is of a quasi-entitlement nature, some budget hawks in Congress view it as an attractive target. Unlike various mandatory entitlement programs such as Social Security and Medicare, where benefits must be provided to all who are eligible to receive them, Pell Grants are partially funded through discretionary spending, which means that the amount of money can be reduced arbitrarily.

Hospital Spending

During a radio broadcast in 1939 during World War II, Winston Churchill described Russia as being a riddle, wrapped in a mystery, inside an enigma. Similar to a series of proposed rules issued by the federal government being enclosed within other rules in the form of a *babushka doll*, spending reductions in one sphere of health care may have ripple effects in unforeseeable ways. The risk is that some effects may prove to have unpalatable consequences.

Hospitals in the United States represent a key ingredient in the goal of meeting the health care needs of patients. Although health spending as a whole has grown each year, as a percentage of total spending on health care services and supplies hospital care declined from 43% in 1980 to the low 30s in percentage in 2009 as was shown in Table 5 earlier in this chapter. Spending growth in this sector was outpaced by growth in health insurance premiums, pharmaceuticals, and other services (AHA 2011).

Medical advances add to the demand for services and their cost. As much as 50% of the rise in health expenditures over the past several decades is due to advances in technology.

The steady growth of the U.S. population and the increase in the number of individuals over the age of 65 will lead to an increased consumption of health care services. "Nearly half of Medicare beneficiaries have three or more chronic conditions, with the most common being hypertension, arthritis, heart conditions, cognitive or mental impairments, and diabetes. Health spending among seniors often peaks during the last six months of life" when hospitalization episodes become more common. As indicated in Chapter 6, the problem of obesity is becoming more prevalent rather than less so. Hospitalization of obese children continues to increase, jumping by "approximately 75% between 2001 and 2005." Costs of their care nearly doubled in that same period.

Hospitals are heavily regulated. Not only must they "comply with thousands of pages of Medicare and Medicaid guidance issued annually," they are accountable to other federal agencies. "For example, the Environmental Protection Agency (EPA) regulates air emissions from medical waste incinerators." Private payers have "requirements for preauthorization, admission notification, utilization review and reporting, as well as different combinations of covered and excluded services, patient cost-sharing, and payment rules." These dictates emanate from more than 1,000 insurance companies plus employers who self-insure. No set standard exists. Thus, hospitals must conform to a wide range of rules from different sources that can change at any time.[209]

Obesity and Health Expenditures

The rising incidence of obesity has a direct relationship with an increase in costs for chronic ailments stemming from this condition such as hypertension, diabetes, heart disease, and stroke. An analysis by the Congressional Budget Office (CBO) indicates how adult obesity affects spending on health care (CBO 2010). As shown in Table 6, different weight categories (underweight, normal weight, overweight, and obese) result in different amounts of health care spending.

Weight Category	Share of Adult Population (%)		Spending per Adult (2009 dollars)		%Change 1987–2007	
	1987	2007	1987	2007	Share	Spending
Underweight	4	2	3,230	4,970	–50	54
Normal	52	35	2,440	4,030	–33	65
Overweight	31	35	2,650	4,260	13	61
Obese	13	28	2,630	5,560	115	111
Not morbid	12	24	2,640	5,330	100	102
Morbid	1	4	2,530	7,010	400	177
All categories	100	100	2,560	4,550	NA	78

TABLE 6. Distribution of Adults and Health Care Spending by Adult, by Body Weight, 1987 and 2008

Source: Congressional Budget Office based on the 1987 National Medical Expenditure Survey and the 2007 Medical Expenditure Panel Survey.

Weight categories used in the table are defined using the body mass index (BMI), which is a measure of weight standardized for height that applies to adult men and women:

- "Underweight (BMI<18.5)
- Normal (> or equal to 18.5 and <25)
- Overweight (> or equal to 25 and <30)
- Obese (> or equal to 30 and <40)
- Morbidly obese (> or equal to 40)"

"How reducing obesity would affect both total (rather than per capita) spending for health care and the federal budget over time is less clear. To the extent that individuals, on average, lived longer because fewer were obese, savings from lower per capita spending would be at least partially offset by additional expenditures for health care during those added years of life. Moreover, the impact on the federal budget would include not only changes in federal spending on health care, but also changes in tax revenues and in spending for retirement programs

---

209. American Hospital Association. The Cost of Caring: Drivers of Spending on Hospital Care, *Trend Watch*, March 31, 2011.

such as Social Security, for which costs are directly tied to longevity. As a result, the net impact of reductions in obesity rates on national health care expenditures and on federal budget deficits would depend on the magnitude of those various effects." CBO did not "address changes in longevity that might arise from a changing weight distribution or the potential impact of such changes on total health care expenditures."

"The relatively rapid growth in spending for obese adults may reflect changes in the health status of the obese population from 1987 to 2007. Adults who are currently obese might be in poorer health than those who were obese in 1987 because advances in medical treatment in recent decades may have reduced the mortality rates for some obesity-related conditions. As a result, some obese individuals with severe health problems who would have died relatively young in past decades are probably living longer and accounting for continued spending on health care that is high even relative to spending on care for other obese adults." [210]

The 2010 Census and Its Implications

The United States has conducted a census every decade since 1890 when the population was 3.9 million. By 1920, the nation reached a size of 100 million and by 1967, there were 200 million inhabitants. As of April 1, 2010, this country had a population of 308,745,538 individuals living in it, which represents 27.3 million persons or a 9.7% increase since the last census was taken. (As of December 17, 2011, the population was listed as 312,791,912.) One projection has the population growing to 400 million by 2039.[211] Depending on immigration trends, the growth could reach 399 million, 423 million, or 458 million by 2050.[212]

In February and March 2011, the first detailed data set of the 2010 census was released. As a result of population growth in some states and declines in others, seats in the U.S. House of Representatives will change. A noticeable difference is that most declines occurred in the northeast and the midwest. New York and Ohio were the biggest losers of House seats. Both lost two of them. Most gains occurred in southern and Sun Belt states. Texas was the biggest winner, picking up four additional seats, while Florida added two.

Election-day analysts like to separate the nation into Red States and Blue States. They assign Red to the Republicans and Blue to the Democrats. By and large, several Blue States lost House seats while several Red States will have greater representation in Congress. Exceptions to the Red-Blue dichotomy exist. For example, Florida is in the south, but in the 2008 presidential election, President Obama was the victor. As shown in the 2000 and 2004 elections, it is a state that can swing either way and has the potential to decide the outcome of the presidential election. Louisiana is a Red State, but it lost a House seat. The reason that occurred may be a reflection of the emigration since Hurricane Katrina devastated portions of the state.

Generally, Republicans tend to be more conservative insofar as they resist efforts to increase the scope of the federal government and the amount of spending generated at that level. Democrats tend to hold opposite views. If these patterns hold true for the coming decade, then advocates of a more active role for the federal government can expect to encounter some increased resistance.

---

210. Duchovny, N. and Baker, C. How Does Obesity in Adults Affect Spending on Health Care? Congressional Budget Office, Economic and Budget Issue Brief, September 8, 2010, 12 pp.

211. U.S. Census Bureau. "2008 National Population Projections," On the Web at www.census.gov/population/www/projections/2008projections.html. Accessed on July 20, 2011.

212. U.S. Census Bureau. "2009 National Population Projections," On the Web at www.census.gov/population/www/projections/2009projections.html. Accessed on July 20, 2011.

State	House Seats 2000	2010	Change
Arizona	8	9	+1
Florida	25	27	+2
Georgia	13	14	+1
Illinois	19	18	−1
Iowa	5	4	−1
Louisiana	7	6	−1
Massachusetts	10	9	−1
Michigan	15	14	−1
Missouri	9	8	−1
Nevada	3	4	+1
New Jersey	13	12	−1
New York	29	27	−2
Ohio	18	16	−2
Pennsylvania	19	18	−1
South Carolina	6	7	+1
Texas	32	36	+4
Utah	3	4	+1
Washington	9	10	+1

In 2010, the population consisted of 74.2 million children under the age of 18. While numerically this figure represents an all-time high, at 24% the proportion is at an all-time low (O'Hare 2011). "The number of children grew by only 1.9 million in 2000-2010" compared to the 1990s when the increase was almost 9 million. In the 1950s, "the nation added 17.5 million children." Over the long term, families have become smaller. An increase in life expectancy has led to a larger adult population relative to children.

"Demographic changes in the size and characteristics of the child population have important implications for the future of the United States. Although the share of children in the population is projected to remain at its current level (24%) over the next 20 years, the share who are ages 65 and older is projected to rise from 13% to 19% over that same period. The increasing costs of providing for an older population may reduce the public resources that go to children. Additionally, some of the subgroups of children that have grown most rapidly over the past decade tend to have the highest poverty and school dropout rates and lowest standardized test performance. These trends raise questions about whether today's children will have the resources they need to support America's burgeoning elderly population." [213] The same can be said for the nation. Will it be able to pay expenses associated with health care of the aged, which increase per capita as the population grows older, as shown in the following table:

TABLE 7. Mean Annual Expenses per Individual, by Age, 2007

Age Group	Per Capita Spending
6-17	$1,496
18-44	$2,754
45-64	$6,138
65 +	$9,696

Source: National Center for Health Statistics, 2011. *Health United States 2010,* Hyattsville, MD: On the Web at http://www.cdc.gov/nchs/data/hus/hus10.pdf. (Expenses include health care and prescribed medication.)

213. O'Hare, W.P. Trends in the Child Population, in Mather, M. et al. First Results from the 2010 Census, Population Reference Bureau, Washington, DC: July 2011, 24pp.

The resource issue has implications for the health workforce. An aging population places more strain on an existing problem in 2011 of not having enough health professionals such as clinical laboratory scientists. Trends such as increasing the educational preparation required to enter practice in the form of moving from one degree level to a higher level, which characterizes many allied health professions, and the creation of clinical doctorate programs may serve as barriers and disincentives to undertaking a health career.

Population Dynamics

The nation will be more racially and ethnically diverse, as well as much older, by mid-century, according to Census Bureau projections:

- "Minorities, now roughly one-third of the U.S. population, are expected to become the majority in 2042, with the nation projected to be 54% minority in 2050. By 2023, minorities will comprise more than half of all children.
- In 2030, when all baby boomers will be 65 and older, nearly one in five U.S. residents is expected to be 65 and older. This age group is projected to increase to 88.5 million in 2050, more than doubling the number in 2008 (38.7 million).
- Similarly, the 85-and-older population is expected to more than triple, from 5.4 million to 19 million between 2008 and 2050.
- By 2050, the minority population—everyone except for non-Hispanic, single-race whites—is projected to be 235.7 million out of a total U.S. population of 439 million.
- The non-Hispanic, single-race white population is projected to be only slightly larger in 2050 (203.3 million) than in 2008 (199.8 million). This group is projected to lose population in the 2030s and 2040s and comprise 46% of the total population in 2050, down from 66% in 2008.
- Meanwhile, the Hispanic population is projected to nearly triple, from 46.7 million to 132.8 million, during the 2008-2050 period. Its share of the nation's total population is projected to double, from 15% to 30%. Thus, nearly one in three U.S. residents would be Hispanic.
- The black population is projected to increase from 41.1 million, or 14% of the population in 2008, to 65.7 million, or 15% in 2050.
- The Asian population is projected to climb from 15.5 million to 40.6 million. Its share of the nation's population is expected to rise from 5.1% to 9.2%.
- Among the remaining race groups, American Indians and Alaska Natives are projected to rise from 4.9 million to 8.6 million (or from 1.6% to 2% of the total population). The Native Hawaiian and Other Pacific Islander population is expected to more than double, from 1.1 million to 2.6 million. The number of individuals who identify themselves as being of two or more races is projected to more than triple, from 5.2 million to 16.2 million.
- In 2050, the nation's population of children is expected to be 62% minority, up from 44%. Thirty-nine percent are projected to be Hispanic (up from 22% in 2008), and 38% are projected to be single-race, non-Hispanic white (down from 56% in 2008).
- The percentage of the population in the 'working ages' of 18 to 64 is projected to decline from 63% in 2008 to 57% in 2050.
- The working-age population is projected to become more than 50% minority in 2039 and be 55% minority in 2050 (up from 34% in 2008). Also in 2050, it is projected to be more than 30% Hispanic (up from 15% in 2008), 15% black (up from 13% in 2008) and 9.6% Asian (up from 5.3% in 2008)." [214]

---

214. U.S. Census Bureau Newsroom. An Older and More Diverse Nation by MidCentury, August 14, 2008. On the Web at http://www.census.gov/newsroom/releases/archives/population/cb08-123.html. Accessed on August 31, 2011.

Age and gender differences in personal health care spending are evident (Cylus 2011). "According to the Census Bureau, 50% of the U.S. population in 2004 was female. However, in that year females accounted for 57% of all personal health care spending. This percentage is not surprising given the sexes' differences in life expectancy: 80.4 years for women compared with 75.2 years for men. In 2004, 58% of the population age 65 and older was female, women accounted for 61% of total personal health care spending in that age group. In the same year, the comparable figures for American women age 85 and older were 70% of the population and 73% of personal health care spending."

"In surveys, women are more likely than men to report that they are in poor health. Researchers have found that females generally have higher rates of illness and more disability days than males and they are more inclined to report symptoms and seek medical care. On a per capita basis, females' spending for health care goods and services exceeds males' spending. Males and females differ in the types of services they use and in the payers that finance their care. The expenditures of males and females also differ, in part because of the higher prevalence of ADD/ADHD (attention deficit disorder/attention deficit hyperactivity disorder) in male children, spending for maternity care by working-age women, and the gender gap in life expectancy." [215]

Rural America

As in previous decades, many rural areas lost population, including much of the Great Plains (an area stretching across the nation's midsection from the Mexican border to the Canadian border) and northern and central Appalachia. Nearly half of the 1,104 counties that lost residents during the 2000s were those isolated from metropolitan areas and had small or nonexistent urban populations—the most rural areas. Several of these counties have been losing individuals for decades: Parts of the Great Plains have seen their population steadily decline since before the Great Depression.[216]

Older industrial areas in the Northeast and Midwest, often referred to as the Rust Belt, also lost population. Many individuals left in search of better job opportunities. Parts of the Rust Belt have been plagued by high rates of out-migration since the 1970s. The nation's shift toward a more service-based economy and its aging population are reflected in the types of counties that have gained or lost population since 2000. Retirement destination counties— ones that are attractive to the age group 60 or older—were among the big demographic "winners." One-third of the 440 retirement counties grew at least 20% (more than twice the national average) between 2000 and 2010. So did one-fifth of services-dependent counties. By contrast, two-thirds of the nation's farming-dependent counties, nearly half of the mining-dependent ones, and one-third of counties reliant on manufacturing all lost population in the last 10 years.

"For counties gaining population, key policy issues often are high housing costs, environmental damage, crowded schools, traffic congestion, and in the case of immigrant magnets, adapting to new cultures and languages. Communities with declining populations face different concerns. Instead of managing growth, they are dealing with the consequences of out-migration, an

215. Cylus, J. et al. Pronounced Gender and Age Differences Are Evident in Personal Health Care Spending Per Person, Health Affairs, Vol. 30, No. 1, January 2011, pp. 153-160.
216. U.S. Census Bureau, "Population Dynamics of the Great Plains: 1950 to 2007," Current Population Reports P25-1137 (2009): 9, On the Web at www.census.gov/prod/2009pubs/p25-1137.pdf. Accessed on July 10, 2011.

increased aging population, job losses, declining tax revenues, and shrinking schools and neighborhoods. A key policy issue for areas with declining populations is how to attract and retain residents—and businesses—in their communities." [217]

The health implications of these changes are quite dramatic. Many older individuals who have the resources to do so migrate to retirement communities. Although they may be healthy when they first arrive, as they progress in age the prospects of their acquiring one or more chronic ailments will increase. Consequently, they will add to the demand for health care services, which can place a strain on state, county, and city budgets. On the plus side, young health professionals will head for these same places. New health professions schools will continue to be built, existing institutions will create new programs and expand enrollment, and job opportunities should increase accordingly.

Unless major changes occur, rural areas present a profile that is almost the exact opposite. Even if educated there, young professionals may elect to migrate to the South and to other Sun Belt states. As an aging cadre of the health workforce leaves jobs through retirement, disability, and death, there may not be a sufficient number willing to replace them. Because many rural counties cover vast areas, health professions schools may be far from these locales. Distance education helps to offset the geography factor, but an initiative in 2011 by the U.S. Department of Education to allow states to limit access of online courses offered by educational institutions in other states may add to the dilemma of severe workforce shortages.

Nearly one in four Americans, approximately 70 million individuals, live in rural areas, but only about 10% of physicians practice there (Gorski 2011). On average, rural inhabitants are "older, poorer, more likely to be uninsured, and suffer from higher rates of chronic health conditions than others. Rural residents are less likely to have employer-provided health care coverage and the rural poor are less likely to be covered by Medicaid benefits than their urban counterparts. Per capita income is $7,417 lower than in urban areas and rural Americans are more likely to live below the poverty level. Increases in health care costs have disproportionately affected residents of rural areas because of this lower income level overall. The disparity in income is even greater for minorities living in rural areas."

Rural areas face a shortage of health care providers, limiting access to health care. These areas "are more than twice as likely as urban areas to be designated by the federal government as Health Professional Shortage Areas (HPSAs): There are 2,157 HPSAs in rural areas, compared with 910 in urban areas."

In the past decade, federal programs such as the National Health Service Corps (NHSC), Area Health Education Centers (AHEC), and Federally Qualified Health Centers (FQHCs) have increased efforts to improve access and lower costs for rural health care. As a key component of these initiatives, registered nurses and advanced practice registered nurses (APRNs) are delivering essential health care services as primary providers and care managers in rural areas. In order for more of these practitioners to participate in serving patients, scope of practice barriers will have to be removed. [218]

217. Economic Research Service, U.S. Department of Agriculture, Briefing Rooms. Measuring Rurality: 2004 County Typology Codes. On the Web at www.ers.usda.gov/Briefi ng/Rurality/Typology/. Accessed on July 10, 2011.

218 Gorski, M.S. Advancing Health in Rural America: Maximizing Nursing's Impact, AARP Public Policy Institute Fact Sheet FS227, June 2011, Washington, DC: 6 pp. On the Web at http://assets.aarp.org/rgcenter/ppi/health-care/fs227-nursing.pdf. Accessed on July 21, 2011.

Family Caregivers

The United States has an impressive array of resources in the form of health professionals, technology which they use, educational institutions that prepare them for entry to practice, and the kinds of facilities in which they work, such as teaching hospitals. Unfortunately, these resources are not available uniformly throughout the country and not every patient has access to them because of such factors as lack of insurance coverage and health illiteracy. Often unrecognized is the extent to which family caregivers augment what exists in the provision of health and health-related services.

"Family support is a key driver in remaining in one's home and in the community, but it comes at substantial costs to the caregivers themselves, to their families, and to society (Feinberg 2011). In 2009, approximately 42.1 million family caregivers in the United States provided care to an adult with activity limitations at any given point in time and about 61.6 million provided care at some point during the year. The estimated economic value of their unpaid contributions was approximately $450 billion in 2009, up from an estimated $375 billion two years earlier."

"The 'average' U.S. caregiver is a 49-year-old woman who works outside the home and spends nearly 20 hours per week providing unpaid care to her mother for nearly five years at an average value of $11.16 per hour. About one in five women report that caregiving strains their household finances and more than four in 10 spend more than $5,000 per year on caregiving expenses." Almost two-thirds of family caregivers are female (65%). More than 8 in 10 are caring for a relative or friend age 50 or older. Caregiver tasks include:

- "Carrying out personal care such as bathing and dressing.
- Being responsible for nursing procedures in the home.
- Administering and managing multiple medications, including injections.
- Arranging for or providing transportation to medical appointments and community services.
- Serving as 'advocate' during medical appointments or hospitalizations.
- Implementing care plans.
- Playing a key role of 'care coordinator' during transitions, especially from hospital to home.[219]

What should be of concern to policymakers is the toll that contributions to family members exert on caregivers themselves. If they are employed, then furnishing care is the equivalent of adding a highly time-consuming, unpaid job. Their social lives and opportunities to enjoy the fruits of various kinds of recreation are severely limited. If duties in the home include helping patients in and out of beds, chairs, bathtubs, and cars, then they are at risk for back injuries. The likelihood of experiencing depression would also appear to be a danger under such circumstances.

What prevails today may not be the same in the future. American family life has changed. Young adults scatter to the four winds and may not reside anywhere near where their parents live. Divorce produces separation between parents and offspring who may live in different parts of the country and women who do not bear children will not be able to count on receiving care from their progeny.

---

219. Feinberg, L. et al. Valuing the Invaluable: 2011 Update, The Growing Contributions and Costs of Family Caregiving, AARP Public Policy Institute Insight on the Issues 51, June 2011, Washington, DC: 28 pp. On the Web at http://assets.aarp.org/rgcenter/ppi/ltc/i51-caregiving.pdf. Accessed on May 31, 2011.

The Cost of Health Disparities

The Joint Center for Political and Economic Studies estimates racial and ethnic disparities to have cost this nation more than one trillion dollars between 2003 and 2006: $229.4 billion for direct medical care expenditures associated with health disparities and another $1 trillion for the indirect costs of disparities (LaVeist 2009).[220] Among the findings in a Centers for Disease Control and Prevention (CDC) *Health Disparities and Inequalities Report* is that, "if non-Hispanic blacks had had the same adjusted rate of preventable hospitalizations as non-Hispanic" whites from 2004 to 2007, it would have resulted in about "430,000 fewer hospitalizations for non-Hispanic blacks and $3.4 billion in savings" (Moy 2011).[221]

"State Offices of Minority Health and health and public health departments employ a variety of approaches to document racial and ethnic health disparities to help advance health equity (Hanlon 2011). In the current fiscal climate, states continue to face budget deficits, and as a result, they are increasingly focusing on identifying and reducing costs, including those associated with health disparities." States can use information about disparities "to improve quality of care for affected populations. By documenting groups with the poorest outcomes and least value for expenditures, state agencies can begin to target resources and interventions for quality improvement and cost savings." Most states are looking for ways "to create efficiencies by improving the value of health care expenditures." [222]

What the Public Thinks About Controlling the Nation's Debt

The Medicare, Medicaid, and Social Security programs account for a total of 43% of spending by the federal government. By the summer of 2011, polls showed that the general public is well aware of the problem of a rising national debt and believes Congress must take action to curb spending. The desire for fundamental change does not mean, however, that there is much support for reducing the ever-rising costs of these programs.

A national survey conducted by the Pew Research Center for the People & the Press on June 15-19, 2011, reveals that there is little support for benefit cuts: "On the broad question of whether it is more important to reduce the budget deficit or to maintain current benefits, the public decisively supports maintaining the status quo." Respondents also oppose making Medicare beneficiaries more responsible for their health care costs or allowing states to limit Medicaid eligibility.

Substantial differences exist by age group. Individuals "age 65 and older are the only group in which majorities say Medicare and Social Security work well. They also say that it is more important to maintain both programs than to reduce the budget deficit." The last finding is of particular interest since that age group always has a good turnout at the voting booths on election day.

---

220. LaVeist, T.A. et al. The Economic Burden of Health Inequalities in the United States, The Joint Center for Political and Economic Studies: September 2009, 20 pp. On the Web at http://www.jointcenter.org/research/the-economic-burden-of-health-inequalities-in-the-united-states. Accessed on July 22, 2011.

221. Moy, E. et al. Potentially Preventable Hospitalizations—United States, 2004-2007, Centers for Disease Control and Prevention. CDC Health Disparities and Inequalities Report. MMWR Vol. 60 (Supplement), January 14, 2011, pp. 80-83. On the Web at http://www.cdc.gov/mmwr/pdf/other/su6001.pdf. Accessed on July 22, 2011.

222. Hanlon, C. and Hinkle, L. Assessing the Costs of Racial and Ethnic Health Disparities: State Experience, Agency for Healthcare Research and Policy, Healthcare Cost and Utilization Project, June 24, 2011, 7 pp.

Which is more important?
  Taking steps to reduce the budget deficit—32%
  Keeping Social Security and Medicare benefits as they are—60%
  Other/don't know—9%

Dealing with Medicare Costs
  Medicare recipients need to be responsible for more costs —31%
  Medicare recipients already pay enough of their health care costs—61%
  Other/don't know—7%

States and Medicaid Eligibility
  States should be able to cut back on Medicaid eligibility—37%
  Low-income Medicaid beneficiaries should not have benefits taken away—58%
  Other/don't know—4% [223]

Medication Adherence and Health Care Costs

"Approximately 133 million Americans live with at least one chronic disease (Roebuck 2011). Because ongoing use of prescription medication is a key component of treatment for chronic conditions, medication adherence—or making sure that patients take the drugs prescribed for them—is a matter of great importance to policy makers, insurance plan sponsors, physicians, and patients. Patients who adhere to their medication regimens enjoy better health outcomes and make less use of urgent care and inpatient hospital services compared to patients with similar medical conditions who are not adherent. Yet despite the evidence of improved outcomes from adherence, the World Health Organization reports average medication compliance rates in developed countries of just 50%."

"By definition, improvements in medication adherence increase pharmacy spending. Health care reformers and payers are therefore interested in knowing whether or not the higher pharmacy costs are more than offset by reductions in the use of medical services. If so, the financial benefit may justify adopting programs that promote compliance or that remove barriers to adherence."

A study provides evidence that medication adherence reduces total annual health care spending for patients with chronic vascular disease. "Benefit-cost ratios range from 2:1 for adults under age sixty-five with dyslipidemia to more than 13:1 for older patients with hypertension."

Savings are realized mainly through reduced inpatient hospital days and emergency department visits. Moreover, adherence effects are more pronounced for patients age 65 and older. "Additional pharmacy spending incurred from adherence is more than offset by the medical savings realized. The question then becomes whether or not policies and programs that are implemented to improve adherence can do so at costs that do not exceed the expected benefits. The cost of an adherence intervention is directly related to the mode of delivery. Complex, coordinated care involving physicians, nurses, and case managers may be both successful and costly. Alternatives that require fewer resources—such as electronic monitoring devices and pharmacist-led patient counseling—have shown promise in improving patients' medication adherence at less expense." [224]

---

223. The Pew Research Center for the People and the Press. Public Wants Changes in Entitlements, Not Changes in Benefits. On the Web at http://people-press.org/files/legacy-pdf/7-7-11%20Entitlements%20Release.pdf, Accessed on July 22, 2011.
224. Roebuck, M.C. et al. Medication Adherence Leads to Lower Health Care Use and Costs Despite Increased Drug Spending, *Health Affairs*, Vol. 30, No. I, January 2011, pp. 91-99.

Health Care Reform and Controlling Health Costs

A ny health care reform must deal with at least three categories of costs: medical errors, defensive medicine, and offensive medicine (Avraham 2011).

- "Medical errors are caused by fatigue, poor judgment, over-confidence, lack of resources, lack of training, and lack of communication. The costs of medical errors include unnecessary hospitalization, injury, loss of income, and suffering. Patients, their insurers, and the hospital all bear the costs of these mistakes.

- *'Defensive medicine'* is excessive care provided to avoid liability. For example, an overly cautious doctor may order a computed tomography (CT) scan when only an X-ray is medically necessary, thus externalizing the extra cost to the patient and his health insurer.

- *'Offensive medicine'* is excessive care which doctors provide in an attempt to maximize reimbursements. These costs usually include minor procedures, but can also include more lucrative treatments such as heart surgery. Costs grow because, among other reasons, patients are insured for their health care costs. Doctors are essentially in an all-you-can-treat system, with the same incentives to save as in an all-you-can-eat restaurant. President Obama has described this as a system of 'warped incentives.' Similar to costs associated with defensive medicine, these costs are borne by both patients and their insurance carriers. Academics have long documented this problem—which economists call 'induced demand'—yet no one has estimated its overall impact. It is suspected, though, that the costs of offensive medicine are higher than the other two types of costs combined." [225]

Geographic Variations in Spending

N o discussion would be complete without referring to geographic variation in health care spending. The topic is controversial and has led health reform advocates to develop ways of providing care more efficiently in all parts of the United States without compromising quality. "Leading up to federal health reform passage, policy makers and researchers devoted much attention to geographic variation in health care use and spending, largely focused on *Dartmouth Atlas of Health Care* research that has found fee-for-service Medicare spending on elderly beneficiaries varies as much as 2.5 times across localities (Bernstein 2011). Some have interpreted *Dartmouth Atlas* findings to mean that care is provided much more efficiently in some areas and that high-cost areas provide care that is no better—and in some cases worse—than in low-cost areas."

"From a policy perspective, some sources of geographic variation in health spending are warranted—or acceptable—while others are not. Warranted sources include input price differences facing medical providers—for example, wages or rent—and the illness burden in different communities. Moreover, if higher spending produced higher quality, it might be warranted. Unwarranted sources of variation include the use of clearly ineffective or inappropriate treatments; the rate of injuries and avoidable complications caused by medical error or mismanagement; and differing levels of fraud. Other sources of variation can be less clear cut. For example, there may be variation in the use of expensive treatment options, where evidence of the treatment's relative effectiveness compared to less-expensive options is uncertain. The use of more—or fewer—expensive treatments in a locality may be related to physician preferences or patient preferences, along with financial incentives or resource constraints."

---

225. Avraham, R. Clinical Practice Guidelines: The Warped Incentives in the U.S. Healthcare System, *American Journal of Law & Medicine*, Vol. 37, Issue 1, 2011, pp. 7-40.

"Depending on one's perspective, some sources of variation may be warranted or unwarranted. For example, a larger portion of Medicare beneficiaries receiving end-of-life care in one part of the country may prefer aggressive, no-holds-barred hospital care, while a larger portion of those in another part of the country may prefer low-cost, palliative care at home. These kinds of patient preferences—sometimes driven by physician preferences—raise larger societal questions about what constitutes appropriate care in a context of limited resources and ever-rising health care costs."

Thus, "the complicated structure of health care delivery makes it difficult to measure and compare health care delivery across geographic areas. Growing evidence suggests that failing to address these complexities adequately may overstate both the extent and implications of geographic variation in health care spending and use." [226] The Affordable Care Act's emphasis on comparative effectiveness research and the creation of accountable care organizations provide examples of approaches that may clarify further the nature of geographic variations in health care spending and suggest ways of limiting or eliminating altogether unwarranted amounts of expenditure.

Closing Thoughts

Complex problems do not admit of easy, painless solutions. The U.S. population is aging as revealed by the steady growth in the number and proportion of individuals age 65 and older. The first wave of 77 million baby boomers became eligible for Medicare and Social Security benefits on January 1, 2011. Their participation in these programs has enormous implications. Not only must ways be identified to pay for their health care costs, the health workforce will have to make necessary adaptations to meet the health care needs of this age group. Changes in American families and the declining population in rural areas will affect how health care is financed and delivered. As older segments of the population increase in size, the percentage of the population consisting of children under the age of 18 will remain stable over the next two decades. A key implication is that proportionately there will be fewer taxpayers to support the costs of providing services for retirees.

---

226. Bernstein, J. et al. Geographic Variation in Health Care: Changing Policy Directions, National Institute for Health Care Reform, Policy Analysis, No. 4, April 2011, 14 pp. On the Web at http://www.nihcr.org/Geographic-Variation.pdf. Accessed on July 17, 2011.

CHAPTER 8:

The Deacon's Masterpiece and Health Care for the Aged, the Infirmed, and the Impoverished

8

Rising costs of the Medicare and Medicaid programs are at the center of concerns about the ability to finance health services. Fraud and abuse represent a serious drain on limited resources. Unnecessary rehospitalizations add to costs, which serves as a good reason to develop efforts to offer care that is better coordinated and of much higher quality.

The *Deacon's Masterpiece* or the *One-Horse Open Shay* by Oliver Wendell Holmes (American, 1809–1894) opens with the following:

> HAVE you heard of the wonderful one-hoss-shay,
> That was built in such a logical way
> It ran a hundred years to a day,
> And then, of a sudden, it—ah, but stay
> I'll tell you what happened without delay,
> Scaring the parson into fits,
> Frightening people out of their wits,—
> Have you ever heard of that, I say?

The poem concludes with:

> —What do you think the parson found,
> When he got up and stared around?
> The poor old chaise in a heap or mound,
> As if it had been to the mill and ground!
> You see, of course, if you're not a dunce,
> How it went to pieces all at once,—
> All at once, and nothing first,—
> Just as bubbles do when they burst.[227] *

Much of health care is devoted to meeting the needs of older persons. A companion group consists of individuals who cannot afford to obtain services because they are impoverished. In response, the government developed Medicare and Medicaid (and a supplementary program called Children's Health Insurance Program) to address the health problems of beneficiaries.

The *aged* in this chapter refers to individuals who are 65 years of age and older. Recognizing fully well that the youngest cohorts in the bracket of the aged often represent a highly vigorous and productive segment of society with few if any physical or mental health impairments, the fact that they are on the shadow side of life's hill places them at risk for various kinds of impairment in the not-too-distant future.

---

227. *The Complete Poetical Works of Oliver Wendell Holmes*, ed. H. E. S. 1895. Boston: Houghton, Mifflin. (*A *shay* is an open, two-wheel, horse-drawn carriage, also termed a *chaise*.)

At this juncture in American history, one fact is indisputable. Medicare, Medicaid, and the Social Security program are on unsustainable trajectories from the standpoint of financing their costs. As the nation struggles to contain its ever-mounting national debt, rather than considering ways of expanding these programs, the challenge is to figure out how to slow their rate of spending. For Social Security, it may mean raising the age for eligibility of benefits. For Medicare, an outcome might be to raise the age for eligibility and to impose more cost-sharing by beneficiaries through higher copayments, deductibles, and co-insurance. Medicaid also may have to suffer the same fate by tightening eligibility criteria, limiting the scope of services, and requiring more cost-sharing by beneficiaries. Quite naturally, there is not much enthusiasm within the general electorate about the adoption of any of these courses of action.

Is the Age of Methuselah Attainable?

A related, but different point of view, would be to develop ways of curbing the progression of disease through improved health care interventions. Some scientists who study the biology of aging believe that someday it will be possible to slow down the aging process substantially as a means of extending productive, youthful lives. Aubrey de Grey is among the most optimistic of all such researchers. He believes that the key biomedical technology required to eliminate aging-derived debilitation and death entirely—technology that would not only slow, but periodically reverse age-related physiological decay, leaving humans young into an indefinite future—is now within reach.

In a book entitled *Ending Aging*, he and his research assistant describe the details of this biotechnology. They explain that "the aging of the human body, just like the aging of man-made machines, results from an accumulation of various types of damage. As with man-made machines, this damage can periodically be repaired, leading to indefinite extension of the machine's fully functional lifetime, just as is routinely done with classic cars. Since it is known what types of damage accumulate in the human body, the next stage will be to produce a comprehensive development of technologies to remove that damage. By demystifying aging and its postponement, they systematically dismantle the fatalist presumption that aging will forever defeat the efforts of medical science." Important targets for a new class of anti-aging therapies would be called SENS, "Strategies for Engineered Negligible Senescence." [228]

Hope springs eternal in the American breast and the aforementioned view reflects a cognitive orientation or world view that science eventually will triumph. That outlook is expressed in many ways such as a *War Against Cancer* that was proclaimed in 1972. A chief vehicle for funding research aimed at curing or slowing down the natural progression of many diseases is the National Institutes of Health. Tremendous strides have been made in attempts to prevent and treat major problems such as cardiovascular disease, but not everyone is sanguine about what the future holds as a result of such efforts.

Genomics and stem cell research are among the advances that hold the promise of improving health status. Perhaps someday it may be possible to produce humans who, from the day they are born to the day they reach their 100th year, will be the equivalent of the one-horse open shay. No matter how well-constructed, however, such a masterpiece will have to withstand the results of poor judgment by individuals who abuse their bodies through intemperate use of food, alcoholic beverages, and illegal drugs, not to mention the damaged bodies that are a consequence of wars, accidents, and natural disasters.

---

228. De Grey, A. and Rae, M. 2008. *Ending Aging: The Rejuvenation Breakthroughs That Could Reverse Human Aging In Our Lifetime.* New York: St. Martins Press.

Other observers are less optimistic about the potential of regenerative medicine to cure or prevent most of life's ills. Daniel Callahan, President Emeritus of the Hastings Center, and his colleague Sherwin Nuland, a Hastings Center Fellow and retired clinical professor of surgery at Yale University, contend that in the United States, diseases are considered things to be conquered. Several assumptions underlie this perspective: that medical advances are essentially unlimited, that none of the major lethal diseases is in theory incurable, and that progress is economically affordable if well-managed. They ask, "what if all this turns out not to be true? What if there are no imminent, much less foreseeable cures to some of the most common and most lethal diseases? What if, in individual cases, not all diseases should be fought? What if we are refusing to confront the painful likelihood that our biological nature is not nearly as resilient or open to endless improvement as we have long believed?"

They note that "mortality rates for the great majority of cancers have fallen slowly over the decades, but we remain far from a cure. No one of any scientific stature even predicts a cure for heart disease or stroke. As for Alzheimer's, not long before President Obama recently approved a fresh effort to find better treatments, a special panel of the NIH determined that essentially little progress has been made in recent years toward finding ways to delay the onset of major symptoms. And no one talks seriously of a near-term cure." [229]

Milestones in Medicare

Along with enactment of legislation to establish the Social Security program in 1935, comparable milestones were reached in 1965 to create the Medicare and Medicaid programs. President Lyndon B. Johnson signed H.R. 6675 (Public Law 89-97) on July 30, 1965 to create Medicare for the aged and Medicaid for the poor. The first person to enroll in the Medicare program was former President Harry S. Truman, who was present for the signing in Independence, Missouri, where his home was located. Coverage began on July 1 of the following year.

A significant addition to the program was made when President Richard M. Nixon signed into law the Social Security Amendments of 1972 (Public Law 92-603). Medicare eligibility was extended to individuals under age 65 with long-term disabilities (who were receiving Social Security Disability Insurance payments for 2 years) and to individuals with end-stage renal disease (ESRD). Benefits were expanded to include some chiropractic, speech therapy, and physical therapy services.

In 1980, the Omnibus Reconciliation Act (OBRA) of that year expanded home health services by eliminating the limit on the number of home health visits, the prior hospitalization requirement, and the deductible for any part B benefits. Hospice services for the terminally ill became an added benefit in 1982. In 2001, individuals with amyotrophic lateral sclerosis (ALS or Lou Gehrig's disease) could enroll in Medicare upon diagnosis.

President George W. Bush signed the Medicare Prescription Drug, Improvement, and Modernization Act of 2003 into law (Public Law 108-173). The Affordable Care Act of 2010 expanded prescription drug and prevention benefits. It also introduced new programs designed to improve the quality and delivery of care.

"The Medicare Part D program, launched in 2006, increased the share of Medicare beneficiaries with prescription drug coverage (Afendulis 2011). This expansion of benefits recognizes that prescription drugs are an indispensable component of care management, particularly for

---

229. Callahan, D. and Newland, S.B. The Quagmire: How American Medicine is Destroying Itself, *New Republic*, Vol. 242, Issue 8, June 9, 2011, pp. 16-18.

chronic disease. The evidence suggests that, even in a narrow time window, better management of certain conditions with prescription drugs can reduce the likelihood of adverse events like hospitalizations and the costs associated with them."

An analysis "demonstrates that increased drug utilization induced by the introduction of Medicare Part D had measurable clinical benefits. Specifically, the change in drug coverage due to the passage of Part D—from 61% in 2005 to 88% in 2006 and 2007 in the analysis sample—led to a reduction of about 42,000 hospital admissions from any of the conditions studied, a 4.1% decline from 2005. This estimate reflects the actual change in drug coverage in the sample due to the introduction of Part D; a larger coverage increase for the entire Medicare population would have increased the estimate of prevented hospitalizations." Because the "analysis is limited to data from the first 2 years of the Part D program, which may not be long enough to identify changes in hospitalization rates, estimates may understate the impact of Part D." [230]

Medicare Program Features

A n excellent source of information about Medicare is the Henry J. Kaiser Family Foundation. That organization's *Medicare Chartbook, 2010* provides reliable data available about the program (Cubanski 2010). The chartbook includes the following information:

Medicare Beneficiaries

As shown in Figure 1, Medicare "covers 47 million people, including 39 million people who are age 65 and older and 8 million nonelderly people with a permanent disability." The oldest members of the baby boomer generation reached their 65th birthday on January 1, 2011. Approximately 10,000 per day for the next 19 years will reach that chronological milestone and become eligible to participate in the Medicare program. Figure 2 shows the demographic characteristics of the Medicare population.

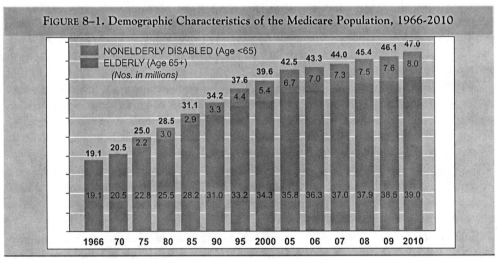

FIGURE 8–1. Demographic Characteristics of the Medicare Population, 1966–2010

Source: Kaiser Family Foundation analysis of Centers for Medicare and Medicaid Services (CMS) data (adapted from Cubanski 2010).

230. Afendulis, C.C. et al. The Impact of Medicare Part D on Hospitalization Rates, *Health Services Research*, Vol. 46, Issue 4, August 2011, pp. 1022-1038.

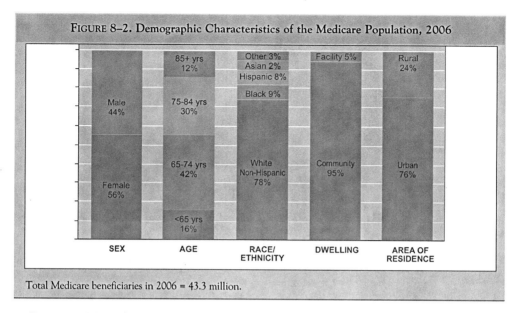

FIGURE 8–2. Demographic Characteristics of the Medicare Population, 2006

Total Medicare beneficiaries in 2006 = 43.3 million.

Between 1966 and 2000, "the number of beneficiaries on Medicare more than doubled and is projected to double yet again to 80 million by 2030." The program serves a population with diverse needs and circumstances. Nearly half of all Medicare beneficiaries live on an income below 200% of the federal poverty level, and those with lower incomes generally report being in poorer health than their higher income counterparts. Figures 3 and 4 show the extent of chronic conditions and self-reported health status: nearly half have three or more chronic conditions, roughly one-third have a cognitive or mental impairment, and more than one-fourth of all beneficiaries report their health status is fair or poor. "More than 2 million Medicare beneficiaries live in nursing homes or other long-term care settings, most of whom are female and nearly half of whom are age 85 and older."

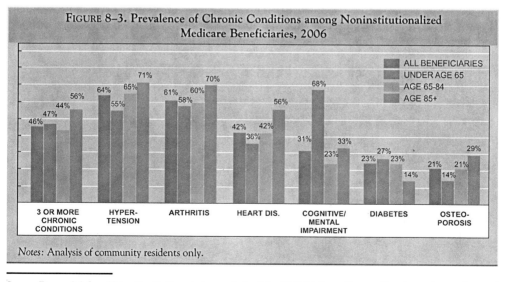

FIGURE 8–3. Prevalence of Chronic Conditions among Noninstitutionalized Medicare Beneficiaries, 2006

Notes: Analysis of community residents only.

Source: Figures 2-3 from Kaiser Family Foundation analysis of the CMS Medicare Current Beneficiary Survey Cost and Use File, 2006 (adapted from Cubanski 2010).

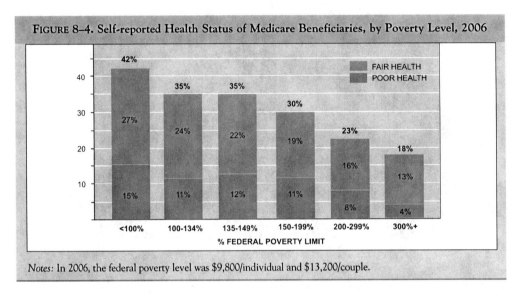

FIGURE 8–4. Self-reported Health Status of Medicare Beneficiaries, by Poverty Level, 2006

Notes: In 2006, the federal poverty level was $9,800/individual and $13,200/couple.

Medicare Benefits, Utilization, and Access to Care

Medicare covers a broad range of health care services, including inpatient and outpatient hospital care, post-acute care such as home health and skilled nursing facility care, physician services, diagnostic testing including preventive services, prescription drug coverage, and hospice care. Medicare-covered benefits typically are subject to deductibles and coinsurance payments. Despite offering a relatively generous benefits package, Medicare provides limited long-term care benefits and does not cover eyeglasses, hearing aids, or dental care. Because health problems tend to rise with age, Medicare beneficiaries generally use more health care services than younger adults.

"In 2006, 82% of all beneficiaries had one or more physician visit, 21% were hospitalized, and 30% had one or more emergency room visit" as shown in Figure 5. "A relatively small share of Medicare beneficiaries report access problems across a broad range of standard measures; however, rates of access problems tend to be higher among certain subgroups, such as those with low incomes, those in relatively poor health, the non-elderly disabled, and beneficiaries without supplemental coverage."

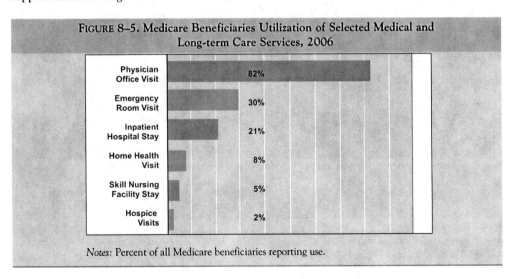

FIGURE 8–5. Medicare Beneficiaries Utilization of Selected Medical and Long-term Care Services, 2006

Notes: Percent of all Medicare beneficiaries reporting use.

Medicare and Prescription Drugs

"Medicare beneficiaries are highly dependent on prescription drugs to manage their acute and chronic health conditions, with 88% of them taking at least one medication in 2006. Since 2006, Medicare has offered access to an outpatient prescription drug benefit (Part D) through private plans, including stand-alone prescription drug plans (PDPs) and Medicare Advantage prescription drug (MA-PD) plans. Assistance with drug plan premiums and cost-sharing is available to beneficiaries with limited incomes and resources."

Medicare Advantage

"Since the early 1970s, Medicare beneficiaries have had the option to receive their Medicare benefits through private health plans, mainly health maintenance organizations (HMOs), as an alternative to the fee-for-service (FFS) Medicare program. Over the past several decades, the role of private plans in Medicare has evolved. Even the name of the program (Part C) has changed, from Medicare+Choice, as it was called in 1997, to Medicare Advantage, as it was renamed in 2003. In 2010, about one in four people on Medicare (24%) were enrolled in a Medicare Advantage plan."

Dual Eligibility: The Role of Medicaid for Medicare Beneficiaries

"Medicaid, the federal-state program that provides health and long-term care coverage to low-income Americans, is also a source of supplemental coverage for roughly one in five Medicare beneficiaries. These beneficiaries are known as *dual eligibles* because they are eligible for both Medicaid and Medicare. Medicaid helps to make Medicare affordable for beneficiaries with low incomes and modest assets by paying premiums and filling in Medicare's cost-sharing requirements and by paying for benefits that are not covered under traditional Medicare. Eligibility for Medicaid assistance is based on a beneficiary's income and resources, with some variation across states. Most dual eligibles qualify for full Medicaid benefits, including long-term care and dental services, which Medicare does not cover."

Beneficiaries eligible for Medicare and Medicaid tend to be in poorer health and have greater medical and long-term care needs than others on either program, as shown in Figure 6. Thus, they "account for a disproportionate share of spending under both programs—36% of Medicare spending in 2006 and 40% of Medicaid spending in 2007."

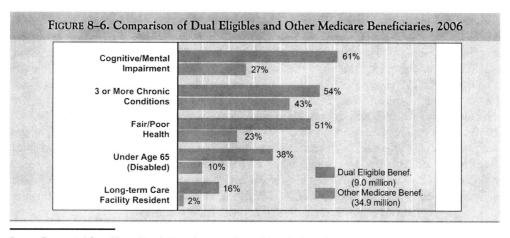

FIGURE 8–6. Comparison of Dual Eligibles and Other Medicare Beneficiaries, 2006

Source: Figures 4-6 from Kaiser Family Foundation analysis of the CMS Medicare Current Beneficiary Survey Cost and Use File, 2006 (adapted from Cubanski 2010).

Supplemental Insurance Coverage

"To help pay for benefits not covered by Medicare and to ease the burden of Medicare's relatively high cost-sharing requirements, the majority of Medicare beneficiaries (90%) have some form of supplemental health insurance. Employer-sponsored coverage was the most common source of supplemental insurance in 2007, followed by Medicare Advantage plans, which typically provide some benefits beyond those covered under traditional Medicare, Medicare Supplemental Insurance policies (Medigap), and Medicaid for those with low incomes and modest assets. ... While more than one-third of all Medicare beneficiaries have additional coverage from an employer, the share of employers offering retiree health benefits has declined, from 66% in 1988 to 28% in 2010."

Out-of-Pocket Spending

"In 2006, Medicare covered just under half (48%) of fee-for-service beneficiaries' total medical and long-term care expenses. Beneficiaries paid, on average, 25% of total expenses out-of-pocket. Of the $4,241 in average out-of-pocket spending per beneficiary, 39% was for premiums, 19% for long-term care, 15% for medical providers and supplies, and 14% for prescription drugs. Out-of-pocket spending on health care increases with advancing age and varies by health status. With health costs rising more rapidly than income for individuals on Medicare, median out-of-pocket spending as a share of beneficiaries' income has increased from 11.9% in 1997 to 16.2% in 2006."

Medicare Spending

"In fiscal year 2010, Medicare spending is expected to total $524 billion, accounting for 20% of national health expenditures, 15% of the federal budget, and 3.6% of the gross domestic product (GDP)" as shown in Figures 7 and 8. "Medicare is responsible for 20% of the $2.6 trillion in total national health care expenditures in the U.S., but 40% of the nation's total home health care spending, 30% of hospital spending, and 24% of prescription drug costs. Inpatient hospital services continue to account for the largest share of Medicare benefit payments (27%), followed by Medicare Advantage plans (23%) and payments to physicians (13%)."

Medicare Financing

"In fiscal year 2010, Medicare revenues came mainly from general revenue (43%), payroll taxes (37%), and beneficiary premiums (13%), with the remaining 7% of revenues from taxation of social security benefits, payments from states, and interest. Part A (the Hospital Insurance Trust Fund) is funded mainly by a 1.45% payroll tax paid by workers and employers (and as of 2011, a 2.35% payroll tax on earnings for taxpayers with incomes above $200,000/ individual and $250,000/couple). The Part B Supplementary Medical Insurance (SMI) Trust Fund is financed by a combination of beneficiary premiums (25%) and general revenues (most of the remainder). Part D is similarly financed; general revenues make up 82% of revenues for Part D, beneficiary premiums comprise 10%, and payments from states comprise 7%. According to the Medicare Board of Trustees' 2010 intermediate assumptions, the Hospital Insurance Trust Fund reserves are projected to be depleted in 2029—a 12-year extension from the previous year's projection of 2017, attributable mainly to Medicare spending reductions and additional revenues included in the Affordable Care Act of 2010." [231] As noted in the previous chapter regarding the CLASS program, revenue projections sometimes prove to be overstated.

---

231. Cubanski, J. et al. *Medicare Chartbook*, 4th edition, 2010, The Henry J. Kaiser Family Foundation, Menlo Park, CA: 115 pp.

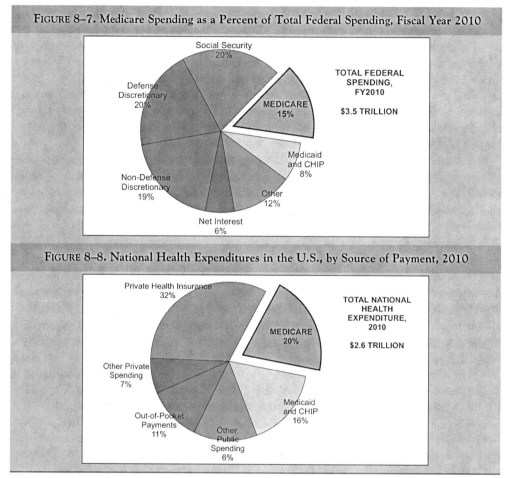

FIGURE 8–7. Medicare Spending as a Percent of Total Federal Spending, Fiscal Year 2010

FIGURE 8–8. National Health Expenditures in the U.S., by Source of Payment, 2010

Source: Figures 7-8 from Kaiser Family Foundation analysis of data from the Congressional Budget Office, The Budget and Economic Outlook: An Update, August 2010 (Figure 7) and CMS, Office of the Actuary, National Health Expenditure Projections 2009-2019, February 2010 (Figure 8) (adapted from Cubanski 2010).

Regional Variation in Medicare Spending

"Geographical variations occur in Medicare spending (Fisher 2009). "Three regions— Boston, San Francisco, and East Long Island, New York—started out with nearly identical per capita spending, but their expenditures grew at markedly different annual rates: 2.4% in San Francisco, 3.0% in Boston, and 4.0% in East Long Island. Although such differences may appear modest, compounding leads to enormous differences in spending levels over time. By 2006, per capita spending in East Long Island was $2,500 more than in San Francisco—which translates into about $1 billion in additional annual Medicare spending from this region alone."

What is transpiring to account for such variations? "It is highly unlikely that these differences in growth could be explained by improvements in health status. Marked regional differences in spending remain after careful adjustment for health and there is no evidence that health is decaying more rapidly" in one city than in another.[232]

---

232. Fisher, E.S. et al. Slowing the Growth of Health Care Costs—Lessons from Regional Variation, *New England Journal of Medicine*, Vol. 360, No. 9, February 26, 2009, pp. 849-852.

A report from the Medicare Payment Advisory Commission (MedPAC) presents "data on the difference between regional variation in Medicare spending and regional variation in the use of Medicare-covered services. Regional variation in Medicare spending per beneficiary reflects many factors, including differences in beneficiaries' health status, Medicare payment rates, service volume (number of services), and service intensity (e.g., magnetic resonance imaging [MRI] versus simple x-ray). In contrast, regional variation in the use of Medicare services reflects only differences in the volume and intensity of services that beneficiaries with comparable health status receive. Although service use varies less than spending, the amount of services provided to beneficiaries with similar resource needs still varies substantially." [233]

The Affordable Care Act of 2010 (ACA) recognizes that "solving Medicare's long-term fiscal crisis requires major payment and health care delivery reforms (Reschovsky 2011). Consequently, the Act supports demonstrations and initiatives (e.g., accountable care organizations [ACOs], bundled payments, patient-centered medical homes) designed to reduce costs and improve care."

"It is important to recognize that Medicare spending is concentrated among a relatively small percentage of its enrollees. The 5% of Medicare beneficiaries with the highest spending account for 43% of total program spending, while the top 25% of spenders, who often have multiple chronic conditions, account for 85% of total spending. Thus, the ability of proposed reforms to 'bend the Medicare cost curve' depends largely on how they affect the costliest beneficiaries."

More than "one in five Medicare beneficiaries receives care in different census divisions during the year and these patients have significantly higher costs. Although the precise reasons for interdivisional care receipt are ambiguous, it suggests that any geographic-based policy needs to be mindful that there are no natural boundaries to local health care markets and that a substantial portion of beneficiaries will use providers in multiple 'markets,' however defined. The results also have implications for accountable care organizations (ACOs) as envisioned in the Affordable Care Act. Beneficiaries are to be attributed, ex post, to ACOs rather than prospectively assigned to them. If care is not concentrated within a narrow number of providers consistently, especially among high-cost beneficiaries, ACO success in improving care and lowering cost may be limited."

"Meaningful efforts to reduce Medicare costs will require policies that specifically address the needs of high-cost beneficiaries." Certain policies "being considered may be more successful in lowering the costs of low-cost rather than high-cost beneficiaries. Consequently, the task of reducing Medicare costs in the aggregate may prove difficult unless reforms can improve health care quality or eliminate unnecessary services for very sick, complex patients." [234]

Medicare-Medicaid Dual Eligibles

In 2008, about 8 million Medicare beneficiaries were enrolled in their states' Medicaid programs (Jiang 2010) as noted earlier. "For these dually-eligible individuals, Medicaid pays for the Medicare premiums and other out-of-pocket expenses such as deductibles and coinsurance, and for Medicaid-only services such as long-term care." As shown earlier in this chapter, Figure 6 provides data on how dual eligibles differ from other Medicare beneficiaries.

---

233. Medicare Payment Advisory Commission. Measuring Regional Variation in Service Use, Dec. 2009, 24 pp. On the Web at http://www.medpac.gov/documents/Dec09_RegionalVariation_report.pdf. Accessed on Aug. 2, 2011.
234. Reschovsky, J.D. et al. Following the Money: Factors Associated with the Cost of Treating High-Cost Medicare Beneficiaries, *Health Services Research*, Vol. 46, Issue 4, August 2011, pp. 997-1021.

"Dual eligibles have been and will continue to be important to both federal and state public policymakers. Care for this population faces unique challenges due to split financial accountability between the two programs, diverse socio-demographic and clinical characteristics, and the related poverty and poor health of the population. These challenges create considerable difficulties for care coordination, which affects both access and quality of care. Lack of access to care, poor quality of care, and inadequate management of health conditions could lead to hospital admissions that are potentially preventable. Identifying conditions that are common reasons for potentially preventable hospitalizations would help guide development of strategies to improve care and patient outcomes while potentially lowering costs."

"Dual eligibles accounted for about one-third of all Medicare hospital stays with a principal diagnosis of pressure ulcers (36%), asthma (32%), and diabetes (32%); and roughly one-quarter of stays for urinary tract infection (UTI), chronic obstructive pulmonary disease (COPD), and bacterial pneumonia. Compared with other Medicare beneficiaries, dual eligibles were more than twice as likely to be hospitalized for pressure ulcers, asthma, and diabetes, 52% more likely for urinary tract infection, and over 30% more likely for COPD and bacterial pneumonia. The top three causes of potentially preventable hospitalizations for dual eligibles were bacterial pneumonia (2,041 stays per 100,000 enrollees), congestive heart failure (1,829 stays per 100,000 enrollees), and COPD (1,179 stays per 100,000 enrollees)."

"Among the nine selected potentially preventable hospitalizations, stays for pressure ulcers had the highest average hospital cost per stay ($15,000), irrespective of dual eligibility. About half of dual eligible stays for diabetes and asthma were among patients ages 18 to 64. However, elderly patients ages 85 and over accounted for one-third of stays for injurious falls and about one-quarter of stays for UTI, bacterial pneumonia, and dehydration. The greatest gap in potentially preventable hospitalizations between dual eligibles and non-dual eligibles occurred among those ages 65 to 74, for which the rate of stays for dual eligibles was nearly 2 to 4 times the rate of stays for non-dual eligibles, except for injurious falls." [235]

Fraud, Waste, and Abuse

"Health care fraud is all about the money (Krause 2010). A small group of offenders may believe the rules simply do not apply to them; a few may be motivated by the thrill of outsmarting a complex regulatory system; and occasionally someone may view fraud as a political act of protest against unwarranted governmental intrusion into health care. But in the vast majority of cases, health care fraud occurs simply because that is where the money is. The United States is estimated to have spent $2.5 trillion on health care in 2009, with over $918 billion of that amount coming from the federal government. Under some estimates, up to 10% of that amount—no one quite knows for sure—might be lost to fraud."

"Fraudsters, prosecutors, and policymakers each internalize fraud-related financial incentives, but in different ways. Health care fraud is primarily a crime of opportunity, an opportunity created by vast sums of money that flow through a complicated health care reimbursement system. As such, there are two primary ways of reducing it: (1) decrease opportunities for fraud to occur, such as by closing loopholes and clarifying regulatory gray areas; or (2) increase the level of deterrence, such as by imposing higher penalties or increasing program oversight, so that

235. Jiang, H.J. et al. Potentially Preventable Hospitalizations among Medicare-Medicaid Dual Eligibles, 2008, Agency for Healthcare Research and Quality Statistical Brief #96, September 2010. On the Web at http://www.hcup-us.ahrq.gov/reports/statbriefs/sb96.jsp. Accessed on August 5, 2011.

someone who encounters an opportunity to commit fraud will calculate that it is not in his or her best interest to do so." [236]

The U.S. Government Accountability Office (GAO) has designated Medicare as a high-risk program since 1990, in part because the program's size and complexity make it vulnerable to fraud, waste, and abuse (King 2010).

- *Fraud* represents intentional acts of deception with knowledge that the action or representation could result in an inappropriate gain.
- *Waste* includes inaccurate payments for services.
- *Abuse* represents actions inconsistent with acceptable business or medical practices.

These three kinds of activities "all can lead to improper payments, overpayments, and underpayments that should not have been made or that were made in an incorrect amount. In 2009, the Centers for Medicare & Medicaid Services (CMS)—the agency that administers Medicare —estimated billions of dollars in improper payments in the Medicare program." [237]

Schemes to defraud the Medicare program have grown more elaborate in recent years (GAO 2008). In particular, HHS has acknowledged Centers for Medicare & Medicaid Services' (CMS) "oversight of suppliers of durable medical equipment, prosthetics, orthotics, and supplies (DMEPOS) is inadequate to prevent fraud and abuse. Specifically, weaknesses in the DMEPOS enrollment and inspection process have allowed sham companies to bill Medicare fraudulently for unnecessary or nonexistent supplies." [238]

"From April 2006 through March 2007, CMS estimated that Medicare improperly paid $1 billion for DMEPOS supplies—in part due to fraud by suppliers." GAO investigators easily "set up two fictitious DMEPOS companies using undercover names and bank accounts. GAO's fictitious companies were approved for Medicare billing privileges despite having no clients and no inventory. CMS initially denied GAO's applications in part because of this lack of inventory, but undercover GAO investigators fabricated contracts with non-existent wholesale suppliers to convince CMS and its contractor, the National Supplier Clearinghouse (NSC), that the companies had access to DMEPOS items. If real fraudsters had been in charge of the fictitious companies, they would have been clear to bill Medicare for potentially millions of dollars worth of non-existent supplies."

The full extent of health care fraud cannot be measured precisely. The "Federal Bureau of Investigation (FBI) estimates that fraudulent billings to public and private health care programs are 3–10% of total health spending, or $75–$250 billion in fiscal year 2009 (Morris 2009). Federal health care programs operate under a 'pay-and-chase' model. Government contractors that process and pay claims for reimbursement generally presume that qualified providers submit claims for medically necessary items or services. The majority of claims are submitted electronically, processed based on predictable edits applied to representations on the claim, and paid claim-by-claim with limited verification that the services were actually provided or were neces-

---

236. Krause, J.H. Following the Money in Health Care Fraud: Reflections on a Modern-Day Yellow Brick Road, *American Journal of Law & Medicine*, Vol. 36, Issue 2/3, 2010, pp. 343-369.
237. King, K.M. Medicare Fraud, Waste, and Abuse: Challenges and Strategies for Preventing Improper Payments, Testimony before the Subcommittees on Health and Oversight, Committee on Ways and Means, House of Representatives, GAO-10-844T, June 15, 2010, 15 pp.
238. U.S General Accountability Office. Medicare: Covert Testing Exposes Weaknesses in the Durable Medical Equipment Supplier Screening Process, A Report to the Senate Permanent Subcommittee on Investigations, Committee on Homeland Security and Governmental Affairs GAO-08-955, July 2008, 24pp.

sary. Additional analysis is needed to determine whether a series of claims, each of which may appear legitimate by itself, demonstrates a pattern of potential fraud or abuse when taken together. The U.S. government generally identifies abusive billings through retrospective analysis after it has paid claims. Although the payment process includes some front-end safeguards, criminals are increasingly sophisticated in detecting and circumventing these measures."

"Although Medicare and Medicaid always have been vulnerable to fraud, the government has identified an alarming surge in fraud schemes and abusive practices in recent years. Drug dealers are switching from trafficking in narcotics to health care fraud, having discovered that defrauding Medicare is safer, more lucrative, and carries a lower risk of detection and prosecution. Law enforcement routinely uncovers complex schemes that span several states and involve dozens of conspirators."

"Health care fraud is attractive to professional criminals because the penalties are lower than those for other organized crime–related offenses (such as those related to illegal drugs); there are low barriers to entry (for example, a criminal can obtain a supplier number, gather some beneficiary numbers, and bill the program); schemes are easily replicated; and there is a perception of a low risk of detection. If reimbursement is high enough and their costs low enough, criminals can reinvest some of their profit in kickbacks for additional referrals, thus using the program's funds to perpetuate the fraud scheme. To combat health care fraud, the government needs to alter the cost-benefit analysis for those considering health care fraud by increasing the risk of swift detection and the certainty of punishment." [239]

The Cost of High Readmission Rates at Hospitals

"Medicare acute care hospital discharge planning is often seen as offering purely clinical, financial, or legal challenges (Marciarille 2011). In reality, the re-engineering of Medicare acute care hospital discharge planning requires overcoming all three: it is a legal, a financial, and a clinical delivery challenge of the utmost importance. With nearly one-fifth of Medicare patients readmitted to a hospital within 30 days of discharge, the failure of discharge and of discharge planning is multi-dimensional. It represents both a financial disaster for the Medicare program and an exacting burden that extracts a high personal toll on Medicare beneficiaries."

"A problem of the magnitude of unplanned Medicare rehospitalizations has some broad patterns: the diagnoses for which beneficiaries are rehospitalized, the lack of outpatient follow-up care, and extraordinary regional variation across the United States."

"One pattern concerns the broad outlines of the diagnoses that are most involved in Medicare rehospitalization. Certain conditions at discharge are disproportionately represented in unplanned Medicare rehospitalizations. The top five medical conditions generating the most readmissions concern: heart failure, pneumonia, chronic obstructive pulmonary disease, psychoses and gastrointestinal problems. Four of these conditions may fairly be characterized as chronic. The top five surgical procedures most likely to require readmission involve: cardiac stent placement, major hip or knee surgery, vascular surgery, major bowel surgery, and other hip or femur surgery."

"A second pattern is the lack of outpatient follow-up care for more than half of patients with a medical discharge who were readmitted within 30 days to the community." These individuals "showed no record of primary care receipt between their original hospital discharge and their

239. Morris, L. Combating Fraud in Health Care: An Essential Component of any Cost Containment Strategy, *Health Affairs*, Vol. 28, No. 5, September/October 2009, pp. 1351-1356.

rehospitalization. A corollary of this second pattern is the high number of medical rehospitalizations following a surgical discharge." [240]

A study showed that "older black Medicare patients had higher 30-day readmission rates than white patients for acute myocardial infarction, congestive heart failure, and pneumonia. These differences were related, in part, to higher readmission rates among hospitals that disproportionately care for black patients (Joynt 2011). These associations persisted even after accounting for a series of potential confounders, including markers of caring for poor patients, suggesting that measured features of hospitals and lower reimbursements alone are unlikely to explain these gaps. Racial disparities in readmissions related to both patient race and the site where care is provided should spur clinical leaders and policymakers to find new ways to reduce disparities in this important health outcome." [241]

The Medicaid Program

Medicaid serves more than 60 million low-income families, seniors, and individuals with disabilities. The federal government pays an average 57% of program costs. States pay the rest. Medicaid always is a prominent issue in Washington, as it is in every state capital. At the state level, Medicaid costs have the potential to crowd out spending on other kinds of social programs such as education. As state budgets collapse under the weight of increased unemployment, which leads to reductions in tax revenues with a corresponding increase in the number of residents becoming eligible for programs such as Medicaid, the dilemma increases in intensity during a recession.

According to a *Medicaid Primer* by the Kaiser Family Foundation, the program originally was conceived as a health coverage supplement only for those individuals receiving cash welfare assistance (Kaiser 2010). Over time, Congress has expanded Medicaid substantially to fill growing coverage gaps left by the private insurance system. Many states have expanded eligibility for the program further and Medicaid has become the cornerstone of all state-level initiatives to broaden coverage of the uninsured. During the most recent economic recession (2007-2009), Medicaid provided a safety-net of coverage for millions more Americans affected by loss of work or declining income. The program now provides benefits to more recipients than any other public or private insurance program, including Medicare. Medicaid is the main payer of nursing home care and long-term care service overall. It also is the largest source of public funding for mental health care. Health centers and safety-net hospitals that serve low income and uninsured patients rely heavily on Medicaid revenues. Medicaid is an engine in state and local economies, too, supporting millions of jobs.

Medicaid provides health coverage for millions of low-income children and families who lack access to the private health insurance system that covers most Americans. The program also provides coverage for millions of individuals with chronic illnesses or disabilities who are excluded from private insurance or for whom such insurance, which is designed for a generally healthy population, is inadequate. Medicaid is the nation's largest source of coverage for long-term care, covering more than two-thirds of all nursing home residents.

Because eligibility for Medicaid is tied to having low income, and enrollment cannot be limited or waiting lists kept, the program operates as a safety-net. During economic recessions,

---

240. Marciarille, A.M. Healing Medicare Hospital Recidivism: Causes and Cures, *American Journal of Law & Medicine*, Vol. 37, Issue 1, 2011, pp. 41-80.
241. Joynt, K.E. et al. Thirty-Day Readmission Rates for Medicare Beneficiaries by Race and Site of Care, *Journal of the American Medical Association*, Vol. 305, No. 7, February 16, 2011. pp. 675-681.

when job loss causes workers and their families to lose health coverage and income, more recipients become eligible for Medicaid and the program expands to cover many of them, offsetting losses of private health insurance and mitigating increases in the number of uninsured.

"It is estimated that for every one percentage point increase in the unemployment rate, Medicaid enrollment grows by 1 million. Enrollment growth has been accelerating in each 6-month period since the most recent recession began in December 2007. The largest 6-month Medicaid enrollment increase on record occurred from December 2008 to June 2009, when 2.1 million additional individuals obtained Medicaid coverage. Between June 2008 and June 2009, enrollment rose by nearly 3.3 million, or 7.5%."

"Over 10 million Americans, including about 6 million elderly and 4 million children and working-age adults, need long-term services and supports. Medicaid covers about 7 of every 10 nursing home residents and finances over 40% of nursing home spending and long-term care spending overall. More than half of all Medicaid long-term care spending is for institutional care, but a growing share—41% in 2006, up from 30% in 2000 and 13% in 1990—is attributable to home and community-based services."

"Medicaid provides 33% of public hospitals' net revenues. Medicaid payments furnish an even larger share of health centers' total operating revenues (37%) and is their largest source of third-party payment. State agencies administer Medicaid subject to oversight by the Centers for Medicare and Medicaid Services (CMS) in the U.S. Department of Health and Human Services (HHS). State participation in Medicaid is voluntary, but all states participate. Federal law outlines basic minimum requirements that all state Medicaid programs must meet, but states have broad authority to define eligibility, benefits, provider payment, delivery systems, and other aspects of their programs. The proportion of the population covered by Medicaid varies from state to state, ranging from 8% in New Hampshire and Nevada to 22% in the District of Columbia."

"Historically, non-elderly adults without dependent children, no matter how poor they are, have been categorically excluded from Medicaid by federal law unless they are disabled or pregnant. States have been able to receive federal Medicaid funds to cover these adults only if they obtained a federal waiver; alternatively, states could use state-only dollars. The new health reform law ends the categorical exclusion of these adults as of 2014, expanding Medicaid eligibility nationally to reach adults under age 65 (both parents and those without dependent children) up to 133% FPL (federal poverty level). An enhanced federal match rate applies for adults newly eligible for Medicaid as a result."

Only American citizens and specific categories of lawfully residing immigrants can qualify for Medicaid. The Personal Responsibility and Work Opportunity Reconciliation Act, enacted in 1996, barred most lawfully residing immigrants from Medicaid during their first 5 years in the U.S., except for emergency treatment. Some states have used state-only funds to cover these legal immigrants during the 5-year ban. Recently, Congress gave states the option to receive federal Medicaid matching funds for lawfully residing immigrant children and pregnant women during their first 5 years in the U.S. As of June 2010, "18 states including the District of Columbia had adopted the option to cover immigrant children, pregnant women, or both, without the 5-year wait. The health reform law does not change any rules about immigrants' eligibility for Medicaid." [242]

Shortly after President Obama took office, his Administration responded to the recession by adding some $90 billion to the Medicaid program. That money came to an end as of July 1, 2011. Consequently, although the unemployment rate hovers around 9% as of December 2011,

---

242. The Henry J. Kaiser Family Foundation. Medicaid: A Primer, Menlo Park, CA: June 2010, 50 pp. On the Web at http://www.kff.org/medicaid/upload/7334-04.pdf. Accessed on August 3, 2011.

states have been forced to cut back payments to providers, limit benefits, and require beneficiaries to pay more for their care. If providers decide to cease treating patients, the latter will have no recourse other than to go to emergency rooms for care, which adds more costs to the health system. Whenever that occurrence takes place, providers try to shift added costs to other patients and private insurers.

Dental Care Under Medicaid

Inadequate payment levels to providers can have an adverse impact on the ability to obtain health care. For example, tooth decay is a common disease among children and adolescents. Although tooth decay can significantly affect quality of life, it often goes untreated. Approximately "24% of children aged 2 to 8 years had untreated dental caries in 1999-2004 (Decker 2011). More than one-third of children are covered by public health insurance, primarily Medicaid and the Children's Health Insurance Program (CHIP). Coverage of dental care for children and adolescents covered by these two programs is required, although states have wide latitude in setting payment rates for providers, including dentists. These rates vary greatly by state."

"Data on states' Medicaid dental fees in 2000 and 2008 merged with data on children's use of dental care from the National Health Interview Survey (NHIS) showed that children covered by Medicaid use dental care less frequently than children with private insurance but the frequency of children covered by Medicaid receiving dental care is associated with each state's provider payment policy. The 2000 Surgeon General's report on oral health documented linkages between oral diseases and ear and sinus infections, weakened immune systems, and other health conditions. Untreated dental conditions have the potential to affect children's speech, social development, and quality of life. Children in families with income below the poverty level have higher prevalence of dental caries than children in higher-income families and their disease is more likely to be untreated."

"Among the reasons that children and adolescents covered by Medicaid do not receive care are low payments to dentists for service, burdensome program administration requirements that are not required by other insurance carriers, and lack of patient education that can lead to frequently missed appointments." One study "supports the claim that low Medicaid payment rates are associated with children and adolescents' receiving less dental care than children covered by private insurance." [243]

Medicaid and Medical Homes

"A patient-centered medical home is an enhanced model of primary care in which care teams, led by a primary care provider, attend to the multifaceted needs of patients and provide whole-person, comprehensive, coordinated, and patient-centered care (Takach 2011). Dissatisfied with outcomes of inadequate quality and plagued by uncontrolled cost growth, more than 38 states are using the patient-centered medical home model to change the way in which primary care is delivered." One study focused on "17 states that are aligning patient-centered medical home standards with incentive payments to support reform in the delivery of primary care. Most states' initiatives are less than 2 years old and their findings have not been published."

---

243. Decker, S.L. Medicaid Payment Levels to Dentists and Access to Dental Care among Children and Adolescents, *Journal of the American Medical Association*, Vol. 306, No. 2, July 13, 2011, pp. 187-193.

"These initiatives use national recognition or state-based qualification standards along with incentive payments to address soaring costs and lagging health outcomes in state Medicaid programs. Even though these initiatives are in their infancy, early results are encouraging. Modest increases in payment to physicians, aligned with quality improvement standards, have not only resulted in promising trends for costs and quality, but also have greatly improved access to care. Several state programs have already demonstrated declines in per capita costs for patients enrolled in Medicaid; increased participation of physicians in caring for Medicaid patients; and high patient and provider satisfaction. These early results give states good reason to continue developing patient-centered medical homes as part of their Medicaid programs." [244]

Long-Term Care

"Aging is a story of change in individuals and families. It is also a story of loss: loss of physical and mental function, loss of family and friends, and loss of a spouse. These losses take place at different rates for different individuals and groups; people and families often adapt to losses with changes in their behavior or environment, making aging a complex and dynamic process (Waite 2010). The experience of aging is quite different for women than it is for men for a number of reasons. Racial and ethnic groups also tend to follow divergent paths during later adulthood. Families provide a key context in which health is produced and challenges to health are met. The health and well-being of each member depends on the health and well-being of the others, since the resources that family members command and the demands they make both depend on their health and functioning." [245]

Medicare and Medicaid "both cover populations in need of long-term care, but they are poorly coordinated. Gaps often exist in some services while there is overlap in others. This can lead to inefficient delivery of services and confusion among program recipients and providers alike (Ng 2010). Spending on post-acute services in Medicare and long-term care services in Medicaid has grown more rapidly than enrollment in either program since 1999. Although growing numbers of patients receive home and community-based services paid for by the two programs, there are wide variations across states and among target groups, indicating that the system of long-term care is in need of structural reform."

"Long-term care refers to a broad range of services and supports for people who need assistance for 90 days or more, including those with chronic illnesses and a variety of disabilities. The need for long-term care spans the age range from children to older persons. Growth in the aged population, especially those age 85 and older, has contributed to a growing need for long-term care. Most long-term care services are provided by informal (unpaid) family caregivers. Formal long-term care involves two main types of services: (1) home and community-based services such as personal care, and (2) institutional care in nursing homes and intermediate care facilities for the developmentally disabled."

"Most formal long-term care services are paid for by government sources. In 2007, of the total $190.4 billion in estimated spending for nursing home and home health care in the United States, Medicare paid for 25%, Medicaid and other public funds paid for 42%, out-of-pocket funds paid for 22%, and private insurance and other sources paid for 11% (excluding hospital-based nursing home spending). The resulting variation among states' budgets and coverage deci-

---

244. Takach, M. Reinventing Medicaid: State Innovations to Qualify and Pay for Patient-Centered Medical Homes Show Promising Results, *Health Affairs*, Vol. 30, No. 7, July 2011, pp. 1325-1334.
245. Waite, L. and Das, A. Families, Social Life, and Well-Being, *Demography*, August 2010 Supplement, Vol. 47, pp. S87-S109.

sions adds to the overall complexity of public programs' services and spending within and across states. The system of providing and paying for long-term care in the United States reflects this piecemeal developmental history and shared federal-state responsibility. The result can be confusion among patients and providers, amid seemingly illogical patterns of insurance coverage and available services." [246]

As the Affordable Care Act unfolds, "most state legislatures are left to ponder how they will ultimately fare, given growing fiscal constraints, increased enrollment in Medicaid and the Children's Health Insurance Program (CHIP), and a political season where government spending is likely to be a prominent issue (Keckley 2010). Appropriately, state leaders must look to promising areas where opportunities for cost savings also improve results: Among these is long-term care (LTC) for the Medicaid population. Left unattended, states' obligation to their LTC Medicaid enrollees has the potential to debilitate government effectiveness. The health care reform bill provides little near-term relief."

Currently, there is no "coordinated, comprehensive system for the provision and financing of LTC services in the United States. For the disabled and elderly who lack personal financial resources, navigating the complexities and regulations associated with LTC decisions can be extremely challenging. No less daunting is the task facing policy makers, whose decisions on behalf of these vulnerable populations directly and dramatically affect both state and federal budgets."

"By design, state-administered Medicaid has become the nation's primary funding source for LTC for those in need. The pressure on states to control costs while making effective decisions regarding the provision of community- versus institutional-based LTC services presents an opportunity to transform LTC as a whole. This transformation assumes a sense of urgency as state and local governments face new and growing fiscal challenges generated, in part, by the needs of an aging baby boom generation. Prior to 1995, elderly residents exceeded 15% of the population in only five states; by 2025, the elderly will exceed 15% in every state except California and Alaska. The number of Americans aged 65 and older will more than double in at least 20 states and then continue to grow."

"The convergence of an aging population and health care reform's mandate for increased access to care will have far-reaching consequences for Medicaid. Not only will it force Medicaid to examine existing benefit programs for the elderly and the poor, it will also push Medicaid to rethink how it can address the full range of elderly needs with the resources it possesses and can mobilize. A key beneficiary of those resources will be patients needing LTC."

"It is estimated that more than 35% of a state's budget will be needed for Medicaid by 2030, of which half will be for LTC services. Research indicates that nursing facility expenditures are not driving this cost escalation, so a push to manage LTC costs by eliminating less-costly home/community care programs could boomerang, with the result that beneficiaries end up requiring more costly institutional care. Health care reform's mandate for increased access is expected to worsen Medicaid's expenditure trend. At a time when unemployment rates remain high, state tax revenues have decreased and state budget deficits have increased, states are being asked to do more with less in regard to health care resources." [247]

---

246. Ng, T. et al. Medicare and Medicaid in Long-Term Care, *Health Affairs*, Vol. 29, No. 1, January 2010, pp. 22-28.
247. Keckley, P.H. and Frink, B. Issue Brief: Medicaid Long-Term Care: The Ticking Time Bomb, Deloitte Center for Health Solutions, 2010, 15 pp. On the Web at http://www.deloitte.com/assets/Dcom-UnitedStates/Local%20Assets/ Documents/US_CHS_2010LTCinMedicaid_062910.pdf. Accessed on August 3, 2011.

The Lewin Group estimates that:

- "Seven percent of Medicaid beneficiaries using LTC account for 52% of total Medicaid spending.
- LTC spending constitutes a substantial portion of state Medicaid budgets—one-third on average and ranging from 23% to 61%.
- The total number of individuals age 65 and over requiring LTC will grow from 7.4 million in 2010 to 16.1 million in 2050.
- Total national LTC spending for individuals age 65 and older of approximately $182 billion will nearly double by 2030 and increase to about $684 billion by 2050.
- The number of patients age 65 and older requiring Medicaid LTC will grow from 2.7 million in 2010 to 4.9 million in 2050.
- Medicaid LTC spending is projected to increase from approximately $64 billion in 2010 to $101 billion in 2030 and $217 billion in 2050."

"From a broader public financing context, total spending for Medicaid, Medicare, and Social Security is projected to climb from 8.4% of GDP to 18.4% by 2050. In addition, Medicaid spending for health care for working age adults and children will greatly increase as a result of expansion of the Medicaid program to cover more uninsured people through the new national health reform law."

"Issues of LTC financing are closely intertwined with other challenges that will need to be addressed to meet the growing need for LTC in the United States, including supporting family caregivers, sufficient supply of the paid LTC workforce, promoting healthy aging, and ensuring access to quality services that meet people's needs. Attempts to address these challenges have generally been fragmented and uncoordinated, focusing on one aspect of the problem or limited to a few providers or states."

Challenges that must be confronted include:

- "Build and maintain an adequate, skilled, and diverse workforce by improving recruitment, retention, and the training of health and long-term care personnel to provide care for the growing population of older people and people with disabilities.
- Support unpaid caregivers through individual counseling, organization of support groups, caregiver training, and respite care." [248]

Federal Health Spending in the Context of a Growing National Deficit

For the greater part of 2011 until August 1, Congress and the Administration were embroiled in debates about raising the national debt level. Failure to do so would have resulted on August 2 in an inability of the federal government to meet all its obligations. Although it seemed unlikely that Social Security recipients would be affected, it was never entirely clear how funding reductions would be applied to groups such as holders of U.S. Treasury securities. By the end of that first week in August, Standard & Poors had downgraded its rating of Treasury securities. One possible effect might be the necessity to raise interest

---

248. The Lewin Group. Medicaid and Long-Term Care: New Challenges, New Opportunities, June 25, 2010, 54 pp. On the Web at http://www.lewin.com/content/publications/Genworth_Medicaid_and_LTC_Final_Report-6.23.10.pdf. Accessed on August 3, 2011.

rates to attract investors. Higher interest rates, in turn, have the potential to choke efforts to boost the economy.

President Obama signed legislation into law on August 2 to raise the nation's debt ceiling and reduce the deficit. As the nation prepared to hit the previous debt ceiling at midnight, the legislation passed the Senate 74-26 and the House of Representatives 269-161. The measure raises the debt ceiling by $900 billion—$400 billion immediately and $500 billion in September 2011, following a presidential request—and enacts cuts of $917 billion over 10 years. While Medicare and Medicaid would not be subjected to the initial reductions, the legislation assigns a Joint Select Committee on Deficit Reduction with the task of recommending $1.2-1.5 trillion in additional savings by November 23. Congress then would have to vote on the recommendations by December 23, and the president could request an additional increase in the debt ceiling of $1.5 trillion if passed.

On November 21, the Select Committee was unable to reach agreement on how to cut $1.2 billion over a 10-year period. If Congress fails to send a balanced budget amendment to the states before the end of 2011, the bill would automatically trigger across-the-board cuts totaling $1.2 trillion in mandatory and discretionary spending beginning in 2013. Medicaid would not be subject to the cuts, but Medicare provider payments would face a reduction of no more than 2% over 9 years (2013-2021). The president would then be authorized to request an additional increase in the debt ceiling of $1.2 trillion.

B ruce Vladek who oversaw the Medicare and Medicaid programs "from 1993 to 1997 has stated that ideas for Medicare savings have been around for years, but have never gotten past the talking stages because of political opposition or because they are simply bad ideas. One especially pernicious proposal appears to have increasing traction among both politicians and policy analysts: the prohibition of *first-dollar coverage* in Medicare supplemental insurance, whether purchased in the individual markets or provided as a retiree benefit."

He believes "this proposal is based on a simple and seemingly self-evident syllogism. Medicare beneficiaries with supplemental insurance that provides them with first-dollar coverage by paying their deductibles and co-payments use more services than the small minority of beneficiaries without such coverage. Hence, forbidding such coverage would reduce use, thereby saving Medicare a pile of money."

"Sometimes this poison pill is sugar-coated, as in the proposal from Senators Joseph Lieberman (I-CT) and Tom Coburn (R-OK). In their plan, the structure of Medicare out-of-pocket liabilities would be altered to create protection against catastrophic out-of-pocket expenses for some, in exchange for higher out-of-pocket liabilities for most beneficiaries. But whatever form the proposals take, they would have seriously adverse consequences for the sickest and most needy Medicare beneficiaries."

The reason health insurance exists in the first place "is to relieve individuals who are not medical experts of the need to figure out whether they can afford any particular medical service. In a rational world, policymakers worried about unnecessary or inappropriate use of specific services would just refuse to pay for those services. In the contemporary American political environment, they might be accused of 'rationing' or creating 'death panels,' so they stay away. Instead, they appear to be willing, once again, to impose the consequences of their inability to control costs on those least able to bear them." [249]

---

249. Vladek, B. A Pernicious Idea: Proposals to Forbid First-Dollar Coverage for Medicare Beneficiaries, *Kaiser Health News*, August 2, 2011.

Health Reform and Prevention

Accccording to a report prepared by different federal agencies, older Americans have long been recognized as having unique social, economic, and health needs. Since the passage of the landmark Medicare Act in 1965, numerous policies and programs have evolved to support and improve the health and quality of life for adults aged 65 and older. "The most recent addition is the 2010 Affordable Care Act, which addresses coverage for clinical preventive services with a U.S. Preventive Services Task Force rating of an A or B, immunizations recommended by the Advisory Committee on Immunization Practices, and numerous additional wellness benefits for older adults. Recently issued rules to implement the legislation call for Medicare to eliminate out-of-pocket costs for previously covered preventive services in January 2011. The new law also entitles Medicare beneficiaries to a free annual wellness visit that includes a schedule of recommended preventive services. Additionally, a few states already have eliminated copayments for some cancer screenings and more are poised to do so." [250]

Many services are under-utilized. While a high percentage of Medicare beneficiaries visit a physician at least once a year and make an average of six visits during the year, many do not receive the full range of recommended covered preventive services. Removing the cost barrier has potential to improve utilization rates; however, there are other significant barriers. It is unlikely that eliminating cost, by itself, will result in widespread use of lifesaving preventive services (Maeshiro 2011).

Major gaps also are evident. In a public health context, these gaps or disparities can occur in the quality of health and health care across age, gender, race or ethnicity, income, education, geographic location, disability, and sexual orientation. In general, low-income Americans and racial and ethnic minorities experience disproportionately higher rates of disease, fewer treatment options, and reduced access to care. The same holds true for the use of evidence-based clinical preventive services among adults aged 65 years and older as well. For example, from January to March 2010, 65% of Hispanic adults and 61% of non-Hispanic black adults reported never having received the pneumococcal vaccination—significantly more than the 35% of non-Hispanic white adults of the same age who reported never having been vaccinated.

"The Healthy People Curriculum Task Force was established in 2002 to encourage implementation of Healthy People 2010 Objective 1.7: 'To increase the proportion of schools of medicine, schools of nursing and health professional training schools whose basic curriculum for healthcare providers includes the core competencies in health promotion and disease prevention.' In 2004, the Task Force published a *Clinical Prevention and Population Health Curriculum Framework* ('Framework') to help each profession assess and develop more robust approaches to this content in their training."

"During the 6 years since the publication of the Framework, the Task Force members introduced and disseminated it to constituents, facilitated its implementation at member schools, integrated it into initiatives that would influence training across schools, and adapted and applied the Framework to meet the data needs of the Healthy People 2010 Objective 1.7. The Framework has been incorporated into initiatives that help promote curricular change such as accreditation standards and national board examination content, and efforts to disseminate the experiences of peers, expert recommendations, and activities to monitor and update curricular content. The publication of the revised Framework and the release of Healthy People 2020 (and

---

250. Centers for Disease Control for Disease Control and Prevention, Administration on Aging, Agency for Healthcare Research and Quality, and Centers for Medicare and Medicaid Services. *Enhancing Use of Clinical Preventive Services Among Older Adults*. Washington, DC: AARP, 2011. On the Web at www.cdc.gov/aging and www.aarp.org/healthpros. Accessed on August 2, 2011.

the associated Education for Health Framework) provide an opportunity to review the efforts of the health professions groups to advance the kind of curricular change recommended in Healthy People 2010 and Healthy People 2020 and to appreciate the many strategies required to influence health professions curricula." [251]

Some Additional Observations About Medicare and Medicaid

Programs in place today in the form of Medicare and Medicaid resulted from a long, complex process that involved both continuity and change. It can be expected that current efforts to reform health care in the U.S. today will entail some combination of building upon what exists and introducing some degree of transformation. The Medicare and Medicaid programs will be at the heart of such efforts as policymakers address issues that involve regional variations in spending, increases in the percentage of patients with chronic conditions, programmatic fraud and abuse, payments for health facilities and personnel, and the mix of practitioners needed to meet the health care needs of the population.

Most discussions of benefit packages focus on the provision and coverage of services for physical problems. Mental health typically does not receive the attention that it deserves. Advocates of benefit expansion often cite problems stemming from addiction to drugs and alcohol. The war in Iraq and Afghanistan undoubtedly will play a role in adding to the ranks of those who already are suffering from addiction while serving in the military or who will acquire a drug or alcohol problem (or both) after being discharged and returning home to civilian life. They also will enter that murky area where different kinds of benefit programs with varying eligibility requirements meet or fail to meet a person's health and health-related social needs.

It should be obvious that providers included in existing benefit packages will fight to block attempts to scale back coverage for their specialties. Conversely, efforts to upgrade such packages open up an intense battle among other specialties that seek to be included. For example, as the 1st session of the 107th Congress drew to a close, HR 2792—the Disabled Veterans Service Dog and Health Care Improvement Act of 2001—was passed by the House in Congress late that year. If enacted, it would make possible the provision of chiropractic care to veterans through all VA medical centers. Physical therapists opposed the expansion on the grounds that new services would reduce funding for other needed services such as those provided by physical therapists. Eventually, HR 2792 morphed into HR 3447 and became Public Law 107-135 on January 23, 2002, thereby enabling chiropractic care to be provided to veterans.

Battles continue each year on Capitol Hill to enable the services of athletic trainers to be included in the Medicare benefit package. The National Athletic Trainers' Association filed a civil lawsuit against the American Physical Therapy Association, citing antitrust laws and related violations.

It doesn't matter whether it's dentists versus dental hygienists, psychologists versus psychiatrists, optometrists versus ophthalmologists, anesthesiologists versus nurse anesthetists, or physical therapists versus athletic trainers—the pie is viewed as being only so large and the theory of the limited good prevails, i.e., the only way that Party A can benefit is by taking away something from party B, or in biblical terms, taking from Peter to pay Paul. Yet, not too surprisingly, there has not been one recorded instance of a complaint ever being made by the Paul group of beneficiaries in this world.

---

251. Maeshiro, R. et al. Using the Clinical Prevention and Population Health Curriculum Framework to Encourage Curricular Change, *American Journal of Preventive Medicine*, Vol. 40, No. 2, February 2011, pp. 232-244.

Under the Affordable Care Act, beneficiaries with Original Medicare can receive recommended preventive benefits and a new annual wellness visit without paying an additional penny out-of-pocket. The Affordable Care Act also is closing the prescription drug donut hole by providing increasing discounts on covered drugs in the donut hole. In 2011, the number of individuals with Medicare benefiting from these improvements is growing:

- "From January 1, 2011 to July 2011 there were 17,336,421 beneficiaries, or 51.5%, with Original Medicare who received one or more free preventive services.

- During the same time period, 1,061,780 Americans with Original Medicare have taken advantage of Medicare's new Annual Wellness Visit, up from 780,000 in mid-June.

- Through the end of June 2011, 899,000 Americans with Medicare have benefited from the 50% discount on covered brand name drugs in the Medicare Part D donut hole—an increase of over 420,000 individuals in the month of June alone.

- The dollar amount of these out-of-pocket savings on drug costs for Medicare beneficiaries has risen to $461 million saved through June 2011—up from $260 million through May 2011, meaning beneficiaries in the donut hole saved over $200 million in the month of June alone." [252]

What the Future May Hold for Health Spending

"In 2014, national health spending growth is expected to reach 8.3% when major coverage expansions from the Affordable Care Act of 2010 begin (Keehan 2011). The expanded Medicaid and private insurance coverage are expected to increase demand for health care significantly, particularly for prescription drugs and physician and clinical services. Robust growth in Medicare enrollment, expanded Medicaid coverage, and premium and cost-sharing subsidies for exchange plans are projected to increase the federal government share of health spending from 27% in 2009 to 31% by 2020." [253]

Apart from the disabled, eligibility for Medicare is tied to Social Security eligibility. "By 2035, there will be 1.9 workers for each Social Security beneficiary, down from 4.9 workers per beneficiary in 1960." This relatively small proportion of workers will bear the tax burden of paying for Medicare, Medicaid, and Social Security. A report from the Congressional Budget Office (CBO) summarizes some of the agency's most recent projections for Social Security and provides background information on the program. [254]

A Kaiser Health Tracking Poll conducted in July 2011 found that health care, particularly Medicare and Medicaid, continues to play a role in the national discussion over the federal budget deficit. In the midst of this debate, the poll found that Americans of all political stripes see a role for both spending reductions and tax increases as part of an overall deficit reduction strategy. Still, few are willing to support major spending reductions in Medicare and a large majority believes the country's budgetary problems can be addressed without cutting Medicare spending. The ongoing debate about the deficit doesn't appear to have had much impact on the public's overall opinion of the health reform law, which remains divided. Despite the fact that

252. Centers for Medicare and Medicaid Services, Medicare Part D Prescription Drug Coverage Gap Discounts. On the Web at http://www.cms.gov/NewMedia/03_partd.asp#TopOfPage. Accessed on August 7, 2011.

253. Keehan, S.P. et al. National Health Spending Projections through 2020: Economic Recovery and Reform Drive Faster Spending Growth, *Health Affairs*, Vol. 30, Issue 8, August 2011, pp. 1594-1605.

254. Congressional Budget Office. CBO's 2011 Long-Term Projections for Social Security: Infographic, August 5, 2011. On the Web at http://www.cbo.gov/ftpdocs/123xx/doc12376/SocSecInfographic_print.pdf. Accessed on August 9, 2011.

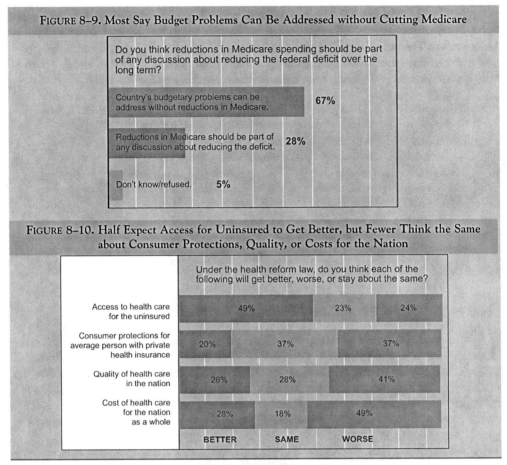

FIGURE 8–9. Most Say Budget Problems Can Be Addressed without Cutting Medicare

Do you think reductions in Medicare spending should be part of any discussion about reducing the federal deficit over the long term?

Country's budgetary problems can be address without reductions in Medicare. — 67%

Reductions in Medicare should be part of any discussion about reducing the deficit. — 28%

Don't know/refused. — 5%

FIGURE 8–10. Half Expect Access for Uninsured to Get Better, but Fewer Think the Same about Consumer Protections, Quality, or Costs for the Nation

Under the health reform law, do you think each of the following will get better, worse, or stay about the same?

	BETTER	SAME	WORSE
Access to health care for the uninsured	49%	23%	24%
Consumer protections for average person with private health insurance	20%	37%	37%
Quality of health care in the nation	26%	28%	41%
Cost of health care for the nation as a whole	28%	18%	49%

Source: Kaiser Family Foundation Health Tracking Poll—July 2011; adapted with permission.

consumer protections were one of the least controversial and most widely supported provisions of the Affordable Care Act, just 20% of Americans think the law will lead to improvements in consumer protections for the average person with health insurance. Half expect access to care for the uninsured to become better under the law.[255]

Closing Thoughts

The One-Horse Open Shay analogy conjures up thoughts of an immediate collapse. The U.S. health care system is not going to capsize all at once, but the ever-increasing costs of health care are on an unsustainable path. Even with the health reform bill that was enacted in 2010, not everybody will be able to obtain health insurance. Those who have coverage may face increased costs in the form of higher deductibles and copayments. Moreover, if consumers have to pay more for coverage, it will drain their ability to spend money for other goods and services such as education. Even more importantly, health expenditures should lead to better health outcomes and a healthier population, which does not always happen.

---

255. The Henry J. Kaiser Family Foundation. Kaiser Health Tracking Poll—July 2011. On the Web at http://www.kff.org/kaiserpolls/8209.cfm. Accessed on August 7, 2011.

CHAPTER 9:
Reforming Health Care

9

Improving the delivery and financing of health care has been a quest of policymakers for several decades. Enactment of health reform legislation in 2010 opened up the prospect of increasing access, improving quality, and curtailing cost growth. Mechanisms stemming from the new law such as accountable care organizations, an independent payment advisory board for Medicare, and a patient-centered outcomes research institute are supposed to achieve these aims. Disputed aspects of the law may either experience attempts by Congress to deny funds needed for implementation or await resolution in the courts.

Some Factors that Influence the Ability to Provide High-Quality Health Care

Patients
Growth in numbers as the population expands in size
Differences by race/ethnicity, gender, and age
Adherence to medication usage and related health care advice
Extent of health literacy
Personal responsibility involving use of food, drugs/alcohol, and tobacco products
Ability to pay for health care
Willingness to take advantage of screening opportunities

Hospitals, Clinics, and Practitioners' Offices
Geographic distribution of facilities and health personnel
Solo practitioners versus group practice
Salaried health professionals versus independent practitioners
Degree of integration of a comprehensive array of services
Protection from frivolous malpractice claims
Ability to avoid the practice of defensive medicine
Use of electronic medical records
Evidence-based practice

Health Workforce
Student recruitment and completion of studies required to enter the workforce
Availability of clinical sites for student training
Maintenance of an adequate supply of faculty
Caregivers similar to demographic characteristics of the population served
Creation of career ladders
Opportunities for continuing education

Role of Government at Various Levels
Providing a health safety net for patients through reimbursement mechanisms
Licensing health professionals
Establishing regulations and standards
Financing research
Preventing fraud and abuse

Health care in the United States is a work in progress and resembles a kaleidoscope in many fundamental ways. At any given time, some components may need more attention than other parts. The Affordable Care Act of 2010 was a monumental piece of legislation that was created to address major aspects of health care in the areas of access, costs, and quality. Given the vast panorama that constitutes the health scene in this country, it is highly unlikely, however, that any piece of legislation will ever be comprehensive enough to address every item needing attention.

Concerns about health care that existed 100 years ago continue to be salient in the second decade of the 21st century. Shown below is a list of major initiatives that have been taken to improve the provision of health care services in the U.S. over the decades.

Major Health Care Initiatives in the 1990s
1910 American Medical Association displays interest in a national health program
1916 American Medical Association recommends a system of national health insurance
1920 American Medical Association declares opposition to such coverage
1927 Committee on the Costs of Medical Care created and issues 26 reports
1934 President Franklin Roosevelt appoints a cabinet-level Committee on Economic Security, which examined costs arising from illness
1935 Social Security Act creates Title V grants for maternal and child health
1935 Social Security Act creates state grants for public health work
1938 Federal interdepartmental committee formulates a national health program
1939 S. 1620 introduced in U.S. Senate to create a national health program
1943 Murray-Wagner-Dingell bill introduced in Congress for same purpose; President Roosevelt and Vice-President Harry Truman support these bills
1948 President Truman concludes that government health insurance is not a possibility
1952 President Truman omits mention of concept in his State of the Union Address
1957 Rep. Aime Forand (D-RI) introduces bill to provide health insurance for the aged
1965 Medicare and Medicaid enacted in July

As mentioned in Chapter 7, additions and modifications to both Medicare and Medicaid have been made over the years. Despite many efforts to enact health reform from the early 1970s until 2010, many noble efforts went down in flames. During that period of time, major initiatives were launched approximately every 20 years.

During the 1970s, key figures such as President Richard Nixon, Senators Edward Kennedy (D-MA) and Russell Long (D-LA), and Congressman Wilbur Mills (D-AR) played prominent roles in trying to enact comprehensive health insurance. The cudgel was taken up once again in a huge way in the early days of the presidency of Democrat William Clinton. Epic battles occurred that dominated the front pages of newspapers, but in the end these efforts petered out and the combatants retreated to the sidelines to await another propitious moment.

A driving factor throughout these decades was the steady growth in the number of the uninsured. Being in that condition did not mean that Americans were deprived of health care. They could obtain it in emergency rooms. What the situation did signify, however, was that health care in that particular setting lacks essential characteristics. It is episodic in nature and continuity of care is wholly absent.

Despite the creation of the Accountable Care Act (ACA) in 2010, many problems still remain. The addition of the uninsured to the ranks of the insured will take place gradually rather than all at once. Not everybody will be included, which means that millions will continue to lack health insurance coverage. The ultimate fate of this legislation has yet to be determined. Some states are opposed to the individual mandate that will require members of the general public to purchase coverage. The issue goes to the U.S. Supreme Court in 2012 for a final determination of the provision's constitutionality. If the court rejects this feature, the rest of the legislation may be in jeopardy.

Public Opinion Toward Federal Health Expenditures

As of July 2011, health care, and particularly Medicare and Medicaid, continued to play a role in the national discussion over the federal budget deficit. In the midst of this debate, the July 2011 Kaiser Health Tracking poll found that there is little appetite for reducing spending on Medicare (Kaiser 2011), as shown in the following two slides.

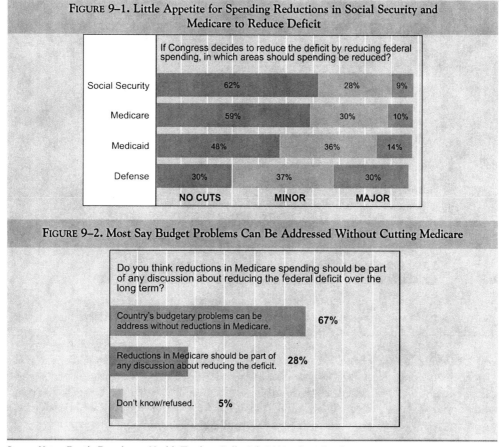

FIGURE 9–1. Little Appetite for Spending Reductions in Social Security and Medicare to Reduce Deficit

FIGURE 9–2. Most Say Budget Problems Can Be Addressed Without Cutting Medicare

Source: Kaiser Family Foundation Health Tracking Poll—July 2011; adapted with permission.

A third slide shows that the public's overall opinion of the health reform law remains divided. As illustrated in the fourth and fifth slides, party affiliation and partisan disagreements are sharply defined. The sixth slide reveals that despite the fact that consumer protections were one of the least controversial and most widely supported provisions of the ACA, just 20% of

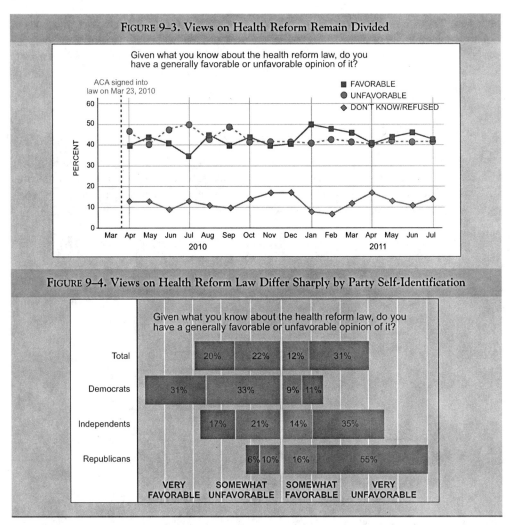

FIGURE 9-3. Views on Health Reform Remain Divided

FIGURE 9-4. Views on Health Reform Law Differ Sharply by Party Self-Identification

Americans think the law will lead to improvements in consumer protections for the average person with health insurance. Only half expect access to care for the uninsured to become better under the law.[256]

Ambivalence on the part of the electorate helps to foster enthusiasm among many Republicans in Congress for jettisoning the ACA in its entirety. Even if this approach fails, there still will be a strong inclination to weaken the law by refusing to provide funding to carry out various provisions. As the federal government strives to cope with reducing the overall national deficit, the ACA will remain a ripe target for spending reductions.

No clear picture exists on how the situation will unfold. The fate of the 2012 election may hang in the balance over such matters. Opponents of an expanded government role in the lives of the citizenry can be expected to vote for Republicans. That party already controls the House of Representatives. If it were to become the majority party in the Senate, President Obama, if re-elected, will find it highly difficult to have legislation that he favors passed. As regulations to

256. Henry J. Kaiser Family Foundation. Kaiser Health Tracking Poll, Publication no. 8209, July 27, 2011.

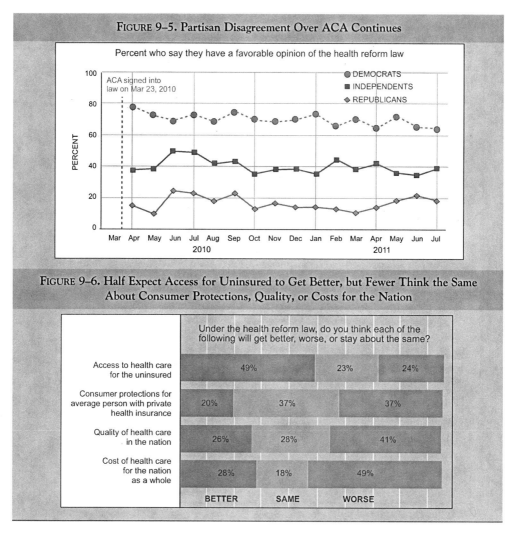

FIGURE 9–5. Partisan Disagreement Over ACA Continues

Percent who say they have a favorable opinion of the health reform law

FIGURE 9–6. Half Expect Access for Uninsured to Get Better, but Fewer Think the Same About Consumer Protections, Quality, or Costs for the Nation

implement the ACA continue to roll out, his adversaries will be ready to pounce on them. In the event he is defeated in 2012 and Republicans control both chambers of Congress and the White House, some major changes may be in store that will affect the ability of the nation to meet the health care needs of the populace.

Most leaders in health care and health care policy believe "traditional safety-net institutions such as community health centers, public hospitals, and faith-based and mission-driven organizations will still continue to fulfill critical roles in the U.S. health system after implementation of the ACA, according to a Commonwealth Fund/*Modern Healthcare* Health Care Opinion Leaders Survey" (Stremikis 2011). As shown in Figure 7, "nearly 7 of 10 respondents believe the new law will effectively improve access and financial protection for vulnerable populations." Figure 8 shows that "70% support policies that would guarantee access to care for undocumented immigrants." Figure 9 indicates support "for improving the quality of care delivered by safety-net providers by ensuring access to enabling services, facilitating the adoption and spread of

Source: Figures 3-6 from Kaiser Family Foundation Health Tracking Poll—July 2011; adapted with permission.

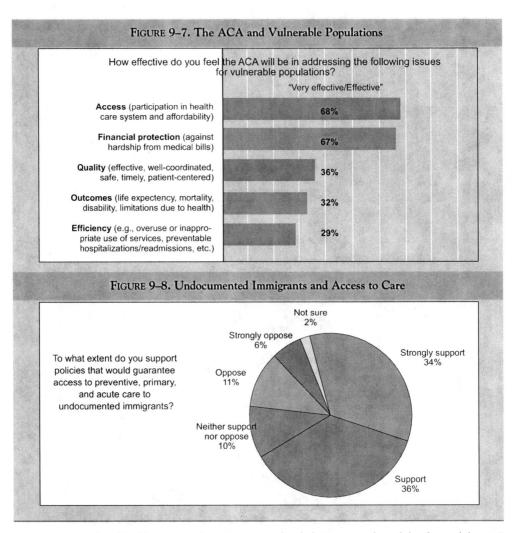

FIGURE 9–7. The ACA and Vulnerable Populations

How effective do you feel the ACA will be in addressing the following issues for vulnerable populations?

"Very effective/Effective"

Access (participation in health care system and affordability)	68%
Financial protection (against hardship from medical bills)	67%
Quality (effective, well-coordinated, safe, timely, patient-centered)	36%
Outcomes (life expectency, mortality, disability, limitations due to health)	32%
Efficiency (e.g., overuse or inappropriate use of services, preventable hospitalizations/readmissions, etc.)	29%

FIGURE 9–8. Undocumented Immigrants and Access to Care

To what extent do you support policies that would guarantee access to preventive, primary, and acute care to undocumented immigrants?

Not sure 2%
Strongly oppose 6%
Oppose 11%
Strongly support 34%
Neither support nor oppose 10%
Support 36%

patient-centered medical homes, and moving toward tightly integrated models of care delivery." Most respondents believe the "health system is currently unsuccessful in achieving equity across the specific domains of access, quality, and outcomes for vulnerable populations" as shown in Figure 10.

Provisions in the new law will "test and promote the spread of delivery system reforms to improve the quality of care within the safety net and across the entire health care system." According to Figure 11, "more than 8 of 10 leaders support expanding opportunities for scholarships and loan forgiveness and providing positive incentives for private sector providers to encourage them to care for vulnerable populations." [257]

The summer of 2009 proved to be an unpleasant period for many members of both chambers. During the August recess at various town hall meetings, voters in an unhappy mood over the prospect of a major overhaul of health care did not hesitate to display strong evidence of their feelings. Chief worries centered around beliefs that proposed legislation would fund abor-

257. Stremikis, K. et al. *Health Care Opinion Leaders' Views on Vulnerable Populations in the U.S. Health System*, The Commonwealth Fund, Pub 1536, Vol. 17, August 2011.

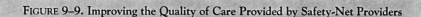

FIGURE 9–9. Improving the Quality of Care Provided by Safety-Net Providers

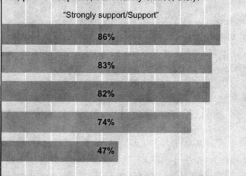

How much do you support the following strategies to improve quality of care that vulnerable populations receive from safety-net providers (e.g., community health centers, public hospitals, community clinics, etc.)?

"Strongly support/Support"

Ensure access to enabling services such as transportation and translation	86%
Facilitate adoption and spread of patient-centered medical homes	83%
Move toward tightly integrated models of care delivery	82%
Use performance-based payment contracting with providers to make them accountable for care they provide to their communities	74%
Facilitate adoption and spread of accountable care organizations	47%

FIGURE 9–10. Rating of U.S. Health System's Performance

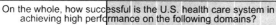

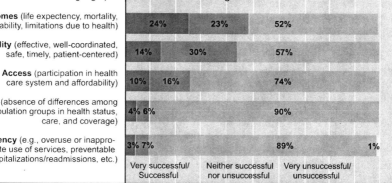

On the whole, how successful is the U.S. health care system in achieving high performance on the following domains?

	Very successful/ Successful	Neither successful nor unsuccessful	Very unsuccessful/ unsuccessful
Outcomes (life expectency, mortality, disability, limitations due to health)	24%	23%	52%
Quality (effective, well-coordinated, safe, timely, patient-centered)	14%	30%	57%
Access (participation in health care system and affordability)	10%	16%	74%
Equity (absence of differences among population groups in health status, care, and coverage)	4% 6%		90%
Efficiency (e.g., overuse or inappropriate use of services, preventable hospitalizations/readmissions, etc.)	3% 7%		89% 1%

FIGURE 9–11. Encouraging Private Sector Providers to Care for Vulnerable Populations

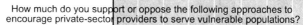

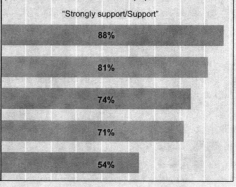

How much do you support or oppose the following approaches to encourage private-sector providers to serve vulnerable populations?

"Strongly support/Support"

Expand opportunities for scholarships and loan forgiveness for providers who practice in health prof. shortage areas	88%
Provide incentives for providers who serve vulnerable populations (e.g., enhanced payment)	81%
Expand funding of enabling services (e.g., transportation, translation) for vulnerable populations to wider range of providers	74%
Permanently increase provider reimbursement rates under Medicaid up to Medicare levels	71%
Condition provider participation in Medicare on Medicaid participation	54%

Source: Figures 7-11 from Commonwealth Fund/*Modern Healthcare* Health Care Opinion Leaders Survey, Aug 2011 (Stremikis 2011); adapted with permission.

tion and, as a result of rationing, would produce the equivalent of death panels that would deny care to the aged and the infirm.

Within Congress, Republicans claimed that health reform legislation would cause the nation to "slide rapidly down the slippery slope toward increasing governmental control of health care" (Grassley 2009). Unprecedented federal mandates would be produced and dozens of new bureaucracies would be created to increase power over individual lives. Another complaint was that emerging legislation in late 2009 would ignore badly needed elements in reform, such as allowing individuals to purchase health insurance across state lines and enacting tort reform to reduce abusive lawsuits that drive up costs.[258]

States as Laboratories for Health Reform—Oregon

Events that transpire at the state level sometimes can serve as guides for what might be carried out nationally. Given the complexity of the nation as a whole and the amount of variability from state-to-state composition of the population, available resources, and a history of successful innovations, there is no assurance that what is effective at that level is transferable to a larger setting. Nevertheless, valuable insights may be gained by analyzing what works and what fails to work in individual states that embark on new endeavors.

Failure by the federal government to enact comprehensive health reform legislation, particularly following the unsuccessful effort to do so in the early years of the Clinton Administration in the 1990s, spurred different states into taking action into their own hands. In doing so, Oregon attracted a tremendous amount of attention. As a means of expanding coverage to the uninsured, a plan involving explicit rationing was implemented that was based on a prioritized list of medical conditions and treatments. The state's novel plan required a "federal waiver to implement a Section 1115 Medicaid demonstration project" (Oberlander 2006). The waiver was not approved until 1993.

All went well initially as shown by a decline in the uninsured rate "from 18% in 1992 to 11% by 1996." By 2002, state officials moved forward to expand the health plan. No new state funds were available, which meant the plan had to be self-financed. The method for doing so was to "provide fewer services for more people. New cost-sharing and premium requirements had a devastating effect on enrollment, which declined. Individuals who failed to pay their premiums were disenrolled from the program and subjected to a 6-month 'lock-out' before they could reapply. Most clients who lost coverage remained uninsured and experienced major unmet needs for medical care."

Difficulties were further compounded when an economic downturn led to a reduction in state revenues. Unlike many other states that have sales taxes, Oregon "derived 70% of its income from personal income taxes," which declined as unemployment increased. "Turnover among state lawmakers weakened bipartisan support for the plan, which came to be viewed increasingly as a fiscal burden. A chief lesson for national policymakers to learn from what happened in Oregon is that the task is not simply to enact coverage expansions, but it is to sustain them." [259]

In 2008, Oregon used a lottery system to allocate "a limited number of Medicaid spots for low-income adults (19 to 64 years of age) to people on a waiting list for Medicaid. Approximately 10,000 of those selected from the 90,000 on the waiting list were enrolled" (Baicker

---

258. Grassley, C. Health Care Reform—A Republican View, *New England Journal of Medicine*, Vol. 361, No. 25, December 17, 2009, pp. 2397-2399.
259. Oberlander, J. Health Reform Interrupted: The Unraveling of the Oregon Health Plan, *Health Affairs Web Exclusive*, December 19, 2006, pp. w96-w105.

2011). A randomized controlled trial provided results that cast "doubt on both the optimistic view that Medicaid can reduce health care spending, at least in the short run, and the pessimistic view that Medicaid coverage won't make a difference to the uninsured." The authors noted that the results are specific to Oregon and that there are limits to the lessons that can be drawn from the experiment.[260]

States as Laboratories for Health Reform—Massachusetts

In April 2006, "the Massachusetts legislature enacted comprehensive health care reform requiring all state residents to carry a minimum level of health insurance, subject to penalties for noncompliance starting in 2008. To make coverage more affordable, the reform expanded Medicaid, subsidized private insurance, and set up the Commonwealth Connector to help individuals find suitable insurance" (Pande 2011).

"Although an estimated 406,000 individuals gained insurance coverage in Massachusetts between June 2006 and March 31, 2009, attributing causal effects to the reforms has been challenging. Living in Massachusetts in 2009 was associated with a 7.6 percentage point higher probability of being insured, a 4.8 percentage point lower probability of forgoing care because of cost, and a 6.6 percentage point higher probability of having a personal doctor compared to expected levels in the absence of reform, defined by trends in control states and adjusting for socioeconomic factors. The effects of the reform on insurance coverage attenuated from 2008 to 2009. In a socioeconomically disadvantaged group, the reforms had a greater effect in improving outcomes on the absolute, but not relative scale."

"Implementation of the national reform could differ substantively. The Massachusetts reforms were passed with essentially universal support; there were only two dissenting votes in both houses of the legislature. This allowed public officials to embark on a widespread social marketing campaign, which could have been responsible for acceptance and success of the mandate. The experience with national reform has been markedly different, with implementation of an individual mandate resulting in polarizing debate and inspiring organized resistance. The penalties for noncompliance with the insurance mandate in the national reform legislation ($695 per person to a maximum of $2,085 per family) are also three to four times higher than in Massachusetts ($218 for an individual and $437 for a family in 2007), which could imply different quantitative effects of the reforms at the national level." [261]

Despite widespread praise for what occurred in the Commonwealth and repeated references to how it served as a model for the ACA, containing costs remains a problem. A report from the Office of the Attorney General identified several factors that should be considered when analyzing cost containment strategies (Coakley 2011):

- "There is wide variation in the payments made by health insurers to providers that is not adequately explained by differences in quality of care.
- Globally paid providers do not have consistently lower total medical expenses.
- Total medical spending is on average higher for the care of health plan members with higher incomes.
- Tiered and limited network products have increased consumer engagement in value-based purchasing decisions.

260. Baicker, K. and Finkelstein, A. The Effects of Medicaid Coverage—Learning from the Oregon Experiment, *New England Journal of Medicine*, Vol. 365, No. 8, August 29, 2011, pp. 683-685.
261. Pande, et al. A.H. Effects of Healthcare Reforms on Coverage, Access, and Disparities: Quasi-Experimental Analysis of Evidence from Massachusetts, *American Journal of Preventive Medicine*, Vol. 41, Issue 1, July 2011, pp. 1-8.

- Preferred Provider Organization (PPO) health plans, unlike Health Maintenance Organization (HMO) health plans, create significant impediments for providers to coordinate patient care because PPO plans are not designed around primary care providers who have the information and authority necessary to coordinate the provision of health care effectively.
- Health care provider organizations designed around primary care can coordinate care effectively (1) through a variety of organizational models, (2) provided they have appropriate data and resources, and (3) while global payments may encourage care coordination, they pose significant challenges." [262]

Apart from good health care, when it comes to encouraging good health, a first-time report card produced by the Boston Foundation and the health policy foundation NEHI indicates a mediocre performance in Massachusetts (Boston Foundation 2011). Their "Healthy People/ Healthy Economy Report Card" graded policies on 14 different health indicators in four key areas: "physical activity, access to healthy foods, investments in health and wellness, and citizen education and engagement. The grades were mixed—no As, five Bs (biking and walking, healthy transportation design and planning, farmers' markets, employee health promotion, school-based Body Mass Index reporting), two Cs (healthy school meals, primary care), four Ds (youth physical activity, food deserts, trans fat policy, health impact assessments), and two Fs (sugar-sweetened beverages, public health funding)."

"The innovative report card is the first in the nation to focus on the effectiveness of public policies that encourage healthy living and controlling and preventing obesity and other chronic illnesses. This first annual report card should serve as a template for other communities and states across the country seeking to hold public officials accountable for the effectiveness and direction of their wellness policies." [263]

Accountable Care Organizations

Section 3022 of the ACA created a shared savings program for Accountable Care Organizations (ACOs) in Medicare. A proposed rule was issued on March 31, 2011. According to the Medicare Payment Advisory Commission (MedPAC), a "shared savings program for ACOs could present an opportunity to correct some undesirable incentives in fee-for-service (FFS) Medicare payment and reward providers who are doing their part to control costs and improve quality. However, creating a well-functioning ACO will require a significant investment of money, effort, and time, and the traditional FFS program will remain an attractive alternative—particularly for providers who are accustomed to being rewarded for the volume of services they provide. It would be a mistake to assess the success of the shared savings program by counting how many ACOs participate in the initial agreement period. A program that builds gradually and is carefully designed to meet the goals of high quality care and slower spending growth is likely to succeed and contribute to the long-term sustainability of the Medicare program" (MedPAC 2011).[264]

---

262. Coakley, M. Examination of Health Care Cost Trends and Cost Drivers, Office of the Attorney General of Massachusetts, Report for Annual Public Hearing, June 22, 2011, 55 pp. On the Web at http://www.mass.gov/ Cago/docs/ healthcare/2011_HCCTD.pdf. Accessed on August 10, 2011.

263. Boston Foundation and NEHI. Mediocre Massachusetts Health Report Card: No A's, Some D's and F's. *Common-Health*, July 19, 2011. On the Web at http://commonhealth.wbur.org/2011/07/massachusetts-health-report-card/. Accessed on August 10, 2011.

264. Medicare Payment Advisory Commission. 2011. Comment Letter on the Proposed Rule for ACOs – June 2011. Washington, DC.

Analysts at PricewaterhouseCoopers (PwC) had some of the following reactions to the proposed regulations:

- "The draft rules favor health organizations that are ACOs in everything but name. Much of the draft rules are based on the experience from the Centers for Medicare and Medicaid Services physician group practice (PGP) demonstration project. Large integrated delivery systems with substantial infrastructure in place will more likely meet ACO requirements than smaller, start-up organizations.
- Quality metrics for ACOs more than double those of any other federal programs, and payments may be reduced if ACOs fail to meet all five quality "domains" totaling 65 metrics. These 65 metrics compare to 32 in the PGP program.
- Beneficiaries are free to seek care outside of the ACO, and they are free to opt out of data sharing. ACOs may not even know the population they are managing until the end of the plan year. Although they will see a prospective list of beneficiaries, up to 25% may turn over in any given year.
- While federally qualified health centers (FQHCs) and rural health centers (RHCs) can't form ACOs on their own, having them as part of an ACO adds a 2.5% to 5.0% bonus.
- Providers can legally form partners within ACOs if their market share is less than 30%. Market share above that threshold may trigger a further review by the Federal Trade Commission or the Department of Justice of the ACO and each of its service lines." According to PwC, "such granular analysis of market penetration may have a chilling effect on the growth of ACOs."

ACOs must select one of two models: a "one-side" model that is all upside or a "two-sided model" that offers higher pay-outs but carries downside risk. Under the latter, ACOs can share up to 65% of the Medicare savings they achieve. Beginning in Year 3 of the program, all ACO participants fall under the two-sided model.

"To share in savings, an organization should spend less on beneficiaries than the benchmark that Medicare sets for that group. ACOs that select the two-sided model should spend at least 2% less to receive any shared savings; the spending reduction in the one-sided model will vary according to the size of the ACO."

Table 1 shown below illustrates the potential gain or loss an ACO might experience in the first year. Estimated impacts of a decrease and increase in spending of 5% against the benchmark for ACOs with 5,000 beneficiaries (ACO 1) and 60,000 beneficiaries (ACO 2) are shown. Under the one-sided model, ACO 1 could receive up to $231,000 with no risk of loss even though it spent more than 5% of its benchmark. This model is available, however, only during the first 2 years of the program. It could receive much more under the two-sided model, nearly $1.3 million. The downside is that if it spent 5% more, it would owe $420,000 to Medicare.[265]

Table 9–1. PwC Analysis of Shared Savings Distributed (Loss)		
	ACO 1	**ACO 2**
Benchmarked cost of care per beneficiary	$8,000	$8,000
Number of beneficiaries	5,000	60,000
One-sided model:		
Assuming 5% cost decrease	$231,000	$7,560,000
Assuming 5% cost increase	N/A	N/A
Two-sided model:		
Assuming 5% cost decrease	$1,300,000	$15,600,000
Assuming 5% cost increase	($420,000)	($5,040,000)

265. PricewaterhouseCoopers. Stalking the ACO Unicorn: What the Proposed Regulations for Accountable Care Organizations (ACOS) Mean, April 2011. On the Web at http://pwchealth.com/cgi-local/hregister.cgi?link=reg/stalking-the-aco-unicorn.pdf. Accessed on August 10, 2011.

Independent Payment Advisory Board

The Affordable Care Act creates a 15-member panel called the Independent Payment Advisory Board (IPAB). Its charge is to recommend a set of Medicare program changes, within certain constraints, if program spending growth exceeds specified targets, beginning in 2015. These targets are estimated to require IPAB to identify nearly $16 billion in savings for the years 2015 to 2019. IPAB recommendations will be sent to Congress under special procedures; disapproval will require a supermajority vote. They may not include changes to increase revenues, beneficiary premiums or cost-sharing, restrict benefits, or modify eligibility criteria. Prior to 2019, certain providers are exempt from reductions.

The IPAB is an important component of the ACA, but it has stirred controversy (Manchikanti 2011). Its purpose is to recommend policies to Congress to help Medicare provide better care at a lower cost, which would include ideas on coordinating care, ridding the system of waste, providing incentives for best practices, and prioritizing primary care. Congress then has the power to accept or reject these recommendations, but it faces extreme limitations, either to enact policies that achieve equivalent savings, or to allow the Secretary of Health and Human Services (HHS) to follow IPAB's recommendations. The impetus for creating the IPAB is that "since 1984, annual medical inflation has exceeded annual overall inflation in every year except 1998. Over this same time period, medical inflation has on average been roughly 2.2 percentage points higher each year than inflation." [266]

Major criticism of the IPAB stems from the perception that it represents an unprecedented usurpation of Congressional authority. On March 29, 2011, a bill was introduced in the Senate by John Cornyn (R-TX) called The Health Care Bureaucrats Elimination Act (S. 668). The proposed legislation has 32 cosponsors. Its purpose is to "remove unelected, unaccountable bureaucrats from seniors' personal health decisions by repealing the Independent Payment Advisory Board." Similar legislation (H.R. 452, Medicare Decisions Accountability Act of 2011) was introduced in the House of Representatives on January 25, 2011 by Rep. David Roe (R-TX). It has 200 cosponsors.

Patient-Centered Outcomes Research Institute

"The Patient-Centered Outcomes Research Institute (PCORI) was established by the ACA to promote comparative effectiveness research (CER) to assist patients, clinicians, purchasers, and policy-makers in making informed health decisions by advancing the quality and relevance of evidence concerning the manner in which diseases, disorders, and other health conditions can effectively and appropriately be prevented, diagnosed, treated, monitored, and managed through research and evidence synthesis" (Manchikanti 2011). PCORI is a private nonprofit, tax-exempt corporation. "The ACA's directive is that the institute shall enter into contracts for the management of funding and conduct of research with government agencies and academic or private sector research entities and that it shall give preference to the Agency for Healthcare Research and Quality (AHRQ) and National Institutes of Health (NIH)."

Similar to other aspects of the ACA, it is not immune to criticism. Opponents view it as a "politically-driven program with the attendant dangers of central planning." Recipients of health care services are seen as being "at risk of having stakeholders who are not scientists or physicians setting the final agenda, using political and financial, rather than medical, criteria.

---

266. Manchikanti, L. et al. The Independent Payment Advisory Board, *Pain Physician*, Vol. 14, Issue 4, July-August 2011, pp. E313-E342.

The entity would be without congressional oversight, freeing it from the usual checks and balances." [267]

"The Institute will convene a Board of Governors consisting of the following: the Director of the Agency for Healthcare Research and Quality (AHRQ) (or designee), the Director of the National Institutes of Health (NIH) (or designee), and 17 members appointed by the Comptroller General: 3 representing patients and consumers, 5 representing providers, 3 representing private payers, 1 representing pharmaceutical companies, 1 quality improvement or health services research independent researcher, and 2 representatives of the federal or state government" (Albright 2011). [268]

Primary Care and the Affordable Care Act

Chapter 11 will address issues pertaining to the health workforce, but a few comments about primary care are worth mentioning in the present chapter. Provisions of the ACA "expand Medicaid to all individuals in families earning less than 133% of the federal poverty level (FPL) and make available subsidies to uninsured lower-income Americans (133% to 400% of FPL) without access to employer-based coverage to purchase insurance in new exchanges (Hofer 2011). This expanded coverage is predicted to increase by 2019 the number of annual primary care visits between 15.07 million and 24.26 million. Assuming stable levels of physicians' productivity, between 4,307 and 6,940 additional primary care physicians would be needed to accommodate this increase."

Since primary care physicians typically serve as the point of entry into the health care delivery system, an adequate supply of them is critical to meeting the "anticipated increase in demand for medical care resulting from the expansion of coverage. The expected increase in primary care utilization resulting from the ACA's expansion of insurance has created new concerns about the number and geographic distribution of providers as well as the ability of providers to deliver care to patients in a timely manner. It will be very difficult to meet the short-term and long-term needs for more primary care physicians simply through changes in medical school and graduate medical education policies." [269]

"With expanded access to primary care for millions of new patients, physicians and policymakers face increased pressure to solve the perennial shortage of primary care practitioners (Jacobson 2011). Despite the controversy surrounding its enactment, the ACA should motivate organized medicine to take the lead in shaping new strategies for meeting the nation's primary care needs. First, physicians and medical professional organizations should abandon their longstanding opposition to nonphysician practitioners (NPPs) as primary care providers. Second, physicians should re-imagine how primary care is delivered, including shifting routine care to NPPs while retaining responsibility for complex patients and oversight of new primary care arrangements. Third, the ACA's focus on wellness and prevention creates opportunities for physicians to integrate population health into primary care practice."

267. Manchikanti, L. et al. The Impact of Comparative Effectiveness Research on Interventional Pain Management: Evolution from Medicare Modernization Act to Patient Protection and Affordable Care Act and the Patient-Centered Outcomes Research Institute, *Pain Physician*, Vol. 14, Issue 3, May-June 2011, pp. E249-E282.

268. Albright, H.W. et al. The Implications of the 2010 Patient Protection and Affordable Act and the Health Care and Education Reconciliation Act on Cancer Care Delivery, *Cancer*, Vol. 117, Issue 8, April 15, 2011, pp. 1564-1574.

269. Hofer, A.N. et al. Expansion of Coverage under the Patient Protection and Affordable Care Act and Primary Care Utilization, *The Milbank Quarterly*, Vol. 89, No. 1, March 2011, p. 69-89.

Several demographic factors will exacerbate the looming physician shortage:

- "First, the nation's population will continue to grow. Between 2006 and 2025, the U.S. Census Bureau projects population growth of some 50 million.
- "Second, the ACA provides access to health insurance for approximately 32 million Americans.
- "Third, the percentage of physicians choosing to enter the field of general internal medicine is declining, while those choosing to exit the field is rising.
- "Fourth, attempts to expand the supply of primary care physicians have had only incremental success. These demographic changes will result in significantly increased demand for primary care, without the corresponding resources to meet the demand." [270]

Impact of the ACA on Specific Diseases Such as Cancer

"Despite the provisions in the health care reform law, decreased access to quality cancer care will remain the most significant obstacle for vulnerable populations (Moy 2011). A major concern with respect to the expansion of Medicaid is that participation of health care providers in Medicaid is in jeopardy, particularly in states that are economically poorer. Some health care providers may be unable to accept additional Medicaid patients because of low reimbursement levels, leading to lower access to health care. Currently, some states are reporting more cuts in Medicaid payments, further reducing the value of this coverage. The law provides for increased reimbursement under Medicaid (to Medicare rates) for primary care services for a limited number of years and for bonus payments for primary care and major surgical services performed in Health Professional Shortage Areas, also for a limited number of years. Neither of these provisions, however, would apply to care for patients with cancer."

"Even more concerning is that there is convincing evidence that adult patients with cancer who are covered by Medicaid have poor clinical outcomes similar to those of uninsured patients. Therefore, Medicaid expansion would not necessarily be expected to improve cancer outcomes among vulnerable populations as the system currently stands. Given the anticipated expansion in the Medicaid population, the quality of care under the Medicaid program may be further compromised. Although it is preferable to provide uninsured patients with some kind of insurance, it is unlikely that simply expanding the Medicaid program in its current form will lead to substantial improvements in patient outcomes."

"Also of great concern is inadequate reimbursement under the Medicaid program. Given the longstanding concern that current Medicaid coverage does not significantly improve individuals' access to quality cancer care, policy makers should consider ways to improve coverage for Medicaid patients. Lower Medicaid reimbursement is particularly problematic in pediatric cancer centers that are mandated to provide a high level of care for all pediatric patients with cancer, regardless of insurance status." [271]

---

270. Jacobson, P.D. and Jazowski, B.A. Physicians, the Affordable Care Act, and Primary Care: Disruptive Change or Business as Usual? *Journal of General Internal Medicine*, Vol. 26, No. 8, August 2011, pp. 934-937.

271. Moy, B. et al. American Society of Clinical Oncology Policy Statement: Opportunities in the Patient and Protection and Affordable Care Act to Reduce Cancer Care Disparities, *Journal of Clinical Oncology*. Published ahead of print on August 1, 2011. On the Web at http://jco.ascopubs.org.libproxy3.umdnj.edu/content/early/2011/08/01/ JCO.2011.35.8903.full.pdf+html?sid=da950656-a2e1-4a34-ac33-24f88118bafb. Accessed on August 10, 2011.

Repeal of the Affordable Care Act

Tremendous clamor preceded the enactment of the ACA and the din never died down after it became the law of the land. Critics assail the legislation based on the belief that the U.S. should not have socialized medicine, the ACA will cost more money rather than lead to cost savings, health care will be rationed, and employers will stop providing health insurance for workers.

As is true of just about every other single aspect of the predicted impact of the ACA, there is little agreement about what employers will do. Unlike the Congressional Budget Office, which estimates that only about 7% of employees currently covered by employer-sponsored insurance (ESI) will have to switch to subsidized-exchange policies in 2014, McKinsey & Company estimates "that overall, 30% of employers will definitely or probably stop offering ESI in the years after 2014. Among employers with a high awareness of reform, this proportion increases to more than 50% and upward of 60% will pursue some alternative to traditional ESI" (Singhal 2011).[272] The report has been criticized in many quarters, but McKinsey stands by its estimates, asserting that its data are based on an opinion survey of corporations rather than individuals.

The future of health reform is unpredictable. Nobody knows who will control Congress and the White House after the 2012 election. Even if Republicans gain control in both chambers and the Oval Office, they can expect a vociferous outcry if they try to repeal the ACA. Individuals tend to be loss-averse and once they obtain a benefit will strenuously resist parting with it. Examples are Medicare beneficiaries who will profit from changes in the Medicare donut hole that will lessen their out-of-pocket expenses, a reversal of prohibitions by insurance companies that deny coverage for children's health care because of preexisting conditions, and youngsters up to the age of 26 who can continue to receive coverage through their parents' health plans.

Related examples can be found among legislators, hospital administrators, academic health centers, and manufacturers of materials used in providing health care (Fuchs 2011). Legislators might oppose reforms "that would make U.S. health care more cost-effective because they seek campaign contributions from health industry stakeholders that benefit from current inefficient arrangements." Any sector that stands to sustain losses by health reform initiatives "will fight harder to oppose change than the more diffuse potential winners will fight to support it."

"Hospital administrators often resist efforts to reduce hospital occupancy for fear that decreases in revenue will jeopardize their ability to cover large fixed costs. The solution requires a change either in the way hospitals and physicians are paid or in incentives for consumers to select lower-cost, high-quality hospitals, or both. Administrators also fear that if they attempt to change physicians' behavior to reduce costs, physicians will admit their patients to other hospitals."

"Academic health centers are typically slow to adopt cost-saving innovations in care delivery because they may conflict with, or be perceived as conflicting with, the centers' research and education missions. Meanwhile, manufacturers of drugs, medical devices, and equipment have the most to lose from the diffusion of more cost-effective care. If a manufacturer has a unique product, it can sell it at a high price that yields a monopoly profit. But since there are alternatives to most medical products, firms seek to create the perception that their products are unique in order to justify high prices."

---

272. Singhal, S. et al. How U.S. Health Care Reform Will Affect Employee Benefits, *McKinsey Quarterly*, June 2011, On the Web at http://www.mckinseyquarterly.com/How_US_health_care_reform_will_affect_employee_benefits_2813. Accessed on August 3, 2011.

"Marketing to consumers and physicians will be much less successful if purchasing and pre-scribing decisions are made by organizations such as managed-care plans or accountable care organizations that are motivated to provide cost-effective care. Such organizations have the incentive and the ability to evaluate competing products and can negotiate with suppliers for the best value. To preserve the present system, manufacturers of health care products spend heavily on federal lobbying." [273]

Regardless of what happens in Washington, DC, over the coming months and perhaps even years, it is likely that time and energy will have to be devoted to finding answers to the follow-ing basic considerations:

- How to provide equitable and comprehensive insurance for all.
- How to insure the population in a way that leads to full and equitable participation.
- How to provide a minimum, standard benefit floor for essential coverage with financial pro-tection.
- How to structure premiums, deductibles, and out-of-pocket costs that are affordable relative to family income.
- How to develop coverage that is automatic and stable with seamless transitions to maintain enrollment.
- How to provide a choice of health plans or care systems.
- How to foster efficiency by reducing complexity for patients and providers.
- How to improve health care quality.
- How to lower overall health care cost increases.

Closing Thoughts

The Accountable Care Act of 2010 is an enormous piece of legislation that became law to reform health care in the United States. Important provisions will go into effect over a stag-gered period of time. Each new step cannot be evaluated properly until it is implemented. Cost, quality, and access stand to be improved as new approaches to financing health care and reshap-ing service delivery unfold. From beginning to end of implementation, thousands of pages of regulations will be produced. Some will be challenged in the courts. Along the way, Congress and state legislatures also may try to reshape portions of the law. All three branches of govern-ment (executive, legislative, and judiciary) will play a role in determining the ultimate effects of the massive undertaking known as health reform.

---

273. Fuchs, V. and Milstein, A. The $640 Billion Question—Why Does Cost-Effective Care Diffuse So Slowly? *New England Journal of Medicine*, Vol. 364, No. 21, May 26, 2011, pp. 1985-1987.

CHAPTER 10:
Patients' Perspectives on Health Care

10

Patients should be at the center of all health care concerns, but differences between them and caregivers can obstruct the provision of high-quality care. The health workforce is faced with the challenge of furnishing care for patients with comorbidities who need a broad range of coordinated services. Patients characterized by health illiteracy will find it difficult to engage in meaningful communication necessary for effective shared decision-making with health professionals.

One way of viewing human life is to see it as a trajectory from the incubator to the incinerator. A critic of that formulation might consider life as a more lengthy passage that begins at the ovum and ends at the mausoleum. Strange as these irreverent descriptions might seem, they serve as a metaphorical basis for major disputes. Every year in Congress, a debate takes place about the wisdom of appropriating money that could be used for abortions. Some "Right to Life" advocates insist that life begins when a human egg is fertilized and that there should not be any attempts to end that life.

For most if not all Americans, life as a patient begins with the administration of the Apgar Test immediately after being removed from one's mother's womb. Being pinched or slapped upon emerging into daylight for the first time can be interpreted as being somewhat rude. Nevertheless, those first 5 minutes are exceptionally important.

The Apgar Test initially is given 1 minute after birth occurs. Five factors are used to assess a baby's condition:

- Activity and muscle tone
- Pulse—heart rate
- Grimace response or reflex irritability
- Appearance or skin color
- Respiration—breathing rate and effort

Each factor is scored on a scale of 0 to 2. Added together, the best possible score is 10. A score of 7-10 generally means that everything is all right. If it is in the 4-6 range, some assistance may be required to facilitate breathing. A score less than 4 will set in motion life-saving measures.

The test is re-administered at the 5-minute mark. If a score of 7 or above is achieved, no other intervention seems necessary. A low score will result in a decision to transfer the baby to a neonatal intensive care unit.

Beginning with taking in the first breath of air after entering the world until the last dying gasp, individuals will experience the role of a patient. Various emotions play a part in how interactions with caregivers are perceived and valued. A child, for example, may be terrified by the thought of having to go to a dentist. A strong, athletic adult male might lose consciousness upon being on the receiving end of a hypodermic needle.

A simple headache can arouse fear of a brain tumor. A chest pain can be interpreted as a warning sign of a heart attack that is about to occur. If symptoms of this nature result in a visit to a health professional or to an emergency room, anxiety can set in while waiting for the results of diagnostic tests. Notification that the results are negative and that doomsday has been postponed helps to create a sensation of elation and gratitude.

Some experiences can produce positive changes in behavior. A painful toothache can lead to a firm resolution to take better care of one's teeth and visit the dentist at regular intervals. A persistent cough among smokers may create a strong desire to seek assistance to cease tobacco use. Being overweight might lead to an inclination to become less sedentary and more physically active.

Apart from one's own health, the health of other family members can result in episodes where it is necessary to interact with health professionals. High fever in a small child can be especially worrisome. An older parent may need support and encouragement in making a decision to undergo major surgery or allow life to take its normal course without the aid of extraordinary measures to extend it.

Sometimes, different health professionals may offer different opinions on a course of action. Depending on where information is sought on the Internet, it may be hard to distinguish the bogus from the legitimate. Consequently, a patient may be in a total quandary about what to do next for himself or herself or for next of kin. Injury, or perhaps even death, may hinge on the kinds of decisions made when circumstances lack clarity.

Being a patient or even being well can present challenges in navigating the world of health care. Often, it is easy to be plagued by doubts and uncertainties about which path to follow either in seeking care or trying to stay healthy. Media reports can contain unreliable information. Disputes exist among reputable practitioners and researchers about the proper course to follow in areas such as prostate cancer treatment and mammography screening, as will be shown in later portions of this chapter.

Nobody remembers these first 5 minutes of life when an Apgar score is being calculated, so it is extremely doubtful that anybody will ever know if babies are capable of having any questions run through their minds then. If it turns out that they are of an inquisitive nature at that tender age, perhaps the best question they might ask on that occasion is, "Did I choose my parents wisely?" The answer to a great degree will be a key determinant of what happens over the next several years.

The Importance of Choosing Parents Wisely

- Parents can transmit inheritable diseases to their offspring.
- Women who use harmful substances in pregnancy tend not to have healthy babies.
- Married men and women tend to be healthier than the unmarried.
- Two-parent families fare better economically than single-parent families.
- Parents with low levels of education may have poor-paying jobs or no jobs.
- Parents who drop out of high school do not have favorable job prospects.
- Parents who smoke can produce an unhealthy home environment.
- Low-income families usually cannot afford high-quality health care.
- Low-income families tend to live in neighborhoods with many health hazards.
- Low-income families tend to live in substandard housing.
- Poor neighborhoods tend to lack quality educational institutions.
- Poor neighborhoods may lack grocery stores with nutritious foods.
- Poor neighborhoods may lack opportunities for physical fitness activities.

Apart from the aforementioned factors, here in the United States some babies enter the world as children of immigrant parents and as the offspring of particular racial and ethnic minority population groups. As patients, they may be at a disadvantage because of a lack of concordance with health care providers. As described in Chapter 2, patients may differ in various ways from their caregivers in areas such as degree of fluency in the English language, health literacy, trust, feelings of frustration, respect, and even age and gender. Depending on the extent of such differences, the quality of health care provided may be less than optimal.

Given such differences, it should not be any dramatic revelation to discover that health professionals and their patients do not interpret particular situations in the same way. A case in point is medical errors. Preventing them is a serious concern. The report by the Institute of Medicine (IOM), *To Err Is Human*, focused attention on the problem, particularly its conclusion that, each year, more Americans die as a result of medical errors made in hospitals than as a result of injuries from automobile accidents (Kohn 2000).[274]

Medical Errors

A survey was conducted of physicians and the public to learn their views on medical errors. The following questions were asked (Blendon 2002):

- "Have you had a personal experience with medical errors made in your care or that of a family member?
- How frequent and how serious is the problem of medical errors as compared with other problems in health care?
- What are the most important causes of medical errors?
- What actions should be taken to prevent medical errors?
- What should be the consequences for a health professional or institution involved in a medical error?"

The results had "implications for national efforts to reduce errors. First, major efforts to change hospital and medical practice are likely to face some important challenges. Even though significant percentages of practicing physicians and the public reported personal experience with medical errors that had serious consequences and despite the media's interest in the problem, medical errors are not viewed by either group as one of the most important problems in health care. The costs of malpractice insurance, lawsuits, and health care costs were considered more important. The public and physicians are concerned about individual cases of medical errors. When the patient is seriously harmed, both groups want some action to be taken. However, both groups believe that the number of in-hospital deaths resulting from errors is much lower than that suggested by the IOM and also believe that a substantial proportion of these deaths are not preventable."

"Second, physicians and the public differ in their beliefs about measures that would be very effective in reducing the incidence of errors. The public appears to believe that a range of proposals aimed at reducing medical errors would be very effective. However, the majority of practicing physicians view only two proposals as very effective: requiring hospitals to develop systems for preventing medical errors and increasing the number of nurses in hospitals."

---

274. Kohn, L.T. et al, editors. 2000. *To Err is Human: Building a Safer Health System*. Washington, DC: National Academy Press.

"In particular, although the physicians surveyed believe that high-volume medical centers have fewer medical errors, only a minority believed that moving patients to high-volume centers would be an effective way to reduce medical errors. This may be due to the belief that errors occur infrequently and that changing medical practice would therefore have a limited effect. Half the respondents in the survey of the public did not see an advantage of high-volume centers, suggesting a need for education of physicians and the public if a strategy based on the volume of procedures is pursued."

The results "point to a substantial difference between the views of physicians and those of the public on the reporting of medical errors to state agencies, a recommendation embraced by a number of national groups. The public sees reporting as a very effective way of reducing errors and wants these reports to be publicly available. Physicians are more skeptical about this proposal and would prefer that reports be kept confidential."

Finally, "the results point to a gap between the views of the public and proposed approaches to preventing medical errors. One of the central statements in the IOM report is that errors should be viewed as due primarily to failures of institutional systems rather than failures of individuals. This is not a premise that the public embraces. The public believes that persons responsible for errors with serious consequences should be sued, fined, and subject to suspension of their professional licenses. Nor do physicians seem to believe that individual health professionals are blameless. A majority of physicians believe that individual health professionals are more likely to be responsible for preventable medical errors than are institutions. Moreover, although few physicians believe that an increase in malpractice suits would be effective in preventing individual errors, many believe that health professionals who make errors with serious consequences should be subject to lawsuits."

The results of the survey "show that the public and, to a lesser extent, physicians hold individual health professionals personally responsible for errors. Although they support a requirement that hospitals develop systems to prevent future errors, the public is unlikely to support the substitution of a system in which individuals are not subject to sanctions." [275]

Mammography Screening

During the first year of the Obama Administration, which began in January 2009, it became evident that with a majority of Democrats in both chambers of Congress, a serious effort would be undertaken to achieve health care reform on a large scale. When President William Clinton embarked on a similar course of action, some opposition to his plan was energized by a series of television ads sponsored by the health insurance industry. In the summer of 2009, other influences took hold and portions of the electorate became highly upset about what they perceived as the kind of health reform the majority political party had in mind.

Their anger and frustration affected their elected officials who conducted town meetings in congressional districts and states across the land in August 2009. One concern was that health reform would result in higher health care costs and the loss of employer-based insurance. Another concern was the possibility that health care would be rationed, even to the extent that "death panels" would be formed to deny access to care by patients in the final stages of terminal illness. During the uproar that continued over the next several months following the summer upheavals, an event occurred that was the equivalent of tossing kerosene on the growing flames.

275. Blendon, R.J. et al. Views of Practicing Physicians and the Public on Medical Errors, *New England Journal of Medicine*, Vol. 347, No. 24, December 12, 2002, pp. 1933-1940.

"On November 16, 2009, the U.S. Preventive Services Task Force (USPSTF) released new breast cancer screening recommendations, resulting in considerable controversy (Squiers 2011). Prior to November 2009, the USPSTF recommended that women aged 40 and older receive mammography screening, with or without a clinical breast exam, every 1–2 years. The new recommendations endorsed biennial mammography screening for women aged 50–74 years. For women aged 40–49 years, they recommended against routine mammography screening, which resulted in considerable media controversy."

"The term *routine* was misunderstood by the public to mean the USPSTF recommended against mammography screening in all women aged 40–49 years. On December 4, 2009, the USPSTF updated the language of their recommendation regarding women under age 50 to clarify their original intent: 'The decision to start regular, biennial mammography screening before age 50 years should be an individual one and take patient context into account, including the patient's values regarding specific benefits and harms.' Reactions to the publication of the recommendations were published in newspapers, professional journals' editorials, and position statements by the American Cancer Society and the American College of Radiology, and occurred against the backdrop of public debate over national healthcare reform, raising concerns about the potential rationing of care through such recommendations."

Most newspaper articles and blog posts expressed negative sentiment (55.0% and 66.2%, respectively). The most common reasons mentioned for being unsupportive of the new recommendations were the belief that delaying screening would lead to later detection of more advanced breast cancer and subsequently more breast cancer-related deaths (22.5%) and the belief that the recommendations reflected government rationing of health care (21.9%)."

"National news stories described the recommendations for women aged 40–49 years almost twice as often as the recommendations for women aged 50–74 years. These results are consistent with previous studies that suggest a media bias in favor of mammography screening, which highlight the challenges that organizations like the USPSTF face in making recommendations that do not necessarily support regular screening and underscore the need for educating journalists and media organizations."

"Despite the media flurry, only 20.3% of women aged 40–49 years and 23.4% of all women in the sample correctly identified the mammography recommendation for women aged 40–49 years. Overall, the new recommendations confused women more than they helped them understand when to obtain a mammogram. Women aged 40–49 years were significantly more likely to be confused about when they should have a mammogram than the older age group. Because the mammography recommendation for women aged 50–74 years (i.e., every 2 years) was not dramatically different from the previous recommendation (i.e., every 1–2 years), this finding is not surprising." [276]

Health Reform Law Viewed as a Benefit to Women

"In 2009, more than 17 million women lacked health insurance coverage in the United States. A disproportionate number of these women were African American or Latino. In addition, many women aged 55 to 64 lack coverage through either their own employment or access to a spouse's plan at a time when they face an elevated risk of long-term and life-threatening illness" (Prickett 2011). Among its many aims, the Affordable Care Act (ACA) of 2010 became law as a means of correcting this deficiency.

276. Squiers, L.B. et al. The Public's Response to the U.S. Preventive Services Task Force's 2009 Recommendations on Mammography Screening, *American Journal of Preventive Medicine*, Vol. 40, Issue 5, May 2011, pp. 497-504.

Generally, women are "less likely than men to have coverage through their own employment or a lack of access to a spouse's employer-sponsored health insurance plan. These two factors, marriage and employment, can lead to greater insurance instability for women. Historically institutionalized gender roles have created a system that places women at a disadvantage relative to men in access to employer-based health benefits because men have traditionally been the primary economic provider in marriage. For example, it is estimated that more than 1 million women lost health insurance because of a spouse's job loss during the first year of the current recession. Disadvantages in employment and the traditional male bread-winner model create unique vulnerabilities for minority group women who have weaker ties to these institutions."

The ACA extends Medicaid to many pre-retirement age women, "but a large portion of pre-retirement age minority women live in states that have especially restrictive existing eligibility criteria, meaning new federal requirements will help to close the gap in insurance rates between minority women and their non-Hispanic white counterparts. Perhaps most important, state Medicaid coverage must meet adequate standards of care as defined by the federal government and it must match the same standard offered as the minimum benchmark package through the Exchanges that will come into existence. Despite these new standards outlined in the health care law, there remains potential for states to implement these standards differently, even more so with many state budgets currently in fiscal crisis and looking for ways to decrease Medicaid rolls. In addition, because of the high concentration of Hispanics in several states, which states ultimately implement the new eligibility thresholds as written could moderate or exacerbate the racial and ethnic disparities in access to health insurance." [277]

The Medical Home—Placing the Patient at the Center of Health Care

The American Academy of Pediatrics (AAP) is credited with the introduction "of the medical home in 1967, initially referring to a central location for archiving a child's medical record. In its 2002 policy statement, the AAP expanded the medical home concept to include these operational characteristics: accessible, continuous, comprehensive, family-centered, coordinated, compassionate, and culturally effective care" (Kellerman 2007).

Beyond the pediatric segment of the population, the patient-centered medical home (PCMH) is viewed as having a whole-person orientation in which "the personal physician is responsible for providing for all of the patient's health care needs or taking responsibility for appropriately arranging care with other qualified professionals." The concept "includes care for all stages of life: acute care, chronic care, preventive services, and end-of-life care. All elements of the health care complex such as hospitals, home health agencies, and nursing homes, along with the patient's family and community-based services, are involved." Care is facilitated by registries, information technology, health information exchange, and other means to ensure that patients get the indicated care, when and where they need and want it in a culturally and linguistically appropriate manner." [278]

Challenges have been raised about the acceptance of the PCMH in addressing chronic illness concerns such as varying definitions across clinical settings, doubts about their scalability to small- to medium-size physician-owned sites, and details about cost-saving capabilities (Sidorov

---

277. Prickett, K.C. and Angel, J.L. The New Health Care Law: How Will Women Near Retirement Fare? *Women's Health Issues*, Vol. 21, No. 5, September-October 2011, pp. 331-337.
278. Kellerman, R. and Kirk, L. Principles of the Patient-Centered Medical Home, *American Family Physician*, Vol. 76, Issue 6, September 15, 2007, pp. 774-775.

2008). Close examination of how terms "such as coordinated, integrated care, enhanced access, physician-directed teaming, and whole-person orientation" shows considerable variation in the number of elements implemented and how they are provided. Moreover, "if the recommended location of the PCMH's multiple care processes is under a personal physician's direction, not only is identifying a responsible physician difficult, but there also is a conspicuous lack of head-to-head studies demonstrating that the PCMH's physician-led elements perform better than similar programs situated elsewhere." [279]

"The PCMH has been proposed by four primary care physician specialty societies; has been endorsed by a range of purchaser, labor, and consumer organizations, including IBM, Merck and Company, the ERISA Industry Committee, and AARP; and is being tested in demonstrations by major public and private health plans, including Medicare, various Blue Cross and Blue Shield plans, UnitedHealthcare, and Aetna" (Berenson 2008). A point stressed is that "there is a need to achieve broader consensus on what medical homes reasonably can be expected to accomplish, and how they can best be developed in different practice environments and supported with altered payment policies." [280]

Health Care Quality

Donald Berwick is a widely acknowledged expert on the topic of health care quality. A physician, he was selected by President Barack Obama to head the Centers for Medicare and Medicaid Services (CMS). Prior to his being chosen, he was President and Chief Executive Officer of the Institute for Healthcare Improvement, an organization located in Cambridge, Massachusetts. His appointment was not met with universal approbation in Congress. Typically, such appointments have to be confirmed by the Senate. Many Republicans expressed their disapproval of his selection because they viewed him as being in favor of health care rationing. He also was perceived as being an admirer of the National Health Service in Great Britain, which is considered by Congressional critics as socialized medicine, a term criticized by political conservatives in the U.S. While Congress was in recess, President Obama appointed him as head of the CMS. Unless he is confirmed by the Senate, he no longer can serve in that capacity beyond the end of 2011. He resigned in early December 2011.

His opinions about PCMHs were expressed in a paper that he wrote in 2009. In it, he stated that "the question remains open about the degree to which medical homes will shift power and control into the hands of patients, families, and communities." He argued for a "radical transfer of power and a bolder meaning of 'patient-centered care,' whether in a medical home or in the current cathedral of care: the hospital" (Berwick 2009).

He described a situation in which he accompanied a close friend who was about to undergo a cardiac catheterization. She was frightened and wanted him to be with her in the lab for the procedure. The request was denied. In asking what was wrong with the picture, he reasoned that most doctors and nurses would answer that what is wrong with that picture is the "unreasonableness of my friend's demand and my own, our expecting special treatment, our failure to understand standard procedures and wise restrictions, and our unwillingness to defer to the judgment of skilled professionals."

---

279. Sidorov, J.E. The Patient-Centered Medical Home for Chronic Illness: Is It Ready for Prime Time? *Health Affairs*, Vol. 27, No. 5, September 2008, pp. 1231-1234.
280. Berenson, R.A. et al. A House Is Not a Home: Keeping Patients at the Center of Practice Design, *Health Affairs*, Vol. 27, Issue 5, September 2008, pp. 1219-130.

He found a lot wrong, "but none of it is related to unreasonable expectations, special pleading, or disrespect of professionals. What is wrong is that the system exerted its power over reason, respect, and even logic in order to serve its own needs, not the patient's. What is wrong was the exercise of a form of violence and tolerance for untruth, and—worse for a profession dedicated to healing—needless harm. The violence lies in the forced separation of an adult from a loved companion. The untruth lies in the appeal to nonexistent rules, the statement of opinion as fact, and the false claim of professional helplessness: 'impossibility.' The harm lies in increasing fear when fear could have been assuaged with a single word: 'Yes.'"

His opinion is that a patient- and family-centered health care system would be radically and uncomfortably different from what exists today. As examples, he cited the following:

"(1) Hospitals would have no restrictions on visiting—no restrictions of place or time or person, except restrictions chosen by and under the control of each individual patient.

(2) Patients would determine what food they eat and what clothes they wear in hospitals (to the extent that health status allows).

(3) Patients and family members would participate in rounds.

(4) Patients and families would participate in the design of health care processes and services.

(5) Medical records would belong to patients. Clinicians, rather than patients, would need to have permission to gain access to them.

(6) Shared decision-making technologies would be used universally.

(7) Operating room schedules would conform to ideal queuing theory designs aimed at minimizing waiting time, rather than to the convenience of clinicians.

(8) Patients physically capable of self-care would, in all situations, have the option to do it."

He also would like to see the word *noncompliance* abandoned since he believes that in failing to abide by health professionals' advice or technical evidence, the patient is indicating something that needs to be heard and learned by practitioners.[281]

His comments bear a relationship to notions discussed in Chapter 2 on the topic of semiotics. The social weight of interaction between patients and providers often is slanted toward health professionals who have the most authority in the relationship by virtue of their greater knowledge of disease and how to treat it. This power imbalance may act as a disincentive to challenge such authority openly. Instead, some patients may take some or all such advice with a grain of salt and go about their business, disregarding what they have been instructed to do.

Patients' Perception of Hospital Care

In one study, the following questions were addressed (Jha 2008):

- "How do U.S. hospitals perform on measurements of patients' experiences?
- Is performance with respect to one element of a patient's experience (e.g., communication with physicians) related to performance with respect to another element (e.g., communication with nurses)?
- Do patients who receive care in hospitals with three key characteristics (being a for-profit hospital, having a higher ratio of nurses to patient-days, and being a nonteaching hospital) report better experiences than patients in hospitals without these characteristics?

281. Berwick, D.M. What 'Patient-Centered' Should Mean: Confessions of an Extremist, *Health Affairs Web Exclusive*, Vol. 28, No. 4, July/August 2009, pp. w555-w565

- Is a hospital's ability to provide patient-centered care related to its performance on measures of clinical quality?
- How variable is the performance of hospitals across regions?"

The results indicated that although "most patients were generally satisfied with their care, there was room for improvement. Patients who received care in hospitals with a high ratio of nurses to patient-days reported somewhat better experiences than those who received care in hospitals with a lower ratio, and hospitals that performed well on the Hospital Consumer Assessment of Healthcare Providers and Systems (HCAHPS) survey generally provided a higher quality of care across all measures of clinical quality than did those that did not perform well on the survey, although the strength of this relationship was modest."

"There were large regional variations in patients' experiences with their care, with Birming-ham, Alabama, performing better than other regions and the New York City area lagging behind." Suboptimal performance occurred in areas "that have been the target of quality-improvement initiatives for some time. Nearly a third of the patients did not give high ratings in the domain of pain control, despite the focus on this area by the Joint Commission. In addition, despite long-standing interest by the CMS and others in reducing the rate of readmission, many patients did not rate their discharge instructions highly. It is less surprising to see that communication about medications was often not rated highly, given reports of difficulties with adverse events related to medications. Poor communication at discharge is likely to exacerbate these problems."

The researchers concluded that the "performance of hospitals is variable and that there are plentiful opportunities for improvement. Public release of data on clinical performance has previously prompted improvements in the quality of clinical care in hospitals." They are hopeful "that regular reporting of performance on patient-reported measures of quality will catalyze similar improvements in patient-centered care." [282]

Communication Differences Between Patients and Providers

The most prevalent cancer among men in the U.S. is prostate cancer. Each year, approximately 186,000 men are diagnosed with it (Rim 2011). "Once diagnosed, men face difficult choices about their care given the lack of clinical consensus about prostate cancer management and the uncertainty of benefits from each treatment option. Without definitive clinical guidelines and strong evidence to support one treatment over another, most professional organizations encourage a shared decision-making approach in which a patient and his health care provider interact to determine the best management for the patient. However, due to the many treatment options available and potential mild to severe side effects of each treatment modality, patients often may receive complex and sometimes conflicting information from several sources about treatment and quality of life post-treatment."

Apart from recommendations made by physicians, "patient decisions and preferences are also often influenced by family members and other caregivers. Cultural differences in communication style may play a role in whether, and to what extent, patients discuss treatment decisions with spouses/caregivers. Communication is a complex process, involving multilevel interactions, understanding of the content of discussion, and the relational aspects of cultures and

282. Jha, A.K. et al. Patients' Perception of Hospital Care in the United States, *New England Journal of Medicine*, Vol. 359, No. 18, October 30, 2008, pp. 1921-1931.

behaviors, which are critical to the decision-making process and for ensuring comprehensive, quality cancer care and outcomes."

"Race/ethnicity and cultural background have critical bearing on how cancer is discussed and processed individually and in partnership." Findings in one study "showed there were racial/ethnic variations in communication among the triad, although not statistically significant at $p = 0.05$. African-American family members more frequently reported feeling encouraged to ask questions about treatment options and also tended to report having independent conversations with the physician compared with whites. Family members of African-American patients reported fewer discussions about treatment options with the patient and appeared to perceive a stronger role in decision-making than white family members. Comparatively, African-American patients also valued recommendations of their family member more than white patients. Although data in the study for this population were sparse, a similarly higher proportion of Hispanic family members compared with all other race/ethnicities 'strongly agreed' their role was to support the patient by helping to arrange meetings with doctors and weigh the pros and cons of each treatment option." [283]

"Other studies that have characterized family involvement with prostate cancer treatment decisions among African-American prostate cancer survivors have also shown that men particularly value their wives' opinions about the best treatment option and that family members generally play an important role in making decisions about the treatment the men receive" (Jones 2008) [284]

"Provision of high quality patient-centered care is fundamental to eliminating healthcare disparities in breast cancer (Karliner 2011). California surgeons and oncologists caring for breast cancer patients report significant communication challenges when caring for limited English proficient (LEP) patients. The majority report less-patient-centered treatment discussions despite equal information-giving. Oncologists, possibly because of the complexity of options, are more likely than surgeons to report less-patient-centered discussions. Additionally, many physicians worry that their LEP patients do not ask all of their questions, and report more difficulty discussing both treatment and prognosis across a language barrier than across differences in culture and education. Use of professional interpreters is associated with more patient-centered communication. Despite this, there is a low rate of use of professional interpreters to bridge the language barrier."

"The first step to solving this problem is for breast cancer physicians across different types of practice settings to recognize that quality of care is compromised without adequate communication, not just of the facts of information but also of the nuances of treatment choices and decision-making. For LEP patients, this communication is dependent on use of professional interpreters rather than on family members, inadequate non-English language skills, or untrained staff. With the large and aging population of LEP patients, access to and reimbursement for professional interpreter services is vital to provision of quality health care not just in California but across the country. In addition, future research should focus on the development of efficacious multilingual communication tools to assist in complex treatment and prognosis discussions and assure that LEP breast cancer patients have all of their questions addressed." [285]

---

283. Rim, S.H. et al. Considering Racial and Ethnic Preferences in Communication and Interactions among the Patient, Family Member, and Physician Following Diagnosis of Localized Prostate Cancer: Study of a U.S. Population, *International Journal of General Medicine*, Vol. 4, 2011, pp. 481-486.

284. Jones, R.A. et al. Family Interactions among African American Prostate Cancer Survivors, *Family Community Medicine*, Vol. 31, No. 3, July/September 2008, pp. 213-220.

285. Karliner, L.S. Language Barriers and Patient-Centered Breast Cancer Care, *Patient Education and Counseling*, Vol. 84, Issue 2, August 2011, pp. 223-228.

Patients and Non-Physicians Providers
Such as Pharmacists

The past few decades can be characterized by many important changes that affect patients and the kind of health care that they receive. An increase in geographic mobility offers one example. Not so long ago, it was common for every member of a nuclear family to use the same physicians and the same dentist. When inpatient care was needed, they all tended to go to the same hospital. Currently, because of changing delivery patterns such as physicians being hired by hospitals and employers switching health plans, there is no guarantee of being able to keep the same physician or dentist even when employees stay at the same job and continue living in the same locale. Until electronic health records become more widely adopted, personal medical records may not undergo a smooth migration from one setting to another.

Another way in which health care is changing is that practitioners other than physicians are playing key roles in the delivery of care. Since it is unlikely that there will be an increase in primary care doctors that matches the growth in the general population, more demand will be placed on physician assistants and nurse practitioners. Another group of health professionals that can play a valuable role in primary care is the nation's pharmacists. Here again is another illustration of the discrepancies that exist between the views of patients and members of this profession.

Pharmacists' responsibilities have expanded significantly over the years, from primarily dispensing and compounding medications to include more patient-care roles (Oyelami-Adeleye 2011). "To an increasing extent, pharmacists are involved in developing, implementing, and monitoring therapeutic plans, counseling patients about medications, and managing patients' medical conditions. An important step towards the expansion of pharmacists' patient-care roles in the U.S. occurred in the 1990s, when the U.S. federal government enacted the Omnibus Budget Reconciliation Act of 1990 (OBRA '90) and mandated that pharmacists provide prescription drug counseling to Medicare recipients. Pharmacy professional organizations have further reinforced these clinical responsibilities through the development of new practice guidelines and initiatives."

"While many U.S. pharmacists have adopted or begun to embrace their new roles, the understanding and acceptance of these roles by patients remain a challenge." In one study, pharmacists and patients disagreed on:

- "The health care professional who should be responsible for adjusting a patient's medication therapy if needed.
- Answering patients' questions about their medical conditions.
- Helping patients to manage their medical conditions better.
- Advising patients about healthy living and preventing disease."

For all four items, the majority of pharmacists felt that both pharmacists and physicians should be responsible for these roles, while most patients attributed these responsibilities to physicians. "If patients do not perceive that pharmacists are or should be responsible for providing services that pharmacists and professional pharmacy organizations feel fall within the pharmacists' responsibilities, the benefits from those services will likely be undermined." Potential barriers to the provision of routine pharmacy care services "that still need to be resolved include differences in pharmacists' comfort level and their own perceived abilities, obtaining sufficient reimbursement for their time, and documenting the beneficial outcomes that would result from service provision across a variety of patients." [286]

Patients and Their Use of Medications

Older patients, in particular, often have comorbidities that require the daily use of several medications. For example to regulate heart rate, lower cholesterol levels, and control atrial fibrillation, a patient may be taking the following: ramipril, nadolol, aspirin, folic acid, amiodarone, Pradaxa®, Lipitor®, and Niaspan®. Include a back strain at some juncture that results in metaxalone being prescribed, and it is easy to envision how a patient can be confused. Remembering when to take all these pills, which may include cutting standard-size tablets in half for a smaller dosage, requires a strong attention to detail. Older patients with vision deficiencies and some memory loss may find it challenging to read labels on medication containers and be able to recall correct usage, especially pills that must be taken twice a day.

Adverse drug events (ADE) are a leading cause of patients heading to emergency rooms and their physicians' offices (Sarkar 2011). "An estimated 13.5 million ADE-related visits occurred between 2005 and 2007 (0.5% of all visits), the large majority (72%) occurring in outpatient practice settings, and the remainder in emergency departments. Older patients (age 65 years and older) had the highest age-specific ADE rate, 3.8 ADEs per 10,000 persons per year. In adjusted analyses of outpatient visits, there was an increased odds of an ADE-related visit with increased medication burden for six to eight medications compared with no medications, and increased odds of ADEs associated with primary care visits compared with specialty visits."

Population-based ADE visit rates increase with age. Adults aged 25–44 years old had a rate of 1.3 per 10,000 persons per year, those 45–64 had a rate of 2.2 per 10,000 persons per year; and those 65 years and older had the highest rate, at 3.8 ADE visits per 10,000 persons per year (Figure 1).

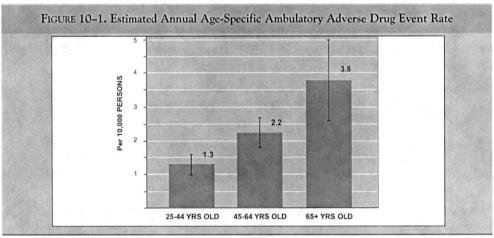

FIGURE 10–1. Estimated Annual Age-Specific Ambulatory Adverse Drug Event Rate

Source: Adapted from Sarkar et al., *Health Services Research* (Sarkar 2011).

---

286. Oyelami-Adeleye, I. et al. Pharmacy Patrons' Awareness of Pharmacists' Education and Routine Patient Care Responsibilities, *Journal of Pharmacy & Pharmaceutical Sciences*, Vol. 14, No. 2, 2011, pp. 306-314.

"At the physiologic level, the use of multiple prescription and over-the-counter medications increases the potential for drug–drug interactions and difficulties with self-administration. Second, multiple studies have documented the inadequacy of medication counseling in ambulatory medical visits and in pharmacy settings. Future research explicitly examining medication counseling and ADE risk is needed. Third, prior studies clearly demonstrate that patients often cannot accurately interpret or carry out medication instructions, clearly increasing potential for ADEs." [287]

The last point highlights the necessity of reducing the rate of health illiteracy in the United States. The U.S. Pharmacopeial Convention has proposed new standards that may be beneficial. They call for larger type size, more white space, clearer instructions, and critical information listed at the top of medication labels (O'Reilly 2011). Steps that physicians can take to lessen the chances of drug mishaps include the following:

- "Counsel patients on the name, dose, indication, and potential side effects when prescribing new medications.
- For each new medicine, use the 'teach-back' method, asking patients to repeat what they understand about the drug, how much to take and when, why they are taking it, and what its potential side effects are.
- Keep an accurate medication list for each patient and ask patients about medications prescribed by other physicians as well as any over-the-counter drugs or herbal supplements they take.
- Reconcile medications after a hospital stay.
- Routinely assess patients for medication side effects.
- Submit adverse events to the *Institute for Safe Medication Practices' Medication Errors Reporting Program*. Also, report serious problems to the Food and Drug Administration's *MedWatch* program." [288]

Physicians and other health professionals have important roles to play in monitoring how patients use their medications. A related consideration is the use of nonprescribed substances. Many patients may not believe it is necessary to indicate that they self-medicate because they were never asked about it. On a routine basis, caregivers should try to obtain a clear picture of steps taken by patients to maintain or improve personal health.

Adverse events represent one set of concerns involving medications. Another important problem stems "from medication non-adherence, the extent to which a person's behavior does not coincide with medical or health advice. Studies have shown that the prevalence of medication non-adherence varies from 8% to 71% (Unni 2011). Numerous factors such as costs of medications, disease conditions, characteristics of the medication regimen, relationship with providers, and psychosocial issues were found to be important in predicting medication adherence. Studies indicate that while 50% of patients on chronic medications are non-adherent, approximately 30% claim forgetfulness as the reason for their non-adherence, thus making forgetfulness a prominent reason for non-adherence. Patients may report reasons for non-adherence such as forgetfulness or carelessness because they perceive them to be socially acceptable responses."

287. Sarkar, U. et al. Adverse Drug Events in U.S. Ambulatory Medical Care, *Health Services Research*, Vol. 46, No. 5, October 2011, pp. 1517-1533.
288. O'Reilly, K.B. Quantifying Adverse Drug Events: Med Mishaps Send Millions Back for Care, amednews.com, June 13, 2011, On the Web at http://www.ama-assn.org/amednews/2011/06/13/pr120613.htm. Accessed on August 19, 2011.

The results of a study "established a significant association between belief in medicines and forgetfulness and carelessness in taking medications. Since forgetfulness and carelessness in taking medications is usually considered as unintentional non-adherence with no reference to the patient's beliefs in medicines, cue-based interventions such as phone reminders or alarms are usually provided to decrease non-adherence. However, results from this study ascertain that such interventions are not likely to impact adherence if beliefs in medicines are contributing to non-adherence." [289]

Shared Decision-Making by Patients and Providers

The example of prostate cancer mentioned earlier in this chapter illustrates that the provision of health care is more complicated than simply having a physician dictate unilaterally a course of treatment to follow, especially when different options are available. The patient himself and members of his family may want to be part of any discussion along such lines.

As the number of conditions with multiple evidence-based treatment options has increased, promoting effective shared decision-making (SDM), a strategy to match families with the most acceptable treatments, has become a public health priority. In this context, the Institute of Medicine highlighted the delivery of patient-centered care, the focus of SDM, as one of six priority areas for improvement in health care for the 21st century and encouraged study of the effectiveness of SDM (IOM 2001).[290]

"In SDM, both clinicians and families participate in treatment decisions, exchange information, express preferences, and jointly determine a treatment plan (Fiks 2011). For this process to be effective in pediatrics, parents of young children and pediatricians must have or develop an understanding of the other parties' perspectives on the child's health condition and its treatment so that communication and ultimately joint decisions reflect the needs, preferences, and goals of families as well as the scientific evidence."

"ADHD (Attention Deficit Hyperactivity Disorder) is the most common neuro-developmental disorder in children and adolescents, with prevalence estimates between 3% and 16%, depending upon the sample and measurement techniques used. ADHD is an ideal prototype for the study of SDM in children's health care for several reasons: there are multiple evidence-based treatment options, including behavior therapy and medication; disparities exist in the receipt of evidence-based treatments; and personal and cultural values influence the acceptability of treatment. Following promulgation of national guidelines from the American Academy of Pediatrics (AAP), pediatricians have increasingly assumed a leading role in managing ADHD. Reflecting the importance of SDM in treatment, these guidelines emphasize involving families in treatment decisions, eliciting treatment preferences, and targeting care to families' goals. Little guidance is provided, however, about how to elicit preferences and goals, how these may differ across the population, and what steps must be taken to implement SDM in pediatric practice effectively."

In a freelisting study, parents of children with ADHD and primary care pediatricians "listed words reflecting their understanding of (1) Attention Deficit Hyperactivity Disorder (ADHD), (2) getting/offering help for ADHD, (3) talking to doctors/families about ADHD, and (4) 'mental health.' Parents' terms reflected ADHD's effects on the child and family, while clinicians

289. Unni, E.J. and Farris, K.B. Unintentional Non-Adherence and Belief in Medicines in Older Adults, *Patient Education and Counseling*, Vol. 83, Issue 2, May 2011, pp. 265-268.
290. Institute of Medicine, Committee on Quality of Health Care in America. 2001. *Crossing the Quality Chasm: A New Health System for the 21st Century*, Washington, DC: National Academy Press.

often mentioned school. Lists suggested differing needs and goals for clinicians and subgroups of parents in SDM: 'time' for clinicians, 'learning' and 'understanding' for non-college-educated parents, and 'comfort' and 'relief' for college-educated parents. Neither parents nor clinicians framed ADHD in the same way as 'mental health.'" The conclusion drawn is that "parents and clinicians, who conceptualize ADHD differently, should negotiate a shared understanding of ADHD as a basis for SDM. Treatment discussions should be tailored to encompass families' varied emotional and educational needs." [291]

To cite another example, in pediatric minor head injury management, the "vexed question of parental competence has long been of concern in pediatrics (Sobo 2003). Children are largely dependent on parents in identifying and addressing health problems. Physicians are, in turn, dependent on parents for helping children fulfill clinical agreements such as taking medicine, being observed, and seeking follow-up treatment. At least in the USA, where individual rights are highly regarded, adult patients are generally vested with freedom of choice regarding their treatment regime. But adults are not free to do as they like for the children they care for. Clinicians must decide whether they can count on parents to institute children's home care plans."

The "competent" parent is the parent that is viewed as reliable in this regard. A study to determine factors that indicate that kind of reliability led to two main findings. "First, parental competence is not interpreted the same by all physicians. It seems to be a context-specific construct. Subgroups of physicians with distinct models may exist. Training may be one key independent variable. Second, physicians who are less certain about how to evaluate parental competence and have less experience making such evaluations may be more likely to order discretionary CT scans. Surgical specialization seems to be a risk factor. Guidelines supporting informed parental competence decision-making (and physician training in this skill) may decrease the number of unnecessary CTs." [292]

Patients are not totally blame-free when unfavorable health outcomes occur. "A growing body of evidence indicates that the earlier health-enhancing behaviors are adopted, the greater the likelihood that chronic illnesses that differentially affect older racial/ethnic minorities can be reduced or prevented (August 2011)."

"One such health behavior, regular physical activity, has been found to be critical for preventing morbidity and mortality, especially among older adults." Specifically regarding physical activity, "middle-aged racial/ethnic minorities generally fared worse than whites, although these disparities diminished in late adulthood." In one study, it was "particularly true among more acculturated, English-proficient minorities, including African American/blacks. These results are consistent with other studies, which have demonstrated racial/ethnic disparities in leisure-time physical activity, such that racial/ethnic minorities, including African American/blacks, Latinos, and Asian/Pacific Islanders, tended to be less physically active compared to whites."

When they come to the United States, "immigrants tend to be healthier, but over time, adopt a less healthy lifestyle. The generally low rates of engagement in physical activity across all racial/ethnic categories highlight the need to consider important barriers to exercise. For example, disparities in physical activity may be a function of health-related factors as well as the lack of environmental and social resources available to these individuals such as the absence of safe public parks or recreational facilities."

---

291. Fiks, A.G. et al. Using Freelisting to Understand Shared Decision Making in ADHD: Parents' and Pediatricians' Perspectives, *Patient Education and Counseling*, Vol. 84, Issue 2, August 2011, pp. 236-244.

292. Sobo, E.J. and Kurtin, P. Variation in Physicians' Definitions of the Competent Parent and Other Barriers to Guideline Adherence: The Case of Pediatric Minor Head Injury Management, *Social Science & Medicine*, Vol. 56, No. 12, June 2003, pp. 2479-2491.

"Physically demanding occupations, which are common among individuals of lower socio - economic status, usually involve less flexible work schedules and fewer opportunities for engagement in leisure-time activities. Although health issues may serve as a barrier to exercise, paradoxically, older adults with a chronic condition may be motivated to exercise, which might partially explain why rates of engagement in moderate activity are higher among this age group. Another possible explanation for the lack of disparities in late adulthood is that these older individuals, regardless of race or ethnicity, may be physically resilient individuals who survived the various chronic conditions and associated disability of middle adulthood." [293]

Taking the Patient's Point of View into Account

A positive development has been a gradual transition in medicine from viewing patients as pathological specimens to individuals who are entitled to state their views about how the treatment that they receive corresponds to their perceptions about the quality of their lives. More and more individuals are living into advanced years and are being kept alive despite the presence of many chronic conditions. The notion of patient-centered outcomes must be taken into account more fully when practitioners are making decisions about which course of treatment to follow.

"For much of the past 200 years, medicine has pursued the positivist goal of erasing the patient from perception (Sullivan 2003). A fully objective view of disease was made possible when the autopsy was integrated into clinical medicine through clinico-pathologic correlation. At the autopsy, disease can be studied and defined independent of the life of the patient as a fully naturalized phenomenon. The patient already is dead, so the diagnosis is not being made for this patient's benefit."

"Patients' daily functioning has had to be rescued from an overemphasis on clinico-pathological correlation. Geriatric medicine has been especially important in this area. Disease diagnosis based on categories derived from tissue pathology may offer little guidance in a geriatric physician's daily work with elderly patients. Given all the diseases that the very old have, it is odd but true that diagnosis and cure almost disappear from the physician's repertoire in caring for these patients. In geriatric medicine, the traditional fight against premature death and objective disease is often the wrong fight. Preservation of function may be crucial to make a life continue to be worth living."

"If patient-centered outcomes such as quality of life unseat the defeat of death and disease as the primary goal of medical care, then physician autonomy will be qualified further. Patient values will shape the goals and the means of medical care. Patients' lives rather than patients' bodies will be the focus of medical interventions. Definitive evaluations of medical effectiveness will occur within patients' lives rather than within doctors' hospitals. Neither society nor individuals can assume where pathophysiology fits into the lives of patients. Citizen-patients must decide what purpose medicine is to serve, just as they do for other social institutions." [294]

"Control of most, if not all, chronic disease requires adequate medical intervention. However, it is neither clinicians nor health systems that manage chronic disease, but rather patients themselves (Clark 2003). Unless psychopathology is present and unless medical care is

---

293. August, K.J. and Sorkin, D.H. Racial/Ethnic Disparities in Exercise and Dietary Behaviors of Middle-Aged and Older Adults, *Journal of General Internal Medicine*, Vol. 26, No. 3, March 2011, pp. 245-250.

294. Sullivan, M. The New Subjective Medicine: Taking the Patient's Point of View on Health Care and Health, *Social Science & Medicine*, Vol. 56, No. 7, April 2003, pp. 1595-1604.

unavailable or of greatly inadequate quality, patients can become expert managers of their conditions." [295]

No shortage of information exists on how caregivers can improve their performance, but patient decisions also must be factored into how the quality of health care is assessed. Some patients fail to have prescriptions filled while others take "drug holidays," i.e., several consecutive days without medication each month. As another example, many individuals who begin an exercise program abandon it within 6 months.

The list of unsatisfactory behaviors is lengthy. The problem is compounded when small children are involved who depend on responsible parents to ensure that medications are taken as required. Adolescence brings on another set of challenges. These youngsters are achieving greater independence and are at an age when they feel invulnerable. Fast driving, binge drinking, drug use, and other forms of risk-taking are among the many acts that result in death and the permanent maiming of members of this group. That kind of behavior does not lend itself too well to adhering to advice from adults regarding the necessity of taking medications and adopting other recommended actions.

"The health care choices of individual consumers and daily management of their own health can profoundly affect health care utilization, costs, and outcomes (Hibbard 2008). While there are sharp differences between advocates of a strong government role in health care reform and those who believe reform should be achieved primarily through the private sector, most health care reformers at least acknowledge that improvements in quality, cost containment, and reductions in low-value care will not occur without more informed and engaged consumers and patients. Payment reform and structural changes to care delivery only address one side of the equation. The other side is consumers and patients becoming more informed decision-makers and managers of their health."

"Activation refers to people's ability and willingness to take on the role of managing their health and health care. The Patient Activation Measure (PAM) was designed to assess an individual's knowledge, skill and confidence in managing personal health. The PAM consists of a 13-item scale that asks people about their beliefs, knowledge, and confidence for engaging in a wide range of health behaviors. Based on responses to the 13-item scale, each person is assigned an 'activation score.'"

"Individuals identified as highly activated according to the measure are more likely to obtain preventive care such as health screenings and immunizations, and to exhibit other behaviors known to be beneficial to health. These behaviors include maintaining good diet and exercise practices; self-management behaviors such as monitoring their condition and adherence to treatment protocols; and health information-seeking behaviors, such as asking questions in the medical encounter and using quality information to select a provider."

"Most importantly, studies show that activation is changeable over time. Consumers who get support for being proactive about their health from their care team, from their coworkers and supervisors, and from friends and family tend to be more activated and to engage in healthier behaviors and choices."

Research on patient activation suggests that individuals go through phases or levels on their way to becoming effective self-managers. These levels also are useful for designing interventions to help them improve their ability to self-manage. Four levels of activation based on the individual's overall activation score have been identified:

---

295. Clark, N.M Management of Chronic Disease by Patients, *Annual Review of Public Health*, Vol. 24, 2003, pp. 289-313.

- "At the first or lowest level, people tend to be passive and may not feel confident enough to play an active role in their own health.
- At the second level, people may lack basic knowledge and confidence in their ability to manage their health.
- At the third level, people appear to be taking some action, but may still lack confidence and skill to support all necessary behaviors.
- At the fourth level, people have adopted many behaviors to support their health, but may not be able to maintain them in the face of life stressors."

Levels of activation are shown in the following table:

Table 1. Level of Activation of U.S. Adults, 18 and Older, 2007	
Level 1 (least activated)	6.8%
Level 2	14.6%
Level 3	37.2%
Level 4 (most activated)	41.4%

Source: HSC Health Tracking Household Survey (Hibbard 2008).[296]

Businesses and the Cost of Health Care

By the end of 2011, ongoing tumult in the financial markets served as a reflection that the U.S. economy remains in the doldrums. Many patients are affected negatively by a high unemployment rate from one month to the next. Even when employed, other individuals have not enjoyed pay raises to the extent that they did so in the past, which can affect their willingness to seek health care and be able to afford it. Another important group consists of those who are not counted in unemployment statistics because they have given up hope and stopped looking for a job. Their ability to pay for health care also is affected adversely.

With the cost of employee health care benefits expected to increase in 2012 at more than twice the rate of inflation, large U.S. employers are planning to have workers share more of the cost, according to a survey by the National Business Group on Health. According to the survey, "employers estimate their health care benefit costs will increase an average of 7.2% in 2012, which is slightly lower than a 7.4% average increase in 2011, but it is on a higher base and it still sharply outpaces the economy's anemic growth and business conditions. To help control those increases and begin driving down costs to avoid the Cadillac tax on benefits that exceed a certain dollar amount, employers are planning to use a wider variety of cost-sharing strategies. (Sometimes referred to as a "Cadillac" or "gold-plated" insurance plan, a high-cost policy is usually defined by the total cost of premiums, rather than what the insurance plan covers or how much the patient has to pay for a doctor or hospital visit. Premium costs can be high for reasons other than generous benefits, including the age, gender, and health status of the customer. In an employer-based plan, premiums are based on the pooled risk of employees and may be higher if many workers are sick, older, female, or live in a region with expensive health costs.)

---

296. Hibbard, J.H. and Cunningham, P.J. How Engaged Are Consumers in Their Health and Health Care, and Why Does It Matter? Center for Studying Health System Change, Research Brief, No. 8, Washington, DC: October 2008, 9 pp.

More than half of respondents (53%) plan to increase the percentage that employees contribute to the premiums, while 39% plan to increase in-network deductibles. Additionally, about one in four employers plans to increase out-of-network deductibles (23%) and out-of-pocket maximums (22%) in 2012." The survey, based on responses from 83 of the nation's largest corporations, was conducted in June 2011.[297]

Closing Thoughts

Placing greater strain on household budgets by increasing the share of health insurance costs that individuals and families must share is not a good prescription for seeking health care services and benefiting from them. To the extent that health care is deferred, more serious health problems are likely to arise at a later date. Even when health care is affordable, interactions that occur between patients and professionals are not always as satisfactory as they should be. Chapter 2 on semiotics and Chapter 4 on race, ethnicity, culture, and geography illustrate the many ways in which caregivers and patients differ from one another. Changes in patterns of health care delivery mean that patients may have to deal in more involved ways with other practitioners such as pharmacists, which may affect the level of trust placed in these professionals and a willingness to engage in shared decision-making with them.

---

297. National Business Group on Health. Majority of Large Employers Revamping Health Benefit Programs for 2012, National Business Group on Health Survey Finds, Washington, DC: August 18, 2011. On the Web at http://www. businessgrouphealth.org/pressrelease.cfm?ID=179. Accessed on August 19, 2011.

CHAPTER 11:

The Health Workforce

11

The health workforce undergoes steady change. An insufficient number of primary care physicians means that other kinds of health professionals will have to be involved in meeting the service needs of the population. Scope of practice disputes in states around the nation may inhibit opportunities to obtain full use of the capabilities of members of different professions. Uncoordinated care must be addressed, especially for patients with comorbidities. Health professionals need to work more effectively as members of teams. Interprofessional education and clinical training should become a standard ingredient in the preparation of practitioners.

The need to have the federal government play a role in ensuring that the nation has an adequate supply of competently prepared health professionals is not a topic that typically generates much interest in Congress and in the White House. Over the past several decades, the main focus has been on containing health care costs and providing health insurance coverage to individuals who do not have it. Medical liability issues also become prominent occasionally from the standpoint of how an overuse of clinical testing as a defense against lawsuits adds to the high cost of health care.

For the most part, an implicit assumption seems to be that if everybody in the population could be given a health insurance card, most health problems would either disappear altogether or become prominently attenuated. Nevertheless, provision of health care requires the presence of practitioners. This factor is one element in the overall equation that does not always receive the amount of attention that it warrants.

Profound demographic shifts over the next two decades will result in significant increases in the demand for inpatient acute care services if current utilization patterns persist. An aging baby boom generation, increasing life expectancy, rising fertility rates, and continued immigration will undoubtedly increase inpatient hospitalizations and significantly alter the mix of acute care services required by patients. The aging of the population will be accompanied by an increase in the incidence and prevalence of chronic diseases. Every state in the union is experiencing an increase in the proportion of patients who are obese, demonstrating the importance of lifestyle and behavioral factors that can have a deleterious impact on health status. As mentioned in Chapter 7, improvements in health care are making it possible for obese patients with serious health problems to live longer, a development that adds to escalating costs.

Health Professions Education and Diversity

As the U.S. population increases in size, it will undergo profound changes. The proportion of non-Hispanic whites will continue to decline at the same time that the segment age 65 and older will become larger. More health care services will have to be provided and the size of the health workforce will have to increase concomitantly as a means of keeping pace with growing demand.

Currently, there is an imbalance between the demographic makeup of the health workforce and the diversity of the patient population needing services. Chapters 2 to 4 of this book discuss the kinds of problems that can develop when caregivers and patients differ in such ways as race and ethnicity, religion, language concordance, degree of health literacy, and socioeconomic background.

Throughout the health professions, a major aim is to produce a more diverse cadre of educators and practitioners. Increasing diversity among them has been identified as a societal imperative, most notably by two blue ribbon panels commissioned by the W.K. Kellogg Foundation in 2003 to conduct a comprehensive review of research and practices (Barnett 2011). A "brief builds on findings from a national study published in the May 2007 report 'Health Professions Accreditation and Diversity: A Review of Current Standards and Processes,' and outlines a set of consensus recommendations for ongoing dialogue and collaboration between health professions accreditors and health professions education institutions' administrative and faculty leaders."

Among higher education institutions, professional schools have a special responsibility to align their educational process with evolving societal needs and priorities. This responsibility is perhaps most clear among health professions education institutions, which are charged with providing their students with the insights and competencies that will enable them to serve increasingly diverse communities.

Three interacting dimensions that are the focus of attention are:

- **"Compositional Diversity**—numerical and proportional representation of population groups from diverse backgrounds.
- **Curricular Diversity**—diversity-related content and pedagogy to promote shared learning and integration of skills and experiences.
- **Institutional Climate**—environment that provides opportunities for shared learning among individuals and groups from diverse backgrounds."

Major recommendations consisted of the following:

Institutional Commitment and Leadership

"Current accreditation standards do not explicitly address the roles and expectations of administrative leadership and faculty in ensuring diversity among faculty, staff, and students or creating an environment that fosters the accrual of the benefits of diversity for faculty, staff, and students from all backgrounds. The lack of attention to this important issue contributes to significant variation in the degree and manner in which leadership is provided to enhance academic processes in this regard."

Admissions

An overriding issue in the "health professions education institutions admissions process is a lack of clarity and consistency in the application of Holistic Review (a type of admissions process in which an applicant's entire file is read and saved as a whole rather than in pieces) as a tool for incorporating diversity considerations in the evaluation of candidates for admission." While a growing number of "these institutions claim to have implemented some form of Holistic Review in their admissions process, there is significant variability in how the reviews are conducted (e.g., use and weighting of criteria, sequencing and application), which leads to questions about the reliability of the approach."

Institutional Climate

Increased understanding of and a "more complete definition of institutional climate that includes recognition of the need for shared learning across groups comprising a health professional education institution" are necessary. Numerous examples exist of "where campus-level special interest groups have been created, but most are student driven and often lack substantive support from schools, programs, and their attendant leaders. All too frequently, there is little attention to cross-fertilization across groups at the general campus level."

Social Contract

A general concern "is the lack of attention and focus on the social contract obligations of higher education. Fulfillment of expectations, particularly in professional higher education, can and should occur on multiple levels which include but are not limited to (a) ensuring optimal alignment of educational content with current and emerging needs in the communities where such education takes place, (b) outreach, engagement, and support for inclusion of students from diverse backgrounds, and (c) conducting research that both advances the field and addresses important societal challenges." [298]

Within each health profession, some challenges are more salient than others. In one situation, a difficulty may be an inadequate number of applicants to academic programs to meet existing and projected health care needs. Nursing and many allied health professions have had to confront that dilemma. In medicine, a major challenge is to attract enough students to embark on careers in primary care. The high cost associated with obtaining a medical degree and the huge debt load that results can serve as an incentive to enter a specialty where income will be higher.

Whenever serious health workforce shortages exist, market forces may dictate an increase in salaries to attract newcomers. If there is a serious imbalance between earnings of a faculty member compared to the income of a practitioner, then for important economic reasons, individuals may leave the academy for a larger pay check.

Depending on the profession, one way of recruiting faculty is to attract individuals who do an outstanding job of mentoring students during their training in clinical sites. Changing careers may entail many key ramifications such as a lower salary and pursuit of a doctorate degree. Simultaneously one may have teaching responsibilities with the expectation that a research project will lead to external funding from sources such as the National Institutes of Health and eventually to publications in respected journals and presentations at conferences.

In a survey conducted of its member institutions by the Association of Schools of Allied Health Professions during the period September-November 2010, concerning the 2010-2011 class starting in Fall 2010, the results from 88 respondents indicated that in 18 of the 19 allied health professions studied, available classroom seats were not filled (ASAHP 2011).[299] The data reflect the fact that some programs in certain professions are not attracting enough applicants. In other instances, there may be a sufficient number of applicants, but vacant seats still are going unfilled because some who apply are unable to meet established criteria such as a strong background in mathematics and the sciences. Another reason is that some youth may be unaware of various allied health careers. Yet another possibility is that different professions in other health fields may appear more attractive.

---

298. Barnett, K. et al. 2010. Health Professions Accreditation and Diversity: A Collaborative Approach to Enhance Current Standards. Commissioned by the W.K. Kellogg Foundation and The California Endowment.
299. Association of Schools of Allied Health Professions. 2010-2011 Institutional Profile Survey, Washington, DC: 2011.

The Health Professions as Moving Targets

An examination of the health professions reveals that they differ in fundamental ways from other vocational pursuits such as law or architecture. A trend in recent years is that in certain professions in order to enter practice, more education and a higher academic degree may be necessary. An example is *dental hygiene.*

New oral health professional workforce models are being developed and some changes require that dental hygiene education shift its focus to attainment of a bachelor's degree (ADEA 2011). One way to expand educational opportunities is in the form of bachelor's degree completion programs, which means that any dental hygienist who wants to earn a bachelor's degree can do so through flexible course schedules and credit transfer. According to the American Dental Hygienists' Association, there are 55 such programs in 32 states.

In dental hygiene, an associate's degree is the most prevalent entry point in the U.S. "Of the 301 Commission on Dental Accreditation (CODA)-accredited programs in 2008-2009, 86% granted associate's degrees." Accreditation standards for education "leading to an entry-level position (a minimum requirement defined as two academic years) have not changed in nearly six decades, which may explain the fairly small numbers of students who directly enroll in a bachelor's degree program." The importance of having a bachelor's degree not only will improve individual upward career mobility, but it also will improve the oral health of the nation by increasing the number of qualified dental hygienists available to serve as educators and leaders.

A "trend across the states has been to expand the scope of practice and decrease supervision requirements for dental hygienists. Many states now permit dental hygienists to perform some procedures without the direct supervision of dentists" as a means of improving access to care by underserved segments of the population. Target groups include "children, older adults, rural area residents, low-income individuals, and those lacking insurance coverage." [300]

Clinical Doctorates

The issue of in which states dental hygienists can provide particular services to certain kinds of clientele leads to a broader consideration of controversies that have existed for many years and undoubtedly will continue well into the future. As an example, the term *doctor* has taken on different colorations that have significant consequences.

One distinction is between a clinical doctor's degree, e.g., MD, and a research doctorate, e.g., PhD. The number of professions that have practitioners with clinical doctorates has expanded in recent years to include nursing, occupational therapy, pharmacy, and physical therapy. Added to the mix are clinical doctoral degrees that were established in earlier periods for groups such as allopathic, osteopathic, and naturopathic physicians, chiropractors, and dentists. Creation of newer clinical doctorate academic programs has led to concerns about the following:

- Creation of substantive changes to an institution's mission
- Availability of academically prepared faculty and necessary resources for new programs
- The increased chasm between entry-level certificate or associate degree programs and doctoral level programs
- Expectations of higher salaries, with the costs passed on to patients and the health system
- The impact on fiscally disadvantaged students

---

300. American Dental Education Association. 2011. Bracing for the Future: Opening Up Pathways to the Bachelor's Degree for Dental Hygienists, Washington, DC.

The last point is especially significant insofar as the more that course credits and length of time required in school increase, the higher will be the cost for students. Many students who fall into the category of ethnic and minority groups will find it even more difficult to obtain such degrees. Ironically, students from disadvantaged backgrounds are the individuals most sought after and needed in many health professions.

An additional consideration is that increasing academic requirements also means increasing resource demands on the institution. Financial models may work in tuition-driven budgeting (either state or private), but expanded academic requirements also may demand facilities and personnel that are difficult to obtain. Faculty shortages are common in many health programs and hiring additional faculty may be difficult to satisfy. Degree elevation may, through regional or professional accreditation, result in demands for raising the credentials of existing faculty. The costs and time frames for faculty to comply are issues that must be addressed.

According to the Association of Schools of Allied Health Professions, "the movement of a profession from undergraduate to graduate degrees or to the doctorate as the required entry-level degree could have a profound effect on institutions with established programs (ASAHP 2009). Many institutions with highly successful health professions programs are not chartered to grant doctoral degrees, or in some cases, any graduate degrees. The implications if they are required to go to a new level and their governing structure will not allow it are serious issues.

"Individuals with a clinical doctorate may not be perceived as holding an appropriate credential for progression into and through academic professorial ranks and tenure at all institutions. In such cases, faculty with the clinical doctorate may only be eligible for clinical faculty appointments tied specifically to teaching clinical practice techniques and supervising student clinical education experiences. In such instances, they should not be expected to produce scholarly outcomes beyond those related to improvements in clinical skills, practice regimens, or clinical education techniques." [301]

The Association also has indicated that "in some cases, there is not a clear distinction between *entry-level doctorates* in professions such as physical therapy and *advanced practice doctorates* in professions such as nursing (ASAHP 2008). Entry-level programs prepare students to achieve the knowledge and competencies of first-time graduates expected by and articulated by their professional associations or, more specifically, by the appropriate specialized accrediting agency."

"Advance practice doctorate degree programs are designed to prepare already credentialed or licensed individuals to practice clinically with competencies above and beyond those expected of entry-level professionals. Moreover, they are distinguished from research doctorates such as PhDs in that they may not require original research leading to a published dissertation. Instead, they may incorporate into the curriculum advanced practice rotations or residencies and a capstone research project demonstrating the student's ability to conduct clinically relevant research appropriate to the advanced diagnostic or therapeutic practices taught in the program. A concern has been that regional accrediting bodies may be unable in all instances to understand the discerning characteristics that distinguish entry-level from advanced clinical doctorates." [302]

---

301. Association of Schools of Allied Health Professions. Potential Impacts of Entry-Level Clinical Doctorate Degrees in the Health Professions, Washington, DC: March 2009, 5 pp.
302. Association of Schools of Allied Health Professions. Descriptive Differentiation of Clinical Doctorates, Washington, DC: February 2008, 4 pp.

Scope of Practice

A part from the widespread use of the term *doctor*, longstanding controversies have existed over which professions are allowed to offer particular services, such as prescribing medications. Legislatures around the United States often are embroiled in such disputes. On occasion, the Federal Trade Commission (FTC) may be petitioned by one of the contending parties to state its opinion on the nature of a legislative change being proposed.

Organized medicine has been at the forefront of efforts to prevent the encroachment of other professions on what it considers its practice domain. The rationale for doing so is for reasons of patient safety.

Examples of Disputants in the Health Professions

Ophthalmologists *versus* Optometrists
Psychiatrists *versus* Psychologists
Anesthesiologists *versus* Nurse Anesthetists
Allopathic and Osteopathic Physicians *versus* Naturopathic Doctors
Allopathic and Osteopathic Physicians *versus* Chiropractic Doctors
Allopathic and Osteopathic Physicians *versus* Podiatric Doctors
Dentists *versus* Dental Hygienists
Chiropractors *versus* Physical Therapists
Physical Therapists *versus* Athletic Trainers

By late 2005 and early 2006, the American Medical Association (AMA) and several medical specialty organizations were forming a national *Scope of Practice Partnership* (SOPP) to marshal resources against the growing threat of expanding scope of practice by nonphysician professions. An aim is to coordinate research to help specialty societies and state medical associations to oppose expansions in nonmedical scope of practice and improve information sharing among the various organizations. Legislative developments around the country are an example of the kind of information to be disseminated as a means of learning what strategies are being pursued by other professions and in mounting opposition campaigns when these groups have bills introduced in state legislatures, which are likely to advance to enactment. The purpose of doing research would be to accumulate national data on differences in training and education, academic requirements, licensure, certification, ethics, governance, and disciplinary processes between physicians and other professionals.

Not too surprisingly, just as every action tends to have a reaction, the *Coalition for Patients' Rights* (CPR) was formed shortly thereafter in 2006. Establishment of this group serves as a basis for monitoring activities of the SOPP and for communicating the view that the health care needs of the public are best served by professionals who have the necessary education and skill levels and that patients should have access to quality health care providers of their choice. The CPR consists of more than 35 organizations representing a variety of licensed health care professionals.

In 2010, the SOPP developed position papers on professions such as audiology and physical therapy. Associations representing these professions found it necessary to respond, particularly to portions of the documents that were deemed inaccurate. In addition to producing these papers, "physicians with the help of AMA model legislation plan to push lawmakers to establish scope of practice review panels to evaluate plans by nonphysician health professionals who wish to expand their practice realm (Sorrel 2010). The panels would be composed of various regulatory board officials, university experts, and other health care advisers to help lawmakers understand the underlying medical, educational, and public policy considerations." Another initiative that involves the AMA is "helping states with model legislation requiring nonphysicians to identify their credentials clearly. For instance, by wearing badges or limiting the use of the term 'doctor.'" [303]

At any given moment in any state, on legislative, legal, and regulatory fronts, professional associations attempt to influence which kinds of health care interventions should be their sole province such as the use of invasive procedures and medication prescription authority. As an example, in August 2011 the Kentucky Medical Association launched a public relations campaign called "MD ID—Know Who's Treating You." The effort will include newspaper and theater advertising, along with appearances on radio and television talks shows. A web-based component features a comparison of the education required for various health professions. Physicians indicated that the campaign was necessary after the 2011 General Assembly rushed through state Senate Bill 110, which allows optometrists to perform certain procedures such as some laser surgeries.

Although most battles occur at the state level, bills occasionally are introduced in Congress. H.R. 451, the *Health Care Truth and Transparency Act of 2011*, was introduced on January 26 of that year. The measure has 45 cosponsors. Unlike many pieces of proposed legislature that amount to hundreds and even thousands of pages, this bill consists of the following after its short title is stated in Section 1:

SEC 2. FINDINGS.

Congress finds that—

(1) many types of health care professionals including physicians, technicians, nurses, physician assistants, and other allied practitioners are engaged in providing services in health care settings, and all of these individuals play an important and distinct role in the health care delivery system;

(2) the exchange of information between patients and their health care professionals is critical to helping patients understand their health care choices;

(3) consumers are often unaware of the differences in, and seek more information about, the qualifications, training, and education of their health care professionals;

(4) evidence exists of patient confusion resulting from ambiguous health care nomenclature and related advertisements and marketing products; and

(5) nationwide surveys conducted in 2008 and 2010 revealed the depth of confusion regarding the education, skills, and training of health care professionals and indicated strong support for regulating the advertising and marketing claims of health care professionals.

SEC. 3. HEALTH CARE SERVICE PROFESSIONAL UNFAIR AND DECEPTIVE ACTS AND PRACTICES.

(a) Conduct Prohibited—It shall be unlawful for any person to make any deceptive or misleading statement, or engage in any deceptive or misleading act, that—

(1) misrepresents whether such person holds a State health care license; or

(2) misrepresents such person's education, training, degree, license, or clinical expertise.

(b) Requirement To Identify License in Advertising—Any person who is advertising health care services provided by such person shall disclose in such advertisement the applicable license under which such person is authorized to provide such services.

(c) Enforcement—A violation of subsection (a) or (b) shall be treated as an unfair or deceptive act or practice prescribed under section 5 of the Federal Trade Commission Act (15 U.S.C. 45). The Federal Trade Commission shall enforce this Act in the same manner, by the same means, and with the same jurisdiction as though all applicable terms and provisions of the Federal Trade Commission Act were incorporated into and made a part of this Act.

---

303. Sorrel, A.L. Organized Medicine Pushes Back on Expansions of Scope of Practice, *amednews*, January 18, 2010.

SEC. 4. *TRUTH IN ADVERTISING STUDY.*

(a) Study—As soon as practicable after the date of enactment of this Act, the Federal Trade Commission shall conduct a study of health care professionals subject to the requirement of section 3(a) to—

(1) identify specific acts and practices constituting a violation of such section;

(2) determine the frequency of such acts and practices;

(3) identify instances of harm or injury resulting from such acts and practices;

(4) determine the extent to which such persons comply with State laws or regulations that—

(A) require oral or written disclosure, to the patient or in an advertisement, of the type of license such person holds; and

(B) set forth requirements for advertisements for health care services with regard to disclosure of the type of license under which such person is authorized to provide such services; and

(5) identify instances where any State public policy has permitted acts and practices which violate section 3(a).

(b) Report—The Federal Trade Commission shall report its findings to Congress not later than 1 year after the date of the enactment of this Act.

SEC. 5. *RULE OF CONSTRUCTION.*

Nothing in this Act shall be construed or have the effect of changing State scope of practice for any health care professional.

SEC. 6. *AUTHORIZATION OF APPROPRIATIONS.*

For the purpose of carrying out this Act, there are authorized to be appropriated to the Federal Trade Commission such sums as may be necessary for each of fiscal years 2012 through 2016.

Given the fact that in any given year, thousands of bills are introduced in Congress, this particular item may never see the light of day in the form of committee action, passage by both chambers, and being signed into law by the President. Nevertheless, it does have potential to arouse considerable attention throughout the various states around the nation. Critics view the proposed law as being more inclined to protect the prerogatives of organized medicine and to criminalize competition than it is about protecting public health. Introduced on behalf of ophthalmologists, it would force optometrists to disclose their licensing status in advertisements and would empower the Federal Trade Commission to investigate them.

The usual basis for any dispute is the matter of the competencies necessary to ensure patient safety, which essentially pertains to the question of who can do what to whom safely and effectively under what circumstances. Earlier sections of this book have demonstrated that health care shortages exist in areas such as the primary care branch of medicine. Physician assistants and nurse practitioners are examples of professions that can fill the void.

The latter group has assumed an increasing role as providers, particularly for underserved populations (Newhouse 2011). A "systematic review of published literature between 1990 and 2008 on care provided by advanced practice registered nurses (APRNs) indicates patient outcomes of care provided by nurse practitioners and nurse midwives in collaboration with physicians are similar and in some ways better than care provided by physicians alone for population groups and in the settings included. Use of clinical nurse specialists in acute care settings can reduce length of stay and cost of care for hospitalized patients. The results of the review indicate that APRNs provide effective and high-quality patient care, have an important role in improving the quality of patient care in the United States, and could help to address concerns about whether care provided by APRNs can safely augment the physician supply to support reform efforts aimed at expanding access to care." [304]

Ultimately what is needed are studies that demonstrate that one group of health professionals can provide safe and effective care that is comparable to the group that is resisting the expansion of procedures by its opponents. An irony is that if state law prohibits certain practitioners from performing certain tasks, then it makes it almost impossible for that group to demonstrate that it possesses the necessary skills. Studies cannot be conducted if practitioners are not allowed to try to prove their capabilities.

One remedy may exist by having more consumer involvement in the resolution of practitioner conflicts over who can do what and to whom. An objective review of evidence by a group of outsiders may make it possible to loosen up some scope of practice restrictions. Another remedy might be to examine what happens in other states. If practitioners who graduate from accredited institutions and who have certification from national organizations are allowed to perform certain procedures safely in states A, B, and C, and there is no evidence that patient safety has been compromised in any way, then states D, E, and F should be able to change scope of practice restrictions that stand in the way of having other health professionals treat patients to the full extent of their powers.

Many disputes attain widespread publicity through legislative changes and action in the courts, but these are not the only combat sites. For example, the Medicare Relative Value Scale Update Committee is a location where primary care physicians have indicated that they should have greater representation on these kinds of bodies relative to procedure-oriented physicians such as surgeons. Decisions made in that policy arena have an impact on reimbursement levels. With the aging of the population and the presence of more comorbidities among members of this group, primary care physicians are required to spend more time with these patients and believe that compensation should reflect that degree of involvement.

Confusing Aspects of Health Care

Attempting to navigate the turbulent waters of which health professionals can do what to whom safely under what circumstances is a daunting task for even the most knowledgeable patients and consumers. Added to the mix are purveyors of various foods, beverages, and health food store products, which claim to create a state of nirvana among users.

A sore shoulder derived from playing tennis or swimming too vigorously can propel patients in any number of directions to seek relief. Sufferers can go to physicians, naturopaths, acupuncturists, chiropractors, physical therapists, athletic trainers, and kinesiotherapists. Each profession may use different treatment modalities in efforts to restore patients to healthy status. Failure to achieve satisfactory results in one domain may serve as an incentive by patients to shift to another kind of health practice. Over-the-counter medications or older medications from the medicine cabinet in one's home also may be used without any health professionals being aware of what alternative measures patients might be adopting. Sometimes, pain may be reduced and recovery enhanced simply by avoiding contact with any health provider, obtaining more rest, and ceasing to perform whatever action is at the root of the problem until a later time when symptoms have completely disappeared.

---

304. Newhouse, R.P. et al. Advanced Practice Nurse Outcomes 1990-2008: A Systematic Review, *Nursing Economics*, Vol. 29, No. 5, September-October 2011, 21 pp.

Another confusing aspect of health care, which affects not only patients but also practitioners and policymakers, is the lack of consistency in terminology. The term *allied health* provides an excellent example. Title 42, Chapter 6A, Subchapter V, Part F, Sec. 295p of the United States Code states that:

> *"The term 'allied health professionals' means a health professional (other than a registered nurse or physician assistant) who has not received a degree of doctor of medicine, a degree of doctor of osteopathy, a degree of doctor of dentistry or an equivalent degree, a degree of doctor of veterinary medicine or an equivalent degree, a degree of doctor of optometry or an equivalent degree, a degree of doctor of podiatric medicine or an equivalent degree, a degree of bachelor of science in pharmacy or an equivalent degree, a degree of doctor of pharmacy or an equivalent degree, a graduate degree in public health or an equivalent degree, a degree of doctor of chiropractic or an equivalent degree, a graduate degree in health administration or an equivalent degree, a doctoral degree in clinical psychology or an equivalent degree, or a degree in social work or an equivalent degree, or a degree in counseling or an equivalent degree."*

Although the statute indicates rather clearly what allied health is not, it fails to specify what it is. The Scope of Practice Partnership (SOPP) formed by some medical organizations lumps every profession outside of medicine as being allied health. Policy papers that are produced in both the private sector and in government agencies often include nursing and pharmacy as being allied health professions. Within the so-called allied health community itself, estimates vary about the proportion of the overall health workforce that allied health represents. Two-thirds is a figure often bandied about at the top of the range, while at the bottom the estimate might be as low as 20%. Whatever number or percentage is used is a function of which resource is relied upon to produce estimates.

Enthusiasm for the term *allied health* is somewhat less than total in some quarters. Whereas two decades ago 40% of institutions belonging to the Association of Schools of Allied Health Professions (ASAHP) had those words included in the title of their school of college, at the end of 2011 that figure is 20%. Over the years, changes have been made to reclassify these entities as Colleges of Health Sciences, Colleges of Health Professions, Colleges of Health and Human Services, and other related designations. In some cases, the modification is necessary because the school or college also includes other professions such as nursing and pharmacy.

In some professional associations, the label is disdained because of the view that each profession is independent, distinct, and not allied to any other profession. Another perspective is that the term is synonymous with the classifications *paramedical* and *paraprofessional*, which are interpreted as being of a second-class status. Confusion exists at many levels. For example, is a pharmacy assistant part of allied health or part of pharmacy? The answer may depend on who is being asked and who responds.

In 1989 an Institute of Medicine (IOM) committee released its report *Allied Health Services: Avoiding Crises* (IOM 1989).[305] Regrettably, many issues discussed in that document remain relevant today, although the environment is quite different. The demand for health care is growing as the nation's population ages and efforts are underway to provide coverage for the millions of Americans who lack health insurance. At the same time, escalating costs have led to a variety of initiatives to make the delivery of health care more effective and efficient. Similar to other professions, the allied health workforce has a role to play in achieving success from these efforts.

Given the importance of allied health in health care reform, the Health Resources and Services Administration (HRSA) provided support for the IOM to hold a workshop in Washington, DC, on May 9-10, 2011, to examine the current allied health care workforce and

---

305. Institute of Medicine. 1989. *Allied Health Services: Avoiding Crises*, National Academy Press, Washington, DC.

consider how it can contribute to improved health care access, quality, and effectiveness (IOM 2011). Organizing questions for the workshop were:

- What is allied health?
- Who is part of that workforce?
- What workforce strategies hold promise to improve access to selected allied health services across the continuum of provider professions?
- How can policymakers, state and federal government, and allied health care providers improve the regulation and structure of allied health care delivery to increase access to care?

Additional questions explored by presenters at the workshop included:

- What is the demand for various allied health workforce professionals?
- How will demand change in the future?
- What are the most effective forms of training and education for allied health workers?
- What is the relationship between allied health workers and other health professionals?
- What is the impact of allied health workers on health outcomes?
- How do regulations governing allied health workers vary from jurisdiction to jurisdiction?
- What are the consequences of this variation?

A workshop report was issued in December 2011 and is available on the Web.[306]

Interprofessional Care and Education

Whether the term used is *interdisciplinary* or *interprofessional*, the concept of having members of different professionals work together harmoniously in teams dates back to the early part of the 20th century. In recent times, events such as the conference *Collaborating Across Borders* (the third one was held in Tucson, AZ in November 2011) and special issues of academic journals have focused on interprofessional education and practice. For example, in October 2010, a Supplement to the Fall issue of the *Journal of Allied Health* was devoted to articles on this topic.

Reasons why better teamwork is needed in health care are described in a report by the Institute of Medicine in which it is noted that "health professionals work together, but display little of the coordination and collaboration that would characterize an interdisciplinary team (Greiner 2003). Many factors, including differing professional and personal perspectives and values, role competition and turf issues, lack of a common language among the professions, variations in professional socialization processes, differing accreditation and licensure regulations, payments systems, and existing hierarchies have decreased the system's ability to function, causing defined roles to predominate over meeting patients' needs."

A key implication is that "health professionals, both those in academic settings and those already in practice, must be educated differently so that they can function as effectively as possible in a reformed health care system—one focused on enhancing quality and safety. Most

---

306. Institute of Medicine. 2011. *Allied Health Workforce and Services: Workshop Summary*. Washington, DC: The National Academies Press. On the Web at http://www.iom.edu/Reports/2011/Allied-Health-Workforce-and-Services.aspx?utm_medium=etmail&utm_source=Institute%20of%20Medicine&utm_campaign=12.08.11+Report+-+Allied+Health+Workforce&utm_content=New%20Reports&utm_term=Non-profit. Accessed on December 9, 2011.

important, professionals will need to break down the silos that exist and seek to understand what others offer in order to do what is best for the patient." [307]

The combined effort of representatives of six health professions education associations resulted in the production of core competencies for interprofessional collaborative practice (Expert Panel 2011). "The transformation in education that is envisioned would enable opportunities for health professions students to engage in interactive learning with those outside their profession as a routine part of their education. The goal is to prepare all health professions students for *deliberately working together* with the common goal of building a safer and better patient-centered and community/population-oriented U.S. health care system."

A framework for moving ahead is four competency domains: (1) Values/Ethics for Interprofessional Practice, (2) Roles/Responsibilities, (3) Interprofessional Communication, and (4) Teams and Teamwork. A series of specific competencies is listed for each domain. Challenges to achieving these outcomes are described. [308]

One challenge has been to bring together students from diverse professions at the same time and place, at similar moments in their professional development, and to expect consistent, appropriate, and meaningful learning to occur (Graybeal 2010).

Barriers to Creating Interprofessional Education (IPE) Programs

- Inability to produce a fundamental cultural shift in an educational institution
- Lack of success in dealing with naysayer faculty
- Inability to develop a mass of key leaders to develop curricula
- Having IPE as an add-on rather than having it incorporated throughout the curriculum
- Lacking at least one administrator who can serve as a champion of the effort
- Inability to devote resources necessary for the undertaking
- Inability to obtain buy-in from professions that have lacked preexisting relationships
- Producing collaboration that is imposed rather than embraced
- Prescriptions by accrediting agencies that can limit curricular modifications
- Difficulty in finding common blocks of time when students can participate
- Implementing IPE in clinical settings with students lacking comparable clinical skills

---

"Another significant challenge is determining ways to develop the evidence base for interprofessional education and its desired outcome, enhanced collaboration in health care teams leading to improved patient outcomes. Consistent measurement within and across institutions will be needed to measure the impact of IPE on patient/client care and the subsequent paradigm shift in the healthcare environment." [309]

Some examples of the design and implementation of interprofessional learning activities are the Jefferson Health Mentors Program[310] and the extracurricular Urban Service Track at the University of Connecticut.[311]

---

307. Greiner, A.C. and Knebel, E., editors. 2003. *Health Professions Education: A Bridge to Quality*—Chapter 2, The National Academies Press, Washington, DC.
308. Interprofessional Education Collaborative Expert Panel. 2011. Core Competencies for Interprofessional Collaborative Practice: Report of an Expert Panel. Washington, DC.
309. Graybeal, C. et al. The Art and Science of Interprofessional Education, Supplement to the *Journal of Allied Health*, Vol. 39, No. 3 (Part 2), Fall 2010, pp. 232-237.
310. Collins, L. et al. The Health Mentors Program: A Longitudinal Chronic Illness Mentorship Program, 2009. On the Web at MedEdPORTAL:http://services.aamc.org/30/mededportal/servlet/s/segment/mededportal/?subid=4062. Accessed on December 7, 2011.
311. Clark-Dufner, P. et al. The University of Connecticut Urban Service Track: An effective academic-community partnership. *Connecticut Medicine*, Vol. 74, No. 1, 2010, pp. 33-36.

"Communications strategies are central to the planning and execution of IPE programs (Weinstein 2010). The diversity of telecommunications-based tools and platforms available for IPE are expanding rapidly. Each tool and platform has a potentially important role to play. Current financial challenges for institutions of higher education also are driving the need for new educational paradigms. Decreased endowments for private schools and state budget cuts for public schools have limited new 'bricks and mortar' construction, faculty hiring, and student enrollment for conventional university training."

"Modern telecommunications make possible higher enrollment and facilitated faculty coverage without the need for new buildings or increased faculty hires. Work on student team projects is possible at any time, rather than being confined to university classroom hours of operation. Faculty office hours can be expanded to permit more timely dialogue between learner and teacher." At the University of Arizona, the features and implementation of a first-of-a-kind amphitheater (the T-Health Amphitheater, or "Telehealth Amphitheater") was designed to serve as the hub for a distributed IPE learning center.[312]

Given the vast nature of health care and education in the United States, it is likely that many useful models will be developed (McCloskey 2011). While some may have unique characteristics that may be difficult to replicate in other settings, the fact that interprofessional cooperation can be demonstrated should serve as an incentive for others to strive to achieve better teamwork. Pioneering courses are being developed at some institutions, such as what was achieved at Boston University in an effort to prepare public health, medical, and dental students for their combined roles in community health settings.[313]

A course offered at that institution serves the following broad goals:

- "To increase and promote collaboration between medicine, public health, and dentistry.
- To strengthen partnerships with community organizations in nearby neighborhoods.
- To prepare health care professionals to be self-reflective and collaborative team members and leaders able to effect change in health systems and in the health communities."

Student Recruitment

In 2010, a $6 million initiative funded by the U.S. Department of Labor was aimed at creating a Healthcare Virtual Career Network (VCN), a platform for students and displaced workers to learn what health professions are available that might match their interests, along with information on what requirements are necessary to enter a particular field and how to fulfill educational requirements. Students and workers differ in fundamental ways. For the latter group, the incentive is to obtain a job, any job for that matter, as soon as possible. Working in the health care field involves a calling to serve others. As the population ages and chronic disease becomes more prevalent, it will take more than just wanting a job to perform effectively in that arena.

In order for the VCN set of activities to be successful, its availability will need to be well publicized. Target groups include state associations of health care human resource directors, one-stop workforce organization centers, high school and college fairs, offices within the U.S.

312. Weinstein, R.S. et al. Technologies for Interprofessional Education: The Interprofessional Education-Distributed "e-Classroom-of-the-Future," Supplement to the *Journal of Allied Health*, Vol. 39, No. 3 (Part 2), Fall 2010, pp. 238-245.
313. McCloskey, L. et al. Public Health, Medicine, and Dentistry as Partners in Community Health: A Pioneering Initiative in Interprofessional. Practice-Based Education, *Journal of Public Health Management and Practice*, Vol. 17, No. 4, 2011, pp. 298-307.

Department of Health and Human Services, conference workshops, libraries, faith-based organizations, unemployment insurance offices, national healthcare associations, community development agencies, and Housing and Urban Development (HUD) centers. Additional targets consist of existing health career websites and military personnel who will embark on new careers after their service in the military ends.

Until fairly recently in the pre-Internet period, there was a relatively low knowledge level by a great many youth about health careers. Fortunately, that situation has changed. A resource such as *ExploreHealthCareers.org* has proven enormously useful to prospective health professions students.

Many factors influence the choice of health careers: job satisfaction, salaries, employment opportunities, status, job security, and exposure to individuals who work in different kinds of health professions. The latter aspect can have a significant downside. In some clinical settings, a student doing field training might hear many complaints about the profession, even to the point of recommendations by disgruntled workers who advise students to choose another profession.

Other factors also can influence an individual's choice to pursue a health care career. An example is career stability, which in a sluggish economy is crucially important. There always will be a great many patients who need health care services. A sense of personal fulfillment associated with being a health care professional can lead to a satisfying career.

Occupational portability is another factor that can have an impact on the health workforce. Many health care providers are limited in moving from state to state due to varying licensure requirements. Other deterrents can include an undesirable commute, long work hours, work load, lack of nearby programs or poorly staffed programs, cost of education, and the length of time involved in the educational program. In addition, some uncertainty may exist such as in the case of the possibility of health reform having an adverse effect on the salaries/earning potentials of medical school graduates. When the debt load is high and the salary potential is relatively low, it should come as no surprise when a medical student aims to become a specialist rather than a family medicine practitioner.

A condition that might deter individuals from picking a health career is working different shifts in a 24-hour facility, which also may include the requirement of being there on weekends and holidays. As healthcare facilities try to cut costs, more job-sharing may occur, which can involve additional learning. In that situation, clinicians would be expected to learn multiple job duties, which may not always generate a corresponding amount of respect and interest.

Role of Government

The Affordable Care Act that was enacted in 2010 acknowledged the importance of the health workforce by creating a commission with a duty to report to Congress and the President about workforce matters. Unfortunately, as 2011 drew to a close, no money had been appropriated and not much can happen until the group receives adequate funding.

Several programs have been developed over the years to recruit minority faculty and students under Title VII of the Public Health Service Act. Administered by the Health Resources and Services Administration (HRSA), entities such as the Health Careers Opportunity Program were designed to attract and help prepare such students academically so that they could pursue a career in the health professions. The problem with many of these programs is lack of sufficient funding.

As an example, a *Health Workforce Information Center* (HWIC) on the Web provides information on health workforce solutions in one centralized and easy-to-access location. Resources available through HWIC's website will help health providers, educators, researchers, and policymakers around the nation to develop strategies to meet future workforce demands. Funded by the HRSA and operated by the University of North Dakota School of Medicine and Health Sciences, the Center offers the latest information on health workforce programs and funding sources; workforce data, research and policy; educational opportunities and models; and news and events.[314]

Site visitors have a broad range of publications and other resources at their fingertips. The site also offers free, customized assistance from information specialists (digital librarians), who will search databases on workforce topics and funding resources, furnish relevant publications, and connect users to workforce experts and federal programs, among others.

Another useful source of information about many health careers in allied health can be found through the Office of Science Education at the National Institutes of Health (NIH). An alphabetical listing of professions is provided, along with a description of educational requirements and median salary data.[315]

Many health care needs in underserved communities are met by the National Health Service Corps (NHSC), which has more money and flexibility resulting from provisions in the 2009 economic stimulus package and the national health reform law. In 2011, qualifying clinicians can receive loan repayment when working part-time and receive credit for teaching. Previously, clinicians had to work full-time and teaching didn't count as service. The stimulus package and the Affordable Care Act are providing nearly $300 million to the NHSC. In addition to physicians, clinicians who qualify for NHSC loan repayment are physician assistants and dental hygienists.

The Health Workforce of the Future

Demographic patterns in the United States will have a huge impact on health professions education and the composition of the health workforce that will be needed for coming decades. Colleges and universities will be challenged to have faculty and students more congruent with these kinds of population changes. A 2011 report from the Brookings Institution shows how the rapid growth of Hispanic and Asian groups and new internal shifts of African Americans are transforming the racial and ethnic demographic profiles of America's largest metropolitan areas ahead of other parts of the country (Frey 2011).

An analysis of 1990, 2000, and 2010 decennial census data for the 100 largest U.S. metropolitan areas indicates that: "non-whites and Hispanics accounted for 98% of population growth in large metro areas from 2000 to 2010. Forty-two of the 100 largest metro areas lost white population, and 22 now have majority 'minority' populations, up from 14 areas in 2000. Among the newcomers to this category are metropolitan New York, Washington D.C., San Diego, Las Vegas, and Memphis." Smaller metro areas and areas outside of metropolitan regions, by contrast, remain overwhelmingly white.

"The aging white population grew by only 1.2% over the 10-year period, giving way to the younger 'new minority' growth engines, fueled by both recent immigration and natural increase.

---

314. Health Workforce Information Center. On the Web at www.healthworkforceinfo.org. Accessed on Accessed on August 3, 2011.
315. National Institutes of Health Office of Science Information. On the Web at http://science.education.nih.gov/Lifeworks. Accessed on August 3, 2011.

The two largest of these new minorities, Hispanics and Asians, each grew about 43%—together accounting for more than 60% of the nation's population growth over the last decade."

"Three-quarters of black population gains from 2000 to 2010 occurred in the South. Atlanta, Dallas, and Houston led all metropolitan areas in black population gains at the same time that the black portion of the population dropped in metropolitan New York, Chicago, and Detroit for the first time."

"Average neighborhood segregation levels held steady for Hispanics and Asians, but declined for blacks from 2000 to 2010. Older and northern metropolitan areas continue to register the highest segregation levels for minority groups. Despite recent declines, blacks remain more residentially segregated than either Hispanics or Asians." [316]

Many individuals who are part of the segment of the U.S. population known as *Millennials*, members of the generation born after 1980, already either are practicing health professionals or are in school preparing to become part of the health workforce. At another point on the age spectrum, the 77 million *Baby Boomers,* who were born in the period 1946–1964, will join the millions of the *Silent Generation* (born in the period 1928–1945) and the *Greatest Generation* (born prior to 1928) who already are part of the Medicare program and are recipients of long-term care health and social services. These generation groups, along with *Generation X* (born in the period 1965–1980), have distinct characteristics that may have an effect on how health care is delivered in coming years.

A study conducted at the Pew Research Center involved four of these groups (Pew 2010). The Greatest Generation was excluded because of an insufficient number of respondents. Shown below are some ways in which the generations are either similar or different.

What Makes Your Generation Unique	
Millenial	**Silent**
Technology use (24%)	WWII, Depression (14%)
Music/pop culture (11%)	Smarter (13%)
Liberal/tolerant (7%)	Honest (12%)
Smarter (6%)	Work ethic (10%)
Clothes (5%)	Values/morals (10%)

Source: Pew Research Center. Millennials—A Portrait of Generation Next, 2011.

Other differences are that Millennials spend much more time using cellphones and the Internet, with the latter employed to post their social profiles and videos of themselves. Age group differences can be the result of three overlapping processes:

1) **"Life cycle effects.** Young persons may be different from older individuals today, but they may well become more like them tomorrow, once they themselves age.
2) **Period effects.** Major events (wars; social movements; economic downturns; medical, scientific or technological breakthroughs) affect all age groups simultaneously, but the degree of impact may differ according to where individuals are located in the life cycle.

---

316. Frey, W.H. The New Metropolitan Minority Map: Regional Shifts in Hispanics, Asians, and Blacks from Census 2010, Brookings Institution, State of Metropolitan America, No. 40, August 31, 2011. On the Web at http://www.brookings.edu/~/media/Files/rc/papers/2011/0831_census_race_frey/0831_census_race_frey.pdf. Accessed on September 15, 2011.

3) **Cohort effects.** Period events and trends often leave a particularly deep impression on young adults because they are still developing their core values; these imprints stay with them as they move through their life cycle." [317]

It is not possible to know yet which formative experiences the Millennials will carry forward throughout their life cycle. Apart from any superficial characteristics or modes of personal behavior, ultimately the kinds of citizens they will be and the quality of the health care that they will provide will be rooted in attributes that may be common to all generations.

These qualities will stem from the values that have been instilled in them by older family members. How they behave will be a reflection of their ability to sustain meaningful relationships with patients as well as with significant individuals in the form of spouses and their own children. Whether it be of a religious nature related to a specific denomination or a more general sense of spirituality, an ethical code will guide their behavior. Their willingness to work in team-based health care will have a direct impact on the success of patient outcomes. Their desire for lifelong learning will influence their ability to stay abreast of the latest developments in health technology. Their embrace of rapid advances in areas such as genomics will aid in the provision of quality health care. Finally, their ability to adapt will determine how effective they will be in the many alterations that will result from major health reform efforts.

Most of the members of this year's entering college class of 2015 were born in 1993, right around the time the Internet became widely available. They are the first generation to grow up taking the word *online* for granted and for whom crossing the digital divide has changed how they access information for class assignments. They have come of age when everything from parents analyzing childhood maladies to breaking up with boyfriends and girlfriends, sometimes quite publicly, has occurred on the Internet.

Each August since 1998, Beloit College has released the Beloit College Mindset List, providing a look at cultural touchstones that shape the lives of students entering college that fall. Originally, the Mindset List was created as a reminder to faculty to be aware of dated references. It helps to serve as a catalogue of the rapidly changing worldview of each new generation. Examples for the class of 2015 are:

- "Grown-ups have always been arguing about health care policy
- Nurses always have been in short supply.
- The only significant labor disputes in their lifetimes have been in major league sports.
- Charter schools always have been an alternative.
- They have broken up with significant others via texting, Facebook, or MySpace." [318]

Because of the economy and such reasons as the declining value of personal investment portfolios due to stock market downturns, some older health workers are postponing retirement. Newcomers to the health professions who are fresh out of school will have to blend in with these older peers. The extent to which they can do so harmoniously will have an impact on the quality of patient care delivered.

---

317. Pew Research Center. Millennials—A Portrait of Generation Next: Confident, Connected, Open to Change. February 2010, 149 pp. Available on the Web at http://pewsocialtrends.org/assets/pdf/millennials-confident-connected-open-to-change.pdf. Accessed on August 22, 2011.

318. Beloit College. Mindset List: 2015. On the Web at http://www.beloit.edu/mindset/2015/. Accessed on September 15, 2011.

Closing Thoughts

I nadequate numbers of health professionals pose a problem for a U.S. population that is growing in size, with significant expansion occurring among the oldest cohorts. Clinical laboratory science practitioners in allied health and primary care physicians offer examples of workforce shortages that exist. The issue of which groups of health professionals are allowed to provide services safely under what circumstances is at the root of scope of practice disputes in states around the nation. The cost of health care will be affected by which professionals furnish care, since personnel at one level such as dental hygienists can provide certain services at lower costs than dentists.

Complementary and
Alternative Medicine

12

Patients who cannot see a remedy in sight for relieving what ails them will be open to using whatever kind of health care holds the prospect of a cure. Immigrants arrive in the U.S. with beliefs about disease causation and best forms of treatment that may differ radically from more conventional approaches to health care in the western world. Such factors play a role in steering patients in the direction of seeking care from complementary and alternative providers.

Folk remedies of one sort or another have been used for centuries. For example, a classic influenza remedy of German-Swiss origin is to sleep in a four-poster bed. Place a hat on one of the posts and drink schnapps. Upon seeing two hats, one's flu symptoms no longer seem to be as annoying.)

In addition to health care services provided by various practitioners and the kinds of products and devices that can be found in places such as health food stores, there is a whole range of home remedies and folk practices that are transmitted from one generation to the next. Onions, for example, are viewed as an excellent remedy for curing the flu and pneumonia. Placing a raw onion in a jar by the bed or boiling one and inhaling it with a towel over the head can work wonders, according to some true believers. Carrying garlic in one's pocket has also been touted to work curative miracles.

Earlier chapters have focused almost exclusively on what typically is considered the conventional end of the spectrum of health care in the United States, i.e., facilities such as hospitals and individual practitioners in the form of physicians, nurses, pharmacists, and allied health professionals. This chapter moves the discussion to another path known as *complementary and alternative medicine* (CAM). It matters little whether one approves of CAM therapies or believes in their effectiveness. The fact is that patients use them.

As successful as conventional health care can be, it does not solve all problems nor does it consistently produce optimal levels of satisfaction among patients. A way of examining the issue of why complementary and alternative medicine is used is to consider two opposing views (Prasad 2009). "The first is that there is no alternative medicine, but only scientifically proven, evidence-based medicine supported by solid data or unproven medicine for which data are lacking." Regardless of the kind of therapy or who delivers it, critical questions are the same:

- "What is the therapy?
- What is the disease or condition for which it is being used?
- What is its purported benefit to the patient?
- What are the risks?
- How much does it cost?
- Does it work?"

The German philosopher Martin Heidegger offered the view that "the essence of technology is *calculative thinking*—the use of objects to achieve some purpose, while the essence of poetry and art is *meditative thinking*—reflecting on the beauty inherent in how things are." His fear was that calculative thinking might someday come to be accepted and practiced as the only way of thinking. Dismissing alternative medicine exemplifies his fears. According to that perspective, the worry is "not that health is an outcome to be optimized by cost-effective, evidence-based medicine, but that this might become *the only way* of thinking about health and that no alternative exists. That health is something more than an unrelenting devotion to outcomes may or may not be the psychological driving force of the alternative medicine movement."

A calculative view of exercising would be that it is done to achieve longevity. A meditative view would be that engaging in this practice is part of an active lifestyle that is healthy. A medicine that is calculative and meditative allows for a pluralistic sense of health and the good life and one that makes sense of illness in the modern age.[319]

Similarly, in looking at the "hows" and "whys" of decision-making about CAM usage, there may be a range of "push" and "pull" factors (Nichol 2011). "Push factors include dissatisfaction with conventional care and perceived harmful effects of conventional treatments; 'pull factors' include desire for more holistic and 'natural' approaches and greater philosophical congruence with CAM. The use of CAM can be a process of seeking meaning in one's illness and regaining or exerting control over one's health and treatment conditions." [320] Many adherents to this perspective believe that true collaboration between conventional and alternative medicine promises patients the best of both worlds.

What Is CAM?

"Complementary and alternative medicine (CAM) covers a heterogeneous spectrum of ancient to new-age approaches that purport to prevent or treat disease (Barnes 2008). By definition, CAM practices are not part of conventional medicine because there is insufficient proof that they are safe and effective. Complementary interventions are used together with conventional treatments whereas alternative interventions are used instead of conventional medicine. Generally, individuals who choose CAM approaches are seeking ways to improve their health and well-being or to relieve symptoms associated with chronic, even terminal, illnesses or the side effects of conventional treatments. Other reasons for choosing to use CAM include having a holistic health philosophy or a transformational experience that changes one's world view and wanting greater control over one's own health. Many types of CAM practitioners try to treat not only the physical and biochemical manifestations of illness, but also the nutritional, emotional, social, and spiritual context in which the illness arises. The overwhelming majority of patients using CAM approaches do so in order to complement conventional care rather than as an alternative to conventional care."

"In 2007, almost 4 out of every 10 adults in the U.S. had used CAM therapy in the past 12 months, with the most commonly used therapies being non-vitamin, non-mineral, natural products (17.7%) and deep breathing exercises (12.7%). American Indian or Alaska Native adults (50.3%) and white adults (43.1%) were more likely to use CAM than Asian adults (39.9%) or black adults (25.5%). Results from the 2007 National Health Interview Survey

---

319. Prasad, V. *Towards a Meaningful Alternative Medicine*, Hastings Center Report, Sept-Oct 2009, pp. 16-18.
320. Nichol, J. et al. Beliefs, Decision-Making, and Dialogue about Complementary and Alternative Medicine (CAM) within Families Using CAM: A Qualitative Study, *Journal of Alternative and Complementary Medicine*, Vol. 17, No. 2, February 2011, pp. 117-125.

(NHIS) found that approximately one in nine children (11.8%) used CAM therapy in the past 12 months, with the most commonly used therapies being non-vitamin, non-mineral, natural products (3.9%) and chiropractic or osteopathic manipulation (2.8%)."

"Children whose parent used CAM were almost five times as likely (23.9%) to use CAM as children whose parent did not use CAM (5.1%). For both adults and children in 2007, when worry about cost delayed receipt of conventional care, individuals were more likely to use CAM than when the cost of conventional care was not a worry." [321]

Alternative medicine was a term commonly used in the latter decades of the 20th century. After the American Medical Association (AMA) disbanded its Committee on Quackery, following a Supreme Court ruling in 1990 that its practices against chiropractors "violated antitrust laws, physicians gradually became more open to medical pluralism (Ruggle 2005). The foremost influence on their changing attitudes was surveys showing that increasing numbers of individuals were using chiropractic" and other health services such as mind-body relaxation techniques. "It became clear that these therapies were serving less as alternatives than as adjuncts to conventional medicine. Accordingly, the term *complementary* appeared and a new acronym gained currency."

After Congressional hearings in the U.S. Senate in 1991, "a bipartisan majority of appropriations committee members decided that the National Institutes of Health (NIH) should investigate the safety and efficacy of alternative medicine and proposed new funding to set up an Office of Unconventional Medicine." Funding was provided to study the safety and efficacy of the more widely used therapies. As appropriations increased, the name later was changed to the National Center for Complementary and Alternative Medicine (NCCAM). [322]

The NCCAM defines complementary and alternative medicine as a diverse group of medical and health systems practices and products that are not presently considered to be part of conventional Western medicine. Complementary medicine is used in conjunction with conventional medicine, e.g., acupuncture to treat pain, while alternative medicine is used in place of conventional Western medicine, e.g., herbs rather than antidepressant medications to treat depression.

CAM practices can be categorized as follows:

- Alternative medical systems (e.g., acupuncture, homeopathic treatment)
- Biologically-based therapies (e.g., non-vitamin, non-mineral natural products and diet-based therapies)
- Manipulative and body-based therapies (e.g., use of chiropractic, massage therapy)
- Mind-body therapies (e.g., relaxation techniques, Yoga, tai chi, qi gong)

"In the United States, disability affects about 1 in 5 persons and this ratio is expected to increase as baby boomers age (Okoro 2011). The economic impact of disability-related cost to the U.S. health care system is substantial." It is not surprising that the use of complementary and alternative medicine (CAM) is prevalent among individuals who have disabling conditions as shown in Figure 1. "Use of CAM therapies by conventional medical providers has increased and will likely become more prevalent as evidence-based therapies are mainstreamed into allopathic medicine."

---

321. Barnes, P.M. et al. *Complementary and Alternative Use among Adults and Children: United States, 2007*, National Health Statistics Reports, No. 12, December 10, 2008, 24 pp.
322. Ruggle, M. Mainstreaming Complementary Therapies: New Directions in Health Care, *Health Affairs*, Vol. 24, No. 4, July/August 2005, pp. 980-990.

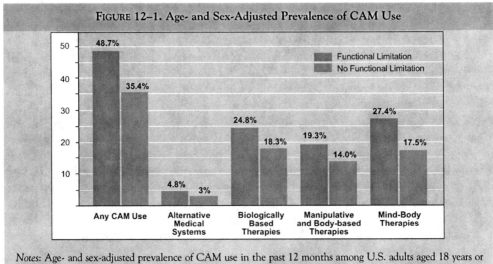

FIGURE 12-1. Age- and Sex-Adjusted Prevalence of CAM Use

Notes: Age- and sex-adjusted prevalence of CAM use in the past 12 months among U.S. adults aged 18 years or older with or without functional limitations. *Source:* National Health Interview Survey, 2007 (Okoro 2011).

"More health care professionals are being exposed to CAM therapies during their medical education, using CAM themselves, practicing in holistic settings with CAM practitioners, or practicing in health care fields that already have adopted evidence-based CAM treatment protocols (e.g., disability service providers). The increased likelihood of specific CAM therapies being covered by health insurance might influence greater use. From 1997 to 2007, visits to acupuncturists increased threefold. Acupuncture is a therapy that has experienced increased coverage by health insurance plans, plus more states are licensing its practice and practitioners. Health insurance coverage might make other CAM therapies cost effective as well." [323]

"The presence of diabetes was a powerful predictor of CAM use." Both pharmacologic CAM (multivitamins, glucosamine, gingko biloba) and nonpharmacologic CAM (chiropractic, acupuncture, healer, and massages) have been reported as being highly used regardless of age, gender, household income, time of diabetes diagnosis, or diabetes complications (Villa-Caballero 2010). In one study, use was higher among subjects with diabetes who see a physician regularly and significantly higher among subjects with more education. Use of pharmacologic CAM and nonpharmacologic CAM was similar across all ethnic groups. The kinds of differences that exist are that Hispanics preferred oral herbs and remedies, along with prickly pear cactus. The latter is viewed as being a more natural and less expensive mode to complement their traditional diabetes treatments. Asians were more likely to prefer the use of healers and gingko biloba.[324]

Who Uses CAM?

A survey of individuals aged 50 and older was conducted (AARP 2010). As shown in the figures that follow, 37% used herbal products or dietary supplements; 22% used massage therapy, chiropractic manipulation, or other bodywork; 9% used mind/body practices; 5% used

323. Okoro, C.A. et al. Use of Complementary and Alternative Medicine among USA Adults with Functional Limitations: For Treatment or General Use? *Complementary Therapies in Medicine*, Vol. 19, Issue 4, August 2011, pp. 208-215.

324. Villa-Caballero, L. et al. Ethnic Differences in Complementary and Alternative Use among Patients with Diabetes, *Complementary Therapies in Medicine*, Vol. 18, Issue 6, December 2010, pp. 241-248.

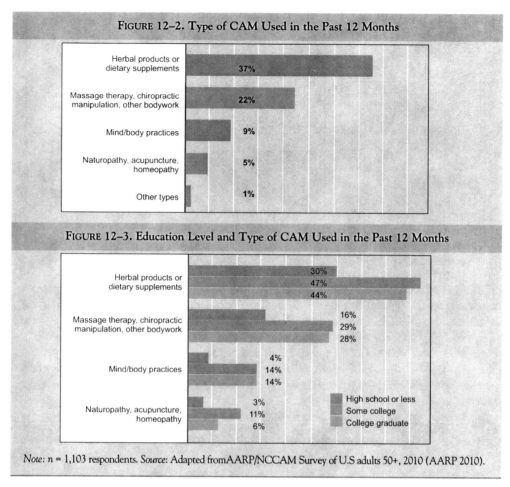

FIGURE 12–2. Type of CAM Used in the Past 12 Months

Herbal products or dietary supplements — 37%
Massage therapy, chiropractic manipulation, other bodywork — 22%
Mind/body practices — 9%
Naturopathy, acupuncture, homeopathy — 5%
Other types — 1%

FIGURE 12–3. Education Level and Type of CAM Used in the Past 12 Months

Herbal products or dietary supplements — 30% / 47% / 44%
Massage therapy, chiropractic manipulation, other bodywork — 16% / 29% / 28%
Mind/body practices — 4% / 14% / 14%
Naturopathy, acupuncture, homeopathy — 3% / 11% / 6%

High school or less
Some college
College graduate

Note: n = 1,103 respondents. Source: Adapted from AARP/NCCAM Survey of U.S adults 50+, 2010 (AARP 2010).

naturopathy, acupuncture, and homeopathy; and 1% used other types of CAM products and practices (Figure 2).

Based on level of education, 30% of those who have a high school education or less reported using herbal products or dietary supplements, whereas 47% of those with some college and 44% of those who graduated from college reported the use of these substances (Figure 3).

When asked why they use CAM practices, the common reasons were to prevent illness or overall wellness (77%), reduce pain or treat harmful conditions (73%), treat a specific health condition (59%), or supplement conventional medicine (53%) (Figure 4).

Among all survey participants, 67% reported that they had not discussed CAM with any health provider. Individuals aged 50 and older were most likely to have discussed CAM with their physician (28%), a nurse or nurse practitioner (12%), physician assistant (12%), pharmacist (9%), chiropractor (2%), or physical therapist (1%) (Figures 5 and 6).

When asked why they did not discuss CAM with their health care providers, the results were: the provider never asked (42%), they did not know they should bring it up (30%), there was not enough time during the office visit (17%), they don't think provider knows about the topic (16%), the health care provider would have been dismissive/told them not to do it (12%), and they weren't comfortable discussing it with a health care provider (11%) (Figure 7).

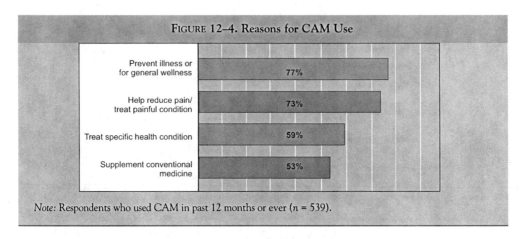

FIGURE 12–4. Reasons for CAM Use

Note: Respondents who used CAM in past 12 months or ever (*n* = 539).

When asked about taking prescription medicine, 63% of CAM users take anywhere from two to five or more of these medications (Figure 8).[325]

The goal of another study was to "document the daily use of complementary therapies of older adults for specific symptoms on days the symptoms occurred for chronic conditions, and for health promotion (Arcury 2011). Data were also collected on the daily use of self-care behaviors such as the use of over-the-counter medicine and rest, and on the daily use of conventional health care such as the use of prescribed medicine. Data collection focused on older adults who lived in three rural counties in south-central North Carolina." The chronic conditions arthritis, heart disease, diabetes, and respiratory disease served as a basis for the study. The

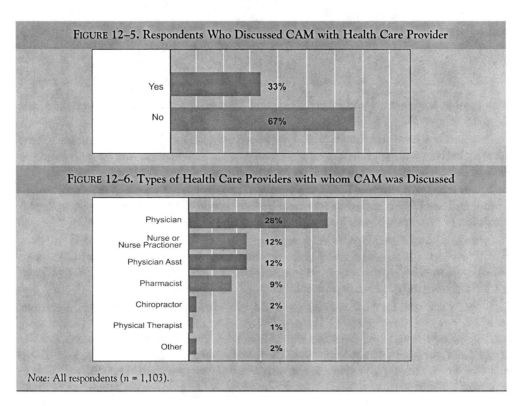

FIGURE 12–5. Respondents Who Discussed CAM with Health Care Provider

FIGURE 12–6. Types of Health Care Providers with whom CAM was Discussed

Note: All respondents (*n* = 1,103).

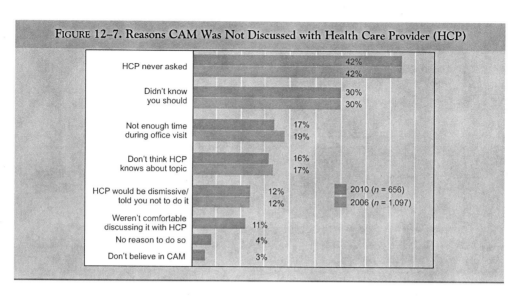

FIGURE 12–7. Reasons CAM Was Not Discussed with Health Care Provider (HCP)

results showed that "85% of the rural older adults who participated in the study had used a home remedy in the past year, 28.0% had used an herb, 28.0% had used a supplement, and 25.5% had used a complementary practitioner."[326]

"In 2007, adults in the United States spent $33.9 billion out of pocket on visits to CAM practitioners and purchases of CAM products, classes, and materials" as shown in the chart in Figure 9 (Nahin 2009). "Nearly two-thirds of the total out-of-pocket costs that adults spent on CAM were for self-care purchases of CAM products, classes, and materials during the past 12 months ($22.0 billion), compared with about one-third spent on practitioner visits ($11.9 billion)."

"Despite this emphasis on self-care therapies, 38.1 million adults made an estimated 354.2 million visits to practitioners of CAM. About three-quarters of both visits to CAM practitioners and total out-of-pocket costs spent on CAM practitioners were associated with manipula-

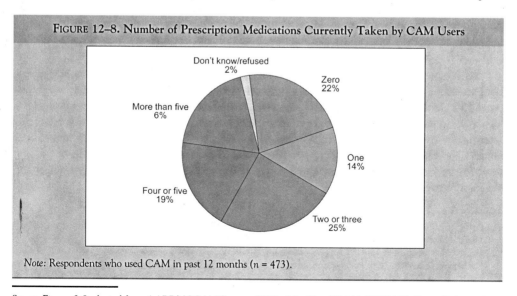

FIGURE 12–8. Number of Prescription Medications Currently Taken by CAM Users

Note: Respondents who used CAM in past 12 months (n = 473).

Source: Figures 2-8 adapted from AARP/NCCAM Survey of U.S adults 50+, 2010 (AARP 2010). Figure 7 also includes data from AARP/NCCAM Survey 2006 AARP 2010).

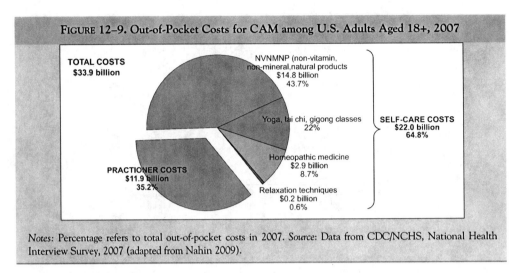

FIGURE 12–9. Out-of-Pocket Costs for CAM among U.S. Adults Aged 18+, 2007

Notes: Percentage refers to total out-of-pocket costs in 2007. *Source:* Data from CDC/NCHS, National Health Interview Survey, 2007 (adapted from Nahin 2009).

tive and body-based therapies. A total of 44% of all out-of-pocket costs for CAM, or about $14.8 billion, was spent on the purchase of non-vitamin, non-mineral, natural products (NVN-MNP)." [327]

Using the 2007 National Health Interview Survey data, researchers found that "pediatric CAM users were more likely to take prescription medications, have a parent who used CAM, and have chronic conditions (Birdee 2010). With the exception of asthma or frequent ear infections, there was higher CAM use among children with common medical conditions or symptoms including attention-deficit/hyperactivity disorder (ADHD), anxiety or stress, allergies, asthma, dermatologic conditions, developmental disorders, fever, gastrointestinal conditions, headaches, insomnia, learning disabilities, musculoskeletal conditions, overweight, psychological conditions, and respiratory infections. Among a subset of children whose parents also responded to the adult survey, a larger percentage of children used CAM if a parental figure used CAM (65%) as compared with children whose parental figure did not use CAM (35%). CAM use was also higher among households reporting a delay in medical care of children because of difficulties in access. Children who missed more school days because of illness reported higher CAM use."

"Use of biologically based therapies was associated with health access difficulties, suggesting that parents may turn to CAM therapies when conventional health care is not readily available. Overall CAM use was associated with prescription medication use in the previous 3 months. Although not significantly associated with the use of biologically based therapies, this raises the potential for drug-herb interaction. Among adults, only half disclose their use of herbal and dietary supplements to a health care provider. Pediatricians and pharmacists need to inquire about use of herbs and supplements when prescribing medications and actively monitor for adverse effects." [328]

325. AARP, NCCAM. Complementary and Alternative Medicine: What People Age 50 and Older Discuss with Their Health Care Providers. *Consumer Survey Report*, April 13, 2010. 14 pp.

326. Arcury, T.A. et al. Daily Use of Complementary and Other Therapies for Symptoms among Older Adults: Study Design and Illustrative Results, *Journal of Aging and Health*, Vol. 23, No. 1, February 2011, pp. 52-69.

327. Nahin, R.L. et al. Costs of Complementary and Alternative Medicine (CAM) and Frequency of Visits to CAM Practitioners: United States, 2007, National Health Statistics Reports, No. 18, July 30, 2009, 16 pp.

328. Birdee, G.S. et al. Factors Associated with Pediatric Use of Complementary and Alternative Medicine, *Pediatrics*, Vol. 125, No. 2, February 2010, pp. 249-256.

Regulatory Oversight Absent

At one time, approval of botanicals was in the domain of the Food and Drug Administration (FDA) (Kemper 2008). Congress circumvented this process by passing the Dietary Supplement and Health Education Act (DSHEA) in 1994. The effort was led by senators in states that manufacture dietary supplements. By doing so, herbs achieved the status of becoming food rather than drugs. The bill was signed into law (P.L. 103-417) by President William Clinton on October 25 of that year.

"According to the DSHEA, manufacturers bear the burden of proof of ingredient safety of dietary supplements. However, unlike pharmaceutical preparations, dietary supplements can be marketed without proven safety or efficacy. A manufacturer does not have to provide the FDA with the evidence on which it relies to substantiate safety or effectiveness before or after it markets its products. For new ingredients, the manufacturer is only required to provide evidence to the FDA that the product is 'reasonably expected to be safe.' Manufacturers of supplements are not required to report any data on adverse events to the FDA. The FDA can demonstrate that a supplement is unsafe only after it reaches the market. The FDA must prove that the product is unsafe before it can restrict a product's use or take other legal action."

"Because of regulations differing from those governing the use of pharmaceuticals, there are concerns about the purity and potency of herbal products and other dietary supplements sold in the United States. Product quality is influenced by many factors, including which portion of the plant is used (i.e., root, stem, leaves, flowers), the time of harvest (i.e., young versus old plants), the handling of the product, and proper identification of the plant. Furthermore, labeling is often inaccurate. To conduct research, the quality of product must be guaranteed, and to compare clinical trials, the similarity of product must be ensured." [329]

Prayer and Spiritual Healing

Prayer is an item that receives some degree of scrutiny in studies of CAM. The results are mixed and it is difficult to sort out many complicating variables. If Christians, Muslims, and Jews all are praying for a patient and recovery or improved health results, which group's prayers were more effective, or did they all contribute equally or not at all? Another uncontrolled variable is the impact of prayer by individuals or congregations that routinely pray for sick and dying persons around the world.

In utilization studies of CAM, rates of use typically are reported for a list of treatment modalities, but "one class of modalities above all tends either to be excluded altogether or, if reported, not followed up in depth (Levin 2011). Use of spiritual healing of various types has been relegated to the margins of health services research on CAM since the earliest days of the field, perhaps because of an understandable desire to dissociate from non-medical therapies, non-professional providers, and treatments without scientifically validated mechanisms of action. Existing data, however, sparse as they are, reveal that the frequency of use of a spiritual healer or reliance on the prayers of others may exceed almost every other CAM therapy. This finding has been validated across racial and ethnic groups in the U.S."

One study indicated that "contrary to common assumptions, use of such healers is not primarily conditioned by sociodemographic disadvantage, serious health need, or lack of access to

329. Kemper, K.J. et al. The Use of Complementary and Alternative Medicine in Pediatrics, *Pediatrics*, Vol. 122, No. 6, December 2008, pp. 1374-1386.

mainstream medical care or insurance coverage. These findings indicate that use of a spiritual healer, whether a faith healer or a psychic, is supplementary to traditional care-seeking behavior. Spiritual healing, whatever its merits or faults, is thus an example of care that is both alternative and complementary." Individuals who have used a spiritual healer are not characterized by "lack of education, marginal racial/ethnic or socioeconomic status, poor health, or lack of other health care options. Efforts to understand this class of healthcare behavior based solely on these sorts of factors are inadequate and do not explain why individuals use such care." [330]

The incorporation of prayer into the definition of CAM has broad implications and should be considered in reference to four key points (Tippens 2009):

> "(1) There needs to be a clear standard for classifying what is and is not considered CAM.
> (2) Use of the broad term 'prayer' fails to distinguish between the diverse forms of spiritual healing used by practitioners and the conventional understanding of the word.
> (3) Defining prayer as CAM potentially inflates the statistics of CAM use.
> (4) These inflated statistics disguise racial-ethnic disparities in CAM use and access to CAM services."

"The ambiguous definition of CAM allows for wide variations of CAM use data, depending on which definition is used. Including prayer in the definition of CAM dramatically increases the percentage of CAM users, particularly among racial/ethnic groups, which leads to two related questions: How should CAM be defined, and does prayer, as distinguished from spiritual healing practices, fit this definition?" [331]

The aim of another study was to "compare religious characteristics of general internists, rheumatologists, naturopaths, and acupuncturists, as well as to examine associations between physicians' religious characteristics and their openness to integrating CAM (Curlin 2009). Naturopaths and acupuncturists were three times as likely as internists and rheumatologists to report no religious affiliation (35% versus 12%), but were more likely to describe themselves as very spiritual (51% versus 20%) and to agree they try to carry religious beliefs into life's dealings (51% versus 44%). Among physicians, increased spirituality and religiosity coincided with more personal use of CAM and willingness to integrate CAM into a treatment program." [332]

Attention Deficit Hyperactivity Disorder

The number of children diagnosed with attention deficit hyperactivity disorder (ADHD) has grown markedly since being recognized as a specific disorder in the 1970s (Sarris 2011). "The prevalence rate of ADHD within Western cultures is approximately 5% and remains the most common psychiatric illness among young children, with an estimated 50% of these children retaining ADHD symptoms for the rest of their lives. CAM frequently is given to children and adolescents for reputed benefits in the treatment of hyperkinetic and concentration disorders such as ADHD. In vulnerable populations, high quality evidence is required to support these claims."

---

330. Levin, J. et al. Prevalence and Sociodemographic Correlates of Spiritual Healer Use: Findings from the National Survey of American Life, *Complementary Therapies in Medicine*, Vol. 19, No. 2, April 2011, pp. 63-70.

331. Tippens, K. et al. Is Prayer CAM? *Journal of Alternative and Complementary Medicine*, Vol. 15, No. 4, April 2009, pp. 435-438.

332. Curlin, F.A. et al. Religion, Clinicians, and the Integration of Complementary and Alternative Medicines, *Journal of Alternative and Complementary Medicine*, Vol. 15, No. 9, September 2009, pp. 987-994.

An assessment was done of current evidence of herbal and nutritional interventions for ADHD using a systematic search of clinical trials meeting an acceptable standard of evidence. Currently, no clear picture emerges about which, if any, CAMs can be recommended for use in treating ADHD. The CAM natural products reviewed provide a mixture of results, with the most promising concerning the minerals "zinc and iron, and the antioxidant botanical French maritime pine bark." [333]

Musculoskeletal Pain

Confronted by life's maladies, individuals who suffer may find it preferable to try any kind of treatment that offers the prospect of relief. In other countries such as Italy, France, and Australia, individuals with chronic musculoskeletal pain (e.g., osteoarthritis) use a topical application of nettle sting (White 2011). As a counter-irritant, a small pain caused by the nettle sting is used to abolish a greater one (hyperstimulation). "Examples of counter-irritants include the shock of an electric eel, scarification, cupping, cauterization, bee venom, and Kromayer ultra violet light." [334]

Osteoarthritis is the most common form of arthritis. A less common form is rheumatoid arthritis. According to the American College of Rheumatology (ACR), "conventional therapies for many conditions in the spectrum of rheumatic and musculoskeletal diseases are not completely effective, have side effects, and can be expensive (ACR 2011). Patients desire less expensive, safe, simple, and effective alternatives. They may feel helpless in the face of unpredictable, progressive, and disabling disease and therefore they seek therapies that offer them control of their illness."

"The ACR recognizes the interest in CAM modalities and supports rigorous scientific evaluation of all modalities that improve the treatment of rheumatic diseases. The College understands that certain characteristics of some CAMs and some conventional medical interventions make it difficult or impossible to conduct standard randomized controlled trials. For these modalities, innovative methods of evaluation are needed, as are measures and standards for the generation and interpretation of evidence. The ACR supports the integration of those modalities proven to be safe and effective by scientifically rigorous clinical trials published in the biomedical peer review literature." Caution is advised for "those not studied scientifically. Healthcare providers should be informed about the more common CAM modalities, based upon appropriate scientific evaluation, and should be able to discuss them knowledgeably with patients." [335]

Results of a national survey showed that most "rheumatologists express favorable attitudes toward most categories of CAM practices relevant to the care of patients with chronic back pain or joint pain (Manek 2010). More than half of the respondents consider common individual CAM therapies to be beneficial and are at least moderately likely to recommend them. However, rheumatologists' opinions regarding the perceived benefit of common CAM therapies and their likelihood of recommending them varied widely across different CAM modali-

333. Sarris, J. et al. Complementary Medicines (Herbal and Nutritional Products) in the treatment of Attention Deficit Hyperactivity Disorder (ADHD): A Systematic Review of the Evidence, *Complementary Therapies in Medicine*, Vol. 19, No. 4, August 2011, pp. 216-227.
334. White, A.R. et al. Patient Consensus on Mode of Use of Nettle Sting for Musculoskeletal Pain, *Complementary Therapies in Medicine*, Vol. 19, No. 4, August 2011, pp. 179-186.
335. American College of Rheumatology Position Statement. On the Web at http://www.rheumatology.org/practice/clinical/position/complementary.pdf#search="complementary and alternative medicine. Accessed on Aug 31, 2011.

ties; percentage of favorable responses ranged from as high as 70% for body work (e.g., massage, shiatsu) to as low as 11% for energy medicine (e.g., Reiki). After controlling for other factors, female sex and being born outside the United States were independently associated with rheumatologists' favorable ratings of perceived benefit and willingness to recommend CAM." [336]

CAM and Some Health Problems Affecting Women

CAM use is common in the United States, "particularly among middle-aged women for symptoms commonly reported during perimenopause" (Cherrington 2003). A study examined the "relationship between women's report of perimenopausal symptoms and the use of CAM and socioeconomic or cultural factors." Among the study group of non-Hispanic white, African American, and Hispanic women, results indicate that "the prevalence of CAM use was 33%. Approximately 94% reported use of CAM therapies and 23% used CAM practitioners. Those who used CAM were younger and better educated. More often they reported pelvic pain and painful intercourse. The only demographic factor to predict use of alternative medicine was education. The types of CAM therapies used varied somewhat by ethnicity, with more ethnic minorities reporting meditation/relaxation/prayer. The use of other CAM therapies did not vary by ethnicity. The majority of women who chose CAM therapies used those that they procured themselves such as herbs and vitamins, independent of a CAM practitioner." [337]

Viewing the situation outside the United States, "self-medication with herbal remedies and 'natural' medications taken by mouth is widespread and growing in the United Kingdom (Gratus 2009). Almost half of women with breast cancer report taking herbal remedies, vitamins, or other supplements during treatment. Among cancer patients in general, 7% report taking herbal medicines. Self-medication may be used to help counteract the effects of cancer treatment, to alleviate symptoms of cancer, to boost the immune system, to deal with another condition, or in the hope of tackling the cancer itself. It may also provide a sense of control or of being actively involved in treatment. However, some herbal medicines may cause problems unrelated to cancer. Black cohosh, used by women taking hormonal medications after breast cancer, is associated in rare cases with serious liver problems."

Because of the possibility of unwanted side effects or interactions, patients with "cancer are generally advised to tell the professionals treating them if they are taking any form of medication, including herbal medicines and supplements. Studies suggest that only about half of them do so and that healthcare professionals themselves may be unable to give informed advice." [338]

How CAM Attracts Users

As indicated in the opening paragraph of this chapter, folk remedies have been used throughout the world for countless generations. Whether certain practices bear the label *folk, complementary, alternative,* or *integrative,* the fact remains that they will continue to be used.

336. Manek, N.J. et al. What Rheumatologists in the United States Think of Complementary and Alternative Medicine: Results of a National Survey, BMC *Complementary and Alternative Medicine*, Vol. 10, No. 5, 2010, 8 pp.

337. Cherrington, A. et al. Association of Complementary and Alternative Medicine Use, Demographic Factors, and Perimenopausal Symptoms in a Multiethnic Sample of Women: The ENDOW Study, *Family & Community Health*, Vol. 26, No. 1, January 2003, pp. 74-83.

338. Gratus, C. et al. The Use of Herbal Medicines by People with Cancer: A Qualitative Study, BMC *Complementary and Alternative Medicine*, Vol. 9:14, 2009, 7 pp.

It seems highly probable that the future will bring newer practices and products into existence as a way of meeting the needs and desires of individuals who want relief from pain or who simply want to feel healthier. Whether old practices or new innovations ever can be shown through research that they actually work effectively is for the most part immaterial because true believers who claim to experience positive effects will continue to use them.

In the Inferno section of Dante's *Commedia Divina*, line 69 in Canto II reads as follows: "*I' son Beatrice che ti faccio andare*" (I who bid you go am Beatrice). Inspired by this sentiment, in the late 1940s an enterprising company in Italy began marketing a laxative called Beatrice as an aid to serve the needs of constipated individuals. Thus, while new products and practices may come into being for the noble purpose of benefiting the human race, in some cases it should be acknowledged that certain purveyors may have a more pecuniary interest in mind.

One of the more colorful examples of marketing a health product can be found in the efforts of Dudley "Coozan" LeBlanc. A popular member of the Louisiana State Senate, he became wealthy by creating a product known as Hadacol. His medicine road show traveled throughout the southern states for many years until the 1950s, featuring a team of carnival performers, musicians, and beauty queens to tout his popular vitamin-mineral tonic. Users claimed that it made them feel good, and well it should have, because it was laced with enough alcohol to immobilize an elephant. When asked how he happened to call his product Hadacol, his response was "*Hadda call it something.*"

Not so long ago, chiropractic was outlawed in Massachusetts. In neighboring cities across the border in New Hampshire, offices of chiropractors lined both sides of the road. Parking lots on the property of these practitioners always had many spaces occupied by vehicles bearing Massachusetts license plates. It took many years in some instances, but eventually that profession became eligible not only to practice in Massachusetts, but also to participate in the Medicare program and in the Veterans Health Administration. As an example of another inroad attained, the Association of Chiropractic Colleges became a member of the Federation of Associations of Schools of the Health Professions (FASHP) in 1997.

Old attitudes die hard, but the more conventional practitioners of today such as allopathic physicians are experiencing greater opportunities through their education and training to expand their knowledge of what other kinds of health professionals have to offer. A study was conducted at two campuses of the Texas Tech University Health Sciences Center to examine the knowledge, attitudes, and use of CAM among primary care providers (Zhang 2010). More than half (56.5%) of respondents were female and younger than 36 years of age.

Overall, "the study revealed a positive attitude towards CAM. More than 60% of the providers would like to refer a patient to a CAM practitioner and about 75% of them believed that incorporation of CAM therapies into the practice would have a positive impact. Providers were most familiar with and felt most comfortable counseling their patients about massage therapy and St. John's wort among all CAM modalities. About 70% of the participants believed that the institution should offer proven CAM therapies to patients." [339]

Another study examined the attitudes of the providers of tomorrow (Abbott 2011). Concluding thoughts from the investigation of a national sample of medical students were that "there is a need for emerging physicians to understand and address the practices of complementary, alternative, and integrative medicine (CAIM), but the results of the survey indicate that significant obstacles remain. While medical students appear receptive to the underlying princi-

---

339. Zhang, Y. et al. A Study to Examine the Attitudes, Knowledge, and Utilization of CAM by Primary Care Professionals in West Texas, *Complementary Therapies in Medicine*, Vol. 18, No. 6, December 2010, pp. 227-232.

ples of CAIM, they may perceive CAIM therapies as not being evidence based. From a policy standpoint, this suggests that for CAIM to be appropriately integrated into conventional health care, more research is needed, particularly research that evaluates the mechanisms, safety, and cost-effectiveness of CAIM therapies. Although future physicians may be willing to use CAIM themselves, many are unwilling to cross the barrier to recommending or using CAIM in their practice until more assessment has occurred."

"Lack of studies evaluating the effectiveness of CAIM may be the principal obstacle to integration by mainstream health care practitioners." Survey investigators believe "medical student education in CAIM must be improved. Development of a more comprehensive and consistent educational approach to teaching medical students about CAIM is necessary if future physicians are to be adequately prepared for their role as health care providers. Just as medical schools have restructured their curricula to reflect the changing practice of medicine and incorporate new fields of study such as HIV/AIDS, gene therapy, and immunology, medical educators must recognize the importance of educating future doctors in health care systems outside of conventional medicine. This education must be guided by appropriate evidence, good science, and an understanding of the differences inherent in various forms of medicine." [340]

Allopathic medical care is somewhat less than perfect. Chapter 10 described health care from the perspective of patients, and Chapter 2 on semiotics pointed out various shortcomings associated with conventional health care. Chapter 14 on the topic of health care quality will illustrate other ways in which health care can be improved. Pain, suffering, and hopelessness are the kinds of forces that stimulate patients to seek any available remedy, no matter how far fetched it may seem. When all tried and true approaches have been used and the situation remains as desperate as ever, patients may try just about anything in their search for some form of relief.

The ability of patients to make an informed choice about treatment options can be hindered by health professionals who cut off discussion of CAM. When that situation occurs, patients will turn to other sources of advice, which may not be reliable. Reasons why patients fail to inform physicians that they are using CAM include worrying how the doctor will respond such as ordering them to cease usage or as a result of their own failing to understand that CAM could interfere with conventional therapy. A culture of self-diagnosis and self-treatment may be enhanced by a mistrust of conventional health care. Adverse effects of prescribed medicines also may be factors driving patients toward using CAM.

The introduction of billable hours by payers and the often highly impersonal nature of large medical centers are just two of many factors that can lead to unsatisfactory kinds of hasty interaction between patients and caregivers. Oftentimes, CAM providers may be in an advantageous position to fill whatever void is perceived to exist. One way of doing so is to spend a sufficient amount of time with patients, without hurrying the encounter and demonstrating a willingness to listen to them.

Allopathic Medicine

Clinical trials often fail to offer a physiologic rationale as a means of explaining how many CAM practices work. Doing so would help investigators to develop a causal hypothesis,

---

340. Abbott, R.B. et al. Medical Student Attitudes toward Complementary, Alternative and Integrative Medicine. Published online April 14, 2011, *Evidence-Based Complementary and Alternative Medicine*, on the Web at http://www.ncbi.nlm.nih.gov/pmc/articles/PMC3147138/?tool=pubmed. Accessed on August 30, 2011.

choose an appropriate control, and rule out placebo effects. Not all CAM interventions are subjected to the rigorous clinical testing that characterizes many allopathic procedures. Patients are unaware of this deficiency, and even if they did know that clinical research is lacking, it probably would not result in their cessation of use of untested products and procedures.

Not that long ago, it took quite an effort to find out what other choices might exist apart from allopathic medicine. Those days are gone. Access to a computer keyboard opens up an enormous vista of health practices that might never have been discovered otherwise. Patients are able to obtain a wide variety of information that is either beneficial or worthless and are in a position to act accordingly.

The term *allopathic medicine* was coined more than 200 years ago by Samuel Hahnemann who began as an MD, but became the founder of homeopathy (Whorton 2004). Experimenting with *cinchona* in the treatment of malaria, or intermittent fever as it was called then, he discovered "that the very drug that provided relief for a serious disease could produce the same symptoms, or something quite close to them, in a healthy person. He discovered the principle of *similia similibus curantur*, or 'like cures like.' He decided that this approach to healing based on similars should be called homeopathy from the Greek roots *homoios* (like) and *pathos* (suffering)."

He used the term *allopathic* to refer to conventional medicine being practiced at that time by MDs. He and other kinds of alternative practitioners employed it pejoratively regarding medicine. Taken from the Greek roots meaning "other than the disease," it was intended among other things to indicate that regular doctors used methods that were unrelated to the disharmony produced by disease and were harmful to patients.[341]

An exceptionally magical word in the contemporary world is *natural*, which many highly skilled marketing experts have applied as a descriptor of various products and practices. If it's natural, then it must be good. Health food stores thrive on marketing natural substances aimed at enhancing health status. A close relative is the term *organic*.

U.S. society is engulfed by news in one form or another about health. The 21st century is a highly therapeutic age where it almost seems un-American not to feel good and be happy. Mental health is the other side of the coin. Ceaseless efforts are applied by all manner of practitioners, including radio and TV gurus, to rid the populace of fear, anxiety, and feelings of worthlessness.

In her book, Barbara Ehrenreich begins with a diatribe on the culture surrounding breast cancer, into which she was plunged after being diagnosed with the disease. She notes that patients who fail to adopt a sunny, positive outlook may be ostracized or browbeaten. She is not convinced that positive thinking has anything to do with one's chances of survival.[342]

Alternatives to traditional health services are attractive to a sizeable segment of consumers. Preference and use are driven by a belief that traditional medicine is not optimal for treating their problems and cost savings are secondary, although still a factor. The Kaiser Health Tracking Poll for August 2011 indicates that among individuals age 18-64, among the insured 19% said that they had problems paying medical bills. Among the uninsured, the figure was 56%. As a result of cost, respondents reported doing the following:

---

341. Whorton, J.C. 2004. *Nature Cures: The History of Alternative Medicine in America*. Oxford University Press, USA.
342. Ehrenreich, B. 2009. *Bright-Sided: How The Relentless Promotion of Positive Thinking Has Undermined America*. New York: Metropolitan Books.

Financial Barriers Facing the Uninsured		
Percent Reporting the Following Due to Cost	Insured	Uninsured
Relied on home remedies or over-the-counter drugs instead of seeing a doctor	26%	68%
Put off or postponed obtaining health care you needed	21%	67%
Skipped dental care or checkups	24%	64%
Not filled a prescription for medicine	20%	54%
Skipped a recommended medical test or treatment	16%	51%
Cut pills in half or skipped doses of medicine	12%	37%
Had problems obtaining mental health care	7%	33%

Source: Henry J. Kaiser Family Foundation. Kaiser Health Tracking Poll, August 2011, 5 pp.

Finally, a new online resource developed in 2011 by the NCCAM is designed to give health care providers easy access to evidence-based information on CAM. With this resource, providers will have the tools necessary to learn about the various CAM practices and products and be better able to discuss safety and effectiveness of complementary and alternative medicine with their patients.[343]

Closing Thoughts

The presence of CAM has helped to change the health care landscape in important ways. The creation of the National Center for Complementary and Alternative Medicine at the National Institutes of Health has made it possible to devote research money to this portion of the health domain. CAM practitioners provide services in the amount of billions of dollars. It is essential to determine the extent to which CAM interventions are effective. The next two chapters focus on health care delivery and quality. Given that many patients use CAM along with conventional health care, it is necessary as a safety matter that such combinations of care do not interact in detrimental ways. A valuable development is that CAM courses are included in the curriculum of many schools of medicine.

---

343. National Center for Complementary and Alternative Medicine. Resources for Health Care Providers. On the Web at http://nccam.nih.gov/health/providers/. Accessed on November 3, 2011.

CHAPTER 13:
Health Care Delivery

13

This chapter on health care delivery and the next one on health care quality share many elements. Generally, they both complement and build on issues that have been described in previous chapters, such as race/ethnicity, geography, health literacy, health care financing, and the health workforce. In recent decades, the delivery of health care has changed greatly under the influence of constraints such as cost and patient preference. This chapter focuses on the new venues and arrangements that have emerged for expanding the availability of health services, including medical homes, retail clinics, urgent care centers, accountable care organizations, medical neighborhoods, and integrated delivery systems

Although it is a text primarily dealing with quality, an Institute of Medicine report contains a set of performance characteristics that pertain directly to health care delivery (IOM 2001). Six specific aims for improvement of health care are:

Safety

"Patients should not be harmed by care that is intended to help them nor should harm come to those who work in health care. Patient safety is freedom from accidental injury. Although not all errors cause injury, accidental injury can be due to error, defined by the IOM as either (1) the failure of a planned action to be completed as intended, or (2) use of a wrong plan to achieve an aim. In health care these errors include, for example, administering the wrong drug. The health care environment should be safe for all patients, in all of its processes, all the time. This standard of safety implies that organizations should not have different, lower standards of care on nights and weekends or during times of organizational change. Specifically, in a safe system, information is not lost, inaccessible, or forgotten in transitions."

Effectiveness

"Effectiveness refers to care that is based on the use of systematically acquired evidence to determine whether an intervention such as a preventive service, diagnostic test, or therapy produces better outcomes than alternatives—including the alternative of doing nothing. Evidence-based practice requires that those who give care consistently avoid both underuse of effective care and overuse of ineffective care that is more likely to harm than help the patient."

Patient-Centeredness

"This aim focuses on the patient's experience of illness and health care and on the systems that work or fail to work to meet individual patients' needs. Similar terms are *person-centered, consumer-centered, personalized,* and *individualized*. Like these terms, *patient-centered* encompasses qualities of compassion, empathy, and responsiveness to the needs, values, and expressed preferences of the individual patient. Some dimensions of patient-centered care are: (1) respect for patients' values, preferences, and expressed needs; (2) coordination and integration of care; (3)

information, communication, and education; (4) physical comfort; (5) emotional support—relieving fear and anxiety; and (6) involvement of family and friends."

Timeliness

"Timeliness is an important characteristic of any service and is a legitimate and valued focus of improvement in health care. In addition to emotional distress, physical harm may result, for example, from a delay in diagnosis or treatment that results in preventable complications. Lack of timeliness also signals a lack of attention to flow and a lack of respect for the patient that are not tolerated in consumer-centered systems in other service industries. It suggests that care has not been designed with the welfare of the patient at the center."

Efficiency

In an efficient health care system, resources are used to get the best value for the money spent. The opposite of efficiency is waste, the use of resources without benefit to the patients a system is intended to help. There are at least two ways to improve efficiency: (1) reduce quality waste, and (2) reduce administrative or production costs. Not all, but many types of quality of improvements result in lower resource use. This is true for improvements in effectiveness that result from reductions in overuse. It is also true for most improvements in safety, which result in fewer injuries. Quality waste from both overuse and errors is abundant in health care and contributes to excess costs."

Equity

"A statement of purpose for delivery of health care services is to reduce the burden of illness, injury, and disability continually; and to improve the health and functioning of the population. The aim of equity is to secure these benefits for all the people of the United States. This aim has two dimensions: equity at the level of the population and equity at the level of the individual. At the population level, the goal of a health care system is to improve health status and to do so in a manner that reduces health disparities among particular subgroups. With regard to equity in care giving, all individuals rightly expect to be treated fairly by social institutions, including health care organizations. The availability of care and quality of services should be based on individuals' particular needs and not on personal characteristics unrelated to the patient's condition or to the reason for seeking care."

Finally, it should be noted that the "six aims are complementary and synergistic. Occasionally, however, there will be tensions among them. Health care institutions, clinicians, and patients will sometimes need to work together to balance competing or conflicting objectives. Two examples are the potential conflict between the aims of patient-centeredness and effectiveness, and the need to balance the aim of equity as applied to the population with achievement of the other aims at the level of the individual." [344]

Health Care Then and Now

An old Italian saying is that it is better to be a mouse between two cats than to be a patient between two doctors. While the provision of health care may have been either ineffective or dangerous in previous eras, important strides have been made over the centuries to develop improved methods of diagnosing and treating a wide range of diseases and injuries.

---

344. Institute of Medicine. 2001. *Crossing the Quality Chasm: A New Health System for the 21st Century*—Chapter 2. Washington, DC: National Academy Press.

The early part of the 1600s was characterized by the plague in Europe. Vaccinations did not exist, so health authorities had to rely on other forms of conventional wisdom (Cipolla 1973). A health officer in Italy by the name of Cristofano di Giulio, of Prato, wrote a manuscript back then with the title *Libro della Sanità*, in which he provided a summary of what he believed a public health officer ought to know in time of plague:

> "It has been proven by experience that to put down an epidemic, first of all it is necessary to resort to the majesty of God and in the intercession of the Holy Virgin and of the Saints. Then it is necessary to observe with every possible diligence the following rules:
>
> - To disinfect with sulphur and perfumes all homes or rooms wherein there has been death or sickness.
> - To separate at once the sick from the healthy as soon as the case of illness is discovered.
> - To burn and take away at once those objects such as have been used by the deceased or by the sick.
> - To shut up straight away all houses wherein there have been infected people and keep them closed for at least 22 days so that those who are segregated inside the houses will not carry the infection to other people."

Despite the absence of microscopy and microbiological knowledge in the 17th century, quarantine practices were employed. Physicians suggested that patients should be treated at a distance with the barber-surgeon of the *lazaretto* (i.e., a pest house for isolating persons believed to have the disease or to be incubating it), shouting from the window the quality, sex, condition of the patient, and the stage of illness. From a safe distance, the physician would shout back the cure. Another belief was that even though a patient had recovered, convalescents remained infectious for some time.

Related public health measures failed to produce salutary outcomes. "Orders for the mass slaughter of dogs and cats, in the belief that the coats of these animals harbored the plague-bearing miasma, made life easier for rats, the creatures eventually discovered to be more closely associated with disease outbreaks. Oddly enough, resorting to the majesty of God often led to crowded religious processions and packed houses of worship, which aided in the rapid transmission of infection." [345]

The aforementioned account represents a mix of prescience and a faulty understanding of etiology. Similar examples abound over the years that display keen thinking coupled with an inability to comprehend the real nature of a health problem. Advances can occur in small and large increments, with the latter often being highly dramatic and significant. An example is the development of vaccines against polio and other scourges that have posed a huge burden on the human race.

Today, while it can be argued that the United States has some of the best health professionals and facilities in the world, there is not much convincing proof to demonstrate that Americans are the healthiest when compared to inhabitants of other nations. "Many advocates of U.S. health reform point to the nation's relatively low life-expectancy rankings as evidence that the health care system is performing poorly (Muennig 2010). Others say that poor U.S. health outcomes are largely due not to health care, but to high rates of smoking, obesity, traffic fatalities, and homicides."

---

345. Cipolla C.M. *Cristofano and the Plague: A Study in the History of Public Health in the Age of Galileo*, Berkeley-Los Angeles: University of California Press; 1973: p. 49.

Cross-national data on the 15-year survival of men and women over three decades were used "to examine the validity of these arguments. The risk profiles of Americans generally improved relative to those for citizens of many other nations, but Americans' relative 15-year survival nevertheless has been declining. For example, by 2005, 15-year survival rates for 45-year-old U.S. white women were lower than in twelve comparison countries with populations of at least 7 million and per capita gross domestic product (GDP) of at least 60% of US per capita GDP in 1975. The findings tend to undercut critics who might argue that the U.S. health care system is not in need of major changes." [346]

The Affordable Care Act (ACA) was enacted in 2010 in the belief of its supporters that the legislation would lead to improvements in health care delivery through mechanisms such as medical homes, accountable care organizations, and increased comparative effectiveness research. Apart from changes in delivery systems, biomedical research in the areas of genomics and stem-cell biology often are proclaimed as having tremendous potential to eliminate various diseases or, at the very least, result in vast improvements in the ways in which they are treated.

Optimism about what the future holds is not universal, however, as shown by the following view, which is that "there is a growing perception that modern medicine is approaching a state of crisis characterized by creative inertia, non-innovation, and non-productivity (Mittra 2009). Compared to the remarkable progress during the first 30 years after World War II, the last three decades have been characterized by a self-congratulatory illusion of progress, the fruits of which have failed to reach our patients. The problem may lie with the fact that the (often lone) clinical innovator of the past who made all the difference to the spectacular progress of medicine during the golden age has been marginalized to the extent that he is now an endangered species. The two definable forces that have led to his alienation are the hegemony of molecular science and the primacy accorded to the *randomized clinical trial* (RCT) in biomedical research. Both these stifle creative originality—the former by an overdependence on complex and technology-driven 'big science' and a flawed founding philosophy, and the latter by putting limits on intellectual expectations and imposing a bureaucratic approach to scientific research."

According to this perspective, "if the golden age was characterized by patient-centric, hypothesis-driven, innovative science often led by the lone investigator, more recent biomedical research is large-scale, glamorous, driven by commercial forces, and non-innovative. The primacy that we have accorded the RCT has stifled other forms of clinical investigations and enquiry that have to do with the individualistic spirit of curiosity, innovation, entrepreneurship and originality—the very human attributes that have historically been at the heart of all scientific discoveries and that featured so prominently in the spectacular breakthroughs of medicine's golden age. Today, the individualistic spirit of scientific curiosity has been replaced by a bureaucratic committee-room mindset that pervades every aspect of the conduct of a RCT and that also marginalizes the role of fortuitous observations that have propelled many medical breakthroughs in the past." [347]

---

346. Muennig, P.A. and Glied, S.A. What Changes in Survival Rates Tell Us about US Health Care, *Health Affairs*, Vol. 29, No. 11, November 2010, pp. 2105-2113.
347. Mittra, I. Why Is Modern Medicine Stuck in a Rut? *Perspectives in Biology and Medicine*, Vol. 52, No.4, Autumn 2009, pp. 500-517.

Sites Where Health Care Is Obtained

"Historically, general practitioners provided first-contact care in the United States (Pitts 2010). Today, however, only 42% of the 354 million annual visits for acute care—treatment for newly arising health problems—were made to patients' personal physicians. The rest are made to emergency departments (28%), specialists (20%), or outpatient departments (7%). Although fewer than 5% of doctors are emergency physicians, they handle a quarter of all acute care encounters and more than half of such visits by the uninsured. Health reform provisions in the ACA that advance patient-centered medical homes and accountable care organizations are intended to improve access to acute care. The challenge for reform will be to succeed in the current, complex acute care landscape." Examples of the kinds of situations that must be resolved if success is to be achieved are as follows:

Timely Access to Care

"One of the biggest barriers to acute care in primary care practice is many office-based practitioners' busy schedules. This makes 'same-day scheduling' and other efforts to ensure access extremely difficult. Busy schedules also discourage primary care physicians from taking extra time to treat patients with complex undifferentiated complaints; they often opt instead to refer such patients to specialists or emergency departments. Finally, hectic schedules reduce the likelihood that physicians will see additional patients after hours."

Patient-Centered Medical Homes

Although provisions of the ACA "should prompt a substantial scaling up of the medical home model, it is unlikely that some of the results achieved in other countries will materialize in the short term in the United States. When the Centers for Medicare and Medicaid Services (CMS) first began funding medical home demonstration projects—well before the new health reform law was enacted—it required the projects to adhere to National Committee for Quality Assurance (NCQA) criteria. The committee set a low bar for access, however, because a grantee only had to have 'written standards for patient access and patient communication' and 'data to show it meets its standards for patient access and communication.' Same-day scheduling was encouraged, but not required. Medical homes did not have to offer evening or weekend availability, and urgent telephone calls could be returned in whatever time frame a practice deemed appropriate."

"Workforce shortages represent another obstacle to expanding access to primary care. Today's primary care physicians are hard pressed to meet existing levels of demand, much less the pent-up needs of the estimated 32 million Americans who will soon acquire health insurance. Entrenched practice patterns constitute still another obstacle to access to timely acute care. Many primary care physicians have come to regard unscheduled visits as a time-consuming disruption to their workday."

Market-Based Approaches

"If health reform fails to achieve its promise of expanded access to care, market forces may drive other solutions. Concierge care, in which subscribers pay an annual fee for the services of a physician, is growing in popularity." A main signature feature is access. "Not only do concierge physicians accommodate same-day scheduling, but most make house calls. Unfortunately, the price of concierge care puts it out of reach for most Americans."

"*Retail clinics* and *urgent care centers* are other market-based approaches. Unless they are electronically linked to local hospitals and primary care practices, retail clinics and urgent care centers are likely to further fragment the delivery of health care. Because they treat only paying patients, they could destabilize local health care markets by drawing revenue-generating patients away from private doctors' offices and emergency departments, leaving the uninsured behind." [348]

Apart from the decline in the proportion of acute care visits to patients' personal physicians, within medicine itself there also have been changes. "From 1997 to 2007, the percentage of visits to physicians who were solo practitioners decreased 21% (Hsiao 2010). During the same period, visits to physicians who were part of a group practice with 6–10 physicians increased 46%. The percentage of U.S. physicians who own their practices has declined over the past two decades." [349]

Although they are similar in some ways, retail clinics and urgent care centers have some different characteristics (Weinick 2010). "Retail clinics, located in retail stores, typically are staffed by nurse practitioners and treat a limited range of health conditions, such as minor infections and injuries. An estimated 29% of the U.S. population lives within a 10-minute drive of a retail clinic, although such clinics are less likely to be located in minority and low-income neighborhoods."

"Urgent care centers typically are freestanding physicians' offices with extended hours; on-site x-ray machines and laboratory testing; and an expanded treatment range, including care for fractures and lacerations. There is some evidence that care at these alternative sites costs less than, and is of comparable quality to, care provided in the *emergency department*." Retail clinics and urgent care centers "provide walk-in care that focuses on acute conditions and exacerbations of chronic conditions. Nurse practitioners and physician assistants work in all three settings. They are the primary providers in retail clinics. About half of urgent care centers nationwide employ physicians trained in emergency medicine." [350]

Retail Clinics and Medical Homes

Two trends would seem to be in opposition (Pollack 2010). "The medical home emphasizes coordination of care, while retail clinics focus on single-visit acute care. Retail clinics might lead to increased fragmentation since a visit to a retail clinic may represent one fewer visit to a medical home. This could undermine a patient's connection to his or her medical home and could prevent the medical home from providing coordinated and continuous care. However, on closer examination it becomes clear that the medical home and retail clinics share a number of core principles."

"The medical home concept emphasizes improved access though open scheduling and enhanced hours. It is staffed by a team of providers, which may include nurses and other health professionals; is led by a personal physician; and focuses on coordination of the patient's care among providers. An integral component is an electronic health record that directly incorporates evidence-based medicine and decision-support tools."

"Retail clinics generally have a limited scope of care, which includes minor infections, such as sore throat and cough, immunizations, and routine preventive screening. For conditions that

---

348. Pitts, S.R. et al. Where Americans Get Acute Care: Increasingly, It's Not at Their Doctor's Office, *Health Affairs*, Vol. 29, No. 9, September 2010, pp. 1620-1629.
349. Hsiao, C-J. et al. National Ambulatory Medical Care Survey: 2007 Summary, National Health Statistics Report, No. 27, Hyattsville, MD: November 3, 2010, 6 pp.
350. Weinick, R.M. et al. Many Emergency Department Visits Could Be Managed at Urgent Care Centers and Retail Clinics, *Health Affairs*, Vol. 29, No. 9, September 2010, pp. 1630-1636.

fall outside their scope of care, retail clinics refer patients to other providers in the community. Almost universally, retail clinics use electronic health records that directly incorporate evidence-based guidelines."

The clinics have faced criticism on a number of fronts. "Perhaps most prominently, physicians and policymakers have worried that the clinics will lead to further fragmentation and will interfere with the medical home. Visiting a retail clinic for acute conditions rather than one's medical home may, over time, erode the patient–primary care physician relationship. In situations where a patient does not have an established relationship with a primary care physician, the opportunity to receive acute care at a retail clinic may lessen the patient's motivation to establish one."

In light of the criticism of retail clinics, the medical home model and retail clinics share many key principles that include: "a focus on improved access to care; the incorporation of electronic health records and evidence-based guidelines; and the use of non-physicians for services that do not require physician-level training. Moreover, both medical homes and retail clinics are 'patient-centered,' although they rely on different definitions of the concept. In the medical home, patient-centeredness focuses on shared decision making and addressing the multifaceted needs of patients. For retail clinics, patient-centeredness relies on convenience, where care is provided in consumer-friendly locations, with extended hours and no appointments."

Some differences are that the "medical home emphasizes comprehensive care, while retail clinics provide only episodic care for acute conditions or preventive care services. In practice, the medical home is typically a single geographic location where care is provided. In contrast, retail clinics provide care at multiple different sites that may be considered largely interchangeable within chains, given the shared electronic health record and highly standardized menu of options. The key difference—and important source of potential conflict—centers on care coordination.

Care coordination, as typically envisioned, addresses the integration of care across all providers for patients with complex chronic illnesses. Care coordination has a different interpretation in the context of the simple acute conditions managed by retail clinics." [351]

Medical Homes and Accountable Care Organizations

"The movement for a revitalized primary care infrastructure envisions transformed primary care practices featuring health information technology, innovative team approaches, and other new models of care. Key policy questions include whether small, independent office practices have the capability and capacity to undergo this type of transformation and whether creation of more organized health care delivery systems is a precondition for the transformation of medical homes and accountable care organizations." Various challenges "may develop as medical homes and accountable care organizations emerge in the care delivery landscape" (Academy Health 2009).

"While the definition of a medical home varies by source, the general construct remains consistent. The medical home model promotes a team-based approach to care of a patient through a spectrum of disease states and across the various stages of life. Overall coordination of care is led by a personal physician with the patient serving as the focal point of all medical activity."

351. Pollack, C.E. et al. The Growth of Retail Clinics and the Medical Home: Two Trends in Concert or in Conflict? *Health Affairs*, Vol. 29, No. 5, May 2010, pp. 998-1003.

The Medicare Payment Advisory Commission (MedPAC) "has defined *accountable care organizations* (ACOs) as a set of providers associated with a defined population of patients, accountable for the quality and cost of care delivered to that population. The providers could include a hospital, a group of primary care providers, specialists, and possibly other health professionals who share responsibility for the quality of care and cost of care provided to patients."

"While the medical home model is centered around a single practice, ACOs are at the other end of the spectrum, housing many practices within one organizing entity. A single ACO could be quite large and cover thousands of patients. Hospitals are not a necessary part of ACOs, but may be a desirable feature. As the structure has been envisioned, patients would not be required to get care from the ACO, but the ACO would be responsible for a patient wherever he or she elected to get care." As described in Chapter 9, ACO members can receive a financial bonus for meeting certain prescribed targets.

Converting the current delivery system to an integrated model of care composed of stand-alone medical homes or multiple medical homes housed within a large ACO structure may encounter the following kinds of challenges:

- "The medical home is a patient-centered model of care. It will take a transformative shift to place the patient at the center of the delivery system, rather than the physician, and provide that patient with high quality, low cost, convenient care.
- Most health care is delivered in small, scattered, office-based practice settings. It is not clear whether a delivery system transformation will be more successful by first developing individual medical homes prior to bringing practices within the umbrella of an organizational structure like an ACO.
- The size of the practice will dictate the approaches needed to effect change. Small independent practices and large integrated groups are both likely to continue to exist within new delivery models. These mixed organizational structures will require different approaches—a combination of internal capacity and external financial incentives to promote change. The challenge is determining how much and what kind of incentives are needed for particular-sized groups.
- While there is an assumption that medical homes will provide better care, it is not clear that demonstration projects will be the ideal test of a medical home's success. First, by its very nature a demonstration is a temporary exercise, which may keep health care providers from fully embracing change. Second, until payment systems are altered to compensate practices for converting to a medical home, change will be slow.
- Timelines must be long enough to realize meaningful results. Focusing, for example, on changes within a practice's quarterly profits may be insufficient. While there will be political pressure to show short-term results, those results may not be determinative of the long-term feasibility of medical homes. In the short term, medical homes may not yield significant positive results.
- A key challenge includes developing structural supports, particularly with regard to staffing. There are no economies of scale for small practices in hiring additional staff.
- Another challenge is lack of knowledge and resources to expand long-term care and acute care coordination.
- Health information technology, independent of other factors, is likely not the 'silver bullet' needed to achieve practice change.
- Providers are not currently trained to work in teams and they are not paid to do so. A better understanding is needed of the skill set and attributes of a workforce functioning in a modern way.
- Primary care physicians are retiring and new medical students are not electing primary care as their specialty. If a reformed health care system is designed to be carried on the backs of primary care providers, who will those people be?
- Currently, there are few redesigned delivery models in which students can train. In school, students learn the traditional practice of medicine. It is not a 'teamness' type of care." [352]

Will Medical Homes Improve Medical Care?

A major premise behind the establishment of medical homes is that they will improve quality. In order to meet the technological requirements of operating at a high level of performance, modern health information systems will have to be used (Bernstein 2010). "Only about 40% of larger practices (with at least 20 physicians) currently use electronic medical records as is necessary to meet the definition of a higher-level medical home, and smaller practices are even less likely to use electronic records. Although both large and small practices need capital and expertise to develop and maintain information systems that characterize higher-level medical homes, small practices may need to be more creative—for example, by sharing with other practices the costs of adopting and maintaining information systems."

Also, "transforming a primary care practice into a medical home can necessitate physicians changing fundamentally their way of practice. Instead of sequential one-on-one patient visits and physician autonomy, medical homes take a proactive population-based approach. Physicians in specialty practices have little incentive to communicate with medical-homes to help them coordinate care and might also resist efforts to manage referrals to specialty services. Finally, consumers may resist what they perceive as restricting their access to specialists or particular services and facilities." [353]

Will Accountable Care Organizations (ACOs) Improve Medical Care?

As ACOs take shape, it will be interesting to see what forms they take and who will be in control of them. Will physician groups or hospitals be the dominant actors? "A move toward ACOs will mean major changes in the structure of physicians' practices, since even physician-group–based ACOs may include one or more hospitals, though they may instead contract with hospitals for specific services chosen on the basis of their relative value (Kocher 2010). Larger ACOs are likely to be contracted directly by payers to manage the continuum of care. They also are likely to bear financial risk, receiving greater payments for the care of chronically ill patients and accepting at least partial responsibility for the costs of specialists' visits, tests, emergency room visits, and hospitalizations. Memories of the inflexible managed-care gatekeepers of the 1990s could lead to theoretically permissive, if practically narrow, networks of providers, although these organizations will need to work closely with a small group of efficient specialists and facilities to achieve their quality and efficiency goals."

Whoever controls the ACOs will capture the largest share of any savings. For physicians to control them, doctors would have to overcome some of the following kinds of hurdles:

- "ACOs will require clinical, administrative, and fiscal cooperation, and physicians have seldom demonstrated the ability to effectively organize themselves into groups, agree on clinical guidelines, and devise ways to equitably distribute money. Since much of the savings from coordinating care will come from successfully avoiding tests, procedures, and hospitalizations, the ques-

352. Academy Health. Medical Homes and Accountable Care Organizations: If We Build It, Will They Come? Research Insights, A Brief Resulting from a Roundtable Discussion at the June 28-30, 2009 Annual Research Meeting, On the Web at http://www.academyhealth.org/files/publications/RschInsightMedHomes.pdf. Accessed on September 8, 2011.

353. Bernstein, J. et al. Medical Homes: Will They Improve Primary Care? Mathematica Policy Research, Inc. Issue Brief, Number 6, June 2010, 5 pp.

tion of how to divide profits among primary care physicians and specialists will be contentious. Proceduralists who would end up losing income are likely to resist key structural changes.

- ACOs will require sophisticated information technology (IT) systems and skilled managers in order to hold clinicians accountable. Historically, doctors have not shown the willingness to assume more capital risk or to invest in overhead.

- Memories of the failed capitation models of the 1990s may make some physicians hesitant to participate." (Capitation refers to a fixed amount of payment per patient, per year, regardless of the volume or cost of services each patient requires).

For hospitals to be in control, the following kinds of hurdles may have to be overcome:

- "They will need to trade near-term revenue for long-term savings. Hospitals are typically at the center of current health care markets, and by focusing on procedures and severely ill patients, most have been fairly profitable. Building an ACO will require hospitals to shift to a more out-patient-focused, coordinated care model and forgo some profits from procedures and admissions. Hospitals' decisions will be further complicated if payers do not change their payment models similarly and simultaneously.

- Hospitals, which have generally struggled to operate outpatient practices effectively, may have difficulty designing ACOs. Acquiring practices and hiring physicians as employees typically reduce physicians' incentive to work long hours and, therefore, reduce their productivity."

"If physicians come to dominate, hospitals' census will decline and their revenue will fall, with little compensatory growth in outpatient services, since physicians are likely to self-refer. This decline will, in turn, lower hospitals' bond ratings, making it harder for them to borrow money and expand. As hospitals' financial activity and employment decline, their influence in their local communities will also wane. It will be hard for them to recover from this diminished role."

"Conversely, if hospitals come to dominate ACOs, they will accrue more of the savings from the new delivery system and physicians' incomes and status as independent professionals will decline. Once relegated to the position of employees and contractors, physicians will have difficulty regaining income, status, the ability to raise capital, and the influence necessary to control health care institutions." [354]

Meanwhile, in a "quest to gain market share, hospital employment of physicians has accelerated in recent years to shore up referral bases and capture admissions (O'Malley 2011). Stagnant reimbursement rates, coupled with the rising costs of private practice, and a desire for a better work-life balance have contributed to physician interest in hospital employment." [355]

Patients in the Context of Changes in Health Care Delivery

Now that a case has been made to some extent about the various ways in which health professionals and the facilities in which they practice may be affected as the health care delivery system continues to evolve, how do patients fit into complex equations that produce uncer-

---

354. Kocher, R. and Sahni, N.R. Physicians Versus Hospitals as Leaders of Accountable Care Organizations, *New England Journal of Medicine*, Vol. 363, No. 27, December 30, 2010, pp. 2579-2582.

355. O'Malley, A.S. et al. Rising Hospital Employment of Physicians: Better Quality, Higher Costs? Center for Studying Health System Change, Washington, DC: Issue Brief No. 136, August 2011, 4 pp.

tain, yet to-be-defined outcomes? As mentioned in Chapter 11 on the health workforce, scope of practice disputes typically revolve around the noble concern of what is necessary to ensure patient safety. Only a hardened cynic would assert that economic factors play a role such that a main safety concern is to protect a portion of health professionals' income stream from encroachment by other kinds of health professionals.

As the unseen guest at many policy discussions, patients should be at the epicenter of health care deliberations. Instead, as policy is formulated and implemented, thereby producing new winners and losers in the overall economic scheme of things, it becomes somewhat easy to forget who should benefit most from whatever unfolds, i.e., patients themselves. Given the kinds of delivery patterns mentioned above such as solo medical practices, retail clinics, urgent care centers, medical homes, and ACOs, how well are these entities going to perform in accomplishing the following?:

- Communicating with patients so that they have a clear understanding of the health care services being provided and the rationale for doing so.
- Supporting patients in self-care and risk reduction practices.
- Involving patients in decision-making so that they fully understand treatment options and any out-of-pocket costs that may have to be met.
- Enhancing patient safety by giving them access to their medical records and making sure that all caregivers for a particular patient have all the necessary information gathered at different times and places.
- Overseeing medication use and furnishing information that will increase the likelihood of health promotion and disease prevention.
- Recognizing and responding to patient challenges stemming from health illiteracy, low levels of education, advanced aging, and other impediments that might compromise the most effective use of health care services.

Thus far, "there has been little discussion about binding patients to ACOs, however, largely because the freedom to choose one's providers is highly valued in U.S. health policy (Sinaiko 2010). The managed care backlash and the rise of preferred provider organizations in the late 1990s have been partially attributed to patients' unwillingness to accept closed physician networks. Most Medicare beneficiaries have not enrolled in private plans that restrict patients'-choice of physicians, even though these plans offer more generous benefits than does the fee-for-service Medicare program. These consumer preferences suggest that policymakers should focus on creating incentives to build patients' loyalty to an ACO."

"One way to do so is to allow patients to share in their ACO's cost savings — for example, through a tiered provider network, which allows patients to pay less at the point of care depending on their choice of provider. Under such an arrangement, physicians would be sorted into tiers according to their ACO affiliation, and patients would pay lower co-payments for visits to physicians within their ACO. One barrier to its effectiveness might be inadequate consumer awareness and low use of the networks. A second method for sharing savings with patients is to charge different premiums depending on whether patients choose to receive their care from an ACO, and if there's more than one ACO option, which one they select."

"Another strategy draws from the lessons of behavioral economics and findings that consumers frequently accept default settings and fail to switch out of them because of procrastination or a belief that a default reflects an expert's recommendation. Private health plans could assign patients to primary care physicians within a low-cost, high-quality ACO as the default, perhaps charging lower premiums or co-payments for visits with these providers, but allow patients to opt out and seek care with other providers if they are willing to pay more out-of-pocket." [356]

Medical Neighborhoods

One way of viewing primary care medical homes is to place them in the larger context of a *medical neighborhood*. "For most patients in the U.S. health care system, the 'medical neighborhood' appears as a diverse array of clinicians and institutions with little or no coordination between them, leaving patients and their families to navigate this system on their own and often to serve as the main conduit of information between the clinicians they see (Taylor 2011). Most patients and their families have little understanding of how their primary care practice coordinates (if at all) with other clinicians, organizations, and institutions in the neighborhood—and often may assume that the system is much more coherent, organized, and coordinated than it is. One approach to decreasing fragmentation, improving coordination, and placing greater emphasis on the needs of patients is the patient-centered medical home."

At its core, a well-functioning medical neighborhood requires basic communication and coordination functions. For example:

- "Specialists need to let primary care clinicians know what type of routine care the patient needs after a surgery or course of treatment.
- Primary care clinicians need to make appropriate referrals and provide specialists with appropriate background information, clinical data on the patient, and goals for the consultation.
- Hospitals need to let primary care teams know when their patients are in the hospital or have visited the hospital's emergency department (ED).
- In general, primary care clinicians and other team members need a broad understanding of each patient's health care needs to assist in coordinating all care, help the patient navigate the system, and ensure that the treatment plans (and prescription medications) of different specialists work together as a whole."

"While the medical neighborhood clearly could and likely should take on other functions as well—such as managing population health and developing better relationships with community services—many believe that efforts to improve the neighborhood should start with the basics, such as getting hospitals to fax primary care clinicians a list of their patients who are in the hospital or ensuring that specialists always communicate back to primary care clinicians about their patients." Similar to many notions that look terrific on paper, however, there are barriers to a high-functioning medical neighborhood.

"The lack of financial incentives for care coordination and the fragmentation of the current system are probably the largest factors in the lack of communication and coordination across key actors in the neighborhood. First, the current fee-for-service (FFS) system limits reimbursement to procedures and those care coordination activities involving direct interaction with the patient (referred to as 'evaluation and management') as well as clinical consultations between clinicians directly involved in that care. Other care coordination activities, which may be undertaken either by non-clinical staff or clinical staff not directly caring for the patient, generally are not reimbursed and thus represent only costs (not revenue) for providers. Second, and perhaps more important, FFS as a general payment approach tends to reward an increased volume of services,

---

356. Sinaiko, A.D. and Rosenthal, M.B. Patients' Role in Accountable Care Organizations, *New England Journal of Medicine*, Vol. 363, No. 27, December 30, 2010, pp. 2583-2585.

but does not recognize efficiency or improved clinical outcomes—providing few incentives for enhancements in care coordination that might result in efficiencies or improved health."

"Other factors, however, also come into play, including limited primary care clinic involvement in inpatient care and the lack of practice norms around clinician communication. A major focus in medical school and other health professions training programs is the ability to make independent clinical judgments and develop expertise in specific areas, and this may contribute to an overall culture in medicine that places relatively less emphasis on coordination, teamwork, and communication, as compared to some other professions. A procedurally focused payment system, combined with a lack of clarity on the respective roles of different types of clinicians in providing patient care, likely has contributed to the specialty-focused and fragmented nature of health care in the U.S., yet little dialogue has been devoted to this topic."

Barriers to Information Flow and Accountability

"No (or few) financial incentives or requirements for care coordination
Lack of staff and time for investment in coordination (at the practice and broader community levels)
Limited primary care clinic involvement in inpatient care
Fragmented, diverse services, rather than an integrated delivery system
Limited financial integration across most providers
Limited health information technology infrastructure and interoperability
Practice norms that encourage clinicians to act in silos rather than coordinate with each other
Complexity of coordination for patients with high levels of need and/or frequent self-referrals
Patient self-referrals about which the primary care medical home is unaware
Misperceptions regarding Health Insurance Portability and Accountability Act (HIPAA) provisions and limits to information exchange" [357]

Integrated Delivery Systems

Health care delivery in the United States has long been characterized by fragmentation at the national, state, and local levels (GAO 2009). "Care is delivered by multiple providers, in multiple care settings, and often without systematic coordination and communication across providers and settings. Fragmentation of care delivery can lead to poor quality of care, medical errors, inefficient delivery of services, higher costs, and patient dissatisfaction. Fragmentation can be especially burdensome for patients with chronic illnesses because of their ongoing care needs and for underserved populations—individuals who are uninsured or medically underserved—because of their financial and other challenges to accessing services."

"One way that hospitals, physicians, and other providers have addressed fragmentation is by forming *integrated delivery systems* (IDS) to improve efficiency, quality, and access to care. An IDS can be integrated across its providers and facilities in aspects such as clinical care, financial management, and human resources. These systems can vary in the way they are organized, with services linked vertically, among different levels of care (e.g., clinic, specialist's office, hospital), or horizontally, across one level of care (e.g., hospitals). They also can vary in the extent to which they are integrated. IDSs can be publicly or privately owned. While public IDSs have a

---

357. Taylor E. F. et al. Coordinating Care in the Medical Neighborhood: Critical Components and Available Mechanisms, White Paper (Prepared by Mathematica Policy Research under Contract No. HHSA290200900019I TO2). AHRQ Publication No. 11-0064. Rockville, MD: Agency for Healthcare Research and Quality. June 2011, 40 pp.

mission of providing care to underserved populations, some private IDSs share this mission and others serve these populations to varying degrees."

"IDSs vary in their organizational configuration and in the continuum of services they provide. They frequently use patient care strategies such as care coordination, disease management, and care protocols. For example, some IDSs serve a patient population that includes a high proportion of underserved individuals and may face financial challenges in doing so. IDSs can be organized in different ways and use various staffing models. Some IDSs are a single entity that includes a delivery system (hospitals, physicians, and other providers) and a health insurance plan."

"Other IDSs include a delivery system, but do not have a health insurance plan. IDSs may employ their own physicians, rely on community-based physicians who are not employed by the system, but are granted use of the hospital facilities and staff, or use a combination of those two approaches. An IDS can be organized at the system level, or it can be more decentralized, having subsystems that organize health care at the local or regional level. These subsystems integrate care within themselves, but not necessarily with other subsystems in the overall system. IDSs can consist of multiple subsystems. Because there is so much variation in the ways that they can be organized, it is difficult to determine the exact number of IDSs in the country; however, millions of Americans receive care from IDSs."

"IDSs offer a continuum of services to a particular patient population or community and can vary in what services are provided within this continuum. For example, some IDSs provide nursing home care within their systems and others do not. Similarly, not all IDSs provide certain specialized services such as organ transplantation or major burn services within their systems."

"Studies have shown that IDSs are more likely to use patient care strategies than are other providers, such as solo practitioners. For example, a national study of the management of chronic illness for patients with asthma, congestive heart failure, depression, and diabetes found that certain IDSs were significantly more likely to use recommended, evidence-based care management processes than were less organized providers. In addition, a study of physician practices in California in the early 2000s found that physicians affiliated with an IDS were more likely to use disease management programs than were physicians in non-integrated medical group practices or small practices."

"Depending on their geographic location and their mission, IDSs serve varying proportions of underserved populations. Individuals who are underserved have higher rates of illness, and they often face barriers to accessing timely and needed care. Patients with limited English proficiency may have problems comprehending health care information and complying with treatment. Rural residents also face barriers to access because of physician shortages in rural areas. Underserved patients may have difficulty obtaining specialty services, including diagnostic services. Integrating care, such as by linking primary and specialty care, can reduce some of the access barriers that underserved population groups experience." [358]

Integrated Care and Mental Illness

Major health problems such as cancer, heart disease, and diabetes play a prominent role in discussions of the necessity of having a health care delivery system that addresses these conditions adequately. Another major set of problems comes under the general rubric of mental illness.

---

358. U.S. Government Accountability Office. Health Care Delivery: Features of Integrated Systems Support Patient Care Strategies and Access to Care, but Systems Face Challenges, Report to Congressional Committees, Report No. GAO-11-49, November 2010, 33 pp.

Mental illness has an impact on all age groups. According to the National Institute of Mental Health (NIMH), an estimated 26.2% of Americans ages 18 and older—about one in four adults—suffer from a diagnosable mental disorder in a given year. Furthermore, researchers supported by NIMH have found that mental illness begins early in life (NIMH 2005). "Half of all lifetime cases begin by age 14 and three-quarters have begun by age 24. Thus, mental disorders are really the chronic diseases of the young." Evidence also shows that the mental health system fails to reach a significant number of individuals with mental illness. Those patients that it does reach often drop out or receive insufficient, uncoordinated care.[359]

Research has improved the ability to recognize, diagnose, and treat conditions effectively. "Many studies have found correlations between physical and mental health-related problems (Collins 2010). Individuals with serious physical health problems often have co-morbid mental health problems and nearly half of those with any mental disorder meet the criteria for two or more disorders, with severity strongly linked to co-morbidity. As many as 70% of primary care visits stem from psychosocial issues. While patients typically present with a physical health complaint, data suggest that underlying mental health or substance abuse issues often are triggering these visits. Most primary care doctors are ill-equipped or lack the time to address fully the wide range of psychosocial issues that are presented by patients."

"Improving the screening and treatment of mental health and substance abuse problems in primary care settings and improving the medical care of individuals with serious mental health problems and substance abuse in behavioral health settings are two growing areas of practice and study. Generally, this combination of care is called *integration* or *collaboration*."

"Integrating mental health services into a primary care setting offers a promising, viable, and efficient way of ensuring that people have access to needed mental health services. Additionally, mental health care delivered in an integrated setting can help to minimize stigma and discrimination, while increasing opportunities to improve overall health outcomes. Successful integration requires the support of a strengthened primary care delivery system and long-term commitment from policymakers at federal, state, and private levels."

"When mental health is integrated into primary care, people can access mental health services closer to their homes, thus keeping families together and allowing them to maintain daily activities. Integration also facilitates community outreach and mental health promotion and long-term monitoring and management of affected individuals." [360]

Health Care Services and Prevention

While billions of dollars are devoted every year to treating patients, a major emphasis must be placed on prevention. Irresponsible use of alcohol products and illicit substances ruins many lives. Carnage on the nation's roadways often results from driving too fast or operating a vehicle while under the influence of drugs or alcohol. Smoking continues to take its toll of human lives in the form of various cancers and respiratory diseases. Unsafe sexual practices provide another example of health problems that can be prevented.

An essential question is how can the U.S. health care system in its many different guises help to save lives? "In recent years, systematic reviews of scientific evidence have identified clinical

---

359. National Institute of Mental Health (NIMH). 2005. Mental Illness Exacts Heavy Toll, Beginning in Youth. Bethesda, MD: National Institute of Mental Health. On the Web at http://www.nimh.nih.gov/science-news/2005/mental-illness-exacts-heavy-toll-beginning-in-youth.shtml. Accessed on September 8, 2011.

360. Collins, C. et al. Evolving Models of Behavioral Health Integration in Primary Care, *Milbank Memorial Fund*, New York, NY: May 2010, 102 pp.

interventions that prevent illness and reduce mortality (Farley 2010). However, time-pressured clinicians are forced to make choices about which of these clinical preventive services to offer during brief clinical encounters. In the U.S., only slightly more than half of recommended health care interventions are provided during the course of normal care. Perhaps the most important improvement in the quality of medical care could be increasing the proportion of individuals who receive clinical interventions that are demonstrated to reduce mortality."

Models predict that "the clinical preventive services that would prevent the greatest number of deaths are those that reduce cardiovascular disease, particularly treatment of hypertension, treatment of hyperlipidemia, and aspirin prophylaxis. These services have the potential to prevent large numbers of deaths because the risk factors they address are common, they are relatively effective in reducing both cause-specific and all-cause mortality in those with these risk factors, and their current utilization is far below achievable levels. Given the uncertainty inherent in the models, the number of deaths prevented by these interventions is far from precise, but overall the results suggest that a wider use of a small number of interventions could prevent tens of thousands of premature deaths a year."

"Primary care needs to be more accessible, and these services should be given higher priority by clinicians, quality officers, and healthcare systems. In particular, electronic record systems that identify patients at risk and generate automated reminders for clinicians and patients, in combination with changes in practice workflow and reimbursement structures, have the potential to increase utilization of these preventive services and should be used more widely." [361]

Achieving access to health care is difficult for many Americans. Universal coverage may not necessarily translate into better access. A report identifies three key obstacles to access: crowded points of entry such as emergency departments, a system that is confusing to navigate, and individuals who inevitably fail to act on their health early (PricewaterhouseCoopers 2009). Consumers are open to trying new means of access and the industry is responding. Solutions discussed include:

- "New means of access like online consultations
- Coordination of care among practitioners by using non-physician providers
- Supportive models such as shared medical appointments that enable patients to learn from each other and from their providers." [362]

Health professionals are in an advantageous position to enhance patient well-being by serving as role models. Data show that only 63.5% of health care personnel were vaccinated against influenza during the 2010-11 season, according to a Centers for Disease Control and Prevention study of 1,931 health care workers (CDC 2011). That rate is a slight increase from the 61.9% who received the seasonal flu vaccine during the influenza A (H1N1) pandemic in 2009-10. Despite the slight uptick, the vaccination rate for health care workers still falls below the Healthy People 2020 target rate of 90%. A potential downside is that unvaccinated personnel who are afflicted with influenza may inadvertently transmit it to patients under their care. [363]

361. Farley, T.A. et al. Deaths Preventable in the U.S. by Improvements in Use of Clinical Preventive Services, *American Journal of Preventive Medicine*, Vol. 38, Issue 6, June 2010, pp. 600-609.
362. PricewaterhouseCoopers' Health Research Institute. Jammed Access: Widening the Front Door to Healthcare, On the Web at http://pwchealth.com/cgi-local/hregister.cgi?link=reg/Jammed_access_Widening_the_front_door_to_healthcare.pdf. Accessed on September 8, 2011.
363. Centers for Disease Control and Prevention. Influenza Vaccination Coverage among Health Care Personnel: United States, 2010-2011 Influenza Season, *Morbidity and Mortality Weekly Report*, Vol. 60, No. 32, August 19, 2011, pp. 1073-1077.

Closing Thoughts

The delivery of health care services has undergone tremendous modifications in the last several decades. Except for patients who can afford concierge care, the days of having a physician visit one's home to provide care are a vestige of the past and are not likely to be repeated in the future. The increased presence of retail clinics and urgent care centers is a valuable asset in expanding the availability of health care services, but only to the extent that they do not add to the amount of fragmentation that already exists. Otherwise, quality may end up being a casualty.

CHAPTER 14

Health Care Quality

14

Several previous chapters, including Chapter 13, have addressed the issue of quality either directly or indirectly. Where a person resides, whether he or she can speak English, and one's cultural and ethnic background are factors that exert a great impact on the quality of health care obtained. The ability to pay for such care is another key variable. Being uninsured or having restrictions placed on which providers are approved to provide care can also affect what is accessible and available. A more serious issue is that health care lacking quality at a sufficiently high level can result in unnecessary rehospitalization episodes, and in worst cases, lead to more serious health problems, including death.

Health care delivery, as discussed in the previous chapter, and health care quality are intimately related to one another. For example, the high cost of health care has led to shortened patient-physician visits. In the context of socially disadvantaged patients, some potential consequences are disparities in patient understanding and satisfaction, low adherence to treatment regimens, suboptimal care, and increased adverse outcomes. Caregivers also may experience more burnout in treating greater numbers of patients in shorter timeframes.

Chapter 11 on the health workforce offers another important dimension. Alternative and complementary practitioners may be dispensing care that fails to meet appropriate standards, but patients seek their services anyway. Personnel shortages in medicine, nursing, and allied health can make life more difficult for the remaining health professionals who attempt to fill the vacuum. They experience additional stress, can become overtired more easily, be more likely to commit errors that compromise health care quality, and have more incentive for leaving the profession at an earlier stage in their careers.

Errors in the Delivery of Health Care Services

Achieving high quality in the delivery of health care services is a goal that occupies the minds of a great many health professionals and health policymakers. Unfortunately, that quest was not always a foremost consideration. A notable early step in the history of quality in health care management occurred with Ernest Codman's pioneering analysis of surgical error (Davis 2011). "In a pattern that resonates to this day, Codman, a Boston surgeon, initiated the first surgical morbidity and mortality conference at Massachusetts General Hospital, and fought for public disclosure of error. His earlier statement that 'every hospital should follow every patient it treats long enough to determine whether the treatment has been successful, and then to inquire 'if not, why not' with a view to preventing similar failures in the future' remains as visionary and disruptive today as it was when written in 1914. In that light, it's perhaps not surprising that his plan to evaluate transparently surgical competence at his hospital was turned down and contributed to his loss of staff privileges." [364]

The topic of medical errors was described to some extent in Chapter 10. An important aspect of quality pertains to the commission of errors and the extent to which not only are they reported, but also the degree to which remediable steps are taken to prevent them from recurring. "Although physicians have been described as 'reluctant partners' in reporting medical errors," a survey of U.S. physicians found that "most were willing to share their knowledge about harmful errors and near misses with their institutions and wanted to hear about innovations to prevent common errors (Garbutt 2008). Physicians found current systems to report and disseminate this information inadequate, however, and relied on informal discussions with colleagues. Thus, much important information remains invisible to institutions and the health care system. Efforts to promote error reporting might not reach their potential unless physicians become more effectively engaged in reporting errors at their institutions."

Many barriers to error reporting identified in earlier physician surveys also were noted in this study, "which suggests that these barriers persist. Physicians were concerned about the confidentiality and legal discoverability of the error information they report. Survey results highlight the importance of developing health care cultures that encourage physicians to report medical errors for quality improvement. A key driver of their willingness to report was their confidence that reported information would be used to make improvements. If physicians have little confidence that this will happen, they are unlikely to seek out opportunities to formally report errors." [365]

"Physicians generally support disclosure; however, many harmful errors are not disclosed to patients (López 2009). Fear of lawsuits, shame, embarrassment, lack of disclosure training, fear of losing patient trust, and uncertainty about how to discuss errors with patients are barriers to physician disclosure." One study revealed that:

- "Fewer than half of the adverse events (AE) reported by patients were disclosed.
- An adverse event was more likely to be disclosed if additional treatment was provided to address the AE during hospitalization.
- Clinicians were less likely to disclose events that were associated with a more prolonged impact on the patient.
- They also disclosed fewer preventable events than non-preventable ones.
- Patients who reported an adverse event and had it disclosed to them gave a higher rating of the quality of their care than patients who reported an event that was not disclosed. Importantly, high-quality ratings continued to be associated with disclosure whether or not the event was deemed preventable." [366]

Although the science of error measurement is underdeveloped, *diagnostic errors* are an important source of preventable harm (Newman-Toker 2009). In considering diagnostic errors, "it is important to distinguish between the error (a process) and the resulting harm (an outcome). Diagnostic error can be defined as a diagnosis that is missed, wrong, or delayed, as detected by some subsequent definitive test or finding. However, not all misdiagnoses result in harm,

---

364. Davis, A. M. Teaching Quality and Cost in the Tumultuous Era of Health Care Reform, *Perspectives in Biology and Medicine*, Vol. 54, No. 2, Spring 2011, pp. 256-266.

365. Garbutt, J. et al. Lost Opportunities: How Physicians Communicate About Medical Errors. *Health Affairs*, Vol. 27, No. 1, January/February 2008, pp. 246-255.

366. López, L. et al. Disclosure of Hospital Adverse Events and Its Association with Patients' Ratings of the Quality of Care, *Archives of Internal Medicine*, Vol. 169, No. 20, November 9, 2009, pp. 1888-1894.

and harm may be due to either disease or intervention. *Misdiagnosis-related harm* can be defined as preventable harm that results from the delay or failure to treat a condition actually present (when the working diagnosis was wrong or unknown) or from treatment provided for a condition not actually present."

Despite their major public health implications, "diagnostic errors have received relatively little public or scientific attention, including from the patient safety community. Misdiagnosis has not featured prominently in patient safety campaigns. In the Institute of Medicine's report *To Err Is Human*, diagnostic errors were mentioned only twice, compared with 70 mentions for medication errors."

"Practical solutions to reduce diagnostic errors have lagged behind those in other areas of patient safety. Computer-based diagnostic decision support systems, often touted as the optimal strategy to reduce misdiagnosis, have not been validated against patient outcomes, and none is in widespread clinical use. Diagnosis is still largely viewed as an individual art rather than evidence-based science. The complexity of diagnostic problems and relative infancy of methods to study misdiagnosis, combined with limited funding for research in diagnostic safety, have further slowed progress." [367]

Adverse medical events (also known as iatrogenic events) are injuries and deaths that are caused by something other than the medical condition for which the patient is seeking care (Goodman 2011). "They are typically divided into three categories, as follows: preventable and negligent; preventable but not negligent; and other adverse events."

"Events in the first category, also called malpractice errors, are injuries or deaths resulting from medical misconduct or lack of adherence to basic minimum standards of care. Examples are performing surgery on the wrong site or leaving a sponge in a patient after an operation. Events in the second category are considered avoidable, although they are not the result of negligence. Some hospital-acquired infections are examples of this sort of medical error. The third category is 'other' events, which are not preventable based on current knowledge and technology. There is no obvious way of avoiding them."

"The category of preventable and negligent adverse events has received far more attention than the other two categories—non-preventable events and preventable but not negligent events. Interest in the latter category is growing, however. New technology, such as electronic health records with alerts for inappropriate medications, may be able to reduce the number of preventable events. The remaining category—other, or non-preventable adverse events— accounts for incidents when doctors and nurses execute procedures flawlessly and equipment functions perfectly, but patients do not heal or respond as expected. Regardless of the category into which an adverse event falls, however, the social cost of a death or injury is the same."

"Currently, patients who are harmed by medical errors have little choice, but to seek compensation through the very imperfect tort system—that is by suing whoever was involved in the adverse medical event." A possible solution might be to offer patients voluntary, no-fault insurance prior to treatment or surgery. They would be compensated if they suffered an adverse event—regardless of the cause of their misfortune—and providers would have economic incentives to reduce the number of such events. [368]

---

367. Newman-Toker, D.E. and Pronovost, P.J. Diagnostic Errors—The Next Frontier for Patient Safety, *Journal of the American Medical Association*, Vol. 301, No. 10, March 11, 2009, pp. 1060-1062.

368. Goodman, J.C. et al. The Social Cost of Adverse Medical Events, And What We Can Do about It, *Health Affairs*, Vol. 30, No. 4, April 2011, pp. 590-595.

A punitive approach to dealing with errors may serve only to compound the situation by encouraging more inappropriate behavior in the form of attempts to cover up wrongdoing. Steady improvements in quality can be realized by detecting errors, developing procedures to prevent their repetition, and disseminating to all parties concerned a description of a problem and how to deal with it properly. The key is to assure perpetrators that they will not be punished for disclosing their mistakes and that such disclosure is welcome.

Health Quality and the Affordable Care Act of 2010

When the Affordable Care Act became law in 2010, its advocates believed that the legislation would result in a monumental effort to increase access to health care by the uninsured, control health care costs, and improve quality. A contrarian point of view is that this government-led movement will lead to a lot of talk about quality, but not necessarily much improvement (Pauly 2011). "A better strategy may be found through 'disruptive innovation,' a market-driven approach that has balanced cost and quality in other industries. An example would be to provide lower-cost substitutes for some aspects of primary physician care, in the form of care at a retail clinic. Consumers might not perceive a clinic as a perfect substitute for physician care, but they might prefer the greater convenience and lower cost. Perhaps a little less quality for a lot less money might be acceptable to consumers and taxpayers to keep medical spending from siphoning off funds required for other needs."

"The closest approximation to health care that was 'a lot cheaper and only a little bit worse' was aggressive managed care in the 1990s. However, a combination of political and market pressures eventually reduced the effectiveness of managed care so that it failed to contain costs—its chief purpose. The provider networks that succeeded it have achieved only modest price discounting. There have been some less drastic changes that have accomplished little beyond inconveniencing some patients and doctors:

- Formularies and triple-tier insurance plans for drugs to push consumers away from high-price brands.
- The movement from inpatient to outpatient care to reduce costs from hospitalization.
- The limited provider networks now prevalent in private insurance, but not Medicare, to narrow consumers' access to a group of providers who agree to observe particular practice standards, accept lower reimbursement, or both."

Yet, these changes have done little to control the rate of growth of health spending.

Retail clinics provide limited services by nonphysician professionals in a more convenient and lower-cost setting. "Such options have been growing and show promise, although their aggregate effects on total spending growth must be modest. A larger impact on cost could come from increased use of specially trained nurses and other professionals as providers of the full range of primary care services. On almost all of the observable dimensions that anyone can identify, nurse practitioners, physician assistants, and other similarly trained professionals can provide primary care that equals the average quality of primary care provided by physicians, but consumers in general need to become aware of this option." [369]

Two possible avenues for reform in the name of enhancing quality of health care are to: 1) eliminate the clutter of unnecessary paperwork, and 2) decrease the gap between effective

---

369. Pauly, M.V. The Trade-Off among Quality, Quantity, and Cost: How to Make It—If We Must, *Health Affairs*, Vol. 30, No. 4, April 2011, pp. 574-580.

treatment methods and the failure to apply them consistently. For example, it's likely that every emergency room in the United States has had its fair share of patients arriving with cardiac problems. By now, it should be possible to expect that aspirin and beta blockers will be administered to these patients more routinely.

The number of forms that they have to complete each day often overburdens nurses and physicians. Apart from the time lost in direct patient care, the sheer volume of paperwork that must be filed in a high-stress environment may help to contribute to the number of errors committed or omissions that take place. Also related to the collection of information about patients is the use of electronic medical records. When a patient must deal with a physician who is covering for one's own doctor, more effective advice could be given if that other practitioner had the ability to obtain access to medical records. Another concern is that personal health records on paper have a way of piling up in clinics and offices. Important notations may not always be transferred to patient charts.

Government's Role in Improving Health Care Quality

In 2011, the Obama Administration launched the *Partnership for Patients: Better Care, Lower Costs*, a new public-private partnership designed to improve the quality, safety, and affordability of health care for all Americans (HHS 2011). The Partnership for Patients initiative brings together leaders of major hospitals, employers, physicians, nurses, and patient advocates along with state and federal governments in a shared effort to make hospital care safer, more reliable, and less costly.

The two goals of this new partnership are to:

- "Keep patients from becoming injured or sicker. By the end of 2013, preventable hospital-acquired conditions would decrease by 40% compared to 2010. Achieving this goal would mean approximately 1.8 million fewer injuries to patients with more than 60,000 lives saved over three years.

- Help patients heal without complication. By the end of 2013, preventable complications during a transition from one care setting to another would be decreased so that all hospital readmissions would be reduced by 20% compared to 2010. Achieving this goal would mean more than 1.6 million patients would recover from illness without suffering a preventable complication requiring re-hospitalization within 30 days of discharge."

Advocates believe that attaining these goals will save lives and prevent injuries to millions of Americans, and has "the potential to save up to $35 billion across the health care system, including up to $10 billion in Medicare savings, over the next 3 years. Over the next 10 years, it could reduce costs to Medicare by about $50 billion and result in billions more in Medicaid savings," which will help place the nation on the path toward a more sustainable health care system.

- "At any given time, about one in every 20 patients has an infection related to their hospital care.
- On average, one in seven Medicare beneficiaries is harmed in the course of receiving care, costing the government an estimated $4.4 billion every year.
- Nearly one in five Medicare patients discharged from the hospital is readmitted within 30 days, affecting approximately 2.6 million seniors at a cost of over $26 billion every year." [370]

---

370. Department of Health and Human Services. Partnership for Patients: Better Care, Lower Costs, April 2011. On the Web at http://www.healthcare.gov/compare/partnership-for-patients/index.html. Accessed on September 18, 2011.

The Affordable Care Act seeks to increase access to high-quality, affordable health care for all Americans. To that end, the law requires the Secretary of the Department of Health and Human Services (HHS) to establish a *National Strategy for Quality Improvement in Health Care* (the *National Quality Strategy*) that sets priorities to guide this effort and includes a strategic plan for how to achieve it (HHS 2011).

"The Strategy will promote quality health care in which the needs of patients, families, and communities guide the actions of all those who deliver and pay for care. It will incorporate the evidence-based results of the latest research and scientific advances in clinical medicine, public health, and health care delivery."

Three broad aims will be pursued to guide and assess local, state, and national efforts to improve the quality of health care:

- "**Better Care:** Improve the overall quality, by making health care more patient-centered, reliable, accessible, and safe.
- **Healthy People/Healthy Communities:** Improve the health of the U.S. population by supporting proven interventions to address behavioral, social, and environmental determinants of health in addition to delivering higher-quality care.
- **Affordable Care:** Reduce the cost of quality health care for individuals, families, employers, and government."

To advance these aims, the plan is to focus on six priorities initially, which are based on the latest research, advice from a broad range of key individuals, and examples from around the country. "These priorities have great potential for rapidly improving health outcomes and increasing the effectiveness of care for all populations." As the National Quality Strategy is implemented in 2011 and beyond, specific quantitative goals and measures will be developed for each priority. They are:

- "Making care safer by reducing harm caused in the delivery of care.
- Ensuring that each person and family is engaged as partners in their care.
- Promoting effective communication and coordination of care.
- Promoting the most effective prevention and treatment practices for the leading causes of mortality, starting with cardiovascular disease.
- Working with communities to promote wide use of best practices to enable healthy living.
- Making quality care more affordable for individuals, families, employers, and governments by developing and spreading new health care delivery models."

"Communities and States have often served as laboratories for expanding health coverage, improving quality, and controlling costs. Those roles will increase in coming years as States take the lead in implementing key parts of the Affordable Care Act such as new State-based Health Insurance Exchanges. These entities will improve health care quality by providing transparent information for consumers and by creating quality standards for health plans."

"Health care delivery in the United States often is not designed around meeting the needs of the patient. Instead, clinical services in many instances are organized around specific clinical conditions and designed with little involvement or direction from the patient. Health care should give each individual patient and family an active role in their care. Care should adapt readily to individual and family circumstances as well as differing cultures, languages, disabilities, health literacy levels, and social backgrounds."

"This kind of person-centered care, which sees a person as a multifaceted individual rather than the carrier of a particular symptom or illness, requires a partnership between the provider and the patient with shared power and responsibility in decision-making and care management. It also requires giving the patient access to understandable information and decision support tools that help patients manage their health and navigate the health care delivery system." [371]

AHRQ has developed a *Patient-Centered Care Improvement Guide* to help hospitals become more patient-centered. It outlines best practices and addresses common barriers to implementing patient-centered care (Frampton 2008). [372]

It is widely documented that Americans often do not receive quality care and certain populations, particularly racial and ethnic minority groups, receive lower quality care on average (Hanlon 2010). AHRQ sponsors the *Healthcare Cost and Utilization Project* (HCUP), "a family of health care databases and related software tools and products developed through a Federal-State-Industry partnership with state government organizations, hospital associations and private data organizations known as HCUP Partners. HCUP databases allow for research about an array of health policy issues and include patient race/ethnicity data. HCUP data can provide national information and they allow for state comparisons using uniformly defined data." [373]

For the eighth year in a row, AHRQ has produced the *National Healthcare Quality Report* (NHQR) and the *National Healthcare Disparities Report* (NHDR). They measure trends in effectiveness of care, patient safety, timeliness of care, patient centeredness, and efficiency of care. New in 2011 are chapters on care coordination and health system infrastructure (AHRQ 2011).

The reports present in chart form the latest available findings on quality of and access to health care. The *National Healthcare Quality Report* tracks the health care system through quality measures such as the percentage of heart attack patients who received recommended care when they reached the hospital or the percentage of children who received recommended vaccinations. The *National Healthcare Disparities Report* summarizes health care quality and access among various racial, ethnic, and income groups, and other priority populations such as residents of rural areas and individuals with disabilities. [374]

The Centers for Disease Control and Prevention (CDC) leads and supports a range of infection prevention activities at the national, regional and local levels. CDC's health care-associated infection prevention activities include developing evidence-based practice guidelines, assessing institution- and provider-level barriers and best practices for adoption of effective practices, developing and disseminating educational materials and toolkits to assist in translating policy into practice, and identifying and evaluating novel prevention strategies. The Healthcare Infection Control Practices Advisory Committee (HICPAC) has provided recommendations for the development of evidence-based guidelines for the prevention of health care-associated infections, including bloodstream infections, surgical site infections, health care-associated pneumonia, urinary tract infections, antimicrobial-resistant infections, and tissue safety issues.

---

371. Department of Health and Human Services. It should be #370.Report to Congress: National Strategy for Quality Improvement in Health Care, March 2011. On the Web at http://www.healthcare.gov/law/resources/reports/quality03212011a.html. Accessed on September 18, 2011

372. Frampton, S. et al. Patient-Centered Improvement Guide, 2008, On the Web at http://www.planetree.org/Patient-Centered%20Care%20Improvement%20Guide%2010.10.08.pdf. Accessed on September 19, 2011.

373. Hanlon C. and Raetzman S. State Uses of Hospital Discharge Databases to Reduce Racial and Ethnic Disparities. Online October 14, 2010. U.S Agency for Healthcare Research and Quality (AHRQ). On the Web at: http://www.hcup-us.ahrq.gov/reports.jsp. Accessed on April 8, 2011.

374. Agency for Healthcare Research and Quality. 2010 National Healthcare Quality and Disparities Reports, AHRQ Publication No. 11-0005, March 2011. On the Web at www.ahrq.gov/qual/qrdr10.htm. Accessed on August 3, 2011.

CDC guidelines are translated into practice in several ways and have served as the basis for national health care quality initiatives such as the *Institute for Healthcare Improvement's 100,000 Lives Campaign* and the *CMS Surgical Care Improvement Project,* which bundles together these guidelines to create best practices to reduce health care-associated infections. These collaborations help to standardize clinical practice, translate policy into practice, and reduce healthcare-associated infections. CDC also provides funding to a network of academic centers, called the *Prevention Epicenter Program,* that work in a collaborative manner to identify novel ways to improve infection control and health care quality and to assess the effectiveness of existing prevention strategies.

The Need for Improvement

A concise overview furnishes an outline of the direction in which health care should move in order for quality to be improved and costs to be constrained (Conway 2009). "The multitude of quality organizations (e.g., National Quality Forum, National Committee for Quality Assurance, Ambulatory Care Quality Alliance) each have made contributions to the quality enterprise, but there is a need to move beyond simply developing more measures and to focus on high-priority metrics such as those that influence outcomes on high-prevalence diseases, demonstrate baseline performance variability, and have potential mechanisms to improve results."

"Current measures often focus on individual patient-clinician interactions at a single point in time and, therefore, undervalue teamwork and patient outcomes over time. Measures focused on adherence to process in single interactions, when implemented widely, may have unintended negative consequences for patients. Measures need to focus more on patients' outcomes over an episode of care such as from hip fracture through recovery."

"Developing the next new device or medication with potential blockbuster status is the current primary driver of the research enterprise. However, clinicians are faced daily with patients who have common ailments for which there is no evidence to guide selection of one therapy or test over another. For clinicians to achieve better, more efficient results, this comparative effectiveness information must be available." [375]

Patients' Views of Health Care Quality

Good quality care requires that procedures and tests be medically appropriate and executed safely—two criteria that often have been the primary focus of quality improvement efforts (Fowler 2011). "However, appropriateness alone does not mean that the care is necessary or desired by the patient. High-quality care must ensure that every procedure, treatment, and test ordered also meet patients' goals for care. High-quality decisions require that patients be fully informed and involved in the decision-making process."

Identifying health problems and laying out reasonable options "are primarily the responsibility of the physician. Patients have the primary responsibility for identifying and conveying their goals and concerns relevant to the decision they are facing. Patients and providers must be receptive to one another."

375. Conway, P.H. and Clancy, C. Transformation of Health Care at the Front Line, *Journal of the American Medical Association,* Vol. 301, No. 7, February 18, 2009, pp. 763-765.

For patients to have a meaningful say in decisions, three essential conditions must be met:

- "They have to be informed. Specifically, they have to be given an objective, unbiased presentation of reasonable options to consider and the pros and cons of those options.
- Once informed, patients have to spend some time to consider their goals and concerns in the consequence of each option.
- They have to have an interaction with providers in which their goals and concerns are shared and incorporated into the decision-making process." [376]

Chapter 2 on semiotics indicates that differences between health professionals and patients from the standpoints of race, ethnicity, age, gender, health literacy, health beliefs, and religion can have a decisive impact on the quality of interaction. Time limits that are imposed on the length of that interaction also play a key role. The ability of providers to communicate options in an understandable manner and the ability to comprehend what is being described are related variables that can influence the outcomes of such decision-making processes.

The case of Mr. J. exemplifies the importance of health literacy in the encounters between patients and health professionals (Paasche-Orlow 2011). In this 76-year-old man, his medical history is significant for hypertension, type 2 diabetes, hyperlipidemia, obesity, and sleep apnea. He began working after finishing the eighth grade. He stopped being employed when his vision failed from complications of hypertension, diabetes, cataracts, and a macular hole. When questioned about his ability to read, he invokes limitations due to his visual deficits.

Clinicians don't know when his blood pressure is high or his diabetes is out of control. It also is unknown if he is or is not taking his medications. "He doesn't really feel that it's a priority to prevent heart disease. Despite numerous discussions, he does not appear to understand what heart disease is, or understands dialysis, or the many consequences that are associated with chronically elevated blood sugars." After not seeing his physician for a lengthy period of time, he said, "Well, I had to go to the hospital." When asked what happened there, he said, "I don't know. But they let me go, eventually." His hospital visit involved chest pain that required cardiac stenting. "He was supposed to be taking clopidogrel to keep his stents open," but did not know a thing about it.

An important lesson to be learned from this illustrated case is that "clinicians can help patients with limited health literacy by removing unneeded complexity in their treatment regimens and in the health care system and by using teach-back methods to assess and improve understanding. Rather than a selective screening approach for limited health literacy, a patient-based universal precaution approach for confirming patient comprehension of critical self-care activities helps ensure that all patients have their health literacy needs identified." [377]

Health Care Professionals, Facilities, and Health Care Quality

More efforts are needed to improve primary care, but there is little time in which to do so (Fiscella 2008). "During 15-minute visits, physicians are expected to form partnerships with patients and their families, address complex acute and chronic biomedical and psycho - social problems, provide preventive care, coordinate care with specialists, and ensure informed

---

376. Fowler, F.J. et al. Informing and Involving Patients to Improve the Quality of Medical Decisions, *Health Affairs*, Vol. 30, No. 4, April 2011, pp. 699-706.

377. Paasche-Orlow, M. Caring for Patients with Limited Health Literacy, *Journal of the American Medical Association*, Vol. 306, No. 10, September 14, 2011, pp. 1122-1129.

decision-making that respects patients' needs and preferences. This is a challenging task during straightforward visits, and, it is nearly impossible when caring for socially disadvantaged patients with complex biomedical and psychosocial problems and multiple barriers to care."

"Constraining care to 15-minute visits for socially disadvantaged patients ensures the perpetuation of health care disparities. Socially disadvantaged patients, often referred to as vulnerable or underserved, are at higher risk for multiple risk factors because of shared social characteristics. They include members of racial and ethnic minority groups and individuals with low literacy and low socioeconomic status. These groups, although distinct, overlap considerably, resulting in concentration of risk for patients."

"Time constraints severely limit informed decision-making and confirmation of patient understanding, and commonly result in omission of discussion of adverse medication effects and costs. For socially disadvantaged patients, who more commonly have multiple, complex, biomedical, and psychosocial problems, care is worse." Treating socially disadvantaged patients "poses unique challenges, requiring more time and greater team work. Communication across differences in language, culture, and health literacy takes time. Socially disadvantaged patients experience worse physical and mental health, including more impairments in vision, hearing, and cognition that slow communication."

"Time pressures may undermine physician empathy and patient trust, particularly among marginalized patients. Discussion of diagnosis and treatment involves exchange of illness-related information, confirmation of patient understanding, complex decision-making, and promotion of behavior change. Each of these tasks may take longer because of differences in language, health literacy, health beliefs, culture, and levels of trust. Participatory decision-making may seem unfamiliar to historically marginalized patients."

As noted in Chapter 2, unconscious physician stereotypes affect care. "Unconscious bias often emerges during periods of stress and time pressure. Physicians, challenged to address the complex needs of patients during a few minutes, more readily simplify these mental tasks by resorting to stereotypical thinking. Busy physicians may attend to data that conform to preconceived notions, such as nonadherence, on the basis of group membership and ignore disconfirming data. In addition, communication with socially disadvantaged patients may result in misinterpretations, even when both parties speak the same language. These misinterpretations are likely to result in lack of agreement about the illness, its treatment, and the patient's role in care. When decision-making is rushed, clinical judgment relies increasingly on heuristics, cognitive short-cuts, that often fail to account for individual needs." [378]

"Hospitalists are physicians whose primary professional focus is the general medical care of hospitalized patients and whose activities include patient care, teaching, research, and leadership-related inpatient care (López 2009). One study found that hospitals with hospitalists are associated with better hospital performance. Because complex factors affect the quality of hospital care delivered to patients, hospitalists are likely to be one of several factors that contribute to high-quality care." Investigators of this kind of health care concluded that "with the continued growth of the hospitalist inpatient care model, further research is needed to delineate the specific hospitalist model characteristics associated with improved quality and outcomes of care. The involvement of hospitalists in the acute care of hospitalized patients may contribute to improved quality of care for patients with common inpatient diagnoses." [379]

378. Fiscella, K. and Epstein, R.M. So Much to Do, So Little Time: Care for the Socially Disadvantaged and the 15-Minute Visit, *Archives of Internal Medicine*, Vol. 168, No. 17, September 22, 2008, pp. 1843-1852.
379. López, L. et al. Hospitalists and the Quality of Care in Hospitals, *Archives of Internal Medicine*, Vol. 169, No. 15, August 10/24, 2009, pp. 1389-1394.

Critical access hospitals (CAHs) play an important and unique role in U.S. health care, caring for individuals who live in rural areas and who might otherwise have no accessible inpatient care (Joynt 2011). "This hospital designation, created by the Medicare Rural Hospital Flexibility Program of the 1997 Balanced Budget Act, resulted from a federal effort to increase resources for small, geographically isolated hospitals, many of which were struggling financially. The legislation defined them as hospitals with no more than 25 acute care beds and located more than 35 miles from the nearest hospital. Hospitals that converted to critical access status became eligible for cost-based reimbursement rather than diagnosis related group-based reimbursement. As a result, margins improved and closures among these small rural hospitals decreased dramatically. More than a quarter of the acute care hospitals in the United States now have the CAH designation."

The designation was created "with the goal of ensuring 'proximate access' to basic inpatient and emergency care close to home for approximately 20% of the U.S. population that still lives in rural communities. The program has been highly successful in protecting access to inpatient care for rural communities, while providing care that receives high scores on patient satisfaction. However, despite broad policy interest in helping CAHs provide access to inpatient care little is known about the quality of care they provide—these hospitals are exempt from reporting to both the Joint Commission performance measure program and the Hospital Quality Alliance national public reporting program. CAHs have less access to capital and fewer health care professionals in their communities, including fewer specialists. Therefore, these hospitals may face equal or greater challenges in delivering high-quality care compared with other vulnerable hospitals, such as safety net hospitals, which have been more extensively studied. Understanding whether the CAH designation has been helpful, in not only improving access, but also in ensuring high-quality care, is a key element in evaluating federal efforts to ensure an effective rural health system."

"Given prior evidence that being a member of a hospital system may be related to improved clinical outcomes, promoting partnerships with health care systems might be a useful strategy to help CAHs. Such partnerships could include on-site rotations by clinicians with specialty training, increased use of telemedicine, or formal referral and transfer agreements—arrangements that allow patients to remain close to home while still facilitating access to specialty care are likely to be particularly well received by patients."

Health professionals are confronted with many challenges in providing quality care. A lack of evidence-based research on the effectiveness of certain procedures can produce some doubt about the wisdom of pursuing a particular course of action. Hurried settings in which a great many patients have to be seen in short periods of time can add to the level of stress. Personnel shortages exacerbate the situation because fewer health professionals are available to perform services that ideally should be carried out by a greater number of providers. The aging of segments of the health workforce adds more burden since each year retirements will occur that may not be matched by a requisite number of newly educated and trained individuals emerging from health professions schools.[380]

Nurses are at the frontline of care in a wide range of settings such as hospitals and clinics. They have long reported that their work conditions are not conducive to providing patient-centered care that is safe and of high quality. This relationship between working conditions and patient safety was recognized by an Institute of Medicine Report (IOM 2003).[381]

---

380. Joynt, K.E. et al. Quality of Care and Patient Outcomes in Critical Access Rural Hospitals, *Journal of the American Medical Association*, Vol. 306, No. 1, July 6, 2011, pp. 45-52.

381. Institute of Medicine. 2003. *Keeping Patients Safe: Transforming the Work Environment of Nurses*. Washington, DC: National Academies Press.

A more recent study found that "job dissatisfaction among nurses contributes to costly labor disputes, turnover, and risk to patients" (McHugh 2011). Survey data showed that much higher job dissatisfaction and burnout among nurses occurred "among those who were directly caring for patients in hospitals and nursing homes than among nurses working in other jobs or settings such as the pharmaceutical industry. Nurses are particularly dissatisfied with their health benefits, which highlights the need for a benefits review to make their benefits more comparable to those of other white-collar employees. Patient satisfaction levels are lower in hospitals with more nurses who are dissatisfied or burned out—a finding that signals problems with quality of care. Improving nurses' working conditions may improve both nurses' and patients' satisfaction and quality of care." [382]

Medical doctors play an extremely important role in meeting the health needs of patients. Two points worth noting are that there are not enough physicians to address the needs of underserved patients such as those who live in rural areas. Generally, controversy ensues whenever any other profession tries to provide a service that previously has been in the domain of organized medicine. Scope of practice disputes abound in many states around the nation, pitting one group of health professionals against another, such as chiropractors and physical therapists or dentists and dental hygienists.

Central to every debate is the issue of which groups of practitioners can provide care that is safe and effective. Determinations of this nature are highly contested, but the outcomes of these disputes have an impact on cost, access, and quality. A related matter considered in Chapter 12 on complementary and alternative medicine is that patients often take action on their own initiative by seeing different kinds of practitioners and by using items that they either purchase in health food stores or concoct on their own. Newcomers to U.S. shores often bring their health beliefs and practices with them. To the extent that all their caregivers are unaware of the full range of services being used by patients, there is a risk that the quality of care will be compromised when adverse reactions occur among incompatible elements of that care.

Another important consideration is the aging of the population. "In the U.S. more than 125 million individuals are living with chronic illness, disability, or functional limitation. The nature of modern medicine requires that these patients receive assistance from a number of different care providers (Bodenheimer 2008). Between 2000 and 2002, the typical Medicare beneficiary saw a median of two primary care physicians and five specialists each year, in addition to accessing diagnostic, pharmacy, and other services. Patients with several chronic conditions may visit up to 16 physicians in a year. Care among multiple providers must be coordinated to avoid wasteful duplication of diagnostic testing, perilous polypharmacy, and confusion about conflicting care plans."

"The particularities of American health care, with its pluralistic delivery system that features large numbers of small providers, magnify the number of venues such patients need to visit. Care must be coordinated among primary care physicians, specialists, diagnostic centers, pharmacies, home care agencies, acute care hospitals, skilled nursing facilities, and emergency departments. Within each of these centers, a patient may be touched by a number of physicians, nurses, medical assistants, pharmacists, and other caregivers, who also need to coordinate with one another. Given this level of complexity, the coordination of care among multiple independent providers becomes an enormous challenge."

---

382. McHugh, M.D. et al. Nurses' Widespread Job Dissatisfaction, Burnout, and Frustration with Health Benefits Signal Problems for Patient Care, *Health Affairs*, Vol. 30, No. 2, February 2011, pp. 202-210.

Coordination failures are common and can create serious quality concerns. For example, "referrals from primary care physicians to specialists often include insufficient information, and consultation reports from specialists back to primary care physicians are often late and inadequate. When patients are hospitalized, their primary care physicians may not be notified at the time of discharge and discharge summaries may contain insufficient information or never reach the primary care practice at all."

As "continuity of care diminishes with fewer primary care physicians, more part-time physicians, and the divorce of inpatient and outpatient practitioners, coordination of care assumes an increasingly central role. Addressing the flaws in care coordination is more difficult than the usual quality-improvement work that takes place within a hospital service or ambulatory care site. Improvement in care coordination requires that different health care entities, sometimes working in competition, perform together. Only then can all care be coordinated for every patient every day." [383]

Lastly, there should be some recognition that delivery patterns from other industries may be worth studying to determine what kinds of practices might be adopted with necessary modifications tailored to health care. The path and progress of a FedEx package can be tracked from the time it is picked up until it is delivered. Meanwhile, a patient who is brought to another part of a hospital for a diagnostic sonography test might be stranded in a corridor awaiting transport to arrive so that he or she can be returned to the original departure point. Another example is that when a patient is transferred from a department on the 14th floor of a hospital to another department on the 5th floor, not all necessary information may accompany this individual and diagnostic tests may be repeated needlessly at the new destination.

Many safety initiatives have been transferred successfully from commercial aviation to health care (Lewis 2011). Yet, among 15 examples of error countermeasures that are used in public transport, many are not used routinely in health care such as the first-names-only rule and incentivized no-fault reporting. The initiatives fall into three themes:

- "safety concepts that seek to downplay the role of heroic individuals and instead emphasize the importance of teams and whole organizations;
- concepts that seek to increase and apply group knowledge of safety information and values; and
- concepts that promote safety by design." [384]

Closing Thoughts

The federal government has initiated several efforts to improve health care quality. Given cost pressures to treat more patients in shorter periods of time, the potential exists for the quality of interaction with providers to be diminished, especially when patients have poor health literacy. Health workforce shortages can lead to burnout, which is not conducive to providing high-quality care. Patients should be able to understand treatment options presented to them. The next chapter describes new technology in the form of devices and procedures that health professionals may recommend even when there is not enough evidence to justify their use. In such instances, patients have to trust in what they are being advised to undergo and hope that the results prove to be beneficial.

---

383. Bodenheimer, T. Coordinating Care—A Perilous Journey through the Health Care System, *New England Journal of Medicine*, Vol. 358, No. 10, March 6, 2008, pp. 1064-1071.
384. Lewis, G.H. et al. Counterheroism, Common Knowledge, and Ergonomics: Concepts from Aviation That Could Improve Patient Safety, *The Milbank Quarterly*, Vol. 89, No. 1, March 2011, pp. 4-38.

The Role of Innovation, Technology, and Research in Health Care

15

The pace of advancements in technology has been quite rapid in recent decades. Some devices such as ventilators and implantable cardioverter defibrillators can prolong life for lengthy periods of time, which is not always a good thing in every instance because of the diminished quality of that life. More research is needed to demonstrate clinical and cost effectiveness of new treatments prior to their widespread use.

This chapter focuses on some advances in technology such as surgical robots, genomics, and information technology. Sometimes, innovations are introduced and adopted before they are proven to be effective. Comparative effectiveness and outcomes research is stressed as a means of reducing the incidence of costly errors and ineffective treatment. This chapter and the final chapter on future trends have much in common. Technological advances are part of the unfolding panorama of health services and treatments that may become standardized care.

Innovations in health care of an organizational nature also hold the possibility of improving the quality of care delivered. Earlier chapters have described the promise that lies behind the creation of accountable care organizations and health insurance exchanges. As of the close of 2011, these notions have yet to be implemented and their effectiveness has yet to be determined. A thought worth keeping in mind is that over the decades, other ways of organizing the delivery of health care such as health maintenance organizations (HMOs) have not completely met what was expected of them when they first were introduced. Even when successful in one venue, there never is an assurance that an organizational innovation will be extended to all geographic areas.

Difficulties are inherent in trying to control costs for health care while simultaneously producing new forms of technology, which may either increase or decrease spending patterns. For example, devices such as stents and advances in pharmacology have led to decreases in expensive hospital stays. The downside is that some new developments prove to be highly costly without improving health status or saving lives in any appreciable way.

Considerable amounts of money are spent for neonatal intensive care. Severely underweight babies who are born to mothers in their early teens or to mothers with severe drug problems can result in massive expenditures to keep these babies alive. Social class, level of education, and poverty are among the factors that create such problems, and technology will be of little avail in solving them or reducing their occurrence.

The aging eyeball becomes less efficient with the passage of time. Instead of purchasing a pair of eyeglasses at a drugstore or at WalMart to magnify the size of the printed word or simply holding the newspaper or book an inch or two more away from the line of vision, expensive surgery

249

frequently might be the option chosen. That choice will add to the pace of increasing health care costs.

Children have a unique gift for looking at photos of their parents when the latter group was much younger and laughing hysterically at hairstyles and fashions that existed in earlier periods. Tattoos are popular these days, but will that remain true in the future, particularly of the variety that covers the neck and limbs? If not, a new type of health care cost will be the removal of these images, and there already is some evidence that a thriving business to provide these services is on the immediate horizon.

Technological and pharmaceutical innovations often are introduced and disseminated widely in short periods of time. In some instances, what originally was designed to solve one kind of health problem may eventually be used in quite different ways, as shown in the following examples.

Mechanical Ventilators

"The technological imperative in American and Western European medicine is sustained through social processes of routinization in which experimental procedures or new technologies quickly come to be considered 'standard' or 'routine' in clinical practice (Kaufman 2000). The meaning of a new biomedical technology changes from experimental to routine as players become habituated to its use. 'Standard of care' is embodied in the newest technologies and 'becomes a moral as well as a technical obligation.'"

"By the early 1970s, the mechanical ventilator or 'breathing machine' was standard equipment in all tertiary medical centers and most community hospitals in the U.S. Through the application of positive pressure, the mechanical ventilator forces air directly into the lungs at a volume and rate adjusted by medical practitioners and maintained by the machine. It thus 'breathes' for patients who have a temporary loss of pulmonary function due to surgery, acute infection, or trauma, or for patients who have a long-term or permanent loss of lung or brain function. Like many technologies before it, the mechanical ventilator was applauded for enabling new forms of treatment such as coronary artery bypass graft surgery and for life prolongation of persons with neuromuscular diseases or adult respiratory distress syndrome." This technology was implemented in hospitals as soon as it was available. "The mechanical ventilator sparked the creation of the intensive care unit and immediately was considered essential technology there."

"By 1975, mechanical ventilation was indicated for a long list of diseases and problems. Its development was inspired by the desire to solve the problem of keeping patients alive through surgery or infection. But from the beginning of its association with intensive care medicine, the mechanical ventilator created troubling outcomes because":

- "It is also capable of keeping people alive for months and years who are in a vegetative state.
- It allows the vital organs of dead persons to remain oxygenated so that those organs can be transplanted later. Brain dead persons who are connected to mechanical ventilators do not look dead, a situation that causes unresolved distress for some families and health professionals.
- Elderly people who have pneumonia or who go into cardiac or respiratory arrest and are resuscitated, easily can be, and sometimes are, placed on mechanical ventilators when they arrive at hospital emergency rooms."

"Unless patients make it clearly known through living wills or other written documents that they do not want their lives prolonged by mechanical ventilation or unless they have advocates who can effectively express to hospital staff the patient's wish not to be placed on a respirator, standard practice throughout the United States is to place the patient on mechanical ventilation if the patient would otherwise die immediately."

"'Choices' that patients, families, and health professionals face when a patient cannot be removed from the ventilator because he or she will not be able to breathe 'naturally' are constructed, then, around the problems of when, why, and how to withdraw ventilator support so that the patient can 'be allowed' to die. 'Choices' are constrained largely by the trap that the mechanical ventilator creates: the perceived responsibility of either prolonging dying 'unnaturally' or 'causing' death proactively. The way in which the technology has come to be used, in addition to a means of enabling surgery or alleviating acute disease, generates a particular form of experience described most often as 'ethical dilemma.' It is the widespread negative public reaction to the mechanical ventilator, more than to any other particular medical technology or procedure, that has sparked the 'right to die' movement across the United States and inspired the cultural cry for 'death with dignity,' that is, death without hi-tech medical prolongation." [385]

Implantable Cardioverter Defibrillators

"The implantable cardioverter defibrillator (ICD) is a small electronic device (like a pacemaker) that monitors heart rate and rhythm and recognizes the onset of life-threatening arrhythmias (Kaufman 2011). When it detects an abnormal rhythm, it delivers timed electrical discharges or shocks to the heart muscle, thereby disrupting and ending a life-threatening rhythm. It is commonly referred to as an 'emergency room in the chest' and functions like the defibrillator paddles used in emergency room resuscitation. A normal rhythm then can resume, either through the pacing function of the device which corrects the rhythm or via the heart's own return to a normal beating pattern."

"Today's implantable cardiac devices, which may include pacing, defibrillating and heart chamber coordination functions (the latter is called cardiac resynchronization therapy or CRT) are examples of a constant re-invention. Most recently, the ICD function often is included with cardiac resynchronization therapy, which helps the two chambers of the heart beat in a synchronized or balanced way, thus relieving the debilitating symptoms of heart failure."

"These multi-function devices can improve cardiac function, reduce debilitating symptoms and treat and prevent lethal rhythms. The development of these 'all in one' devices makes it easy for physicians to suggest to patients that they should consider adding the ICD function when they are offered or advised to get a pacemaker and a resynchronization device. The important point here is that the ICD, invented and then first used to prevent patients from dying prematurely, while still young, is now implanted primarily in older patients, often as part of a multi-function device, mostly with no plans for its impacts on end of life care or for its eventual deactivation in the elderly near death. The expanded means of the ICD, coupled with its expanded use, have contributed to an altered end—a socio-medical emphasis on diminishing the risks of death, regardless of advanced age or disease state. The pursuit of that end precludes or complicates individual physician and patient choice. The goal of avoiding death in ever older, sicker patients fosters, also, new pathways to death and new qualms for patients and families facing the responsibility of choosing one form of dying over another."

---

385. Kaufman, S.R. In the Shadow of "Death with Dignity": Medicine and Cultural Quandaries of the Vegetative State, *American Anthropologist*, Vol. 102, No. 1, March 2000, pp. 69-83.

The irony is that while the ICD "prevents sudden death from a potentially fatal arrhythmia," the kind of death many claim to want in late life, yet, "in doing so, it contributes to prolonged dying," which simultaneously makes it a "technology of life extension and dying even though success in averting sudden death now often leads to prolonged dying with the worsening symptoms of heart disease and may cause a death traumatic for both patients and families due to repeated shocks during the dying transition."

Four powerful socio-cultural engines drive a great deal of the open-ended technology use for the elderly in the U.S.:

- "Clinicians are aware that treatments for the very old can be a double-edged endeavor, yet they want and feel obligated to provide life-extending options, sometimes regardless of a patient's age or extreme frailty.
- Older persons, some of whom are ambivalent about living on and on with deteriorating health, do not easily want to authorize their own deaths by proactively stopping or rejecting a (potentially) life-saving therapy, for that is what saying 'no' to technology has come to imply.
- Families do not want the responsibility of saying 'no' to life-extending interventions for their loved ones and, of course, they are hopeful that treatments can extend meaningful life.
- Importantly, bioethics discourse often excludes the effects of life-prolonging/death-prolonging technologies on families and the fact that clinical practice today tends to ethically 'offload' decision-making about 'life' and 'death' to patients and families."

"Procedure-driven health care finance arrangements guide everyone in the U.S. toward more and more technology use. Innovative technologies that prolong some lives will continue to emerge, to be approved for insurance coverage and to be, thus, ethically necessary. As both the means and the ends of cardiac and other technologies evolve, societal ambivalence—about value, cost effectiveness, the idea of a 'natural' life span, and how much intervention is appropriate at ever older ages—will remain." [386]

In one study, investigators "found that a substantial number of ICDs were implanted in patients who were similar to those who either were excluded from major clinical trials of primary prevention ICDs or shown not to benefit from ICD therapy in other trials (Al-Khatib 2011). Such patients not only have more comorbidities than patients receiving an evidence-based device, but they are at a higher risk of in-hospital death and any postprocedure complication." Considerable variation was observed "in non–evidence-based ICD implants by site. The rate of non–evidence-based ICD implants was significantly higher for nonelectrophysiologists than electrophysiologists. There was no clear decrease in the overall number of non–evidence-based ICD implants over time. As such, more efforts should focus on enhancing adherence to evidence-based practice." [387]

Surgical Robots

"Technological innovation in health care is an important driver of cost growth. Doctors and patients often embrace new modes of treatment before their merits and weaknesses are fully understood (Barbash 2010). These technologies can lead to increased costs, either because

386. Kaufman, S.R. et al. Ironic Technology: Old Age and the Implantable Cardioverter Defibrillator in US Health Care, *Social Science & Medicine*, Vol. 72, No. 1, January 2011, pp. 6-14.
387. Al-Khatib, S.M. et al. Non-Evidence-Based ICD Implantations in the United States, *Journal of the American Medical Association*, Vol. 305, No. 1, January 5, 2011, pp. 43-49.

they are simply more expensive than previous treatments or because their introduction leads to an expansion in the types and numbers of patients treated."

"A wide range of procedures are now performed by means of robot-assisted surgery." Some were "already being performed laparoscopically before robots were introduced. Various nonsurgical treatment alternatives for localized prostate cancer exist, with similar long-term outcomes and varying side effects such as incontinence and impotence. Existing analyses suggest that as compared with open surgery, robot-assisted surgery does not diminish the frequency of these adverse events. However, substantial short-term benefits in postoperative recovery that are associated with robot-assisted procedures may encourage patients with localized cancer to opt for surgical intervention rather than alternative nonsurgical interventions or watchful waiting." [388]

"Prior literature has documented significant increases in aggregate use of surgical procedures with the adoption of new surgical technology, even in the absence of evidence for superior clinical outcomes (Makarov 2011). Prior literature has also demonstrated that patterns of technology adoption and healthcare utilization may vary substantially across regions. However, little is known about technology adoption and consequent regional level changes in healthcare utilization."

"For several reasons, use of the surgical robot (da Vinci Surgical System, Intuitive Surgical, Sunnyvale, CA) for radical prostatectomy to treat prostate cancer is an excellent example to study the effect that surgical technology adoption has on the utilization of surgical procedures."

- "The surgical robot is very expensive. Its purchase price ranges from $1 million to $2.25 million, along with an annual service contract of $140,000, and disposable instruments costing $1500 to $2000 per case.
- The surgical robot is of controversial marginal benefit for the treatment of prostate cancer. Reports of its clinical efficacy have been mixed, with some suggesting improved outcomes (especially decreased length of stay and decreased intraoperative blood loss) and others suggesting either no benefit or actual detriment as compared with open surgery or standard laparoscopy.
- Despite its expense and questionable benefit, the surgical robot has been widely adopted for the treatment of prostate cancer. It was reported that in 2009 more than 85% of men undergoing RP had robotic surgery.
- Hospitals continue to acquire the surgical robot for new indications such as gynecologic, thoracic, and gastrointestinal surgery. The effect of the diffusion of the surgical robot on the care of patients with prostate cancer is unclear."

A study revealed that "regions with more hospitals having acquired surgical robots by the end of the study period demonstrated a significant increase in [radical prostatectomy] compared with those regions without any robot-owning hospitals. Patients should be aware that if they seek care at a hospital with a new piece of surgical technology, they are more likely to have surgery than at a hospital without the technology. As empowered consumers of healthcare, they should also be wary of marketing efforts aimed to capture their business by advertising technology as a proxy for quality."

"Physicians should be aware that they may see fewer patients if they practice at a hospital which is a late adopter of technology. Hospital administrators should be aware that the purchase of new technology will increase surgical volume, but this increase may not be sufficient to compensate for that technology's cost and may have little demonstrable quality benefit for patients." [389]

388. Barbash, G.I. and Glied, S.A. New Technology and Health Care Costs—The Case of Robot-Assisted Surgery, *New England Journal of Medicine*, Vol. 363, No. 8, August 19, 2010, pp. 701-704.
389. Makarov, D.V. et al. The Association between Diffusion of the Surgical Robot and Radical Prostatectomy Rates, *Medical Care*, Vol. 49, No. 4, April 2011, pp. 333-339.

Innovations Evolving from Genomics, Stem Cell Research, and Regenerative Medicine

The mapping of the human genome has produced great optimism about the prospect of using genetic testing to lower morbidity and mortality through early disease detection and targeted surveillance and prevention strategies. "Genomewide association studies, in which hundreds of thousands of single-nucleotide polymorphisms (SNPs) are tested for association with a disease in hundreds or thousands of persons, have revolutionized the search for genetic influences on complex traits (Manolio 2010). Such conditions, in contrast with single-gene disorders, are caused by many genetic and environmental factors working together, each having a relatively small effect and few if any being absolutely required for disease to occur. Although complex conditions have been referred to as the geneticist's nightmare, in the past 5 years genomewide association studies have identified SNPs implicating hundreds of robustly replicated loci (i.e., specific genomic locations) for common traits."

"Genomewide association studies have proved successful in identifying genetic associations with complex traits. This reasonably unbiased approach to surveying the genome has opened doors to potential treatments by revealing the unexpected involvement of certain functional and mechanistic pathways in a variety of disease processes. Although the approach has proved powerful in identifying robust associations between many SNPs and traits, much additional work is needed to determine the functional basis for the observed associations so that appropriate interventions can be developed."

"Despite the limitations of using data obtained from these studies to assess the individual patient's level of risk for a particular condition, genomewide scans may be useful in initiating counseling about nongenetic risk factors or perhaps in screening for a high risk of many conditions at once. Continued efforts to identify genetic variants that influence the response to drugs may yield new associations that could be used to tailor drug selection and dosing to the profile of the individual patient, particularly if it becomes possible to query these data through a user-friendly interface when a medication is ordered. The substantial challenges of incorporating such research into clinical care must be pursued if the potential of genomic medicine is to be realized." [390]

"Rapid technological advances are decreasing DNA sequencing costs and making it practical to undertake complete human genome sequencing on a large scale for the first time (Drmanac 2011). Complete human genome sequencing is becoming available at increasing scale and decreasing cost, thanks to massively parallel genomic micro- and nanoarrays. In 2010, multiple studies based on sequencing dozens to hundreds of complete human genomes were completed or initiated. With the more than 400 genomes/month sequencing capacity available at Complete Genomics, combined with the expanding capacity of National Human Genome Research Institute-funded U.S. genome centers, the Wellcome-Trust Sanger Institute in Europe, and BGI in China, thousands of individual genome sequences are expected to be analyzed in 2011."

"The number of genomes sequenced has grown dramatically over the last few years from <100 in 2009 to >2000 in 2010 and is projected by the journal *Nature* to reach approximately 25,000 in 2011, including low-coverage genomes. It would not be surprising if within the next five years, we see the annual number of complete human genomes sequenced rises to over a mil-

---

390. Manolio, T.A. Genomic Medicine: Genomewide Association Studies and Assessment of the Risk of Disease, *New England Journal of Medicine*, Vol. 363, No. 2, July 8, 2010, pp. 166-176.

lion. Obtaining complete genetic and epigenetic information at this scale, coupled with routine transcriptome sequencing and various functional studies, will lead to an increasingly comprehensive understanding of disease development at the molecular level." [391]

A reasonable question to ask is where public health fits into the equation of genomic medicine. "The mission of public health is to improve health from a population perspective and its unit of intervention is the 'population,' an approach seemingly at odds with the 'one person at a time' vision of genomic medicine (Khoury 2011). Some suggest that applications of human genomics will be made at the clinical level, not through population screening. Some have even argued that there will be very little role for genomics in public health once we know the environmental and social causes of disease."

"In a time of diminishing resources, new technologies can divert needed resources away from what can be done today in delivering basic public health services and addressing social and environmental determinants of disease. However, the practice of genomic medicine (and medicine in general) occurs at multiple levels of intervention including patient-provider dyads, healthcare organizations, families, communities, and state and federal policies and regulations, all appropriately viewed by the Institute of Medicine as part of the 'public health system.' Moreover, as genomics ventures more and more into primary prevention and health promotion with the emergence of the direct-to-consumer movement, we are going to see an increasing role for public health practitioners in providing health education information and policy frameworks for protecting consumers and minimizing costly and unnecessary healthcare expenditures."

"Because public health has a population focus with an eye toward the most vulnerable segments of the population, it will have a major role in ensuring the success of genomic medicine. The public health functions provide an important basis for furnishing an appropriate balance between the forces of 'premature translation' (i.e., use of nonvalidated or potentially harmful genomic information in practice) versus 'lost in translation' (i.e., the endless study and evaluation of new technology with limited access across the population)." [392]

Genomic Medicine and Incidentalomas

The occurrence of incidentalomas can be illustrated by the following series of events that happened involving one patient. Following a heart attack, this individual underwent a routine test that involved the inspection of the carotid arteries. They were fine, but the procedure revealed a node on the thyroid. A subsequent test revealed that a hyperthyroid condition existed even though no symptoms had manifested themselves. To rule out a carcinoma, the patient had a biopsy, which proved to be negative. An endocrinologist erringly prescribed a medication to treat a hypo- rather than a hyperthyroid condition. The consequences were rapid weight loss of 20 pounds in 1 month followed by wild bouts of arrhythmia. A cardiologist indicated that continued use of the medication might have been fatal.

The phenomenon "known as *incidentalomas* has the capability of producing cascade effects, which refers to a process that proceeds in stepwise fashion from an initiating event to a seemingly inevitable conclusion" (Deyo 2002). Regarding medical technology, a chain of events can

---

391. Drmanac, R. The Advent of Personal Genome Sequencing, *Genetics in Medicine*, Vol. 13, No. 3, March 2011, pp. 188-190.

392. Khoury, M.J. Public Health Genomics: The End of the Beginning, *Genetics in Medicine*, Vol. 13, No. 3, March 2011.

be unleashed by "an unnecessary test, an unexpected result, or patient or physician anxiety, which results in ill-advised tests or treatments that may cause avoidable adverse effects and/or morbidity. Examples include discovery of endocrine incidentalomas on head and body scans; irrelevant abnormalities on spinal imaging; tampering with random fluctuations in clinical measures; and unwanted aggressive care at the end of life. Common triggers include failing to understand the likelihood of false-positive results; errors in data interpretation; overestimating benefits or underestimating risks; and low tolerance of ambiguity. Excess capacity and perverse financial incentives may contribute to cascade effects as well. Preventing cascade effects may require better education of physicians and patients; research on the natural history of mild diagnostic abnormalities; achieving optimal capacity in health care systems; and awareness that more is not the same as better." [393]

- "First, physicians will be overwhelmed by the complexity of pursuing unexpected genomic measurements.
- Second, patients will be subjected to unnecessary follow-up tests, causing additional morbidity.
- Third, the cost of genomic medicine will increase substantially with little benefit to patients or physicians (but with great financial benefits to the genomic testing industry), thus throwing the overall societal benefit of genome-based medicine into question."

"Genomic medicine is poised to offer a broad array of new genome-scale screening tests." However, these tests may lead to the discovery of multiple abnormal genomic findings "analogous to the 'incidentalomas' that often are discovered in radiological studies (Kohane 2006). If practitioners pursue these unexpected genomic findings without thought, there may be disastrous consequences."

"Physicians know that as the number of tests increases, the chance that a spurious abnormal test result will arise also increases. They also know that it is difficult to ignore abnormal findings and they often must embark on a sequence of more expensive tests to investigate the findings. Furthermore, the significance of an abnormal finding is related to the prevalence of disease in the population from which the tested patient is drawn. Therefore, if the risk associated with the finding was established in a population with a high prevalence of disease, the rate of false-positive results when testing in a population with a lower rate of disease will be much higher." [394]

For some conditions such as Huntington disease, genetic testing is highly predictive, but for "multifactorial diseases such as colorectal cancer and Alzheimer disease, genetic testing is less determinative and more 'predispositional' in nature (Heshka 2008). In these cases, genetic risk prediction can help identify individuals at increased risk, but doing so may result in increased distress, anxiety, and stigmatization." [395]

The National Institutes of Health created a public database that researchers, consumers, health care providers, and others can search for information submitted voluntarily by genetic test providers (NIH 2011). The Genetic Testing Registry (GTR) aims to enhance access to information about the availability, validity, and usefulness of genetic tests. Presently, more than 2,000 genetic tests are available to patients and consumers, but there is no single public resource that provides detailed information about them. GTR is intended to fill that gap. It is currently

---

393. Deyo, R.A. Cascade Effects of Medical Technology, *Annual Review of Public Health*, Vol. 23, 2002, pp. 23-44.
394. Kohane, I.S. et al. The Incidentalome: A Threat to Genomic Medicine, *Journal of the American Medical Association*, Vol. 296, No. 2, July 12, 2006, pp. 212-215.
395. Heshka, J.T. et al. A Systematic Review of Perceived Risks, Psychological and Behavioral Impacts of Genetic Testing, *Genetics in Medicine*, Vol. 10, No. 1, January 2008, pp. 19-32.

in development, with a projected launch in early 2012. Once operational, GTR will provide access to information about genetic tests for inherited and somatic genetic variations, including newer types of tests such as arrays and multiplex panels. Information about tests will be primarily based on voluntary data submissions by test developers and manufacturers.[396]

Regenerative Medicine

Chapter 8 provided a perspective on regenerative medicine and the promise held by its proponents that a healthy lifespan is achievable well beyond the age of 100. "Interventions to replace undeveloped, destroyed, or degenerated tissues are not new (Trommelmans 2010). Regenerating tissue was thought to be impossible, so that aiming to do so presents a significant shift in the goal of medicine. Regenerative medicine employs three strategies":

- "Inducing the body's inherent regenerative capacities in vivo through the application of growth factors and/or stem cells.
- 'Tissue engineering,' or creating complex structures in vitro containing cells and custom-made scaffolds to implant in the patient.
- Recolonizing donated, decellularized structures with patient-derived cells and implanting them in the patient."

"Regenerative medicine has been enthusiastically received as it promises to make further interventions redundant. Also, it may provide solutions for as-yet-untreatable conditions and it may benefit anyone from neonates (possibly even fetuses) to the elderly. All medical fields have embraced it, from dentistry and orthopedics to neurosurgery and cardiology. Its growth is based on increased knowledge of cell—and especially stem cell—biology and biomaterials, and on the increasing prevalence of degenerative diseases."

"While the principles of regenerative medicine are easy to explain and the possible benefits even easier to appraise, relatively few products have made it into clinical trials, and even fewer into therapy. So far, we know some of the 'vocabulary of tissue formation—the genes, cells, growth factors, and extracellular environment involved—but we know very little the 'syntax' of healthy and affected tissues":

- "How these elements interact during the tissue formation process.
- How the native tissue (healthy and affected) interacts with the new.
- Whether these interactions are unique for each individual or common for all persons."

"For now, regenerative medicine is more akin to tissue *handicraft* than tissue engineering; products are developed on a case-by-case basis, and most research energy is spent on identifying and combining the pieces of the puzzle, then translating these findings into a therapeutically active product."

"Another challenge for the development of regenerative medicine is that it is not being pursued by the usual actors—the big pharmaceutical companies that have the money, infrastructure, and clinical trial experience to bring a therapy to market. Rather, the driving forces behind regenerative medicine are cell biologists and biomaterials experts, many of whom are not

---

396. National Institutes of Health. Genetic Testing Registry. On the Web at http://www.ncbi.nlm.nih.gov/gtr/. Accessed on December 3, 2011.

acquainted with bioethical issues." Ethics committees often are unfamiliar with regenerative medicine, "which may make it difficult to design ethically acceptable clinical trials on regenerative medicine." Another factor is the "considerable time it takes to go from bench to bedside —if the bedside is ever reached." [397]

Organ Transplantation

Among the various interventions to prolong human life, organ transplants represent another avenue to pursue. Double-lung transplants for cystic fibrosis (CF) sufferers offer an example that is replete with key issues to resolve. "Within the modern culture of control, patients and physicians seek to shape the uncertainty of prognostications concerning the course of disease and the anticipated effects of therapeutic and surgical interventions" (Maynard 2006). Decisions are made within a complex framework:

- "The denial of death and disability in technological modernity.
- The consequent emphasis on cure and saving life at any cost rather than the management of chronic illness.
- The extent to which health and illness constitute identity.
- The problems of CF patients conceiving their life narrative when life will be short."

Two important questions are: "(1) Do patient beliefs in the progress narratives of medicine overshadow other considerations, and (2) Are biotechnologies such as organ transplant a calculated gamble on a better life or an uncertain reliance on biomedical expertise?"

"Not every patient will have a successful transplant as defined by 2 or 3 years of life post-surgery with normal lung functions. A more unfavorable outcome could be further disability and death. Risks versus benefits may be uncertain and a series of strategic choices can lead patients down quite different pathways."

"The spectacular successes and miserable failures associated with transplants produce an arena with no easy answers and many questions—questions of negotiating disability in an ablelist society while encountering limits to health and mortality amid the potential offered by new, chimeric embodiments, embodiments that offer the opportunity to relocate one's individual narrative within mainstream cultural imperatives that valorize health. How do individuals negotiate in a world of constraints and possibilities, limits, and opportunities? In the world of cystic fibrosis and lung transplants, how are subjectivities and identities produced and transformed amid modernity's progress narratives? How do linkages of personal and technological futures produce complex dilemmas involving risk and opportunity, appropriation and loss?" [398]

Health Information Technology

This branch of technological developments has many sub-branches such as electronic health records (EHRs), electronic prescribing of medications, and text messaging between pro -

---

397. Trommelmans, L. The Challenge of Regenerative Medicine, *Hastings Center Report*, Vol. 40, No. 6, November-December 2010, pp. 24-26.
398. Maynard, R.J. Controlling Death—Compromising Life, *Medical Anthropology Quarterly*, Vol. 20, No. 2, June 2006, pp. 212-234.

viders and patients. An issue worth pondering is the extent to which digital solutions will enhance the quality and safety of health care. A systematic review of systematic reviews was conducted to shed light on this matter (Black 2011).

The conclusions reached were that "there is a large gap between the postulated and empirically demonstrated benefits of eHealth technologies. In addition, there is a lack of robust research on the risks of implementing these technologies and their cost-effectiveness has yet to be demonstrated, despite being frequently promoted by policymakers and 'techno-enthusiasts' as if this was a given. In the light of the paucity of evidence in relation to improvements in patient outcomes and the lack of evidence on their cost-effectiveness, it is vital that future eHealth technologies are evaluated against a comprehensive set of measures, ideally throughout all stages of the technology's life cycle. Such evaluation should be characterised by careful attention to socio-technical factors to maximise the likelihood of successful implementation and adoption." [399]

A stimulus for wider use of EHRs occurred with President Barack Obama's American Recovery and Reinvestment Act, which made available $19 billion in incentives for their adoption. The Health Information Technology for Economic and Clinical Health (HITECH) Act of 2009 includes funds to stimulate adoption of EHR. The Congressional Budget Office estimates net payments of approximately $30 billion for Medicare and Medicaid incentives over the life of the program (CBO 2009).[400] "A sizable portion of these payments will be made to hospitals that are able to demonstrate 'meaningful use' of a 'certified' EHR. Using EHRs to improve quality is an example of meaningful use" (Jones 2010).

"The CBO projects that these incentives will induce 25% more U.S. hospitals to adopt an EHR that would not have done so otherwise. An expected benefit of EHR adoption is improved quality of care. However, much of the current knowledge about the relationship between health IT and hospital quality comes from a few hospitals that may not be representative of the broader set of hospitals being targeted by the HITECH incentives." [401]

"Health information technology (IT), such as computerized physician order entry and electronic health records, has potential to improve the quality of health care. But the returns from widespread adoption of such technologies remain uncertain (McCullough 2010). Changes in the quality of care following adoption of electronic health records were measured among a national sample of U.S. hospitals from 2004 to 2007." The use of computerized physician order entry and EHRs resulted in significant improvements in two quality measures, with larger effects in academic than nonacademic hospitals. "The conclusion drawn was that achieving substantive benefits from national implementation of health IT may be a lengthy process."

"Under these circumstances, policies focused on improving the efficacy of health IT in nonacademic environments might be beneficial. There are a number of potential policy alternatives. For example, improved interoperability standards might increase health IT value. Many electronic health record systems have difficulty sharing information. This is an area where markets might benefit from increased government intervention. If physician-hospital integration is

---

399. Black, A.D. et al. The Impact of eHealth on the Quality and Safety of Health Care: A Systematic Review, *PLoS Medicine*, Vol. 8, Issue 1, January 2011, 15 pp.

400. Congressional Budget Office (CBO) Letter to the Honorable Charles B. Rangel, Chairman Committee on Ways and Means, U.S. House of Representatives. January 21, 2009. On the Web at http://www.cbo.gov/ftpdocs/99xx/doc9966/HITECHRangelLtr.pdf. Accessed on September 30, 2011.

401. Jones, S. S. et al. Electronic Health Record Adoption and Quality Improvement in US Hospitals, *American Journal of Managed Care*, Vol. 16, Special Issue, December 2010, pp. SP64–SP71.

the source of context dependence, then increased interoperability or, possibly, information exchanges might improve the value of health IT in non-academic settings. Alternatively, investments in the evidence base for decision-support protocols might also increase the efficacy of health IT." [402]

M ore than a decade of experience with one medical group's general internal medicine clinic EHR "has shown that it provides clinicians with increased efficiency in documentation, more rapid and timely access to tests and procedure findings, and useful preventive services alerts for patients" (Webb 2010). Apropos of Chapter 2 on the topic of semiotics, another finding was that "the attention required to enter and access EHR information in the examination room can potentially detract from the quality of interpersonal communication with patients. Physicians may avoid spending the time required to clean up and update EHR medication screens during a particular visit, old prescriptions are left on lists, drugs that were prescribed by other medical specialists or alternative providers are not entered, and newly ordered prescriptions may be hastily discussed with patients."

Nevertheless, "the advent of the EHR offers the potential for primary care practices to adopt new approaches to eliminating medication discrepancies, while also providing patients with easy-to-understand instructions about new prescriptions that will enhance medication safety and adherence. Because the EHR is in use during each patient visit, it is possible to easily review current medication lists. Patients receive an EHR medication list of their current medications at check-in, allowing them to review any discrepancies before their physician visit." Also, to improve patient understanding of their new medications, information sheets can be printed for patients "when they are prescribed a new medication."

A study conducted of patients in this particular setting yielded pilot data that were used to develop a better strategy to improve medication reconciliation and patient knowledge about patient regimens. Using real-time review and access to educational materials afforded by the EHR, a higher standard of care is expected "that will require no significant additional time or effort over the long run." [403]

Prior to and following interactions with health professionals in clinical settings, patients have ample opportunities to seek and locate information of interest to them. Friends, coworkers, and relatives are one source viewed as being credible. The Web opens up a world of information, some of it excellent and some of it absurd, depending on the source.

New information that is acquired can have an impact on the dialogue between patients and clinicians. An example is that a patient may know of the existence of a particular diagnostic test and stress during a discussion with a practitioner that he or she wants it, even though doing so never crossed the health professional's mind because the choice is not an appropriate one. If trust exists in the relationship, the clinician might be able to convince the patient of the lack of value of undertaking such a procedure in light of what appears to be the nature of the health problem. Otherwise, if the practitioner is being viewed as too stubborn and behind the times, the patient will head to another venue to obtain what is deemed personally necessary.

---

402. McCullough, J.S. et al. The Effect of Health Information Technology on Quality in U.S. Hospitals, *Health Affairs*, Vol. 29, No. 4, April 2010, pp. 647-654.

403. Webb, J.R. et al. Can Electronic Health Records Help Improve Patients' Understanding of Medications? *American Journal of Managed Care*, Vol. 16, No. 12, December 2010, pp. 919-922.

Patients' Use of the Web for Health Information

P otential advantages and disadvantages of using the Web as a resource are as follows (Wald 2007):

Advantages
- "Health information on the Web may make patients better informed, leading to better health outcomes and more appropriate use of health service resources.
- Web health information offers opportunities to improve the physician-patient relationship by sharing the burden of responsibility for knowledge and enhancing communication in general.
- Accessing and reflecting upon Web information and considering preferences prior to the clinical encounter can lead to more efficient use of clinical time.
- A participatory decision-making model, which includes a Web-informed patient can add validity to the concept of 'informed consent' and foster informed decision-making.
- After their visit with a physician, Web-based patient information may serve to augment the information provided during the visit.
- The Web can serve as a vehicle for patients to access their own health records.

Disadvantages
- The quality of health information on the Web can be highly variable.
- Some socioeconomically groups may have limited access to the Web.
- Use of Web health information may impact liability. Providers potentially can be held liable for not meeting a standard of care identified through the Web."
- Clinicians may experience conflict with more assertive patients who insist on courses of action that they learned about on the Web.[404]

Electronic Communication Between Patients and Providers

T he exchange of e-mail between physicians and patients is considered a potential tool to improve physician-patient communication and, ultimately, patient care. Results of a study reported in October 2010 indicated that despite indications that many patients want to send e-mail to their doctors, physician adoption and use of e-mail with patients remains uncommon (Boukus 2010).

"Overall, about one-third of office-based physicians reported that information technology was available in their practice for e-mailing patients about clinical issues. Of those, fewer than one in five reported using e-mail with patients routinely; the remaining physicians were roughly evenly split between occasional users and non-users. Physicians in practices with access to electronic medical records and those working in health maintenance organizations (HMOs) or medical school settings were more likely to adopt and use e-mail to communicate with patients compared with other physicians. However, even among the highest users—physicians in group/staff-model HMOs—only 50.6% reported routinely e-mailing patients."

Developments occur rapidly and data that are reported in various studies often are quickly superseded by more recent information, which is a reflection of how rapidly some innovations

---

404. Wald, H.S. et al. Untangling the Web—The Impact of Internet Use on Health Care and the Physician-Patient Relationship, *Patient Education and Counseling*, Vol. 68, No. 3, November 2007, pp. 218-224.

are adopted. It is reasonable to conjecture that by October 2012, these figures will be substantially higher.[405]

Health professionals have an opportunity to broaden their awareness and understanding of new developments in health care. The widespread adoption of iPads and iPhones makes it possible to communicate with peers all around the world and extract information from the Internet without having to be bound to an office computer. Teleconferencing has many uses such as in conducting electronic grand rounds and participating in continuing education offerings. Practitioners in remote areas no longer have to experience the deficit of being geographically isolated from health science centers. Much of what is developed in those venues can be transmitted to health professionals in other places.

mHealth

Mobile health (mHealth) is the use of mobile phone technology to deliver health care. Mobile phone technologies that have been used for mHealth include, but are not limited to, text messaging, video messaging, voice calling, and Internet connectivity. "mHealth innovations have been developed that address an array of issues such as improving the convenience, speed, and accuracy of diagnostic tests; monitoring chronic conditions, medication adherence, appointment keeping, and medical test result delivery; and improving patient-provider communication, health information communication, remote diagnosis, data collection, disease and emergency tracking, and access to health records" (Cole-Lewis 2010).

An example of rapid adoption is the use mobile telephones. By the end of 2008, one estimate was that there "were an estimated four billion mobile phone subscribers worldwide compared to only one billion 6 years earlier." Mobile phone text messaging is a potentially powerful tool for behavior change because it is widely available, inexpensive, and instant. Mobile phones have had a considerable impact in developing countries. Communication by mobile phone is less expensive than alternative options such as landline telephones or standard Internet. Inhabitants of Africa and Asia who never had access to traditional phone communication now use mobile phones on a regular basis. A related fact is that across the world, there is increased access to the Internet via mobile phones. For many users, "the mobile phone is currently the primary mode of accessing the Internet."

The various strengths of text messaging are offset to some extent by some weaknesses. "A potential drawback to the use of text-message-based mHealth interventions is potential marginalization of certain populations such as those that are illiterate or do not have access to a mobile phone for financial reasons. However, these limitations may be reduced as mobile technology advances." Voice response systems and pictures could be used instead of text for individuals whose literacy has limitations.[406]

More current data on mobile phones appeared in one of a series of papers in August 2011 in the report *Innovating for More Affordable Care* (Sandhu 2011). "More than three-quarters of the world's 5.3 billion mobile phones are located in the developing world. Much of the innovative thinking in mHealth is coming from programs that target populations outside the United States, often in developing countries. Now in a twist of fate, the innovations emerging

---

405. Boukus, E.R. et al. Physicians Slow to E-Mail Routinely with Patients, Issue Brief, Center for Studying Health System Change, No. 134, October 2010. On the Web at http://www.hschange.org/CONTENT/1156/?words=boukus. Accessed on September 27, 2011.

406. Cole-Lewis, H. and Kershaw, T. Text Messaging as a Tool for Behavior Change in Disease Prevention and Management, *Epidemiologic Reviews*, Vol. 32, 2010, pp. 56-69.

from the developing world could prove to be a significant springboard for innovation in the developed world."

"One prominent example is GE's portable ultrasound device. Traditional ultrasound machines cost upwards of $100,000, but a GE team in China designed a device for the Chinese market that plugs into a laptop and costs as little as $15,000. The difference was not just in the product's price, but also in its target customers and uses. Instead of being designed for large hospital imaging centers and a range of uses, it was targeted to rural health clinics interested in detecting enlarged livers and gallstones. This innovation drove further innovation in GE's imaging products, including a handheld ultrasound that retails for less than $8,000 and is available in India and the United States, among other countries."

"Although several mHealth programs are operating in developing-country markets, only a few prominent mHealth innovations in the United States have been imported from abroad. Among the most notable are *Vitality GlowCaps* and *GreatCall Medication Reminder Service*, both of which are working to improve medication adherence. The stakes are high. Not following prescribed medication instructions adds an estimated $258 billion to $290 billion annually to U.S. health care costs, or up to 13% of total health care expenditures. In particular, medication adherence is a major problem for the elderly, contributing to one in five Medicare beneficiaries discharged from a hospital being readmitted within 30 days."

"Vitality GlowCaps and GreatCall Medication Reminder Service do similar things, but work differently. The GlowCap device fits over commonly used prescription bottles, and it flashes and sounds when the time comes to take a pill. If the patient forgets, the product then uses an embedded wireless chip to offer a phone or text reminder. The system can even alert a friend or family member, automatically call in a refill, and notify patients' doctors about how well they're taking their medicines. The device came several years after a similar product known as *SIMpill* was developed in South Africa. A related service that works primarily through phone reminders and customer service is the GreatCall Medication Reminder Service, available as of 2010 on Jitterbug cell phones, which are designed to be particularly easy to use. The service helps the elderly remember to take all their medications at the right times." [407]

Outcomes Research and Comparative Effectiveness Research

Technological advances can be expected to continue to occur that have the potential to improve health status. Just as certainly, some of them will be adopted, despite any firm evidence to the contrary that they are superior to the devices and approaches that preceded their entrance upon the scene. A remedy to the problem is to conduct research that demonstrates the effectiveness of technological newcomers.

Comparative effectiveness research (CER) has emerged as a major theme in health care reform. "Unfortunately, there is a widespread lack of understanding about what it will do and fear that it will do more harm than good (Mushlin 2010). These concerns include threats to individual physician's autonomy and professionalism, and fears that care will be rationed based on such findings. This type of research has existed for a long time and has been known by various names, such as health services research, clinical epidemiology or outcomes research. However, there are certain aspects that have emerged as most important within the context of health care reform with its emphasis on expanding insurance coverage, health system and reimbursement changes,

---

407. Sandhu, J.S. Opportunities in Mobile Health, in Innovating for More Affordable Health Care, Stanford Social Innovation Review, August 2011, p. 14-17. On the Web at http://stanford.ebookhost.net/ssir/digital/12/ebook/1/download.pdf. Accessed on September 26, 2011.

disease management, and health information technology. CER has been suggested as a part of the strategy in healthcare reform for improving outcomes and helping to curb the growth in costs."

Many entities in the U.S. are already involved in CER activities. "Examples include the work of the *Effective Healthcare Program* currently ongoing at the Agency for Healthcare Research and Quality (AHRQ), as well as the activities undertaken at the Centers for Medicare and Medicaid Services, the Veterans Administration, the National Institutes of Health, and the Office of the National Coordinator for Health Information Technology. Yet, it was only when the federal government substantially increased the investment in CER through the American Recovery and Reinvestment Act of 2009, that national interest in this topic emerged. Congress allocated $1.1 billion to the NIH, the Department of Health and Human Services, and AHRQ to be spent over a 2-year period to initiate and disseminate CER."

Several definitions for CER have been proposed in the medical literature. "However, the most widely accepted is that of the Institute of Medicine (IOM) Committee on Comparative Effectiveness Research, which was commissioned by Congress and which released its report in June 2009. According to the report, CER is defined as: '*the generation and synthesis of evidence that compares the benefits and harms of alternative methods to prevent, diagnose, treat, and monitor a clinical condition or to improve the delivery of care. The purpose of CER is to assist consumers, clinicians, purchasers, and policy makers to make informed decisions that will improve health care at both the individual and population levels.*' The IOM report emphasized that CER research should focus on selected clinical areas and aspects of the health care delivery system. The report identified 100 study topics related to a range of diseases and systems that are of most importance to the health of the U.S. population." [408]

A reasonable question to ask is if there is sufficient capacity in the clinical enterprise to conduct such studies. The following conditions must be taken into account in order to answer this question (Giffin 2010):

- "Between 2001 and 2007, the number of registered clinical investigators declined 3.5%. The average age of principal investigators is increasing. Only 8% of principal investigators in industry trials are currently under age 40, and the rate of replacement is inadequate to sustain current research levels. For 85% of the physicians who participate in a clinical trial, it is a one-time experience."

- Limited incentives exist "for academic physicians to engage in clinical research. The financial and career rewards for conducting trials often are not commensurate with the challenges that investigators face. The current academic funding and promotion model does not place a high value on clinical research, and many academic researchers must carve out time from other duties to conduct studies. Investigators face stiff challenges when developing and executing clinical trials. These include a multilayer review process that often takes months or years to move from proposal to funding, inefficient Institutional Review Board processes, and complex intellectual property arrangements.

- Community physicians are also discouraged from participating in clinical trials because of the administrative burdens added to already busy practices. Staff time must be diverted to a wide range of study-related activities, such as entering data, scheduling patients for study-related visits and tests, separately storing study-related drugs, and completing administrative paperwork.

- For both academic and community physicians, financial reimbursement often does not compensate for the level of effort and administrative burden involved and insurers may not cover many extra costs associated with clinical care for research participants.

408. Mushlin, A.I. and Hassan, M.K. Comparative Effectiveness Research: A Cornerstone of Healthcare Reform, *Transactions of the American Clinical and Climatological Association*, Vol. 121, 2010, pp. 141-155.

- Another measure of clinical trial capacity is the availability of patients to participate in trials. According to data on industry-sponsored trials, it is increasingly difficult for investigators to enroll patients. An Institute of Medicine (IOM) report on the National Cancer Institute's Cooperative Group Program found that only about 60% of National Cancer Institute–sponsored Phase III trials are completed, mainly because of an inability to recruit sufficient numbers of patients."

Thus, an expansive program of comparative effectiveness research is likely to run into this supply constraint, resulting in three possible scenarios:

- "The capacity to conduct comparative effectiveness research could be expanded by diverting resources from other research priorities.
- Alternatively, the current research capacity could be stretched, by finding ways to conduct research more efficiently.
- Another option is expanding research capacity by making it more attractive for physicians and patients to participate in clinical trials." [409]

Apart from the aforementioned challenges, even if CER endeavors are carried out successfully, there remains the issue of ensuring that results are disseminated and implemented. "The delivery system isn't structured to rapidly absorb and adapt new information to support the changes being implemented" (Esposito 2010).[410]

Confusing Terminology

It is not uncommon for terms such as *comparative effectiveness research, health technology assessment,* and *evidence-based medicine* to be used as though they mean the same thing. The lack of consistency and clarity, and even the misuse of basic words and terms of evidence-based activities, leads to unnecessary disagreements among key groups concerning their appropriate role in health care decision-making (Luce 2010).

Moreover, the terms *efficacy* and *effectiveness* often are used interchangeably, which is erroneous. *Efficacy* refers to the question, "Can it work?" A health care intervention is considered "efficacious when there is evidence that the intervention provides the intended benefit when administered to carefully selected patients according to prescribed criteria, often by experts in a research setting. The evidence of efficacy typically comes from well-controlled randomized clinical trials."

An intervention is considered *effective* when the question "Does it work?" is answered successfully. Being effective means that benefits occur when an intervention is administered "in routine clinical practice settings. Some of this confusion can be traced to the FDA's authorizing legislation and regulations in which the terms *efficacy* and *effectiveness* are often used interchangeably, so *effectiveness* is used when *efficacy* is intended." [411]

---

409. Giffin, R.B. and Woodcock, J. Comparative Effectiveness Research: Who Will Do the Studies? *Health Affairs,* Vol. 29, No. 11, November 2010, pp. 2075-2081.
410. Esposito, D. et al. Using Comparative Effectiveness Research: Information Alone Won't Lead to Successful Health Care Reform, Mathematica Policy Research, Inc Issue Brief. No. 2, December 2010, 3 pp.
411. Luce, B.R. et al. EBM, HTA, and CER: Clearing the Confusion, *The Milbank Quarterly,* Vol. 88, No. 2, 2010, pp. 256-276.

"To date, both public and private research enterprise has predominantly funded efficacy research (Djulbegovic 2011). Comparative effectiveness research holds promise to generate much-needed effectiveness data. However, given the large number of important clinical questions, it will not be possible to provide reliable empirical efficacy, effectiveness, and cost-effectiveness data for every question to help guide individual decision-making. Instead, practitioners will continue to rely on inductive reasoning to apply the results of the study ('group averages' from an efficacy trial) to individual patients who often differ in important ways from patients enrolled in the efficacy trial (e.g., these patients may be older, have co-morbid conditions, or might be using multiple medications)."

"A logically insolvable problem then arises, because there is no guarantee that the treatment effects observed in one group of patients can be repeated with certainty in future patients. Decades of clinical experience have demonstrated that the application of group trial data to individual patients is permissible by using efficacy as effectiveness data, provided there is a rationale for exchangeability of the past and future events and the characteristics and circumstances of the patients are sufficiently similar. However, there is no mathematical, precise resolution of what constitutes 'sufficiently similar' patients."

"Determination of similarity, which in practice often is based on paying attention to the PICO framework (i.e., whether the differences between patients [P], interventions [I], comparators [C], and outcome(s) [O] observed in the setting and circumstances of the trials are similar enough to allow application of the trial results to individual patients in real-world settings), is a matter of judgment confounded by uncertainty about predicted effects. Relying on efficacy data to draw conclusions about effectiveness and feasibility of application of trial data to individual patients remains one of the most important sources of clinical uncertainty. The use of inductive inferences (such as relying on the PICO framework) can help reduce some uncertainty, but ultimately cannot completely eliminate it." [412]

Consumers' Understanding of Research Findings

"Passage of the Affordable Care Act of 2010 has now laid the groundwork for major reforms, including greater use of evidence-based medicine, shared decision-making, comparative effectiveness research, evidence-based benefit design, and transparency of cost and quality information." Combined, these diverse efforts are referred to as "evidence-based health care" (Carman 2010).

"Although much attention has been focused on the roles of governments, employers, insurers, and providers in evidence-based health care, less attention has been paid to the critical role of consumers. Their attitudes and beliefs about evidence-based health care, and their understanding and acceptance of it, will help determine its success or failure. If consumers don't understand it or reject it, or if they see it as an invalid basis for making decisions about providers and treatments, the most ambitious goals of this movement may fail."

"Increasingly, consumers are being asked to use evidence to manage chronic conditions, choose between treatment regimens, and select providers and health plans. In some respects, consumers are rising to the challenge. Research shows that decision aids, which provide information about options and outcomes, can help increase consumers' confidence with decision making and improve their understanding and knowledge of treatment options. If consumers are

412. Djulbegovic, B. and Paul, A. From Efficacy to Effectiveness in the Face of Uncertainty: Indication Creep and Prevention Creep, *Journal of the American Medical Association*, Vol. 305, No. 19, May 18, 2011, pp. 2005-2006.

more involved in decision making generally and self-management of health conditions, the results can be improved adherence to treatment, increased use of screening, increased patient satisfaction, better health outcomes, and lower health care costs."

"Consumers' current knowledge, beliefs, attitudes, and experiences related to health care are often incompatible with evidence-based approaches. In addition, consumers have deep concerns about how physicians and other providers will respond to questions about the appropriateness of treatments, the basis for referrals to specialists and hospitals, or the cost of treatment."

"Effective communication with and support of consumers is essential to improving the quality of health care and containing health care costs. Clearly, consumers will revolt if evidence-based efforts are perceived as rationing or as a way to deny them needed treatment. Policy makers, employers, health plans, providers, and researchers will thus need to translate evidence-based health care into accessible concepts and concrete activities that support and motivate consumers." [413]

Intelligent and Judicious Use of Innovations

Even when new ideas are sound and result in the creation of beneficial practices that save lives and reduce costs, many years can elapse before they experience widespread use. An example is administering beta blockers and aspirin upon a heart attack patient's arrival at a hospital. An opposite event is that some new forms of technology essentially may be worthless, but a medical center will implement them in order to avoid losing market share to a neighboring facility. Pressures arising from patients who demand the latest innovations, combined with the persuasive powers of prestigious members of a medical center's board of trustees, almost always guarantee that such purchases will be made. An example described earlier in this chapter is surgical robots.

It is important that the availability of electronic health information should not provide a rationale for having a reduced amount of face-to-face interaction with patients. In the matter of quality, it should be obvious that potential risks are involved in substituting technology for time actually spent with patients. As evidenced by Facebook, text messaging, the incessant use of cell phones and other modern vehicles for communicating fast updates, many individuals are quite comfortable interacting with others electronically. It is easy to see how this fascination with modern devices can change how newer generations of health care practitioners and patients might possibly interact with one another.

Some medical testing may be analogous to the situation involving auto repairs. When fixing one broken part, it is common to be advised that action should be taken to repair something new that is detected. More often than not, laypersons are not in an advantageous position to assess the quality of the information being given about the actual risk of something else going seriously wrong unless a newly discovered problem is attended to right away.

It is likely that the volume of some diagnostic procedures could be reduced as a means of lowering health care costs and lessening patient discomfort, but the impetus to conduct tests can be driven both by patients and providers of such services. Consumer demand can be a strong incentive to continue practices that do not necessarily lead to improved patient outcomes. Direct advertising to consumers has shown to be an effective means of stimulating such demand.

---

413. Carman, K.L. et al. Evidence That Consumers Are Skeptical about Evidence-Based Health Care, *Health Affairs*, Vol. 29, No. 7, July 2010, pp. 1400-1406.

Americans are preoccupied with their health. A reflection of their interest and concern may be seen in the volume of local and national television news segments that are devoted to the topic as well as the special sections that appear each week in major daily newspapers across the country. It is not unusual to see a high blood pressure testing apparatus in supermarkets. How often the machines are tested for accuracy is conjectural. Meanwhile, what happens if a person has a high blood pressure reading while shopping? Should this individual drop the asparagus and rush to the nearest emergency room?

Returning to a premise discussed earlier in this book, to what degree does health care equate with health? Technological advances in health care have contributed to longer lifespans. Certainly, demonstrable effects can be shown in modern day cardiac interventions, but what about for the population as a whole? Apart from health care, what is the impact of the following on increasing the lifespan:

- A rising standard of living
- Improved housing
- Wider availability of nutritious foods at affordable prices
- Reduced pollution
- Better sanitation
- Smoking cessation
- Increased exercise
- Use of seatbelts
- Safer motor vehicles
- Meaningful jobs
- Shorter workdays
- A shift from dangerous occupations in mining and manufacturing to a more service-oriented economy

An old Latin saying is *post hoc ergo propter hoc*, i.e., "After this, therefore because of this." New technology is introduced and a beneficial result may occur; but there still might not be any connection between the two sets of events.

Closing Thoughts

The pace of change in technology is quite rapid. Copying machines became available in libraries in the 1960s, which was considered an exceptional innovation back then. Today, students are a few short strokes of a computer keyboard away from downloading information from all over the world. Projections about the future have to include the possibility that developments in genomics and regenerative medicine will enhance personal health status. As in the past, many innovations will be rushed to the adoption stage without any evidence that they are superior to what already exists. Efforts to contain health care costs will have to be incorporated into approaches aimed at demonstrating cost and clinical effectiveness of interventions prior to their widespread distribution and use.

CHAPTER 16:
Perspectives on the Future

16

The U.S. population is changing in many ways such as the disproportional amount of growth in the old-est cohorts, which will test the ability of the nation to provide appropriate and affordable health care. Disputes about personal versus societal responsibility for the causes of health problems can be expected to continue. Some individuals will engage in risky behavior harmful to health and ignore advice about how to improve personal health status. Future technological developments will affect the cost, quality, and availability of health care services.

Danish physicist Niels Bohr once noted, "Prediction is very difficult, especially if it is about the future." The previous 15 chapters of this book have touched upon a great many topics that have implications for the future, such as:

- The fate of health reform as expressed in the Affordable Care Act of 2010
- Changing demographics, with the U.S. population growing older and less non-Hispanic white in composition
- Innovations in health technology and in the ways health care is delivered
- Increasing access to health care by extending health insurance to the uninsured
- The degree to which alternative health practices will become more complementary and inter-grative
- The kinds of practitioners who will deliver needed health care services
- Patient-provider shared decision-making

In many important respects, the past is prologue. A good example is that the previous century was characterized by a great many debates about the main causes of poor health status. One side of the argument points in the direction of blaming social conditions and institutions, such as "industrialization, urbanization, secularization, and the breakdown of the extended family" (Leichter 2003). Poverty, which has many deleterious effects on health status, was viewed throughout that period as being a result primarily of an economy "insufficiently abundant to provide subsistence for all the able-bodied, and a social order that inequitably distributed what wealth there was."

A countervailing view shifts the onus of responsibility to individual behavior. Instead of blaming society with its purported "racism, declining moral standards, and capitalism" frame-work, avoidable morbidity and premature mortality were seen as attributable to "personal care-less and imprudent lifestyle choices." [414] Debates along such lines can be expected to continue

---

414. Leichter, H.M. "Evil Habits" and "Personal Choices": Assigning Responsibility for Health in the 20th Century, *The Milbank Quarterly*, Vol. 81, No. 4, 2003, pp. 603-626.

well into the future. Depending on one's point of view, obesity, substance abuse, and improper use of motor vehicles by driving at excessive speeds are considered to be more personal than societal kinds of problems.

Worrisome Health Conditions

A problem that seems to be increasing rather than decreasing is attention deficit hyperactivity disorder (ADHD) among children aged 5–17 years. The long-term effects have yet to be determined, but they are deserving of watchful concern. Data released in August 2011 by the National Center for Health Statistics, a unit within the Centers for Disease Control and Prevention (CDC), are as follows:

- The percentage of children ever diagnosed with ADHD increased from 6.9% to 9.0% from 1998–2000 through 2007–2009.
- ADHD prevalence trends varied by race and ethnicity. Differences between groups narrowed from 1998 through 2009; however, Mexican children had consistently lower ADHD prevalence than other racial or ethnic groups.
- From 1998 through 2009, ADHD prevalence increased from 7.5% to 10.3% for children with family income less than 100% of the poverty level and from 7% to 10.6% for those with family income between 100% and 199% of the poverty level.
- From 1998 through 2009, ADHD prevalence rose from 7.1% to 10.2% in the Midwest and South regions of the United States [Figures 1–3].[415]

Infectious Diseases

Chapter 1 contained a description of the sense of optimism that prevailed in mid-20th century about the imminent prospect of eradicating infectious diseases. Subsequent outbreaks to the present day such as HIV infection and AIDS offer evidence that such a sunny outlook was unwarranted. The U.S. medical community became aware of AIDS 30 years ago (Dieffenbach 2011). "Since then, the global HIV and AIDS pandemic has caused approximately 60 million infections. Experts estimate that more than 25 million individuals have died of AIDS and more than 33 million currently are living with HIV infection or AIDS."

"As the third decade since AIDS was first recognized comes to an end, extraordinary advances have occurred in the understanding, treatment, and prevention of HIV infection and AIDS. As a result of these successes, it is now time to focus on future challenges. Paramount among these is reaching the goal of truly controlling and ultimately ending the HIV and AIDS pandemic. To that end, AIDS researchers and public health personnel worldwide are aggressively pursuing three key areas of scientific research:"

- "Given the availability of highly effective therapeutic regimens for HIV infection, the first challenge is efficiently identifying a maximum number of HIV-infected persons through voluntary HIV testing and initiating antiretroviral therapy (ART).
- Scientists are trying to develop a cure for HIV infection, which would alleviate the need for lifelong ART.

---

415. Akinbami, L.J. et al. Attention Deficit Hyperactivity Disorder Among Children Aged 5-17 Years in the United States, 1998-2009, NCHS Data Brief No. 70, August 2011, 7 pp.

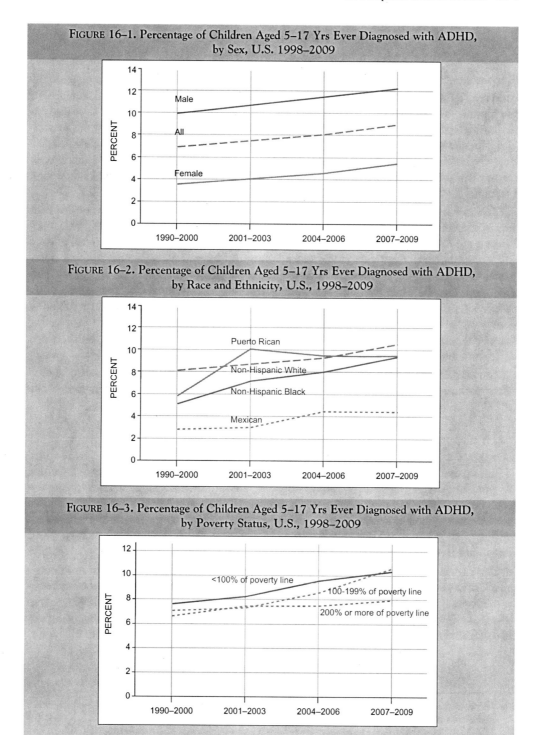

FIGURE 16–1. Percentage of Children Aged 5–17 Yrs Ever Diagnosed with ADHD, by Sex, U.S. 1998–2009

FIGURE 16–2. Percentage of Children Aged 5–17 Yrs Ever Diagnosed with ADHD, by Race and Ethnicity, U.S., 1998–2009

FIGURE 16–3. Percentage of Children Aged 5–17 Yrs Ever Diagnosed with ADHD, by Poverty Status, U.S., 1998–2009

Source: Figures 1-3, CDC/NCHS Health Data Interactive and National Health Interview Survey (adapted from Akinbami 2011).

> • Preventing new cases of HIV infection, which currently number approximately 2.6 million per year globally, is critical to any attempt to end this pandemic." [416]

Apart from infections as devastating as AIDS, public health authorities throughout the world are required to maintain a constant state of vigilance. For example, a less visible irritant that represents a cause for concern is the arrival in the United States of the Asian tiger mosquito, *Aedes albopictus*, an insect that is "more vicious, harder to kill, and unlike most native varieties, bites during the daytime (Mir 2011). It also prefers large cities over rural or marshy areas." It can be found in small artificial containers such as tires, toys, cans, and concrete structures. In Hawaii, this mosquito was responsible for transmitting dengue fever, a sometimes fatal viral infection." [417]

"The global spread of the invasive species *Aedes albopictus* is of growing public health concern in Europe (Neteler 2011). Originating from southeast Asia, it has colonized the Indo-Pacific area, Africa, the Americas, and Europe over the last 30 years. Global dispersal of eggs, which can survive drought periods for several months, occurred through international transportation of used tires. It is proved to be a competent vector for a number of pathogens and parasites. For example, it can transmit the chikungunya virus as primary vector, the dengue virus, eastern equine encephalitis, and yellow fever. In Europe, there is an urgent need for intensive monitoring and development of an early warning system to predict and monitor the spread of this species, especially after the chikungunya outbreak in the Emilia-Romagna region of Italy in 2007 when more than 200 human cases were reported." [418]

More locally, efforts to evaluate the effectiveness of a public health educational campaign to reduce backyard mosquito-larval habitats in New Jersey are described in a study (Bartlett-Healy 2011).[419]

Diagnostic Testing

The uproar that occurred in 2009 over the release of updated mammography screening guidelines suggests that diagnostic testing represents another fruitful ground for waging disputes. For example, "serum prostate-specific antigen (PSA) testing arrived on the scene more than 20 years ago, offering great promise for the early detection and treatment of prostate cancer (Friedrich 2011). Yet, even after 2 decades of experience with this seemingly simple blood test, debate continues to swirl over how and when—and if—it should be used."

"Prostate cancer appears in a large percentage of men as they age, but is indolent most of the time. Critics emphasize that PSA screening is an imperfect tool because it does not differentiate clinically significant tumors from ones that would never cause harm. The result is overdiagnosis and overtreatment. Defenders say that PSA testing is a more rational, evidence-based approach that can help detect and treat the disease early in men who would die of the dis-

416. Dieffenbach, C.W. and Fauci, A.S. Thirty Years of HIV and AIDS: Future Challenges and Opportunities, *Annals of Internal Medicine*, Vol. 154, No. 11, June 7, 2011, pp. 766-772.

417. Mir, A. Attack of the Urban Mosquitoes, *The Wall Street Journal*, July 20, 2011, pp. D1-D2.

418. Neteler, M. et al. Terra and Aqua Satellites Track Tiger Mosquito Invasion: Modelling the Potential Distribution of *Aedesa albopictus* in North-Eastern Italy, *International Journal of Health Geographics*, 2011, 10:49, 13 pp.

419. Bartlett-Healy, K. et al. Source Reduction Behavior as an Independent Measurement of the Impact of a Public Health Education Campaign in an Integrated Vector Management Program for the Asian Tiger Mosquito, *International Journal of Environmental Research and Public Health*, Vol. 8, No. 5, May 2011, pp. 1358-1367.

ease."[420] An element of the controversy that is shared in common with mammography is the ages at which screening is most effective.

Use of Vaccines to Prevent Disease

Few propositions can be made with certainty about what the future will bring. One statement that can be made with great assurance is that the children of today will be the adults of tomorrow. As such, whatever health problems they have in their youth may continue into adulthood. Thus, it would be in the best interests of both individuals and of society as a whole if certain preventable conditions are stopped from ever making their appearance.

Childhood diseases that once were a scourge in the United States are preventable through vaccination practices. An example is measles, which was eliminated—i.e., the absence of endemic transmission—in the late 1990s as a direct result of high coverage using the measles, mumps, and rubella (MMR) vaccine. "Measles is a highly contagious, acute viral disease that can lead to serious complications and death (CDC 2011). Endemic or sustained measles transmission has not occurred in this country despite continued importations." [421]

"Vaccines represent one of the greatest achievements of science and medicine in the battle against disease (Kennedy 2011). As a result of advances in developing vaccines and including them as a standard of care, most diseases that are preventable by vaccination are at record low levels in the United States. In the past 10 years controversies about vaccines and autism, the best number of injections to be administered during a single visit or over the course of the first years of life, and vaccine ingredients have been among the topics prompting concern from parents, the media, policymakers, and others about the safety of recommended immunizations as well as the vaccination schedule. Despite their beneficial impact on health and well-being, vaccines have had a long history of arousing anxiety."

"The rapid growth of the Internet and social media such as Twitter and Facebook have made it easier to find and disseminate immunization-related concerns and misperceptions. Adding to the confusion are questions about the effectiveness of influenza vaccines; the necessity of vaccines such as those for chickenpox and hepatitis B; and the safety of certain vaccines such as whole-cell pertussis for whooping cough, oral polio, and rotavirus for the most common and severe form of diarrhea." [422]

National visibility about some pros and cons of vaccination occurred during a September 2011 televised debate involving Republican candidates for President of the United States when two contenders sparred over the merits of routinely administering Merck's human papillomavirus (HPV) vaccine, Gardasil, to girls starting at 11 or 12 years of age. The vaccine protects against four strains of HPV, the most common sexually transmitted infection in the U.S. and the major cause of cervical cancer.

Opposition to HPV vaccination mandates can take different forms (Colgrove 2010), as shown in the following list that is based on a study by key informants in states that were actively engaged in legislative and policy deliberations about the HPV vaccine:

---

420. Friedrich, M.J. Debate Continues on Use of PSA Testing for Early Detection of Prostate Cancer, *Journal of the American Medical Association*, Vol. 305, No. 22, June 8, 2011, pp. 2273-2276.
421. Centers for Disease Control and Prevention, Measles—United States, January–May 20, 2011, *Morbidity and Mortality Weekly Report*, Vol. 60, No. 20, May 27, 2011, pp. 666-668.
422. Kennedy, A. et al. Confidence About Vaccines in the United States: Understanding Parents' Perceptions, *Health Affairs*, Vol. 30, No. 6, June 2011, pp. 1151-1158.

Reasons for Opposition to HPV Vaccination Mandates

"At the time that mandates were initially proposed, the HPV vaccine had been on the market for only a few months. Many legislators and advocates, along with some public health officials and representatives of medical societies, felt that long-term safety data were needed before mandatory vaccination could be justified.

Some social conservatives objected to a compulsory policy because they believed that protecting teenagers against a sexually transmitted disease might undermine prevention messages that emphasize abstinence. Furthermore, respondents indicated that requiring a girl to be vaccinated at the age of 11 or 12 years would force parents to have discussions about sex before they or their children were ready.

The fact that HPV is not contagious through casual contact in the classroom setting emerged as a distinct theme. According to many respondents, the purpose of vaccination mandates is to prevent the spread of contagious disease in schools, not to use school attendance as a lever to achieve other public health goals.

A factor that soured many policymakers on mandates was consternation over the involvement of the vaccine's manufacturer, Merck, in the policy process. Merck undertook a multifaceted marketing campaign to promote the passage of mandate legislation. Representatives of the company met with legislators and hired political consultants to promote the vaccine.

At $320 for a full course of three doses, Gardasil was considerably more expensive than other required vaccines. Although the federal Vaccines for Children Program covers the cost of the vaccine for eligible youth up to the age of 18 years and most private insurers stepped forward quickly to cover it, respondents reported concerns that some families could not afford the vaccine and that it would consume too great a share of states' Medicaid and public health budgets."

"In addition to concerns about the HPV vaccine, decisions about mandates were also strongly influenced by three factors related to the vaccine policymaking process more generally. First, respondents indicated that mandate proposals tapped into generalized antipathy toward governmental coercion. According to these objections, the bar should be set quite high for any governmental intrusion on individual or parental autonomy." The debate among the general public "also was influenced by general anti-vaccination activism by organizations and individuals who believed that vaccines cause autism and other health problems in children. Although these groups could not plausibly argue that Gardasil might cause autism, they reportedly were using HPV as a tool to focus on vaccine safety issues. Finally, aspects of the policymaking process itself contributed to the failure of mandate proposals." [423]

The specter of autism has been at the root of much opposition to vaccination programs. On February 2, 2010, the *Lancet* officially retracted the 1998 paper by Andrew Wakefield proposing a connection between receipt of the measles-mumps-rubella (MMR) vaccine and autism (Poland 2010). Prior to the retraction, "most co-authors on this paper had removed their names from the work—recognizing it as flawed. In addition, the U.K. General Medical Council concluded that Wakefield had 'shown callous disregard,' abused his position of trust, and acted in dishonest, misleading, and irresponsible ways in the conduct and report of this study. Unfortunately, Wakefield had surprising success in shaping a generation of parents' attitudes towards MMR vaccine in particular, and vaccines in general."

---

423. Colgrove, J. et al. HPV Vaccination Mandates—Lawmaking amid Political and Scientific Controversy, *New England Journal of Medicine*, Vol. 363, No. 8, August 19, 2010, pp. 785-791.

Rarely does a research paper such as the Wakefield article make so many headlines or have such large population effects on human behavior. "The U.K. and U.S. press quickly reported, headlined, and sensationalized this report and its claims—repeatedly—over years. The public received such information uncritically and many of them, particularly those who were parents of autistic children, accepted the theory of an association between vaccination with MMR and autism. Celebrities promoted the findings as fact, and were given a bully pulpit and an aura of legitimacy by the press and other celebrities. The result was a tragic, heart-breaking, and embarrassing public health tragedy hard to fathom in the late 20th and early 21st century of rational thought."

"Fearful, mistrustful, and uncritical parents began delaying and then refusing MMR vaccines. Some took the view that the trivalent vaccine was the problem and opted for immunization with monovalent vaccines. Others did not return for second doses, leaving their children with less than effective levels of protection. Predictably, a sufficient susceptible population developed and outbreaks of these previously controlled diseases occurred in the U.S. and the U.K. Children were injured, hospitalized, and most tragically, died. Tens of millions of dollars were wasted on repeated research studies to refute Wakefield's contention of an association between MMR vaccination and the development of autism. Time and attention were directed away from rational, scientific pursuit of more reliable and probable cause(s) of autism and toward a fatally flawed notion." [424]

Predictions about what will occur in the future are fraught with uncertainty, but if recent history serves as any reliable guide, it appears highly unlikely that opposition to vaccination programs will die down any time soon. For example, "despite the recommendation from the Centers for Disease Control and Prevention (CDC) that children between the ages of 6 months and 18 years be vaccinated against influenza annually, vaccination rates remain suboptimal" (Flood 2010). Among respondents in a study who reported sometimes or never vaccinating their child against influenza, "barriers to vaccination were more variable. The most common barriers were low perceived risk of influenza (46.0%), the perception that the vaccine caused influenza (44.0%), and side effects caused by the vaccine (36.6%)." [425]

A related concern is that increasing numbers of parents are following alternative vaccination schedules that differ from the recommended vaccination schedule for their young children (Dempsey 2011). Following an alternative schedule leads to undervaccination and increases the risk of contracting vaccine-preventable diseases. The results of a study indicate that "at the national level, >1 of 10 parents reported following a vaccination schedule other than that recommended by the CDC for their young children." [426]

Immunizations are a cornerstone of the nation's efforts to protect the public from a host of infectious diseases. Though generally very rare or very minor, there are side effects, or "adverse effects," associated with some vaccines (Stratton 2011). The Institute of Medicine (IOM) reviewed a list of adverse events associated with eight vaccines to evaluate the scientific evidence about the event–vaccine relationship. Using epidemiological and mechanistic evidence, the committee developed 158 causality conclusions, assigning each relationship between a vaccine and an adverse health problem to one of four causation categories. Overall, the IOM

424. Poland, G.A. and Spier, R. Fear, Misinformation, and Innumerates: How the Wakefield Paper, the Press, and Advocacy Groups Damaged the Public Health, *Vaccine*, Vol. 28, No. 12, March 11, 2010, pp. 2361-2362.
425. Flood, E.M. Parents' Decision-Making Regarding Vaccinating Their Children Against Influenza: A Web-Based Survey, *Clinical Therapeutics*, Vol. 32, No. 8, August 2010, pp. 1448-1467.
426. Dempsey, A.F. et al. Alternative Vaccination Schedule Preferences among Parents of Young Children, *Pediatrics*, Vol. 128, No. 5, November 2011, pp. 1-9.

committee concluded that few health problems are caused by or clearly associated with vaccines.[427]

A key issue in making decisions about whether or not to vaccinate children hinges on the concept of trust, which occurs at two levels. Parents who trust the advice of their pediatrician would appear to be more inclined to undertake what is recommended for their offspring. At a more general level, trust in information promulgated by government agencies also can be influential. Sometimes, that trust may diminish when predictions fail to come true. A national alert in 2010 about the lethal danger of the H1N1 influenza was warranted, but when widespread devastation failed to occur, the incident for some critics may have been just one more manifestation of why it is hard to place trust in the authorities.

An important thing to keep in mind, however, is that at the heart of establishing a government in the first place is to provide safety for its citizens. Apart from diplomatic and military functions to protect the nation from harm imposed by outsiders, in the domestic realm there is a responsibility to provide safeguards against the ravages of natural events such as hurricanes and floods that can be mitigated in their effects. Mistakes may be made in carrying out its various assignments because of inadequate amounts of information or even in making improper judgments based on available facts, but government at all levels must be perceived to some degree as existing to serve the best interests of the citizenry. A failure to believe otherwise could produce unfavorable consequences, particularly in the realm of failing to avoid preventable disease through interventions such as vaccination programs.

Genomics and Connectomics

Chapter 15 contained information about genomics. The launching of the Human Genome Project a decade ago was accompanied by much fanfare—so much so that it became widely expected that personalized medicine would emerge within a few years of the completion of the project. "When this outcome didn't materialize, the project experienced something of a backlash, asserting that the public had obtained little in return for its investment and ignoring basic scientific insights" (Nature Neuroscience 2010).

Connectomics is a relative newcomer to the scene of developing greater insights into the nature of disease. In September 2010, "the first grants under the Human Connectome Project, totaling $40 million over 5 years, were awarded by the U.S. National Institutes of Health (NIH). In the public arena, striking, colorful pictures of human brains have accompanied claims that imply that understanding the complete connectivity of the human brain's billions of neurons by a trillion synapses is not only possible, but that it also will directly translate into insights for neurological and psychiatric disorders. Such grand claims are dangerous because, although a better understanding of brain connectivity is a vital tool for understanding brain function, the immediate gains for therapy from such projects are far from clear."

"Given the challenges that this field is facing, it seems ill-advised to present connectomics as providing immediate answers for disease when it is clear that it is a long-term goal that will require the continued support and collaboration of the neuroscience community and the taxpaying public." [428]

---

427. Stratton, K. et al, editors. *Adverse Effects of Vaccines: Evidence and Causality*, Institute of Medicine of the National Academies, Washington, DC: August 25, 2011. On the Web at http://books.nap.edu/ openbook.php?record_id=13164. Accessed on October 7, 2011.

428. Editorial. A Critical Look at Connectomics, *Nature Neuroscience*, Vol. 13, No. 12, December 2010, p. 1441.

Genomics itself will continue to accelerate at a rapid pace. "Researchers are producing genomewide data sets on ever-expanding study populations (Hudson 2011). Broad access to these data, stored samples, and electronic medical records are accelerating an understanding of the role of genes, environment, and behavior in health and disease. Translational research is converting new knowledge into diagnostics, targets for drug development, and new insights about how to prevent and treat disease. The challenge is to ensure that innovation in research and medicine is equaled by innovative policies that foster science and discovery while protecting and respecting research participants and patients."

"The successful integration of genetic testing into medicine requires an educated health care workforce, protections against inappropriate disclosure and discriminatory use of genetic information, and an oversight system that ensures the accuracy and reliability of genetic tests, particularly tests that provide results pertinent to important medical decisions. The dramatic increase in the number, complexity, availability, and medical relevance of genetic tests has created many regulatory challenges as well as opportunities for change."

"In a world of electronic medical records, there is a dual challenge of usefully incorporating genetic information while also protecting patient privacy. Consumers, health care providers, insurers, and regulators face a difficult balancing act to protect the privacy of genetic and other health information while also ensuring its availability and use for medical decision making." [429]

A wholly unregulated sphere of commercial activity is the marketing of genetic tests (Wizemann 2011). As many as 2,000 different kinds of tests are on the market for the benefit of individuals who want to know their risk for cancer or for other less-threatening conditions such as risk of hair loss. Ten years after the sequencing of the human genome, scientists have developed genetic tests that can predict a person's response to certain drugs, estimate the risk of developing Alzheimer's disease, and make other predictions based on known links between genes and diseases. Genetic tests have yet to become a routine part of medical care, however, in part because there is not enough evidence to show they help improve patients' health. The IOM held a workshop to explore how researchers can gather better evidence more efficiently on the clinical utility of genetic tests.[430]

Exaggerated claims by purveyors of some tests can lead to unnecessary lifestyle changes. Since many tests are quite expensive, an immediate divide is created between those individuals who can afford them and those who cannot. A related concern is that a test result can lead to an overestimate of the danger of a risk factor while leading to an underestimate of more threatening factors such as smoking behavior or environmental conditions.

Rejuvenative Technology

What if success is achieved involving rejuvenative technologies and humans are able to live healthy lives until the age of 150? The assumption is that both physical and mental health would thrive over the decades, but what if that state of nirvana is not reached simply because of life's vicissitudes? Family life would be multi-generational, with the emphasis on *multi*. How many career changes would be necessary since the occupation of today might become obsolete decades later? Occupational challenges could result in the necessity of return-

---

429. Hudson, K.L. Genomics, Health Care, and Society, *New England Journal of Medicine*, Vol. 365, No. 11, September 15, 2011, pp. 1033-1041.

430. Wizemann, T. and Berger, A.C. *Rapporteurs. Genetic Evidence for Genomic Test Development: Workshop Summary*, Institute of Medicine of the National Academies, Washington, DC: 2011, On the Web at http://books.nap.edu/openbook.php?record_id=13133. Accessed on October 7, 2011.

ing to school for additional education. Will doing so be affordable and what disruptions might it cause in family life? Might not junior and his great-great-great grandfather share the same dormitory room in college? What if the chosen occupation is miserably boring and the prospect of retiring with benefits is a mere 90 years in the future? Another good question is how will the accumulation of life's stresses over such a lengthy period affect one's mental health?

Cancer, cardiovascular diseases, and infectious diseases receive significant amounts of coverage in the medical literature and by the media. Mental health disorders also can prove to be a heavy burden for patients. Whether or not rejuvenative technologies have the potential to remove these maladies altogether or lessen their prevalence most certainly is a debatable proposition. Humans live their lives amidst a plethora of daily stresses, including whether or not a shaky economy will be consistently strong enough to meet regular needs such as the provision of jobs. Otherwise, poverty carries with it various associated woes, including the burden of poor mental health.

Examples of Mental Health Conditions
Panic disorder
Social phobia
Simple phobia
Manic depressive disorder
Obsessive-compulsive disorder
Drug abuse/dependence
Alcohol abuse/dependence
Personality disorders
Schizophrenia
Bipolar disorder
Dementia (age >65 years)[431]

Any of these conditions can have a devastating impact on the well-being of an individual sufferer. It is difficult to imagine what the effects would be if an individual had to experience one or more of these problems for 10 or more decades.

Rationing

The enactment of health reform legislation in 2010 fueled apprehension among critics of the law that its implementation would lead to rationing of health care. The term "death panels" has been invoked as a mechanism for committees to decide who shall live and who should be allowed to die.

A similar situation occurred in 1960 when a nephrologist at the University of Washington devised a shunt that would allow those suffering from kidney failure to be hooked to a dialysis machine that could keep them alive for many years (Callahan 2011). "Few machines were available and there were many more candidates for their use than could be accommodated." A procedural solution was devised in the shape of committee action to determine medical criteria for selecting candidates and then deciding on a case-by-case basis which ones would receive dialysis treatment. Controversy over this solution came to an end in 1972 when Congress passed legislation providing Medicare coverage for treatment, but not for other lethal conditions such as cancer and heart disease.

---

431. Eaton, W.W. et al. The Burden of Mental Disorders, *Epidemiologic Reviews*, Vol. 30, 2008, pp. 1-14.

Within the bioethics community, there is a fair degree of consensus that if not at once, then sooner or later, rationing will be necessary (the steady rise of cost inflation will necessitate it); "bedside rationing will not be acceptable (too open to bias and erratic criteria); rationing will have to be done at the policy level (mainly out of the hands of individual doctors and patients); and at that level there will have to be a decision-making procedure (most likely committees of some kind will make transparent decisions). Health reform legislation does not do much to stem the steady stream of expensive biologic drugs for cancer care and costly medical devices for heart disease, many of which cry out for some rationing. How many new cancer drugs costing between fifty and one hundred thousand dollars for just a few extra months of life can be afforded?" [432]

The Challenge of Enhancing Patient-Provider Shared Decision-Making

Chapter 2 on the topics of semiotics illustrates many differences between patients and health care practitioners that can compromise the quality of care provided. Racial/ethnic differences, health illiteracy, and socioeconomic disparities all contribute to the challenge of having effective shared decision-making between patients and providers occur. "Major discrepancies exist between patient preferences and the medical care they receive for many common conditions (O'Malley 2011)."

"Shared decision-making (SDM) is a process where a patient and clinician faced with more than one medically accepted treatment option jointly decide which option is best based on current evidence and the patient's needs, preferences, and values. Barriers exist to wider use of SDM, including lack of reimbursement for physicians to adopt it under the existing fee-for-service payment system that rewards higher service volume, insufficient information on how best to train clinicians to weigh evidence and discuss treatment options for preference-sensitive conditions with patients, and clinician concerns about malpractice liability."

Another challenge to engaging patients in SDM "range from low literacy to fears they will be denied needed care." The health reform law established a process to encourage SDM, but Congress has not appropriated money to implement it. [433]

At the Crossroad of Higher Education and Health Care

A considerable amount of the content of this book has been on health professionals and the care that they provide. Prior to entering practice, these individuals must attend academic institutions to learn necessary knowledge and skills. As a result, what occurs in the education domain can have an impact on what happens in the health domain.

Health care and higher education intersect in important fundamental ways (Elwood 2011). The two entities can be viewed as meeting at a crossroad, which may be envisioned as constituting two intersecting multi-lane highways complete with on ramps, off ramps, passing lanes, and breakdown lanes. Some lanes also may be characterized by the movement of vehicles that only can be sighted periodically. For example, federal budgets and decisions on appropriations usually are seen at specific intervals during the year.

---

432. Callahan, D. Rationing: Theory, Politics, and Passions, *Hastings Center Report*, Vol. 41, No. 2, March-April 2011, pp. 23-27.
433. O'Malley, A.S. et al. Policy Options to Encourage Patient-Shared Decision Making, National Institute for Health Care Reform, Policy Analysis No. 5, September 2011, 10 pp.

As an illustration, on October 28, 2010, the Department of Education issued the final "Program Integrity" rules. They were scheduled to take effect on July 1, 2011. The rule package contained the following regulation on distance education:

> *If an institution is offering postsecondary education through distance or corresponding education in a State in which it is not physically located or in which it is otherwise subject to State jurisdiction as determined by the State, the institution must meet any State requirements for it to be legally offering distance or corresponding education in that State. An institution must be able to document upon request from the Department that it has such State approval.*

States are one of three mechanisms involved in educational quality assurance, along with accreditation and federal reviews and audits. These jurisdictions can vary considerably in their requirements. For example, states with more restrictive ordinances may see fit to declare out-of-state institutions ineligible to offer postsecondary instruction via distance learning. A ruling of this nature could have a negative effect on the health workforce. If, for example, a particular state does not have academic programs for certain health professions, students in that state either could move to another state for educational purposes or choose a different health profession. If the latter were to occur, it would help to reduce the size of the workforce in some professions and possibly exacerbate current and projected personnel shortages. A clearer picture of actions that states will take should emerge in coming months. For the present, the regulation has produced a great deal of uncertainty and concern for administrators in many institutions around the United States.

In July 2011, a U.S. District Court judge for the District of Columbia struck down a portion of the Education Department's controversial "state authorization rule." Opponents across the higher education spectrum view the rule as an overreach of federal power. They cite the cost of seeking authorization in every state where they enroll students as a prohibitive factor.

S. 1297 was introduced in the U.S. Senate in 2011. It is a version of the Protecting Academic Freedom in Higher Education Act (H.R. 2117), the House bill to rescind the Department of Education's credit hour and state authorization regulations that went into effect on July 1. Similar to the House bill, the Senate measure has three main provisions: 1) a repeal of the state authorization regulation, which significantly expands and complicates existing federal requirements for an institution to operate legally within a state; 2) a repeal of the new federal definition of a credit hour; and 3) a ban prohibiting the education secretary from promulgating a rule to establish a federal definition of a credit hour in the future. How the situation eventually will be resolved remains open to speculation.

Apart from the influence of the Department of Education, academic institutions also benefit from grants and contracts provided by various components of the National Institutes of Health and other federal agencies to conduct research. The fruits of these investigations often translate into enlargement of the knowledge base and eventually into improved kinds of patient care.

In the health domain, a different kind of crossroads sighting would be in the form of a convoy. An example is P.L. 111-148, the Affordable Care Act (ACA), a massive piece of health reform legislation that became law in March 2010. In more than 1,000 places, it reads "the Secretary shall...." Referring to the Secretary of Health and Human Services (HHS), the law will result in a steady flow of thousands of pages of rules and regulations.

Another ongoing stream of traffic is represented by the number of individuals who reach age 65 and become eligible for participation in the Medicare program. Beginning on January 1,

2011, an average of 10,000+ persons a day began reaching that age and others will continue to do so every day over the next 19 years. Known as the baby boomers, individuals born between 1946 and 1964, they have the potential to place considerable strain on the ability of the United States to provide health and health-related social services.

The breakdown lanes always prove fascinating to observe. Vehicles in that part of the highway either are stalled there for given amounts of time or they permanently become disabled and have to be removed. The following are examples:

- Medicare Catastrophic Coverage Act
- Ergonomics rules
- Patient Bill of Rights
- Stem cell research
- National Health Workforce Commission

The *Medicare Catastrophic Coverage Act* was designed to protect beneficiaries from ruinous costs associated with the use of outpatient prescription drugs and long-term care. The House of Representatives approved the legislation by a vote of 328-72 on June 2, 1988. Six days later, the Senate gave its approval by a vote of 86-11. President Ronald Reagan signed it into law (P.L. 100-360) on July 1. Not long after that event and the celebratory uncorking of bottles of champagne as legislators heaped praise on one another, the intended beneficiaries began to learn of its contents. Becoming apoplectic, they were instrumental in having the House vote to repeal the legislation on October 4, 1989. The Senate unanimously followed suit on November 22 of that same year. President George Bush *père* complied by signing the death certificate.

The final days of the Clinton Administration in 2000 were devoted to rushing through a set of rules to protect employees from ergonomic risk factors in general industry workplaces. The Occupational Safety and Health Administration (OSHA) issued its final *Ergonomic Program* standard late that year. The final rule became effective on January 16, 2001. Amid a considerable amount of controversy, 2 months later the Congressional Review Act was invoked to nullify the regulation. The vote in the Senate was 56-44 and in the House it was 223-206 to support a resolution that was signed into law (P.L. 107-05) by President George W. Bush.

The late 1990s and the early part of the 21st century were characterized by heated debates on Capitol Hill about the wisdom of having a *Patient Bill of Rights* become law. The effort was viewed as a constructive means of correcting perceived abuses by managed care companies that denied coverage for health care services. Following much sound and fury, exhaustion and futility eventually led to the proposed legislation being eased through the door of oblivion and out of sight.

Advocates believe that *stem-cell research* holds great promise for curing various conditions, but depending on one's perspective from a moral and ethical standpoint, there is not universal agreement on how far investigations of this nature should be pursued. The most recent Bush Administration advised caution and placed restrictions on the kinds of research that could be carried out using federal funds. Shortly after President Obama occupied the Oval Office, he reversed these curbs.

The Affordable Care Act (ACA) of 2010 resulted in the creation of a large number of commissions and advisory bodies. An example is the *National Health Care Workforce Commission*, a group of 15 appointees whose assignment will be to make recommendations to Congress and the President about health workforce issues. As of December 2011, no funds had been appropriated for the Commission. Until money becomes available, that vehicle will remain in the breakdown lane.

Enactment of the ACA represents a major step on the road to broaden the base of the citizenry that possesses health insurance coverage. Yet, it must be recognized that individual and community health status are the product of a complex array of social, geographic, and economic factors. Achieving improvements is not something that the health sector is capable of doing on its own.

Increasing access to health care has the potential to add to costs and dilute quality. Ways to offset these hazards exist in the form of conducting research to determine which health interventions work effectively and which ones should be discontinued. Along with increasing access through the ACA, population dynamics ensure that the overall population will continue to grow in size. Both trends will present capacity problems for the way that the health workforce currently is structured. Practice acts in states around the country serve to limit rather than expand the number of health personnel needed to provide services. The legal right to treat patients should be based on competency and the ability to furnish safe treatment effectively rather than upon being a member of a specific profession. Eliminating such barriers offers the promise of increasing access to care, maintaining high standards of quality, and saving money.[434]

Moreover, there is the growing recognition of the necessity of having health professionals work together in teams. Fostering and attaining an appropriate level of interprofessional education and practice is a major goal to achieve. Much work needs to be done and important steps are being taken in that direction. The future should display signs that success is being achieved in producing a health workforce that performs to its optimal capabilities.

Raising the education level of the overall U.S. population requires closing the educational gaps among racial/ethnic groups and by gender (Kim 2011). Although the members of the younger generation of some racial/ethnic groups are more likely to attain college degrees than their predecessors, it is not the case across all groups. Other findings include: the high school completion rate for young people has not improved much and college enrollment gaps have widened among racial/ethnic groups during the past two decades.[435]

Demography—Race and Ethnicity

Ideally, changes in the workforce will occur that mirror the changing demographic profile of the United States. If in the not-too-distant future, whites will no longer be in the majority, then it would be advantageous to have a workforce more reflective of the population. Meanwhile, there currently is a need, as there will be in the future, to produce health professionals who not only have a keen understanding of the different cultures represented by patients, but also have the necessary skills to provide quality care to individuals who may differ by race and ethnicity.

Many kinds of health professionals are educated at the 2-year level in community colleges. A paper from the National Bureau of Economic Research (NBER) is based on detailed administrative data from one of the largest community colleges in the U.S. to quantify the extent to which academic performance depends on students being of similar race or ethnicity to their

434. Elwood, T.W. At the Crossroad of Higher Education and Health Care, *Journal of Allied Health*, Vol. 40, No. 2, Summer 2011, pp. 57-63.
435. Kim, Y.M. Minorities in Higher Education: Twenty-Fourth Status Report 2011 Supplement, October 2011, American Council on Education, Washington, DC: 21 pp.

instructors: "The performance gap in class dropout and pass rates between white and minority students falls by roughly half when taught by a minority instructor. In models that allow for a full set of ethnic and racial interactions between students and instructors, African-American students perform particularly better when taught by African-American instructors."[436] At all levels, in the classroom and in the clinical setting, it would be advantageous to foster greater participation of individuals in the health workforce whose numbers are reflective of either current or future population dynamics.

Building on Past Achievements

"During the 20th century, life expectancy at birth among U.S. residents increased by 62%, from 47.3 years in 1900 to 76.8 in 2000 and unprecedented improvements in population health status were observed at every stage of life (CDC 2011). In 1999, the MMWR (*Morbidity and Mortality Weekly Report*) published a series of reports highlighting 10 public health achievements that contributed to those improvements." In 2011, a second report assessed advances in public health during the first 10 years of the 21st century. Public health scientists at the CDC were asked to nominate noteworthy public health achievements that occurred in the U.S. during 2001-2010. From those nominations, the following 10 achievements, in no particular order, were selected:

Vaccine Preventable Diseases:

"The past decade has seen substantial declines in cases, hospitalizations, deaths, and healthcare costs associated with vaccine-preventable diseases. New vaccines (i.e., rotavirus, quadrivalent meningococcal conjugate, herpes zoster, pneumococcal conjugate, and human papillomavirus vaccines, as well as tetanus, diphtheria, and acellular pertussis vaccine for adults and adolescents) were introduced, bringing to 17 the number of diseases targeted by U.S. immunization policy."

Prevention and Control of Infectious Diseases:

"Improvements in state and local public health infrastructure along with innovative and targeted prevention efforts yielded significant progress in controlling infectious diseases. Examples include a 30% reduction from 2001 to 2010 in reported U.S. tuberculosis cases and a 58% decline from 2001 to 2009 in central line-associated blood stream infections."

Tobacco Control:

"Since publication of the first Surgeon General's report on tobacco in 1964, implementation of evidence-based policies and interventions by federal, state, and local public health authorities has reduced tobacco use significantly. By 2009, 20.6% of adults and 19.5% of youths were current smokers, compared with 23.5% of adults and 34.8% of youths 10 years earlier."

Maternal and Infant Health:

"The past decade has seen significant reductions in the number of infants born with neural tube defects (NTDs) and expansion of screening of newborns for metabolic and other heritable

---

436. Fairlie, R. et al. A Community College Instructor Like Me: Race and Ethnicity Interactions in the Classroom, NBER Working Paper No. 17381, September 2011, On the Web at http://www.nber.org/papers/w17381. Accessed on October 7, 2011.

disorders. Mandatory folic acid fortification of cereal grain products labeled as enriched in the United States beginning in 1998 contributed to a 36% reduction in NTDs from 1996 to 2006 and prevented an estimated 10,000 NTD-affected pregnancies in the past decade, resulting in a savings of $4.7 billion in direct costs."

Motor Vehicle Safety:

"Motor vehicle crashes are among the top 10 causes of death for U.S. residents of all ages and the leading cause of death for individuals aged 5–34 years. From 2000 to 2009, while the number of vehicle miles traveled on the nation's roads increased by 8.5%, the death rate related to motor vehicle travel declined from 14.9 per 100,000 population to 11.0, and the injury rate declined from 1,130 to 722; among children, the number of pedestrian deaths declined by 49%, from 475 to 244. These successes largely resulted from safer vehicles, safer roadways, and safer road use. Behavior was improved by protective policies, including effective seat belt and child safety seat legislation."

Cardiovascular Disease Prevention:

"During the past decade, the age-adjusted coronary heart disease and stroke death rates declined from 195 to 126 per 100,000 population and from 61.6 to 42.2 per 100,000 population, respectively, continuing a trend that started in the 1900s for stroke and in the 1960s for coronary heart disease. Factors contributing to these reductions include declines in the prevalence of cardiovascular risk factors such as uncontrolled hypertension, elevated cholesterol, and smoking, and improvements in treatments, medications, and quality of care."

Occupational Safety:

"Significant progress was made in improving working conditions and reducing the risk for workplace-associated injuries. For example, patient lifting has been a substantial cause of low back injuries among the 1.8 million U.S. health-care workers in nursing care and residential facilities. In the late 1990s, an evaluation of a best practices patient-handling program that included the use of mechanical patient-lifting equipment demonstrated reductions of 66% in the rates of workers' compensation injury claims and lost workdays and documented that the investment in lifting equipment can be recovered in less than 3 years."

Cancer Prevention:

"Evidence-based screening recommendations have been established to reduce mortality from colorectal cancer and female breast and cervical cancer. Several interventions inspired by these recommendations have improved cancer screening rates. Through the collaborative efforts of federal, state, and local health agencies, professional clinician societies, not-for-profit organizations, and patient advocates, standards were developed that have significantly improved cancer screening test quality and use."

Childhood Lead Poisoning Prevention:

"In 2000, childhood lead poisoning remained a major environmental public health problem in the United States, affecting children from all geographic areas and social and economic levels. Black children and those living in poverty and in old, poorly maintained housing were disproportionately affected. In 1990, five states had comprehensive lead poisoning prevention laws; by 2010, 23 states had such laws. Enforcement of these statutes and federal laws that reduce hazards in housing with the greatest risks has significantly reduced the prevalence of lead poisoning."

Public Health Preparedness and Response:

"After the international and domestic terrorist actions of 2001 highlighted gaps in the nation's public health preparedness, tremendous improvements have been made. In the first half of the decade, efforts were focused primarily on expanding the capacity of the public health system to respond (e.g., purchasing supplies and equipment). In the second half of the decade, the focus shifted to improving the laboratory, epidemiology, surveillance, and response capabilities of the public health system." [437]

These achievements are notable and comparable efforts must continue as a means of witnessing more success in the decades that lie ahead. Problems associated with mounting national debt will have to be alleviated, however, since the nation cannot meet its obligations as well as it could if interest payments on that debt represent an expanded portion of public expenditures.

The fate of the Affordable Care Act will hang in the balance of a decision that will emerge from the U.S. Supreme Court in 2012 on the matter of the constitutionality of the individual mandate section of the law. If it is ruled unconstitutional, the effect on the rest of the law could be quite dramatic and not particularly in a positive way.

As they have since the early days of the founding of the Republic, Americans will debate the merits of having a strong, centralized government as opposed to one that encroaches less on states' rights, and by extension individual rights. Disputes of that nature often spill over to the health arena as evidenced by controversies over vaccination policy. Events in the future will help to determine if a proper balance can be struck between allowing individuals to hold sway over their lives while simultaneously ensuring the safety, welfare, and improved health status of the public at large through a judicious combination of meaningful initiatives in both the governmental and private sector spheres.

Closing Thoughts

Some infectious diseases have been brought under control while new ones continue to appear. Vaccination has been shown to be effective in preventing and controlling the spread of many infectious diseases, but segments of the public oppose protecting their children in this manner. Regenerative medicine holds the prospect of extending the human lifespan, but stresses and strains that result in mental health problems will not be eradicated so easily. This chapter closes with a list of significant past achievements in public health that can be used as building blocks for successful interventions in the future.

---

437. Centers for Disease Control and Prevention. Ten Great Public Health Achievements—United States, 2001-2010, *Morbidity and Mortality Weekly Report*, Vol. 60, No. 19, May 20, 2011, pp. 619-623.

Epilogue

As stated in the Introduction, several major imperatives provide a framework for this book:

- A *Demographic Imperative* takes into account that the U.S. population is experiencing dramatic growth in the oldest age brackets. Because of immigration, newcomers will continue to arrive in this country and many will bring with them beliefs about the causes of disease and the best ways of treating it, both of which may be quite different from conventional western health care practices.

- An *Epidemiological Imperative* stems from the realization that old age for many individuals is accompanied by chronic disease and it often is in the form of multimorbidity (the simultaneous presence of different types of diseases and types of diagnoses). The entire population also is at risk of infectious disease. Influenza outbreaks provide an illustration of the devastation that can result from their occurrence. Failure to take advantage of pediatric vaccination programs carries with it an associated risk of being afflicted with serious ailments that can have lifelong consequences. Personal habits and practices are associated with other major kinds of health problems such as obesity and dependence on harmful substances.

- An *Economic Imperative* points to the necessity of slowing down the escalating growth in health care spending, which threatens to reduce funds needed for other useful purposes by individuals and by society as a whole. The aging of the population represents a relentless force that will exert a major impact on the volume and cost of health care and related social services that will have to be delivered.

- A *Technological Imperative* recognizes that the steady production of costly new devices and procedures will place a strain on the ability to contain the rate of rising health care expenditures. Complicating this issue is the need to conduct research to ascertain whether new developments are both cost effective and clinically effective before being adopted on a large scale basis.

- A *Health Workforce Imperative* recognizes that a proper distribution of health professionals by specialty and by geographical location is essential to maintaining a well-functioning service delivery system. Important prerequisites are having an educational system capable of producing graduates with the necessary knowledge and skills, along with a means of making such education affordable, especially for members of disadvantaged groups.

Underlying these imperatives is the necessity of recognizing the supreme importance of placing a strong emphasis on having a *Prevention Imperative*. Societal influences play an instrumental role in this regard by creating mechanisms to educate consumers about ways to stay healthy and also by enacting measures to reduce pollution and exposure to various environmental hazards. Members of the general public have their own contributions to make by attempting to live a healthy lifestyle, adhering to treatment regimens, and by avoiding behaviors such as smoking that can lead to serious chronic health problems involving heart disease and cancer.

Health professionals have an important part to play in the broad area of prevention. Dental hygienists furnish a good example by their insisting to patients the importance of improved oral health through regular flossing and proper brushing of teeth. Other health professionals such as nuclear medical technologists may spend fairly lengthy periods of time with patients when administering tests. Conversations can be enhanced by discussing topics such as weight control and smoking cessation programs. When in the clinical setting, patients may be more receptive to messages that could lead to healthy changes in lifestyle. Apart from treating ailments, health professionals are in an advantageous position to recommend prevention measures that have the potential to improve the health status of patients. Thus, educational programs need to include curriculum components that will enable practitioners not only to treat disease, but to feel knowledgeable and comfortable enough to engage patients in discussions of lifestyle changes that would be beneficial for one's health.

The eminent biologist J.B.S. Haldane suggested that there are four stages of acceptance in the advancement of science:

- This is worthless nonsense.
- This is an interesting, but perverse point of view.
- This is true, but quite unimportant.
- I always said so.

The chapters that precede this epilogue may serve to foreshadow ways in which Haldane's remarks might apply to health care in the United States as of the end of 2011. Just as there are many ways in which the health domain functions suitably, there also are many aspects that cry out for improvement.

A major effort to alleviate health care problems in the U.S. became law in 2010 when health reform legislation was enacted. Controversy that preceded this event has not diminished. Portions of the law such as the creation of accountable care organizations and the imposition of an individual mandate to require Americans to purchase health insurance are either hailed as strokes of brilliance or viewed as completely ridiculous. Both sides of the argument cannot be right, and at some point in the future it is possible that what might be considered a horrible example of social engineering today may prove eventually to be an outcome viewed as a stroke of genius commanding universal approval. At that juncture, the conclusion will be, "I always said so" and every policymaker will take credit for possessing keen foresight.

Between now and some future point when substantial improvements in personal and community health status become a reality, it would be of value to take certain observations into account. In October 2011, a poll conducted by the Kaiser Family Foundation showed that public support of the health reform law hit an all time low that month (Rau 2011). "The poll found that 51% dislike the law and only 34% favor it." The dissatisfaction is mostly due to a decrease in backing from Democrats. Recall that not a single Republican in Congress voted in favor of this legislation. Lack of enthusiasm among Republican voters reflects such negativity insofar as only 11% believe the law is a good thing.[438]

---

438. Rau, J. Public Support of Health Law Drops Sharply, Kaiser Health News, October 28, 2011. On the Web at http://www.kaiserhealthnews.org/Stories/2011/October/28/health-reform-poll-obama-kaiser-foundation.aspx. Viewed on November 18, 2011.

Ohio is often viewed as a bellwether state in national elections. Voters who went to the polls there in October 2011 chose by a two-to-one margin to endorse a constitutional amendment that attempts to exempt Ohioans from the federal law's individual mandate. They are not alone in expressing that sentiment and the future of the mandate will be decided in 2012 when the issue goes before the Supreme Court of the United States. If it is rejected by a majority of justices, ripple effects could be damaging to other aspects of the health reform law. If healthy persons choose not to purchase health insurance, then a higher proportion of policy holders with health problems will result. The increased cost of covering them may prove to be exceedingly difficult.

A survey conducted in 2011 by the consulting firm Deloitte furnishes a backdrop to the challenges involved in efforts to reform health care (Deloitte 2011). The results are:

- "Most consumers (76%) feel they do not have a strong understanding of how the health care system works.
- Over half (51%) of all consumers believe that 50% or more of health care spending is wasted.
- One in three (34%) believes that the performance of the U.S. health care system is worse today compared to 5 years ago.
- Only 22% of consumers give the health care system a favorable grade of "A" (3%) or "B" (19%).
- Three in four (75%) say the recent economic slowdown has had some impact on how much they are willing to spend on health care services and products.
- Three in five (63%) say their monthly health care expense limits their household's ability to spend money on other essentials, such as housing, groceries, fuel, and education.
- One in four (25%) says they decided not to see a doctor when sick or injured.
- 14% provide constant care for a family member; 36% have provided this care for more than 2 years." [439]

Family life in the United States undergoes steady change. According to the Pew Research Center, "barely half of all adults in this country are currently married, a record low. In 1960, 72% of all adults ages 18 and older were married. That figure is 51% in 2011" (Cohn 2011).[440] Research has shown that married couples tend to live longer and to enjoy a more favorable health status. Whether due to divorce or a failure to be married in the first place, this alteration in family life also will affect the ability of family members to provide care for one another.

The aged are now a greater portion of the population than at any time since the Census Bureau began keeping track. According to the 2010 census, there were 40.3 million individuals who are age 65 and older as of April of that year, a rise of about 15% since 2000. The nation as a whole grew by only 9.7%.

As described earlier, costs of the entitlement programs Medicare and Medicaid are unsustainable. Older persons are the beneficiaries of both programs, with Medicaid bearing the heavy burden of paying for long-term care. Around the nation, states are devising ways of limiting their exposure to Medicaid cost increases by cutting payments to physicians, reducing or

---

439. Deloitte. 2011 Survey of Health Care Consumers in the United States: Key Findings, Strategic Implications. On the Web at http://www.deloitte.com/assets/Dcom-UnitedStates/Local%20Assets/Documents/US_CHS_2011 ConsumerSurveyinUS_062111.pdf. Accessed on December 2, 2011.

440. Cohn, D. et al. 2011. Barely Half of U.S. Adults Are Married—A Record Low. Washington, DC: Pew Research Center.

ending optional benefits such as dental care, tightening prescription drug formularies, and enacting or hiking copayments by patients.

As the U.S. economy declined, the new Obama Administration responded by successfully working with Congress to provide stimulus funding. Medicaid funds were enhanced by $103 billion from fiscal 2009 to 2011, but that money supply has dried up, which resulted in the aforementioned steps taken by states to reduce program costs.

A report released in mid-December 2011 by NEHI and the WellPoint Foundation indicates ways in which a leaner, more efficient future of high value health care and improved health for all Americans can be attained (NEHI 2011). "Much of the health care provided today is inefficient, ineffective, and ultimately wasted." The document is intended to support health care leaders' efforts to lower health care costs by identifying seven specific areas of waste and inefficiency that together drain $521 billion from the system each year and it describes steps that could be taken to curb this unnecessary spending without an adverse impact on quality of care.

"Every year, millions of Americans arrive at an Emergency Department (ED) to seek care for a non-urgent condition. They arrive with asthma flare-ups, diabetic complications, the common cold, the flu and even cases of the sniffles. Some are uninsured, but many are not. Some lack a primary care provider, but many have a regular source of health care. For thousands each day, the ED is their first source of health care, not their refuge in an emergency. The consequences of this overuse are well established: overcrowded emergency rooms, uncoordinated care and billions of dollars in unnecessary health care spending. Data suggest that more than half of the 130 million annual ED visits are avoidable, for conditions that can be treated in urgent care clinics, primary care offices and by thoughtful prevention. Successful adoption of proven practices and implementation of policy actions together offer the potential to make millions healthier and save $38 billion currently wasted on unnecessary visits to the ED, money which can be reinvested to bring us closer to the goal of high value health care." [441]

It should be noted that health care will continue to represent a shifting terrain. Chapter 1 indicated that a health problem known as anxiety gradually came to be looked upon as depression. Some evidence suggests that a change may be starting to go in the opposite direction back to anxiety. In that same chapter, it was noted that "a weight considered 'ideal' in 1942 would have been 'desirable' in 1959, 'acceptable' in 1985, and 'overweight' in 2000. Today, the gold standard for weight assessment in the Western world is the body mass index (BMI). However, even using this assessment tool, from 1990 to 2000 the upper limit of healthy weights has changed from 27.8 kg/m² to 24.9 kg/m² and has variably modified its cut-off range for healthy weight on the basis of age and gender." [442]

Fibromyalgia, which was discussed in Chapter 2, presents another example of how intriguing alterations may occur with the passage of time. Only a few decades ago, the fibromyalgia syndrome was of little interest to clinicians and the general public. "At the beginning of the 21st century, it has become a diagnostic category that includes large numbers of people, predominantly women. Why did its boundaries expand so rapidly?" The answers include a convergence of the following:

---

441. NEHI and WellPoint Foundation. A Health Care Leader's Guide to High Value Health Care. On the Web at http://www.nehi.net/bendthecurve/sup/documents/Health_Care_Leaders_Guide.pdf. Accessed on December 15, 2011.

442. Jutel, A. Classification, Disease, and Diagnosis, *Perspectives in Biology and Medicine*, Vol. 54, No. 2, Spring 2011, pp. 189-205.

- Broad social and intellectual currents
- Internal developments within medicine
- The appearance of a self-conscious women's movement and the rise of self-help patient advocacy groups
- The medicalization of everyday life problems
- The rise of an increasingly important pharmaceutical industry and its marketing of drugs
- Active intervention of federal agencies

The combination of these factors resulted "in a dramatic expansion of the numbers of persons" diagnosed with fibromyalgia. Yet, to this day "the diagnosis has remained highly contested, and there are competing etiological theories and therapies." [443]

Smoking exacts a great toll on human life. Despite the risks involved, many college students embrace the habit enthusiastically. The high cost of cigarettes, mainly as a result of increased taxes, has helped to spawn another industry. Instead of the customary kind of cigar that takes a long time to smoke, the new version is smaller and much less expensive flavored variations are being manufactured. They can be smoked in about the same amount of time it takes to enjoy a cigarette. College students were flocking to this new product in 2011.

Everything about health care undoubtedly will change in the next decade and in those that come after it. This book addresses some dimensions of the health domain that may prove helpful in understanding future events as they transpire.

A related matter of concern is which kinds of health professionals will be allowed to treat patients. States around the nation are embroiled in disputes over who can do what to whom safely under what circumstances. Apart from considerations of providing health care of comparable quality, this issue has a bearing on whether any cost savings can be achieved by using one kind of practitioner rather than another.

A major deficiency is that there is no adequate mechanism for producing a national profile of the health workforce that can be used to assess supply and demand across a broad group of professions. The ability to conduct workforce planning does not exist. Given the changing demographic picture, it is essential that a data system be developed as a means of ascertaining what kinds of health professionals are needed and in what numbers. A related concern is the importance of producing enough faculty members to educate future practitioners and to conduct the kinds of research needed to advance the knowledge base and to assess the health effectiveness and outcomes of health care interventions.

---

443. Grob, G.N. The Rise of Fibromyalgia in 20th-Century America, *Perspectives in Biology and Medicine*, Vol. 54, No. 4, Autumn 2011, pp. 417-437.

Index